Fighting for the Butcher

British Troops Fighting in General Mangin's Xe Armée, July-August 1918

Richard Willis

Helion & Company

Helion & Company Limited
Unit 8 Amherst Business Centre
Budbrooke Road
Warwick
CV34 5WE
England
Tel. 01926 499 619
Email: info@helion.co.uk
Website: www.helion.co.uk
Twitter: @helionbooks
Visit our blog at blog.helion.co.uk

Published by Helion & Company 2023
Designed and typeset by Mary Woolley (www.battlefield-design.co.uk)
Cover designed by Paul Hewitt, Battlefield Design (www.battlefield-design.co.uk)

Text © Richard Willis 2023
Images open source unless individually credited
Maps drawn by George Anderson © Helion & Company Ltd 2023
Front Cover: Contemporary postcard of General Mangin. (Author's collection)

Every reasonable effort has been made to trace copyright holders and to obtain their permission for the use of copyright material. The author and publisher apologize for any errors or omissions in this work, and would be grateful if notified of any corrections that should be incorporated in future reprints or editions of this book.

ISBN 978-1-915113-68-9

British Library Cataloguing-in-Publication Data.
A catalogue record for this book is available from the British Library.

All rights reserved. No part of this publication may be reproduced, stored in a retrieval system, or transmitted, in any form, or by any means, electronic, mechanical, photocopying, recording or otherwise, without the express written consent of Helion & Company Limited.

For details of other military history titles published by Helion & Company Limited contact the above address or visit our website: http://www.helion.co.uk.

We always welcome receiving book proposals from prospective authors.

For Chloe, Ella, Lucy

The book would not be possible without the love and support of my wife and daughters. They have been a constant source of encouragement during the many hours I have been absent researching and writing my first book. I love you all. xxx

Bert Bloor

55071 Sergeant Harold Bertram "Bert" Bloor of the 34th Battalion Machine Gun Corps was wounded on the 1st August 1918 during the fighting around Beugneux. Born on Valentine's Day 1900, he was a native of Hockley in Birmingham and left his job as a cycle factory hand to enlist under age in Coventry in March 1916 when he was barely 16 years of age. He had been serving in France since April 1917, rising to the rank of Sergeant, an unusual accomplishment for someone so young. He was severely wounded in the neck and back and evacuated first to No.63 Casualty Clearing Station at Senlis and then by British ambulance train to No.12 General Hospital, Rouen, where he succumbed to his wounds and died on the 11th of August 1918, aged 18 years 6 months. Bert is buried in St. Sever Cemetery Extension, Rouen and is my mother-in-law's first cousin.

Dave O'Mara

Dave was a historian of the Great War and an expert on the French Army of 1914-1918. Known as @croonaert on Twitter, Dave was one of the most helpful, knowledgeable and giving historians you could possibly encounter, yet he was always modest, wearing that knowledge lightly. Nothing was ever too much trouble to answer, however miniscule or technical the question and I lost count of the times that Dave assisted me in my research, helping me to make sense of events and bringing them into their correct context. Dave died suddenly at the end of January 2022 aged 50 and he will be sadly missed by all who knew him.

This book is dedicated to my family and to Bert and Dave.

Contents

List of Maps		vi
1	Fighting for 'The Butcher'	7
2	The 34th Division	9
3	Reorganisation of the 34th Division/Operation *Michael*	13
4	Blunting the German knife – Fighting back during Operation *Georgette*	20
	4.1 The *Blücher-Yorck* and *Gneisenau* offensives	22
	4.2 The Allies plan their own counterpunch	28
	4.3 Operation *Hammerschlag* – The 'Hammer blow'	33
5	All Change for the 34th Division	35
	5.1 101st Brigade	39
	5.2 102nd Brigade	42
	5.3 103rd Brigade	43
6	Operation *Marneschutz-Reims* – The Germans Decoy Operation *Friedensturm* (Peace Offensive)	49
	6.1 Planning Operation *Friedensturm*	49
	6.2 Scope creep and conflicting objectives undermine Ludendorff's plans	52
7	Operation *Hagen* and Operation *Friedensturm*	54
	7.1 Attack Particulars	54
	7.2 French preparations for the defence of the Marne	56
	7.3 15 July – A bridge too far	57
	7.4 16 July	59
	7.5 17 July	60
8	18 July – The Massive Allied Counteroffensive	62
	Counteroffensive	62
9	July 1918 – The Danger Remains	66
	9.1 Payback time and learning to co-operate, but is it too late?	69
	9.2 Offensive action orders issued to the GAR and GAC on 12 July	72
	9.3 Leadership and staff disruption on the eve of the attack	80
	9.4 A god-awful traffic jam and a logistics nightmare	81
	9.5 0435 hrs – Battle commences	83

		9.6	French cavalry finally get into action	84
		9.7	Mangin makes an audacious decision	85
		9.8	0400 hrs, 19 July – The battle recommences	87
10	Relieving the Exhausted French *38e Division*			99
		10.1	Prelude	99
		10.2	Attack Order of Battle	110
		10.3	102nd Brigade makes good progress but 101st Brigade is stalled	112
11	24-27 July, All Quiet on (this part of) the Western Front			120
		11.1	Pétain and Mangin	120
		11.2	24 July: Minor adjustments to the line	125
12	Aftermath of the Battle of Soissonais and the Ourcq			132
		12.1	Marne pocket reduced	132
		12.2	34th Division Order of Battle, 29 July 1918	135
		12.3	General scheme	138
13	Rolling the Dice and Pushing for a Decisive Victory			147
		13.1	Halt or gamble?	147
		13.2	Into action again	148
		13.3	103rd Brigade enters the fray	153
		13.4	Phase II – Advancing towards the Brown Line objective	157
14	One more push to finally break the defenders?			168
15	30-31 July: Time for a rethink?			173
16	1 August: Monumental events			184
17	Paying the 'Butcher's bill'			202
		17.1	Summary of casualties sustained, 22 July-3 August	202
		17.2	The significance of the capture of the ridge north of Grand Rozoy and Beugneux and the action of the British 34th Division	206
		17.3	34th Division casualties, including major engagements	207
		17.4	Message from General Penet	215
		17.5	Mangin's General Order No.343	220

Appendices:
I	34th Division Order of Battle, 4 July 1918	222
II	34th Division casualties	226
III	German Order of Battle, July 1918	232
IV	Allied formations engaged 18 July-6 August 1918	240

Bibliography 241
Index 246

List of Maps

Map 1. Severing the German jugular vein – Order of Battle on 18 July 1918.   61
Map 2. Marne Salient on 20 July 1918.   90
Map 3. The Marne Salient on 22 July 1918.   92
Map 4. Marne Salient on 25 July 1918.   126
Map 5. Marne Salient on 27 July 1918.   131
Map 6. The shrinking 'poche' during the Battle of Soissonais and the Ourcq, 18-28 July 1918.   134
Map 7. Attack plan for 30 CA on 29 July 1918   136
Map 8. 34th Division objectives, 29 July 1918.   146
Map 9. Situation at 21:00 on 29 July 1918.   158
Map 10. Advance of 34th Division, 1 August 1918.   183
Map 11. Marne Salient, 1 August 1918.   186

1

Fighting for 'The Butcher'

"At the beginning of July 1918 I was convinced, I confess it, that before the 1st of September our adversaries would send us peace proposals … We expected grave events in Paris for the end of July. That was on the 15th. On the 18th even the most optimistic among us understood that all was lost. The history of the world was played out in three days."[1]

It is well known that the fortunes of war swing from one side to the other as the momentum shifts, usually on the back of offensives and whether they are successful or not. But only on very rare occasions do they swing so decisively, and almost never over such a short period of time, as happened in July and early August 1918.

The Second Battle of the Marne was one such event, with the momentum shifting over the space of just a few days from the Germans – who had launched their fifth massive attack of the 1918 Spring offensives, codenamed Operation *Marneschutz-Reims*, on 15 July – to the Allies when the latter launched their own equally ferocious counteroffensive on either flank of the Marne salient, the start of the little-known Battle of Soissonais and the Ourcq. The plan was for the Franco-American forces to attack without the usual preliminary artillery bombardment, using massed tanks to push rapidly from either flank and sever the jugular vein in the neck of the *poche* (pocket), closing it entirely and cutting off the retreat of the German army trapped inside. But why were four British divisions involved in this counteroffensive, with two of them – the 34th and 15th (Scottish) divisions – under the direct command of the notorious French General Charles Mangin, known by his men as 'The Butcher'? And why was Mangin, a man who had previously been sacked not once but twice, now spearheading the first Allied counteroffensive of 1918?

To say that 'The Butcher' had a chequered career during the Great War is something of an understatement: he went from hero to villain and back again in his desire to attack at any and every opportunity. He also had a difficult relationship with virtually all of his superiors throughout the war, with most of them disliking him and some actively detesting him. Invariably, the feeling was mutual, resulting in regular bouts of insubordination, which led to Mangin being relieved of duty during the Battle of Verdun in 1916. Reinstated prior to the disastrous Nivelle

---

1 German Chancellor Georg Von Hertling, cited in Pershing, John J., *My Experiences in the World War*. Volume II (1931), p. 472. Quoted in Harbord, James G., *The American Army in France: 1917–1919* (Boston: Little, Brown and Co, 1936), p. xiv.

Offensive in 1917, he was somewhat scapegoated and sacked for a second time, only to return on 16 June 1918 to command the French *Xe Armée*. His immediate superior, General Émile Fayolle, commanding the *Groupe d'armées de Resérve* (GAR, Army Group Reserve), called him "a devil of a man",[2] while the General-in-Chief of the French Army, Henri Philippe Pétain, loathed him, believing him to want nothing but personal glory and to have little if any regard for the fate of his men, the very antithesis of Pétain's more caring and paternalistic character. Yet despite these obvious obstacles, Allied Generalisimmo Ferdinand Foch and French Prime Minister Georges Clemenceau, whilst acknowledging his shortcomings (of which there were many), recognised that Mangin was ideally suited to the task ahead of spearheading the counteroffensive against the Germans from the left flank of the salient. The narrative also seeks to realign the perception of Pétain away from being caricatured as a pessimist verging on defeatist to someone who enthusiastically endorsed Mangin's proposal for the counteroffensive, agreeing that the operation presented an excellent opportunity for fruitful exploitation and the most effective parry to the imminent German offensive.[3]

When the first phase of the counteroffensive opened in the mist at 0435 hrs on the morning of 18 July 1918, with five French armies (*Xe*, *VIe*, *IXe*, *Ve* and *IVe*) involved – and with Mangin's *Xe Armée*, comprised of 10 divisions in the first line and six in the second, acting as the spearhead – 'The Butcher' had opted to replace the usual preliminary bombardment with a creeping barrage accompanied by massed tanks to ensure surprise. In the event he was completely successful, with the Germans suspecting nothing and seeing their forward positions quickly overrun before they were even aware that an attack had commenced. The advance on the first day, with the veteran *1e Division d'infanterie marocaine* (1re DIM) sandwiched between the double strength US 1st and 2nd divisions, was nothing short of spectacular, advancing an unprecedented 8km on the 18th alone. The Germans, temporarily wrong-footed, gave way, with thousands of men being taken prisoner in the confusion. But they quickly restored order, rushing reserve divisions to plug the gaps in their line and holding off the attackers of *Xe Armée*. Further progress ensued towards the objective of Fère-en-Tardenois in the centre of the salient in the following days, but progress noticeably slowed as each of the attacking divisions became increasingly worn out due to the fierce fighting and casualties sustained. The battle now needed an urgent injection of fresh reserves in order to sustain the momentum, with Foch ordering two British reserve divisions from Lieutenant General Sir Alexander Godley's XXII Corps – the 15th (Scottish) and 34th (New Army) divisions – to alter their destination mid-journey and come under command of the French *20e* and *30e Corps* respectively, part of Mangin's *Xe Armée*, to add the necessary impetus to press on and capture the objective.

---

2 Emile Fayolle, Cahiers secrets de la Grande Guerre (Paris: Plon, 1964), 15 August 1918, p. 297.
3 GQG AFGG2, 8 Juillet 1918, 623-1847, p. 357.

2

The 34th Division

In the post-war published history of the 34th Division, written by Lieutenant Colonel J. Shakespear, he describes it as a typical New Army Division, one of six created by the War Office for the Fifth New Army in December 1914. Originally numbered the 41st Division, when the original Fourth New Army was broken up in April 1915, it was renumbered as the 34th Division and its units converted for training and to provide replacements.

The composition of the 34th Division in July 1915 was as follows:

- The division had three brigades: 101st Brigade, 102nd (Tyneside Scottish) Brigade and 103rd (Tyneside Irish) Brigade.
- 152nd Brigade Royal Field Artillery was raised in Nottingham.
- 160th Brigade Royal Field Artillery was raised in early 1915 by the Mayor of Sunderland.
- 175th Brigade Royal Field Artillery was raised in Staffordshire.
- 176th Brigade RFA (Howitzers) was raised in June 1915 in Leicester.
- Divisional Ammunition Column was raised in Nottingham during the summer of 1915, with few of the men having any experience of horsemanship.

34th Division insignia

- 207th, 208th and 209th Field Companies, Royal Engineers, were raised in Norwich by the mayor.[1]

In June 1915 the arrival of Second Anglo-Boer War veteran, 53-year-old Major General Edward Ingouville-Williams, CB, to take command of the 34th heralded its 'birth' as a proper division, and at the start of January 1916 it embarked for France, spending the remainder of the war on the Western Front.[2] The division comprised a number of locally raised 'pals' battalions, notably the Tyneside Scottish and Tyneside Irish, but also the Manchester Scottish and the Grimsby Chums.

The 34th Division's first major action was on 1 July 1916, the infamous first day of the Battle of the Somme, when it was engaged in the attack on La Boiselle. Ingouville-Williams was a colourful character. Known as 'Inky Bill' by his men, he was a stern disciplinarian who worked them hard, but was also described as having a tender heart, looking after the wellbeing and comfort of those under his command.[3] At 1900 hrs on 22 July 1916, he was walking to meet his car at Montauban from Contalmaison when, at the southern end of Mametz Wood, he was caught in a German artillery barrage, hit by a piece of shrapnel and killed instantly. Buried at Warloy cemetery the following day, Inky Bill was yet another example of a general killed in the field and as far from the caricature of a *château* general as it was possible to be.

His successor was 51-year-old Major General (Cecil) Lothian Nicholson, CMG, a former Lieutenant Governor of Jersey and Governor of Gibraltar.[4] Nicholson had been in France since 1914, firstly serving as commander of 2nd Battalion, East Lancashire Regiment, in 8th Division between November 1914 and June 1915, being wounded during the Battle of Neuve Chapelle in March 1915. He was then promoted to Brigadier General commanding 16th Brigade, part of 6th Division, in June 1915, seeing further action at Hooge in August that year.[5] Nicholson arrived at divisional headquarters on 25 July 1916 to take command of 34th Division, a role he would hold until he became General Officer Commanding (GOC) the Eastern Division of the British Army of the Rhine in March 1919. Nicholson quickly got to grips with the 34th Division, and taking his lead from his predecessor, made his presence known to his commanders, as well as being visible at the front. At one point he spent seven hours touring front-line positions during the Battle of Arras in April 1917.[6] During the autumn of 1917, the now weakened division was spared much of the mauling suffered by many of those to the north, becoming involved only in more minor operations, including the removal of the Germans from their observation points in

---

1 Shakespear, Lieutenant Colonel John, *The Thirty-Fourth Division, 1915–1919: The Story of its Career from Ripon to the Rhine* (London: Witherby, 1921), pp. 2–3.
2 Shakespear, p. 1. He devotes 18 pages of the narrative to the events from April to August 1918. See also, *The Long Long Trail* <www.longlongtrail.co.uk/army/order-of-battle-of-Divisions/34th-Division/>
3 Shakespear, p. 65; 'Worcestershire Regiment', <www.worcestershireregiment.com/wr.php?main=inc/o_ingouville_williams>
4 Having recently been appointed Companion of the Order of St Michael and St George (CMG) by the King the previous month. *London Gazette*, 3rd June 1916. *Army Commands 1860* <https://www.gulabin.com/armynavy/pdf/Army%20Commands%201860-.pdf>
5 Imperial War Museum: *Private Papers of Major-General Sir (Cecil) Lothian Nicholson, KCMG, KCB*.
6 Shakespear, pp. 107–08.

Major General Nicholson

the Hargincourt Valley from 26–29 August.[7] The division estimated that 90 percent of its 400 casualties were caused by shellfire after the position had been captured.[8]

But in late 1917 it could be spared no longer, and 34th Division transferred to XIV Corps, part of Gough's Fifth Army, taking over the line on 14 October near Alouette, at the edge of Langemarck, in the Ypres salient. Their time in the front line was mercifully short-lived, being relieved on the 23/24 October, Shakespear commenting that no division ever left the salient with regret. Conditions were described as wretched; even at the best of times, life was sheer misery for all in the line.[9] A further time in the line was, if anything, even more unpleasant: "Our positions were simply a line of shell holes full of water. The conditions were past speaking about, mud and filth up to the neck."[10] Their time in the Ypres salient during October, spending 18 days in the forward area, had cost the division nearly 1,800 battle casualties, with

7 Shakespear, pp. 146–47.
8 Shakespear, p. 151.
9 Shakespear, pp. 156–57.
10 Major C. Anderson, cited in Shakespear, pp. 159-60.

a further 880 evacuated sick.[11] By the end of the 1917, 34th Division had suffered a total 18,500 casualties during the year.[12]

11 Shakespear, p. 164.
12 Shakespear, p. 168.

3

Reorganisation of the 34th Division/Operation *Michael*

During February 1918, with numbers reduced by heavy casualties from the previous year and struggling to retain its fighting strength, the 34th Division was reorganised. Several of the regiments of the Northumberland Fusiliers, so central to the history of the division, were amalgamated and grouped together into 102nd Brigade. The pioneer battalions were reorganised into three companies, whilst the division was expanded by the addition of a fourth machine gun company (240th Brigade Machine Gun Company) to form the 34th Battalion Machine Gun Corps (MGC, amalgamating the 101st, 102nd, 103rd and 240th Companies) on 19 February 1918 under the command of Lieutenant Colonel E.H. Kendrick, DSO, who on its formation had transferred from the 11th Suffolks.[1] For a time, and perhaps the only time in his entire military service, General Nicholson indeed became a Château General, spending a few happy days (in spite of exceptionally cold weather) well behind the lines in a château in the pretty French village of Le Cauroy, 30km west of Arras, as the guest of the Count and Countess Kergohlay.

Sensing the impending danger, General Pétain was extremely keen to increase his reserves, requesting the British to take over more of the French front and for the newly arriving Americans to be fed into French divisions. Haig agreed to a limited expansion of the British front as far as the River Oise, with General Hubert Gough's Fifth Army extending southwards. Pétain, however, was less successful with General John J. Pershing, who flatly refused to allow his American Expeditionary Forces (AEF) troops to serve within the French ranks in any form of amalgamation. Clemenceau, the wily politician, appealed over Pétain's head to US President Woodrow Wilson, but to no avail; Wilson supported Pershing fully in his refusal.[2] Meanwhile, on 3 March, the Germans and Russians signed their peace accord with the Treaty of Brest-Litovsk, finally ending hostilities between the Central Powers and the Russians and allowing the *Oberste Heeresleitung* (OHL, Supreme Army Command) to begin to release divisions across to the Western Front in even greater numbers. First Quartermaster General Erich Ludendorff was now able to focus all of his energies on beating his foes in the west. In reality, the military weakness of the crumbling Russian resistance had allowed the Germans to commence this transfer of divisions from east to west several months before, but with the signing of the peace

---

1 Shakespear, pp. 168-69 and TNA WO 95/2451: 34th Battalion, Machine Gun Corps.
2 Ryan, Stephen, *Pétain the Soldier* (London: Thomas Yoseloff, 1969), pp. 150–51.

treaty, they now enjoyed additional industrial and agricultural assets from which to support their military ambitions. Several coalfields and much of Russia's heavy industry passed into German hands, and equally importantly, the Russians had also abandoned the vast wheat fields of the Ukraine.[3]

Both Ludendorff and Field Marshal Paul von Hindenburg were keen to exploit their numerical advantage on the Western Front before the arrival of American troops in sufficient number tipped the balance back in favour of the Entente. At the start of March 1918, the Germans had a total of 192 divisions compared to 173 for the Allies, with the number rising steadily through the month. Three entire German armies – von Below's Seventeenth, von der Marwitz's Second and von Hutier's Eighteenth – had amassed 63 divisions, 6,200 guns and more than 1,000 aircraft for the attack.[4] On 5 March, 34th Division was once again in the front line, near Gommiécourt and Bullecourt in the St Quentin area. The German Operation *Michael* commenced on 21 March along a 103km front from the River Scarpe in the north to the Oise in the south, with 50 German divisions attacking 26 British divisions in General Gough's Fifth and General Byng's Third Armies. The disparity between attackers and defenders was not just in manpower: the Germans also had superior firepower, with 6,608 guns and 3,535 trench mortars in their attack – firing 3,200,000 rounds on the 21st alone – more than triple the number of British guns (2,686).[5] Under immense German pressure along a front he could not possibly hope to sustain, Haig was forced to formally request assistance from the French at midnight on the 21st. Understanding the seriousness of the situation facing the British, Pétain responded rapidly and decisively by sending north his *IIIe Armée* with *5e Corps d'armée* (*5e CA*) and *2e Corps de cavalerie* (*2e CC*), with six divisions despatched immediately, and 1er Armée following behind, French aircraft ordered to fly hundreds of bombing sorties above German positions. The total French force was 12 infantry and five cavalry divisions, plus 20 regiments of heavy artillery, with Fayolle ordered to take command of the southern portion of the defence. As this included two corps from British First Army as well as the arriving French forces under Fayolle's overall command, Haig was consulted, but readily agreed to the French plan. More reinforcements followed a couple of days later, a total of 23 French divisions joining the defensive battle.[6]

The 34th Division found itself at the epicentre of the massive enemy onslaught on the 21st, the sheer pressure of superior numbers of attackers forcing it to withdraw with the loss of the ruined village of Ecoust. After some of the fiercest defensive fighting the 34th Division experienced in its time on the Western Front – lasting 16 hours – it was finally able to retire sufficiently far to enable it to reorganise as best it could along a new line from St Leger Wood to the southern end of Croisilles Switch North.[7] The German assault recommenced in misty conditions the following morning, with the attackers again utilising their storm troop tactics of bypassing points of resistance, attempting to outflank them and taking them in the rear. By early afternoon, the pressure had once again forced a general retirement by the 34th Division towards the third-line trenches, which continued well into the evening, only ceasing when the Germans

---

3   Greenhalgh, Elizabeth, *Foch in Command* (Cambridge: Cambridge University Press, 2011), p. 294.
4   Clayton, Anthony, *Paths of Glory* (London: Cassell, 2003), pp. 162–65.
5   Zabecki, David, *Operational Art and the German 1918 Offensives* (Cranfield: Cranfield University, 2004), pp. 86–88.
6   Doughty, Robert, *Pyrrhic victory* (Cambridge: Harvard University Press, 2005), pp. 430–36.
7   Shakespear, p. 190.

could not discern friend from foe in the darkness. The exhausted and depleted remnants of the division were replaced by troops of 31st Division and withdrew on the night of 22/23 March, having been driven back by 5,000 yards (4.6km) and suffered 3,179 battle casualties, almost all of which were between the 21st and 22nd.[8] They were not alone; across the entire front things were in near disarray, the front line having been pushed back 5km on the 21st, another 5 the following day and, alarmingly, a total of 16km on the 23rd. Resistance now looked especially patchy in Gough's Fifth Army (for which Gough would be sacked and removed from command five days later), which was giving ground at an unsettling rate and creating a growing breach between Fifth Army and the French on their right.

Circumstances, however, were about to change dramatically for the better for the Allies, as the speed of advance had meant that the Germans had begun to outrun their supply lines, slowing their advance. Much of the success in halting the German attack was also due to the urgent and rapid deployment of three French divisions, a battalion of chasseurs and a regiment of heavy artillery, which had been transported north almost as soon as the attack had commenced, coming into action on the 23rd. The decision to make them ready to move was made by Pétain late in the evening on 21 March. Even though he had not yet been given the go-ahead by Haig, he understood that this was a very dangerous moment and he could not afford to delay his response. The approval came at noon the following day, Pétain issuing the order immediately, and by the following afternoon the three French divisions had arrived, with *125e Division* already in action. He also ordered the reactivation of the GAR under Fayolle, placing *Ier* (under General Marie-Eugène Debeney) and *IIIe* (commanded by General Humbert) *Armées*, together with whatever remnants of Gough's Fifth Army that might still remain, under Fayolle's command, while seven more divisions arrived by road and rail on the 23rd. By 26 March, just five days after Operation *Michael* had commenced, some 16 French divisions were engaged in the battle from the Somme to the Oise, with a further 27 *en route*, testament to both the speed of French planning and their effective logistics in transporting such a large force so rapidly north to support their struggling ally. As Greenhalgh points out, Pétain had done far more than he had promised in the mutual support arrangements, and actually far more than even Haig had asked for. This was due to him being the one commander who made the correct assessment of both the danger and the level of support needed for his ally in order to make a telling contribution.[9]

Pétain was determined to use his troops in a critical mass, rather than throw them in piecemeal in small numbers to be eaten up by the fierce fighting. A large amount of the credit therefore must go to Pétain for his decisive leadership at this critical time, with the Supreme War Council having no reserves to offer the British (since neither Haig nor Pétain had agreed to provide any) and a council being no use in a crisis.[10] One element in particular demonstrates that yet again he was an astute commander, making the correct decision at this key moment. By the time Operation *Michael* ground to a halt and was stopped by Ludendorff, the French had 34 infantry and six cavalry divisions engaged in the battle along a 50-mile front, representing more than a third of the entire French Army assisting the British, many arriving and being thrown into battle without their artillery as it was unable to move at the same pace as the infantry. Nowhere

---

8   Shakespear, pp. 197–98.
9   Doughty, p. 439. Ryan, p. 159, mentions 20 French divisions. Greenhalgh, Elizabeth, *The French Army and the First World War* (Cambridge: Cambridge University Press, 2014), pp. 274–76.
10 Greenhalgh, *Foch in Command* (2011), p. 298.

in his thinking did he show any sign of either caution or pessimism, yet this, together with the French contribution, are invariably lost amongst the numerous Anglophile historians who call Operation *Michael* a purely British victory. This fact is underlined by the number of French casualties: 20,175 killed or missing and 37,278 wounded.[11]

Ryan is not uncritical of Pétain, saying that his intervention should have been faster and with even more divisions sent north,[12] Ryan's conclusion is, however, incorrect; French intelligence expected a German attack in Champagne to commence at any time, and given the number of divisions he had already sent north, it is difficult to see from where Pétain could have sent more troops. He might have been able to bring a few divisions from the eastern sectors, but these would not have arrived in time, and time was of the essence. At the end of the day, this was an attack on the British front, and it should have been Haig and the British, not Pétain and the French, who shouldered the lion's share of responsibility for providing whatever additional reinforcements and reserves they could muster. The French High Command was all too aware that the danger still remained. Clemenceau and Pétain had agreed that if it came to a matter of splitting the British and the French, with the former retreating to the Channel ports and the French towards Paris, then the vital interests of the nation would come first and they would defend the capital at all costs. It was therefore vital to close any gaps emerging between the two armies and prevent them being cleaved apart. But to do so would require Pétain to order his troops to disengage from the battle, withdraw the left flank and move south to create this shield in front of Paris, something he was not prepared to do. Whilst Clemenceau as Premier might be solely concerned with saving France, Pétain was entirely focused on the task at hand: re-establishing contact with the British to his left and staunching the widening gap between the allies, especially Gough's disintegrating Fifth Army. He could thus stop further German progress after their successful and frighteningly rapid penetrations into large swathes of allied territory, enabling the Allies to defeat the enemy in a battle already underway. As Ryan correctly points out, Pétain was a pragmatist and exceptional organiser, and planning for the worst is not the same as accepting it.[13] So Pétain set to work to regain the initiative on behalf of the British. At Foch's urging he ordered General Fayolle, recently appointed by Pétain to command the GAR, to immediately commence an operation to maintain or, where needed, restore contact between the French and British from the Somme to the Oise. He put at Fayolle's disposal two armies, *Ier Armée* (Debeney) and *IIIe Armée* (Humbert), comprising a total of 40 divisions, together with large quantities of artillery. This was the entirety of the French reserves available to Pétain. Here was yet another example that contradicts Pétain's supposed caution. In reality, when the moment arrived, time and again he made decisive and (with the benefit of history) correct operational and tactical decisions. Fayolle put it aptly: Foch supplied the plan, Pétain the means and Fayolle himself the execution.[14]

The reversal on the Somme had significantly weakened Haig's position amongst the Allies, but ironically it had had a similar result for Pétain, despite the undoubted contribution of the French Army. But since he still believed the main attack was due to fall on the French sector, he was correct to stick to his beliefs, even if he was a lone voice. Clemenceau believed the time

---

11   AFGG 6/2, 552, cited in Greenhalgh (2014), pp. 277–79.
12   Ryan, p. 159.
13   Ryan, p. 161.
14   Greenhalgh (2015), p. 279.

was right for a unified command, but felt that Pétain was not the right man for the job, being too timid in action and lacking ideas, but conceding that he well understood the mentality of his men. In essence, the French Premier felt that his Commander-in-Chief was an administrator rather than a leader, and he needed someone with more imagination and dash.[15] At a fraught and fractious conference at Doullens Town Hall on 26 March, a disconsolate and almost beaten Pétain, believing that the main thrust of the German attack was still to come, gave a bleak but honest portrayal of the current situation, simply stating that "the Germans will defeat the English in open country; after which they will defeat us as well".[16] Whilst this was an entirely realistic and candid assessment of recent events and the state of the Allies, who had little to be optimistic about, many in the room saw it as typical of Pétain, painting an overly pessimistic picture. Clemenceau, shocked at what he had just heard, openly questioned Pétain's state of mind. Some perceived the weariness of the French people epitomised in Pétain and wanted something different from the person charged with co-ordinating allied efforts to repulse the German offensives and win the war.[17] So when it came to Foch's turn to speak, he was the complete antithesis to the subdued Pétain, brimming with energy and animatedly pointing out that whilst things had certainly gone badly for the British, the battle was not yet over and neither had it been a decisive German victory. He added that his plan was very simple: "I would fight without a break. I would fight in front of Amiens. I would fight in Amiens. I would fight behind Amiens. I would fight all the time, and by force of hitting, I would finish by shaking up the Boche; he's neither cleverer nor stronger than we are." He concluded with the clarion call: "We must fight where we are! We must not give an inch of ground!"[18] Whilst Foch spoke virtually no English,[19] relying on translators to relay his messages, on this occasion his vigorous body language did the talking for him and no one in the room was left in any doubt of his intentions.

It is untrue to say that Pétain momentarily lost a sense of proportion, which had serious implications for his strategy; nor had he seemed unwilling to assist his main ally. Having sounded out the British in the days preceding the meeting, the wily Clemenceau now chose his moment to suggest the time was ripe for a single unified Allied commander. Both Haig and Pétain were obvious candidates, but it was unlikely either would accept being subordinated to the other. It was now that Pétain's character traits of realism, pragmatism and occasional pessimism – which he had displayed just moments earlier – made the difference. What was needed was unifying a candidate who could bring together the strengths of both the French and British to fight together more effectively to defeat the Germans, and it was Douglas Haig who suggested Foch. The 66-year-old Foch was quickly agreed upon and appointed as Commander-in-Chief of the Allied armies, with the responsibility to co-ordinate their activities, and he immediately set about his task with a series of meetings that day. Clemenceau had achieved a massive political

---

15   Greenhalgh (2011), p. 306.
16   Poincaré, Raymond, *Au service de la France – Victoire et armistice* (1930), p. 88; Watson, David, *Georges Clemenceau: a Political Biography* (New York: David McKay, 1974), p. 303 cited in Neiberg, Michael, *Foch* (Washington: Brassey Inc., 2003), p. 63 and Raymond Poincaré, AS 10:88 (entry for 26 March 1918), cited in Greenhalgh (2011), p. 307.
17   Nick Lloyd, *Hundred Days* (London: Penguin, 2013), p.22.
18   Liddell Hart, Basil, *Foch: The Man of Orléans* (Boston: Little Brown, 1932), p. 275 cited in Neiberg (Foch), p. 63 and Atkin, Stephen, *Pétain* (London: Longman, 1998), p. 34.
19   Greenhalgh (2011), p. 337.

and military coup, resulting in what he saw as the ideal command situation. The French Army remained under the immediate command of General Pétain, "whose known prudence would ensure that French blood would be expended parsimoniously, while all the allied armies … would be under the overall command of a French officer whose known propensity for offensive action without an inhibiting concern for losses ensured a dynamic prosecution of the war effort".[20] Their characters, whilst hugely different, were exactly right for the roles that they were asked to play: Pétain the planner and organiser versus Foch, who had spent his career thinking about the wider situation and what he could do next to influence events towards victory. In future, the three heads of the Allied armies would focus on tactics, with overall strategy transferring to Foch.[21] Pétain's tactical thinking was based on his belief that attacks could only progress by limited means as far as the second defensive positions, and that a breakthrough was no longer realistic or possible at this point in the war, since it would always result in casualty levels which were neither acceptable nor sustainable.

Foch's First Directive, published as soon as he became Generalissimo, stated that he wanted to create a '*masse de manoeuvre*', with strong defensive positions established to defend Amiens, and crucially to maintain a connection between the two national armies. Where troops had been made available, these should be kept in reserve, ready to move to wherever they were needed. A Second Directive was published on 3 April, outlining his offensive strategy involving a double counterattack to take the fight to the Germans. The British would attack on the Somme, pushing the Germans back eastwards, away from Amiens, whilst the French would attack at Montdidier, pushing the Germans north. If successful, the offensive might eventually converge around St Quentin, recapturing much of the ground lost during Operation *Michael*.[22] Foch, like Haig, Nivelle and Mangin (but unlike Pétain), still believed that a breakthrough and a subsequent strategic exploitation were absolutely possible and attainable, especially with new technology in the hands of the Entente and the arrival of American troops in number. After all, hadn't they just witnessed something very similar by the Germans, who – but for better logistics, troops and tactics – might have done exactly that and broken through the Allied lines at Amiens and severed the vital railway communications?

A further conference at Beauvais on 3 April ratified Foch's role, giving him slightly wider powers as Strategic Director of the Allied armies, with Haig and Pétain still in tactical command of their respective forces. The French Army in the north, fighting with the British in Flanders, came under Foch's direct command, who ordered them to take to the offensive in order to keep the Germans off balance and forestall another enemy attack. Both Pétain and Fayolle, the latter commanding the GAR, complained separately to President Poincaré about Foch's conduct of the operation, which went against Pétain's meticulously organised attacks. Foch had had little option but to throw French troops into poorly prepared attacks, not unlike the disastrous ones that Nivelle had begun a year previously, and Pétain was worried that the men would see a return to the old, failed ways, morale would rapidly evaporate and mutinies would follow. He had done so much to restore the morale of his *poilus* (infantrymen) and was not going to do anything to undermine or jeopardise that. Fayolle added that such attacks had proved costly failures in the past, and that in 1918 a different approach was needed. But lessons

---

20   Ryan, p. 162.
21   Atkin, p. 34.
22   Directive Générale no.2, 3 April 1918, AFGG 6/1, annex 1374 cited in Greenhalgh (2011), pp. 310-11.

had been learned; on the ground in Flanders, French officers were conducting a very different style of attack from those of Nivelle. Whatever Foch had urged, attacks were now much more methodical and no one any longer heeded the old mantra of 'defend your ground at all costs' if they came under determined attack.[23]

23 Ryan, pp. 164–65.

4

Blunting the German knife – Fighting back during Operation *Georgette*

Moving north, 34th Division re-entered the line in what had been a relatively quiet sector near Armentières on the River Lys on 30 March. Unfortunately, the move coincided with the launch of the Germans' next offensive a few days later. In spite of the fact that the Allies had got wind of the planned attack, they had had little time in which to plan a spoiling attack of their own. Operation *Georgette*, the focus of the massive German attack, fell on the Lys sector, beginning at 0415 hrs on 9 April, with 36 divisions from von Quast's Sixth and von Arnim's Fourth armies.[1] The preliminary bombardment had started at 2030 hrs the previous evening with a heavy targeting of Armentières using a combination of high explosive and yellow cross mustard (yperite) gas, resulting in 900 casualties for the 34th Division. Once again, Haig was forced to beg for help from the French, rather ungraciously demanding that they immediately take steps to relieve part of the English front and take an active part in the battle. From Haig's point of view, the British were again shouldering the entire effort of defending the second German offensive and once more receiving no assistance from the French. This time though, Pétain had Foch to help plead his case, pointing out that the French had provided almost a third of their divisions during Operation *Michael* and that they would do the same again if required, agreeing to send four divisions immediately under the newly formed *Detachment d'armée du Nord* (DAN).[2]

Unfortunately for the tired and depleted 34th Division, which had hoped to be able to recover, rest and refit in a quiet sector. The River Lys ran very close to the division's rear, with only seven bridges affording escape, so a number of temporary bridges had to be hastily constructed.[3] The actual front held by 34th Division was not attacked, except for hostile shelling, but the Germans managed to cross the Lys at 1500 hrs at Bac-Saint-Maur, just west of the division's positions. Reinforced by 74th Brigade, which was rushed to Steenwerck during the afternoon, the division pushed forward during the evening and into the night with a hastily organised counterattack, the aim of which was to force the Germans out of Croix du Bac and back across the River Lys. Fresh attacks began in the darkness around 0200 hrs on the 10th, with some British reinforcements arriving during the night, but these attacks were only partially successful owing to the difficulty

---

1   Clayton, p. 167.
2   AFGG, p. 338, cited in Doughty, pp. 443–44.
3   Shakespear, p. 203.

of identifying the enemy in the dark.⁴ Once daybreak arrived, the Germans began a strong flanking attack at 0800 hrs, with large numbers of troops pushing forward and slowly forcing the exhausted British remnants back by mid-afternoon to the western edge of Erquinghem–Lys and to Steenwerck, where fierce hand-to-hand street fighting took hold in the town.

To the north, the Germans had captured Ploegsteert and the strategically vital highpoint of the Messines ridge, resulting in the division being caught in a pincer from north and south which was being progressively squeezed by the advancing enemy. General Nicholson was left with no option but to withdraw and retire to the north bank of the River Lys, which he reluctantly ordered to commence at 1500 hrs. Once most of the men had crossed, and with the Germans following up closely behind, orders were received for the bridges to be blown, allowing the men to slip away. Unfortunately, a number of men were left stranded on the wrong side of the river who had no option but to surrender and be taken prisoner. Once across the river, the remaining officers set about collecting men into a composite hodgepodge force and hastily began to reorganise their defences in Nieppe. Further severe German pressure again drove the 34th Division backwards, this time towards the Nieppe system, with the action swaying backwards and forwards throughout the day, but eventually the superior numbers of the enemy began to tell, the division falling back to Pont d'Achelles that evening and from there to a line running from De Seule to the north-western edge of Bailleul by midnight on the 12th/13th. A flanking attack then forced yet another retirement by the division, all the time taking casualties as they withdrew.

Relief, in every sense of the word, came at 1230 hrs when the order was received for the remnants of the division to be relieved by 176th and 178th Brigades of the 59th (2nd North Midland) Division on the night of 14/15 April after seven very long and arduous days of fighting. With a strength now of only 4,500 infantry and another 2,500 in reserve, the division was a shadow of its former self. Yet even though it was exhausted and depleted, it was still called upon to remain ready to repel further enemy attacks and it wasn't until 0800 hrs on 21 April – after 12 days of fighting – that General Nicholson was finally able to withdraw the division fully, being replaced in the line by the French *133e Division*. Casualties had been severe: between noon on the 8 April and noon on the 21st, the 34th Division lost 195 officers and 4,743 other ranks, of which 30 officers and 243 other ranks had been killed; wounded and missing men made up the majority of the casualties.⁵ The gaps in the ranks were quickly filled with replacements, many of whom went to the worst-affected infantry battalions, but with the situation still dangerous, there was precious little time to rest or train the newcomers.⁶

It is worth stating that the Germans threw 152 divisions into these first two offensives,⁷ but despite the number of troops (many of whom were the elite *sturmtruppen*) being overwhelming, neither attack had been decisive. Once again, a good deal of the credit for stopping the progress of Operation *Georgette* should go to the French and to Foch and Pétain, particularly the latter, who immediately despatched a force of three cavalry and four infantry divisions to the west of

---

4   Shakespear, pp. 212–14.
5   Shakespear, pp. 246, 250. Nicholson was temporarily in command of a much larger force during the April offensive, with his units suffering casualties numbering 325 officers and 7,154 other ranks between 8 and 21 April.
6   Shakespear, pp. 198, 201–02.
7   Michelin, *The Americans in the Great War. Volume 1. The Second Battle of the Marne* (1919), p. 3.

Amiens, allowing the British to move their troops towards the fighting further north. Here again was clear evidence of Pétain's prompt and decisive action, striking the right balance between supporting his ally with additional forces and protecting his own front. If anything, he had denuded the French lines to the absolute bare bones, having just 46 divisions in the line and another 12 in reserve between the River Oise and Switzerland, together with three untried American divisions, having sent 47 divisions north to aid the British.[8] But this cut little mustard with British High Command, who firmly believed they had borne the heaviest burden of the two German offensives, while the French did too little to support their ally. This may have been sour grapes at the efforts of the BEF in stemming the attacks or it may have just been because the attacks *did* fall on the British front. Nor was it helped by the French inability to hold onto Mount Kemmel: no sooner had they occupied the hill, than they were thrown off it by a fierce German attack. Either way, it created a degree of ill-will and suspicion between the two nations to a level rarely seen since the start of the war. The truth, however, is that the French had twice come to the aid of the British in large numbers, with 41 French divisions engaged on the British front in March and April, suffering more than 92,000 casualties during a German offensive fought in British-held territory and it is disingenuous to suggest anything otherwise.

4.1 The *Blücher-Yorck* and *Gneisenau* offensives

It was now clear to both the French and British that they required a reserve force of sufficient scale to be able to make a decisive intervention, and crucially it had to be mobile and ready to move at a moment's notice to wherever the next fighting broke out. Pétain therefore formally created the *Détachment d'armée du No*rd (DAN) on 18 April, to give the required structure and organisation necessary for the French forces of nine infantry and three cavalry divisions fighting in the north. The DAN was placed under Foch's overall command the following day. Understanding the need to bolster his reserves, Foch made plans to increase the number of divisions further, not just as a grab for power or to increase his authority, but in order to have sufficient resources to switch to the offensive when the time was right. On top of the dozen French DAN divisions, he also secured three divisions from General Maistre in *Xe Arm*ée and seven from General Micheler in *Ve Armée*, to be placed at strategic points along the front, close to where they were likely to be needed in the short-term, but also in the optimum locations for taking to the offensive.[9]

The difficulties brought about by the two German offensives on the British front were straining relations between the national commanders, and in turn between them and Ferdinand Foch. Haig had proposed reducing his number of British divisions by nine, but Foch was having none of it, whilst Pétain never missed an opportunity to state the contribution of the French in saving the British 'bacon'. But Pétain too expressed regret at having to use his reserves to bolster the weak British lines, thereby increasing the risk on his own front, whilst General Pershing remained adamant that he would never allow his US troops to be amalgamated with either the French or the British. Then there was the political dimension to deal with, with Clemenceau furious that most of the American troops now arriving were being put into the British rather than the French sector. All of this left Foch in something of a bind, since without

---

8   Greenhalgh (2011), pp. 312–22; (2014), p. 310.
9   Greenhalgh (2011), pp. 335–36.

better co-operation at both the political and military level, he would have no chance of moving over to the offensive in 1918.[10] Concerns over the state of Allied manpower were at the forefront of many of these discussions, with each commander having a different interpretation of how to deal with the issue. Whatever the solution, the situation was certainly critical. The French Army, already short of 250,000 men at the start of the year, had suffered 340,000 casualties since March, leaving it perilously understrength. The British, having borne the brunt of the first two assaults of the German Spring offensives, were arguably in an even worse position, and the Americans simply weren't bringing anywhere near enough troops across the Atlantic. The French now estimated that there were only seven German divisions facing the Belgian Army, but 200 opposing the British and French armies, who could muster just 162 divisions between them. The British manpower crisis in the spring had worsened, with 145 battalions broken up in order to strengthen the remainder and the removal of one battalion from each brigade but British losses were outweighing the supply of American troops.[11] None of this should downplay the losses by the Germans from their attacks, but the imbalance in numbers had now become a critical factor and the Allied leaders needed to do something different if they were to outlast the Germans for the rest of the year.

Despite everyone's concerns over future plans, matters closer to home still had to be addressed. Throughout April and May, Haig remained convinced the next German attack would take place in Flanders. Pétain, however, did not; he calculated that the next attack would come on his Champagne front, with the Germans trying to probe for any French weaknesses. Against the urgings of the French Commander-in-Chief, Foch instead decided to place the available reserves in Flanders and on the Somme close to Amiens, ready to repulse any German offensive, be it in the north or the south. Neither Operation *Michael* nor Operation *Georgette* had been decisive. Indeed, some argue that they were both German defeats, since neither conquered any real strategic objectives, just swathes of shell-worn battlefields. The Entente forces were down, but not yet out, and in reality it was worse for the Germans: they had used up most of their *sturmtruppen* in the attacks and now had a much longer front to defend, all with fewer troops in the line, leaving it thinly held in many places and therefore ill-equipped for further offensives. German divisions were still flowing from east to west, but these would all need time to train and equip for the next offensive, and with the expansion of both *Michael* and *Georgette*, the Germans required a longer period of recovery before they could mount their next offensive, giving the Allies vital breathing space to rest and recuperate.

Haig still believed the next German attack would come on his already weak front. After all, wouldn't the logical thing be for the Germans to try to knock out an opponent who was already reeling from two heavy blows? But neither Pétain nor Foch agreed with Haig's assessment, believing the next attack would fall on French lines, which would probably force the Allies to move reserves south, giving the Germans time to exploit their advantage before the DAN reserves arrived. It was rather like a perverse game of cat and mouse, with the Allies frantically trying to identify the exact location of the next offensive before the Germans struck. However when the Germans did attack at 0340 hrs on 27 May, it was not in the north as Haig had

---

10   Greenhalgh (2011), p. 325.
11   Clayton, pp.180–81.

suspected, but on the quiet but vulnerable Chemin des Dames sector between the cities of Soissons and Reims, just as Pétain and Foch had predicted.

Up until this point, the Chemin des Dames could be characterised as one of those sectors where 'live and let live' became the watchword for both sides but interspersed with episodes of extreme violence during the Nivelle Offensive in April 1917.

The German Operation *Blücher-Yorck* in the Chemin des Dames began almost a month after *Georgette* had been wound down, allowing the Allies four vital weeks to make their defensive preparations. It commenced along a front of 43km at 0100 hrs on 27 May with a short but fearsome Bruchmüller artillery bombardment of just two hours and 40 minutes, involving over 4,000 guns firing to a depth of 10–12km behind the front, much of the bombardment featuring gas, with the infantry from 17 elite[12] and specially trained *sturmtruppen* divisions of von Below's First and von Boehn's Seventh armies smashing into the weak and under-strength Franco-British defensive positions, which quickly gave way. The 17 German attack divisions were supported by more than 20 in reserve. There had been some intelligence that German troops were massing along the Chemin des Dames, but this had come too late to do anything about it. In many parts of the front, surprise was almost complete and the attackers had little difficulty making progress, killing or capturing around 50,000 troops from General Denis Duchêne's *VIe Armée*, many of whom were from the five British divisions of Hamilton-Gordon's IX Corps, recuperating in the area after the heavy fighting on the Lys. Additionally, 800 guns were captured, a good indication that the artillery were indeed surprised and unable to get their guns away before capture. Foch had suggested setting up a *roulement* scheme to Haig in April, whereby tired British divisions would be rotated out of the line and placed in quiet French sectors, and the British Commander-in-Chief had agreed. Haig immediately saw the benefit of such a scheme, in spite of opposition from General Sir Henry Wilson, Chief of the Imperial General Staff. But Foch's offer was not an entirely selfless one, as he had identified an opportunity to free up some French divisions for his General Reserve and for the counteroffensive he was now planning.[13]

In early April 1918, General Duchêne had decided that establishing effective defence in depth would not be possible due to the geography of the Chemin des Dames. He fundamentally disagreed with Pétain's directive around defence in depth and consequently had too many troops in forward positions when the Germans attacked. With the defences quickly overrun and the retreating troops in near disarray, the Germans were able to cross the first and second positions without difficulty and with few casualties in the initial waves of their attack. Matters weren't helped since *VIe Armée* held an unusually long length of front, totalling 90km from the River Oise to the edge of Reims, with each division holding a wider front than normal. Pressing on rapidly southwards, the Germans began to create a breach in the Allied line, which increased to a 40km-wide chasm during the latter part of the day as they advanced. Such was the unheralded progress that the Germans managed to seize the bridge across the River Aisne at Oeuilly at 0940 hrs, crossing over it with the help of specially designed long ladders brought up for the task. They covered a distance of 6km in just six hours before pushing on a further 14km by nightfall, with some units even having crossed the River Vesle as darkness fell. The French had

---

12 Greenhalgh (2011), p. 349, says 29 attack and 10 trench divisions. Clayton, p. 168, has the figure at 43 divisions.
13 Blanchard, David, *The Annihilation of the British IX Corps on the Aisne, 27th May 1918* (Unpublished MPhil thesis, 2016); Greenhalgh (2011), pp. 343-44 and Greenhalgh (2014), pp. 287, 294.

failed to blow the bridges across the Aisne and Vesle because they were overrun so quickly that they'd been unable to transmit orders for their destruction to the units manning the bridges. By the end of the first day of the offensive, the Germans had advanced 20km, crossing three rivers along the way as they took advantage of French confusion. The River Vesle was no River Marne, being no more than 15 yards wide, making its crossing difficult but by no means impossible. But like most of the rivers in the area, it had steep slopes on either bank, making it easy to defend but more challenging to attack. By nightfall on day two of the offensive, the Germans had entered Soissons and advanced another 10km south of the Vesle.[14]

The original plan had been for *Blücher-Yorck* to be a diversionary attack to draw French troops south and away from Flanders, the location for Operation *Hagen*, which Quartermaster General Ludendorff believed would definitively split the British and French armies, pushing the British back to the Channel ports and into the sea. But the undoubted success of *Blücher-Yorck* and the unprecedented advance his troops had been able to cover opened up hitherto new opportunities, luring Ludendorff into a rapid reassessment of his plans and the fatal decision to rethink and amend them. So instead of consolidating and halting the operation having gained his objective of the River Vesle, the Germans would throw five more divisions into the battle and the offensive would continue south towards the River Marne, and maybe – if luck was on his side – even get close enough to threaten Paris once again. German intelligence indicated that there appeared to be little in the way of French resistance ahead of him, bar some exhausted, disorganised and weak French *poilus* manning thin lines of hastily erected defences, which he hoped could be brushed aside just as he had on the 27th. On the evening of the 28th, the Kaiser, Crown Prince Wilhelm, Hindenburg and Ludendorff met to discuss the operation, with Ludendorff presenting his revised plans for the next phase.[15]

Unfortunately for Ludendorff, he had made a fatal miscalculation, misjudging the weakness of the French. In spite of concentrating an overwhelming force of 47 divisions during the battle, against the equivalent of 60 French or British divisions, once again the attack, whilst being a spectacular early success and making advances unheralded on the Western Front since 1914, had like the two earlier attacks not been decisive. Not only was Pétain able to release 10 infantry and three cavalry divisions of *Ve Armée* to the front in order to restore the line and stem the advance, if anything the resolve of the French appeared to have stiffened and this time there was no repeat of the mutinies and disobedience of the previous year. The ordinary *poilus*, having recognised the threat to the French capital, seemed more resolute and determined than ever. But fighting on open ground was extremely difficult and alien to many of the French troops, with only the survivors from the summer and autumn of 1914 having any experience of such battlefield conditions and how to combat the German tactics. For the Entente, the crisis point was reached in the final two days of May, with Reims virtually encircled, Soissons having been lost and the Germans even managing to get some troops across the Marne at Dormans. Although the Germans might be able to press on south of the river, each day the level of resistance stiffened, the result of Pétain's decision to organise the defence in the bottom of the new salient, including the US 2nd and 3rd divisions. This eventually forced the Germans to halt along a 20km stretch of the north bank of the Marne, having outrun their supplies and running

---

14 Doughty, p. 449. Clayton, p. 169; Neiberg, Michael, *The Second Battle of the Marne* (Bloomington: Indiana University Press, 2008), p. 177 and Greenhalgh (2014), p. 295.
15 Michelin (1919), p. 8

dangerously short of everything from manpower to food, preventing them from pressing on across the river with any meaningful number of troops. Additionally, the Moroccans of the *1re DIM*, *35e* and *51e* French divisions held their ground south of Soissons, even managing to reoccupy Courmelles and the banks of the River Crise.[16] Equally important had been Pétain's forceful command to Franchet d'Espèrey to defend Reims, rather than evacuating the city as d'Espèrey had originally ordered.[17] The city was covered by the near-impregnable Le *Neuvillette Ligne*, which offered strong protection to the defenders.[18] The stubborn but ultimately successful defence of Reims had meant that the Germans could not use the city and its important railway line to resupply the salient and required them to construct a new railway line instead, which would take time to complete.

German casualties had initially been very low and the prospects had looked good for the OHL, but with each kilometre of territory they captured losses had rapidly mounted, giving Ludendorff little choice but to halt the advance. Worse still, by altering his plan for *Blücher-Yorck* and pressing on beyond its original objectives, he was now forced to order OHL and Crown-Prince Rupprecht to delay the follow-up *Hagen* operation in Flanders, which could not now start until the middle of July at the earliest. Nevertheless, it had been the most rapid advance on the Western Front, amounting to 55km by the evening of 1 June and capturing much of Château-Thierry, leaving the Germans just 56km from Paris, the closest they had come to the French capital since the autumn of 1914. It left the Quartermaster General basking in a huge sense of satisfaction about how events had unfolded, and no doubt certain of his tactical genius. After all, it had been a remarkable effort, especially considering that almost all of the roads ran east–west rather than north–south, with precious little in the way of decent road or rail communications in the area.[19] The only problem was that he'd used up most of his elite *sturmtruppen* in the process, and despite being able to transfer more of his troops from east to west, his manpower resources required to occupy the newly formed huge Marne salient were becoming decidedly thin.

The attack, whilst being a stunning initial success in gaining massive amounts of territory from their enemy, was in reality yet another strategic failure, since little of actual real value (aside from the 50,000 Allied prisoners and 800 guns) was captured. Yet it had severely tested French defences, and these had been found wanting. The battle had absorbed a total of 37 divisions in defence, including five British divisions from IX Corps, with 17 being totally exhausted and requiring immediate relief. Aside from Soissons and parts of Château-Thierry, no other sizeable settlements were captured, and much of the area taken was farmland with little in the way of heavy industry or manufacturing which might help to sustain the German war effort. Indeed, on two counts it was the Germans who suffered most. Firstly, the losses of their trained *sturmtruppen* were massive, estimated at around 130,000 casualties – a figure that they could neither sustain nor easily replace.[20] Secondly, the British had not actually sent any troops to the aid of the French, apart from IX Corps, which was recuperating in the area prior

---

16   Michelin (1919), p. 9
17   Greenhalgh (2011), p. 361.
18   Michelin (1919), p. 9.
19   Greenhalgh (2011), p. 353. Doughty, p. 452.
20   Marix Evans, Martin, *1918: The Year of Victories* (London: Arcturus, 2002), p. 105; Greenhalgh (2011), p. 353 and Doughty, p. 452.

to the battle. The Germans also had another problem to contend with: the advance had been so rapid that they had all but outrun their supply lines, meaning that they had insufficient supplies and ammunition to press the attack beyond the Marne.[21] Just behind the German front lines, they brought up their massive railway guns and were able to shell Paris, resulting in a number of casualties and causing panic on the streets of the capital. The threat was so strong that even some Government departments began to move to safety out of range of the guns. Writing on 14 June, Crown Prince Wilhelm wrote that intercepted letters revealed the French Government was planning to transfer south to Bordeaux, whilst French banks were moving important documents out of the capital. Large numbers of Parisian civilians were reported at the city's train stations and seen leaving with their belongings. For the Germans, the firing of what was known as the Paris Gun on the French capital was thus having a material impact on the morale of the population there.[22]

After this latest reversal, Pétain told one of his divisional commanders, General Serrigny, that he expected to be relieved of his command. Serrigny disagreed, saying that it had been Foch who had taken all of the French reserves and the fault therefore lay with the Generalissimo, not with Pétain. Somewhat mollified, Pétain replied by saying that if it came to a choice between him and Foch, then he would resign since Foch was necessary for the eventual victory and Pétain would do nothing to sap his authority. To support Serrigny's view, it is important to outline that the Commander-in-Chief had made a crucial and timely intervention on 1 June, which is often overlooked when historians talk about Pétain's personality deficiencies. On 31 May, Franchet d'Espèrey had ordered Ve Armée to evacuate Reims in order to use these troops for the defence of the Marne. Upon hearing this, Pétain immediately telephoned *Ve Armée* headquarters to countermand the order, telling the officers that they were to resist where they stood and if necessary use violence against their own men to ensure they didn't lose the city.[23] Foch was well aware of the risks to his military career from this latest reversal, but he remained resolute, saying that whilst the house was shaken, the foundations were holding and that importantly, they would continue to hold. Crucially, both Foch and Pétain still retained the full confidence of Clemenceau, who urged the French Parliament to continue to fight, even though Paris might be threatened, saying: "I shall fight in front of Paris; I shall fight in Paris; I shall fight behind Paris."[24] Whilst Pétain was privately often circumspect and downbeat, in public and to his subordinates at least, he was showing new-found positivity, telling his staff officers that the latest attack would be contained and the worst was now over. It was here that one of his key character traits really came into play, namely that of calmness and levelheadedness. Unlike Foch or Haig, or indeed both of his predecessors, Pétain remained unflustered however difficult the situation might appear, which helped him to make the right decisions and never panic.[25] He concluded by stressing that if they could hold the foe during June, then by July, with American

---

21 Zabecki, p. 286.
22 General Service Schools, *The German Offensive of July 15, 1918* (Fort Leavenworth: General Service Schools Press, 1923), p. 17. This is generally known by the title *Marne Source Book* and will be referred to as this from here onwards.
23 Guy Pedronici (ed.), *Histoire militaire de la France*, vol. 3 (Paris: PUF, 1992), p. 376 cited in Greenhalgh (2014), p. 296.
24 Serrigny, pp. 480–81 quoted in Ryan, p. 168 and Herbillon, quoted in Greenhalgh (2011), pp. 354–56.
25 Atkin, p. 15.

troops arriving in their thousands and tanks rolling off the production lines, they would be in a position to go over to the offensive and then "the victory will be ours".[26] *"J'attends les chars et les Américains"* (I am waiting for the tanks and the Americans) – a phrase that he had first coined as far back as December 1917 –, was about to come true.[27]

4.2 The Allies plan their own counterpunch

Both Foch and Pétain recognised that the huge Marne salient created by the German advance to the River Marne during Operation *Blücher-Yorck* presented a unique opportunity to strike back at the Germans; but only if they could do so quickly. There was, as always, a difference of opinion between the two commanders. Whereas Foch wanted to make a pre-emptive strike, attacking the enemy before they could attack again, Pétain preferred a different approach, favouring the Napoleonic tactic of allowing the enemy to attack first, then responding with well-directed counterpunches, preferably in a different location from the German attack, since this would cause additional problems for German logistics. For the time being at least, whilst Foch was the Allied Generalissimo, thus holding the balance of power, it was Pétain who held all of the cards in terms of the tactics of the French Army under his command, and he preferred the latter option. Foch would have to bide his time and just hope that Pétain would be proven correct.[28] Allied communications into the salient were much stronger than German communications, and critically they still held the important railway centres of Reims, Châlons and Epernay. But it was Soissons at the north-western tip of the salient, in Mangin's *Xe Armée* sector, which was the key hinge to the whole salient, the hub which connected all the rail centres with each other. In contrast, the Germans could only rely on two small railway lines – one running north–south from Soissons to Château-Thierry and the other west–east from Soissons to Reims.[29] All German trains had to pass through Soissons, and the line to Reims was still in Allied hands, meaning that there was one clear and obvious choice for the main thrust of the counteroffensive. With both the western and eastern flanks firmly held by the French, if they were able to attack with speed before the Germans could prepare any significant defensive positions, then they might be able to close the neck of the pocket, severing the jugular vein and trapping 40 divisions of the German Army inside the salient. Failing that, they might (as a bare minimum) be able to squeeze the salient from all sides, progressively choking it of supplies and forcing the enemy out of the poche, hopefully as quickly as they had occupied it in the first place. Pershing too had identified the vulnerability of the new Marne salient, urging his staff to "look at that balloon" on the maps laid out in front of him, with only a single railway line and road to transport all of the men, guns, ammunition and food for the German forces. Pershing later pointed out this opportunity to both Foch and Clemenceau on 23 June.[30]

---

26   Ryan, pp. 168–69.
27   Menat, Candice, *Les Chars et les Américains* (HAL, 2013).
28   Neiberg (2003), p. 72.
29   Neiberg (2003), pp. 82–84 ; Mangin, Charles, *Comment finit la Guerre* (Revue des deux mondes 1920), pp. 193–94 and Doughty, p. 466.
30   Palmer, Frederick, *Our Gallant Madness* (Garden City, NY: 1937) cited in Nelson, James Carr, *The Remains of Company D* (New York: St Martin's Press, 2009), p. 169.

Foch therefore ordered Pétain and the French *Grand Quartier Général* (GQG) to commence preparations for a counteroffensive operation to recapture the salient. The plan was ambitious, even audacious: Mangin's *Xe Armée* and Degoutte's *VIe Armée* would drive eastwards, whilst *IXe Armée* under the newly appointed General Antoine de Mitry would throw the enemy back across the Marne between Château-Thierry and Dormans and drive them north. Berthelot's hard-pressed *Ve Armée* to the east, meanwhile, would do whatever it could to push the Germans westward, but this was not expected to be much. The hope was that the four armies would converge along the neck of the *poche*, trapping or cutting off the enemy inside, with *Xe* and *Ve Armées* having the critical role of closing the trap across the neck of the pocket. With any luck, a breakthrough of the German lines into open country beyond, if possible assisted by cavalry, would create panic within the ranks of the disorganised and disorderly enemy troops. Foch proposed the four armies, totalling 54 divisions, almost 800 tanks and 1,700 aircraft, would attack along the entire salient, a distance of 105km, and ordered Mangin, who had been identified as the spearhead of the counteroffensive, to begin intensive planning for an attack.

However, no sooner had the Chemin des Dames offensive wound down on 5 June, than the Germans opened up their next attack on the 9th: Operation *Gneisenau*, which aimed to extend *Blücher-Yorck* west, straightening out the front between the two bulges in the line, thereby linking the Marne and Amiens salients, enabling the Germans to free up some of their forces and releasing pressure on their supply lines which ran down the western side of the salient. With a growing shortage of reserves, this had only ever been intended as a minor operation to straighten the line. Once again, the intention was to draw Allied reserves south towards the threatened front, with von Hutier's Eighteenth Army attacking, this time against General Humbert's *IIIe Armée* on the River Oise between Montdidier and Noyon. However, almost constant meddling and interference by Ludendorff, trying to micro-manage every aspect of the planning, had led to the original objectives being extended, but without any additional troops being deployed. In nearly every aspect, the planning for Operation *Gneisenau* was inferior to that for *Blücher-Yorck*. Staff work was less rigorous than before, whilst ammunition and particularly petrol were in short supply, suggesting that the heavy artillery would probably be less effective. Manpower too was getting weaker, with a major outbreak of influenza affecting many divisions preparing for battle.

Then on 3 June, a German radio transmission was intercepted, and after 26 hours of intensive work, French cryptologist Georges Painvin and his small team deciphered the message, which indicated the likely location for the attack was between Montdidier and Noyon. The French were further alerted to the imminent attack by a captured German aviator, allowing Humbert to partially withdraw some of his forces away from the front line at the last minute, reducing the potential casualties from the artillery bombardment. But just as had been the case with Duchêne's *VIe Armée*, Humbert had not been able to move enough troops back and had crammed too many in the first position (with half the infantry within 2,000 metres of the front line). When the Germans attacked with 15 divisions across a 37km front after another fearsome Bruchmüller artillery bombardment, they thus quickly overran the first and second positions, with the French *58e* and *125e divisions* giving way and falling back, allowing the Germans to advance 14km in little more than two days and threatening Compiègne, with some German units even managing to cross the River Matz. The French *2e CA* suffered particularly badly, with it being all but destroyed.[31] After having been forced by Fayolle and Pétain to instigate the defence-in-depth system, Humbert had hastily made a partial reorganisation of his defences. Unfortunately, time had run out before these could be completed. Nevertheless, where they were in place the defenders generally performed much better, resisting the enemy attacks for much longer than elsewhere and vindicating Pétain's defensive strategy.

With the French having decoded an intercept which gave them an early warning of the intended location of the offensive, Foch had decided to move some of his reserve divisions from the north to the Aisne to support Pétain, much to the disgust of Haig, who believed that he was being denuded of vital French troops. Haig's mood became even more angry when Foch ordered five American divisions which had been training in the British sector to return to the American sector in Alsace in order to free up French divisions for the defensive operations around Compiègne. With Haig still believing an attack in Flanders was imminent, he finally snapped when Foch ordered three British divisions to replace three from the French reserves of *Xe Armée*, which also moved south, threatening to invoke April's Beauvais agreement and declaring that it was a "waste to send half-trained American troops to the French sector and that British troops were being used up to the last man in order to give the French courage to fight!"[32] A furious row broke out at a meeting at the French War Ministry in Paris on 7 June, with Foch, Haig and Clemenceau all in attendance. After much recrimination and many raised voices, a number of key points and positions were clarified, not least the misunderstanding by Haig that Foch had taken away some of his reserves; he'd just asked them to be moved closer to where they might be required. Ever the charmer, Foch eventually got his way, allowing him to move four reserve divisions behind *IIIe Armée* and another three behind Mangin's *Xe Armée*.

The advance created another smaller salient, with General Fayolle's GAR intending to attack both sides of the new pocket, but the plan fell through when the French front line collapsed, triggering a more general withdrawal. The newly rehabilitated General Mangin, having been promoted from command of *9e Corps d'armée* to command *Xe Armée* on 7 June, met with Fayolle and Debeney on the 10th at Fayolle's headquarters at Noailles, with Foch arriving later that day, followed by Pétain. Fayolle ordered Mangin to prepare a counterattack against the German right flank to be carried out "as soon as possible", with Foch urging Mangin to attack the following day, 11 June. Having discussed the plans before his arrival, Mangin was asked when he would be ready to commence the attack, and both Fayolle and Pétain were taken aback when he said that he would commence the operation the next day. A wry smile came across the Generalissimo's face because he knew that 'The Butcher' was a man of his word; if he said that he could do it, then it was as good as done. Fayolle baulked at the mere idea of launching a counterattack so soon, believing it impossible for Mangin to get his divisions in place in time, but when pressed again by Foch, he too eventually agreed, issuing the order for the counterattack at 1600 hours on 10 June. For his part, Pétain said nothing, either in support of Fayolle or to back up Mangin, preferring to keep his own counsel. His silence spoke volumes to Fayolle, who saw that one man (Foch) was pushing for the counterattack, whilst the other (Pétain) was reluctantly accepting it. Despite Mangin having precious little time to organise the operation, he remained convinced that an attack was entirely possible in the timeframe he'd been given. Fortunately for 'The

---

31   Fayolle, Maréchal Émile, *Cahiers secrets de la Grande Guerre* (Paris: Plon, 1964), p. 121.
32   Haig diary, 3-4 June 1918, cited in Greenhalgh (2011), p. 367.

Butcher', by chance, General Estienne, commander of the *Artillerie Spéciale* (AS), the French tank service, was also at Fayolle's HQ and the two men left together to work up the detailed plan for the attack. Mangin eventually decided to use four of his five divisions for the attack (the *129e*, *152e*, *165e* and *48e*), with the fifth (the *133e*) held back in reserve.[33]

The five divisions, plus two regiments of field artillery and a brigade of British armoured cars of *Groupement Mangin*, was augmented by four *groupements* of tanks for the first large-scale use of French tanks in 1918. Two airborne squadrons were used for infantry liaison/artillery spotting, and a further two for air-superiority and bombing. The launch of *Groupement Mangin*'s surprise counterattack without the customary preliminary bombardment on 11 June is often held up as the precursor to the much-bigger Marne offensive of 18 July, yet this precedent is in reality false. Given the impossibly short lead time and the inevitable logistic difficulties of getting artillery into position, Mangin only had 45 (out of 72) field artillery batteries and 20 (out of 26) heavy artillery batteries available when the bombardment began at 1030 hrs on 11 June, with him only being able to issue his orders to the infantry at midnight. Unsurprisingly, Mangin subsequently ordered a delay of 30 minutes to 1100 hrs for the infantry assault. This meant that whilst it was intended to be a simultaneous artillery/infantry attack with no preliminary bombardment, which almost all previous attacks had, in reality when the assault occurred, it did so after a 30-minute preliminary hurricane bombardment.[34]

Nevertheless, despite the insanely short amount of planning time and the lack of artillery, the attack quickly pushed back the surprised Germans, who lost much of the territory they had gained at the start of *Gneisenau*. Mangin, true to character, wanted to press home the advantage, requesting to use the *133e Division* that was held in reserve. But Pétain forbid it and just as true to character, Mangin went ballistic, declaring to Fayolle that he could not understand why his plan for further exploitation had been overturned.[35] Foch and Pétain called a halt to the attack on the 13th, believing that it had done what they had intended – forcefully hitting back at the Germans – but worrying that a continuation might result in further unnecessary casualties for little gain now that they no longer had the element of surprise. The *152e Division* in particular suffered heavy casualties, losing 60 officers and 2,500 men in the counterattack. But as much as anything else it had been a psychological victory. It also restored Pétain's spirits, and he was noticeably much more upbeat in the following days. Unfortunately his good mood didn't last long, because on the 18th he attended a meeting alongside Fayolle and a grouchy General Humbert, who said that he had little faith in the troops under his command and that he wanted to use his reserves to relieve some of his tired divisions. Unusually for Pétain, he lost his temper and balled at Humbert, saying that his army commander was entirely responsible for the losses during the battle and that only Mangin's prompt action had saved his skin from being sacked![36]

After Mangin's sacking in 1917, the inquiry recommended that this "brilliant commander" needed to cool his "excessive zeal".[37] Nevertheless, when Clemenceau became Prime Minister in November 1917, one of his earliest actions was to take the decision to restore Mangin for a

---

33 Gale, p. 83. Greenhalgh (2011), p. 370. Fayolle, p. 121.
34 Gale, p. 86.
35 Fayolle, p. 121.
36 Fayolle, p. 121 and Greenhalgh (2011), p. 370.
37 Rapport de la Commission d'Enquête instituée par Lettre Ministérielle, No.18.194 du 14 Juillet 1917, p. 29 and SHD 5N255.

third time, initially in command of *9e Corps* in December 1917, believing him to be the 'right sort of general' to make the most of the offensive plans being developed for the following year. Having been earmarked for army command once again, Mangin was quickly promoted, first to command *9e Corps* and then on 7 June 1918 once again to army command, this time in charge of *Xe Armée*.

The attack on 11 June was considered to be a striking success, with further smaller follow-up assaults for the next two days pushing the Germans back 3km across a front of 8km. Just as the German Matz offensive was being halted by Ludendorff on the 13th, Mangin ordered a series of small operations to consolidate the front line, having captured 600 German prisoners and much equipment in the previous two days. The French had taken 11,000 casualties during the Matz attacks and lost 69 out of 144 tanks, most of which were to German field guns. In the period from 27 May to 16 June, the French lost almost 140,000 men in the two battles, as well as more than 200 guns.[38] The guns they could replace, the experienced soldiers less so, but they would have to find an answer, with another German offensive certain to happen sooner or later. One answer might be the arrival of American troops, starting to land in France in large numbers, who, albeit inexperienced and under-trained, were adding some much-needed spirit and a vital infusion of blood to the Entente.

The *Groupe d'armées du Nord* (GAN, Army Group North), recognising that a number of tactical deficiencies resulted from the hasty mounting of the counterattack on 11 June, circulated a note about the battle to all senior French commanders within days of its close. Given the nature of planning for the attack, there was little opportunity for reconnaissance, which had they not known the territory they were attacking, might have proven fatal. Second, if tanks were to support the infantry, they in turn needed to be supported by the artillery, and there was a need to improve the level of protection given to the tanks by French field artillery, a number of tanks having been destroyed by German field guns. However, infantry would still play the main role, and only infantry could occupy ground. Thirdly, the relatively low number of tanks involved in the Matz offensive meant that each tank was fired on by multiple German guns. If the French could put more tanks onto the battlefield, then this would dissipate the impact on each tank, increasing their chances of survival. Lastly, as in previous attacks, many of the tanks were knocked out before they arrived at the 'start line', so the French needed to find a way to get more of them into battle. They had employed smoke, but this had only been partially effective, mainly because the Germans were alerted by a preliminary French bombardment. What they needed was to increase the element of surprise.[39] The key to the French counteroffensive would be to maximise the element of surprise, and Mangin discerned that if he could coordinate a sufficient number of tanks, then his forces could strike with no preliminary bombardment at all.

---

38 Greenhalgh (2014), p. 304.
39 Gale, Tim, *French Tanks of the Great War* (Barnsley: Pen and Sword, 2016), pp. 102–03.

4.3 Operation *Hammerschlag* – The 'Hammer blow'

Elsewhere on the front, Operation *Hammerschlag* was put into action by the Germans at 0330 hours on 12 June with a 90-minute artillery preparation, with five divisions in the front line and three in the second from Seventh Army attacking westwards towards Compiègne at 0500 hours. The French, having been alerted to the attack prior to its commencement, had been able to pull back most of their artillery and at least some of their infantry. Resistance quickly stiffened and several local counterattacks on the second day forced Ludendorff to halt the offensive around noon on the 13th after barely a day and a half of fighting. The operation had yielded little in terms of territory but inflicted significant casualties on the French. Crown Prince Wilhelm's staff later concluded that *Hammerschlag* had been doomed to failure because the Germans had been unable to bring up sufficient supplies of ammunition for the attack, making the rolling Bruchmüller bombardment much less effective than previous offensives. The period after 13 June saw almost continual localised fighting by both sides, with the front moving back and forth as territory was captured and then lost as each side sought to gain the upper hand and improve their positions. One particular episode worth noting came about when General Mangin ordered a series of smaller attacks by *20e* and *30e Corps d'armée* between Soissons and the Savières brook, a small tributary which fed into the River Ourcq, which included crossing the brook in preparation for a much bigger offensive. Mangin's rationale for doing this was clever and insightful. Firstly, it improved his position in advance of the impending attack, removing the Germans' ability to observe his troops; and secondly, by only launching very small-scale attacks, he attempted to lull the Germans into thinking the sector had gone quiet and that nothing much was about to happen. This might then lead the Germans to remove some of the troops further south, to support the attacks along the Marne. Even if the Germans did suspect the French were preparing a larger attack and chose to leave their forces in place, the number of different parts of the front being attacked would hopefully keep the enemy guessing where exactly along the front the attack would fall, meaning that they couldn't risk moving their troops in case they were wrong. It was also a powerful signal, demonstrating that the French were no spent force and still very capable of launching their own attacks. This, Mangin hoped, would give renewed confidence to both his troops and to the wider audience beyond. Each attack was able to capture surprisingly large numbers of German prisoners: 1,100 on 28 June, 1,000 more on 3 July, 350 on the 8th and another 520 on 9 July. Together, this amounted to a quarter of a full German division, with the Germans finding it increasingly difficult to find replacements.[40] More significantly, this indicated that German troops were prepared to surrender rather than to fight, potentially a significant signal of worsening morale among the enemy, something that Mangin was keen to exploit and to inform his superiors about.

For a period, it looked like the situation along the front had developed into something of a 'phoney war', with both sides making small attacks but not wanting to show their hand. Nevertheless, one side was bluffing, just waiting for the right opportunity to strike. Both French and German prisoners often talked of knowledge of impending attacks, but this usually

---

40 Greenhalgh (2014), p. 312. Fayolle, p. 122.

included little in the way of concrete details and was usually not much more than rumour and speculation.[41]

Operation *Gneisenau* should be remembered as a strategic failure for the Germans, but also for the first time during 1918 a tactical failure as well, since they had failed to capture any of the rail lines they needed to supply the Marne salient. Not only had they not relieved the pressure on the *poche*, but they had expended another 25,000 casualties, troops invaluable and irreplaceable to their cause. While this was 10,000 lower than the estimated 35,000 French casualties, many of whom had been taken prisoner and would now need feeding in captivity, unlike the Entente, the Germans were now unable to replace their losses; manpower was becoming a critical constraint. If they could not halt the number of men falling ill with influenza, which looked unlikely, then they faced a very difficult summer and Ludendorff's plans for Operation *Hagen* would be in tatters. OHL quickly sought to justify the failure of the *Hammerschlag* offensive by changing the objective of the attack, from one of improving the position and conquering territory, to that of a diversion and relief of Operation *Gneisenau*. However, what territory it did occupy would now need to be defended, meaning there would be fewer troops available for the *Marneschutz-Reims* operation. As part of this defence, Seventh Army stressed the need to arrange a strong formation in depth, including tank defence; a clear suggestion that the area was vulnerable to attack.[42]

---

41 Marne Source Book, p. 16; Zabecki, p. 428; Army Group German Crown Prince, Noon and Evening Reports, (12 June 1918), Combat Arms Reference Library File: Extracts from the War Diary of the Army Group German Crown Prince, May 27 to June 15, 1918, Bose Wachsende Schwierigkeiten, p. 176 cited in Zabecki, p. 428 and Neiberg, p. 84.
42 Marne Source Book, p. 205. Zabecki, pp. 429-30.

5

All Change for the 34th Division

Battle casualties for the British 34th Division were especially heavy during March and April 1918, as the table below reveals:[1]

	Killed		Wounded		Missing		Total	
	O	OR	O	OR	O	OR	O	OR
January	2	23	9	175		3	11	201
February	2	4	1	8			3	12
March	20	192	56	1,005	62	1,844	138	3,041
April	31	254	135	2,202	40	2,397	206	4,853
May		8	5	46			5	54
June							0	0

Following Imperial Germany's first two offensives, which had pushed the BEF almost to the brink, Field Marshal Sir Douglas Haig decided to withdraw 23 British divisions from Palestine to bolster his forces on the Western Front and reduce every brigade from four to three battalions. A total of 145 battalions were disbanded, alongside three full divisions.[2] Between 21 April and early May 1918, 34th Division (minus its artillery) formed part of Hunter-Weston's VIII Corps, the artillery remaining with V Corps, with the troops of the division employed in digging defensive trenches from Abeele to Watouat in preparation for the next German attack, expected to fall on the Ypres salient. With the division unable to replace its heavy losses from March and April, the army commander visited General Nicholson to inform him that, owing to lack of reinforcements, it had been decided that the division be reduced to a training establishment to assist in training of American troops, the infantry of the division reduced to cadres. This was said to have knocked the stuffing out of General Nicholson. The reduction to cadre strength commenced on 9 May and was completed by mid-May, with each infantry

---

1   Shakespear, p. 294.
2   *Western Front Association* <https://www.westernfrontassociation.com/media/5558/201805.pdf page 2>
    Takle, Patrick, *Nine Divisions in Champagne* (Barnsley: Pen and Sword, 2015), p. 224.

battalion consisting of just 10 officers and 45 other ranks, while the headquarters and brigades moved to the Lumbres training area, 40km from Boulogne on the Channel coast.[3] As part of the orders, several battalions were to be disbanded, having served with 34th Division since its arrival in France, and Nicholson felt their loss keenly.

On 12 May, the 34th Division transferred to XXII Corps, under Lieutenant General Alex Godley, who had been in command of the corps since its creation in December 1917. A number of senior command changes also took place. Lieutenant Colonel J.G. Dooner, Royal Artillery, became the Division's GSO1, with Major J. Hunter becoming GSO2. Command of 101st Brigade moved to Brigadier General W.J. Woodcock, and Brigadier General E. Hilliam moved from 15th Division to command 102nd Brigade. On 5 June, XXII Corps was notified by British GHQ that it had been assembled astride the River Somme for the purpose of securing the junction with the French, or if the need arose, to be rapidly despatched to the south in the event of a hostile attack on the French front. If this move south was required, then XXII Corps would come under the orders of a French commander, and it was instructed to comply to those orders as if they had emanated from British Command. The following day 12 June, 37th and 58th Divisions transferred into XXII Corps and instructions arrived shortly afterwards from General Debeney's French *Ier Armée* in the event that the French were attacked. Further transfers happened on 16 June, with 63rd (Royal Naval) Division joining from Third Army, with the 12th (Eastern) Division going the other way.[4] Later that day, further instructions were received from *Ier Armée* firming up 37th Divisional orders for it to come under tactical command of *Ier Armée* and to occupy the *deuxième position* behind the French *31e CA*. It was immediately clear that General Godley was being pulled in two different directions, and that trying to satisfy both British High Command and his new French masters was going to prove a challenge that would stretch his organisational and diplomatic skills to the limit. British Intelligence reported that the Germans had not moved many divisions south after the recent fighting and still had a number of divisions in reserve on Crown Prince Rupprecht's front. Haig remained concerned that an attack would fall on the British sector around either Ypres or Arras, and on the 16th he appealed to Foch for the return of XXII Corps to British command, repeating his request two days later when the pair met in person at Mouchy-le-Châtel.[5] However, the arrival of French reserves behind the French *Ier Armée* on 19 June meant that this order was never commenced, with Foch instructing XXII Corps to remain in its original positions astride the Somme for the time being, but to remain prepared to move south if the need arose.

From 17 May until 27 June, 34th Division was tasked with training troops from the newly arrived American Expeditionary Forces, including the 28th (Keystone) Division and 78th (Lightning) Division from 2 June and 80th (Blue Ridge) Division on 13 June, all of which were more than twice the size of their British equivalents. On 5 June, the 34th Division was transferred to VII Corps. Orders were then received on 19 June to reconstitute as a First Line Division with infantry from Egypt. Initially, the 6th Inniskilling Fusiliers, 5th Connaught Rangers, 6th Leinster Regiment and 2/4th Somerset Light Infantry were transferred from the 14th to the 34th Division. However, due to medical reasons, this was short-lived and they were

---

3   Shakespear, pp. 250–51, mentions 7 June 1918, but this date is contradicted by TNA WO 95/2439: Adjutant and Quartermaster General.
4   TNA WO 95/9742: XXII Corps, June 1918.
5   Greenhalgh (2011), p. 394.

withdrawn to the Lines of Communication on 24 June; only the Somersets survived, becoming the division's pioneer battalion. On 23 June, the first infantry battalion joined the division, the 2nd Battalion Loyal North Lancashire Regiment, followed the next day by the 2/4th Queens, the 4th and 7th Cheshires and the 1st Herefords. Further moves took place in the coming days, with instructions explaining that the division was being transferred to Second Army. All of the division's artillery and Field Companies, Royal Engineers returned.

Returning from a short period of home leave on 25 June refreshed and re-energised, General Nicholson immediately set about the task of rebuilding 34th Division with vigour, relieved to hear the news that the formation would once again be a front-line fighting force. Knowing that he might still have to spend time training the American forces, there is no doubt that he found the idea of action much more to his liking than baby-sitting these untrained and inexperienced doughboys, even if his new infantry battalions had been fighting a very different war in Egypt, Palestine and Africa and had only just arrived on the Western Front. On 28 June, the division was again transferred – albeit briefly – to II Corps, Second Army. The 34th Battalion MGC (having been temporarily training with Fourth Army), the 1/5th Battalion King's Own Scottish Borderers, 1/8th Battalion Scottish Rifles and 1/5th Battalion Argyll and Sutherland Highlanders also joined the division on 28 June, with 2/4th Battalion Queen's (Royal West Surrey) Regiment, 1/4th Battalion Royal Sussex and 1/4th Battalion Cheshire Regiment arriving the following day, followed finally by the 1/7th Battalion Cheshire Regiment and 1st Battalion Herefordshire Regiment on 30 June, arriving in billets in the Bambecque area.[6] Greenwood calls the reconstituted 34th Division a "hotchpotch of units from India, Egypt and Palestine, together with some Gallipoli veterans", with the implied criticism that they were disorganised and inexperienced. Neiberg similarly describes the 34th Division as comprising tired veterans and complete novices, the majority of whom had never seen action before.[7] However, neither was actually the case, and it should not be forgotten that aside from the infantry, the other units had served together within the 34th Division for most of their time on the Western Front, several of the infantry battalions having served alongside each other in both Gallipoli and Egypt.

In early July 1918, Godley's XXII Corps also underwent a significant reconstitution, becoming Haig's reserve corps, but placed under Inter-Allied control. Shorn of its ANZAC troops, it now comprised four British divisions – the 15th (Scottish), 34th, 51st (Highland) and 62nd (West Riding) divisions – passing into GHQ Reserve on 11 July. Although under Haig's overall control, in reality the instruction for its deployment would now be coming from Generalissimo Foch, with the corps likely to be thrown in wherever the next German offensive might fall. Now convinced that the attack would be on the French front, on 12 July Foch wrote to Haig once again, telling him that he had moved the reserve force behind the French front and that he wished to move two of Godley's reserve divisions to safeguard the junction between the British and French armies and prevent any rupture, requesting three further British reserve divisions to move into the territory vacated by the two divisions which had moved south. Haig, however, had gone on leave to England for eight days from 6-14 July and the matter was dealt with by his subordinates at British GHQ, with Haig's Chief of Staff, General Sir Herbert

---

6   TNA WO 95/2436: General Staff, 34th Division, 28 June 1918.
7   Greenwood, Paul, *The Second Battle of the Marne* (Shrewsbury: Airlife, 1998), p. 96. Neiberg, p. 24.

Lawrence, authorising the move in his absence. Upon his return from leave on the 14th, Haig was angry with the decision taken by Lawrence and telegraphed Foch, asking for an urgent meeting to discuss the matter and to put his case to the Generalissimo.[8] It is revealing that Haig was always resistant to using British divisions to bolster the French line, having sent virtually no troops south when the French were attacked in May and June and threatened again in July. This is in stark contrast to the supposedly conservative and cautious Pétain, who had not hesitated to throw all of his available reserves into both the March and April battles on the British front to help stem the German advances. However, once again Foch and Pétain had guessed correctly, anticipating the location of the next attack to be on the Marne salient and the Champagne region, so when Haig arrived to see Foch at Mouchy-le-Châtel on the 15th, the fifth German offensive had already begun. In spite of the fighting having broken out that morning, with the Germans reported to have crossed the Marne, Foch was in good spirits when he met with Haig. He promised to return the British troops from XXII Corps if they were not needed, for example if the British front was attacked, but he was confident that this would not be necessary.[9] So confident now was Foch that he insisted the best answer to the forthcoming German attack was the immediate and massive counteroffensive by Mangin's *Xe Armée* and Degoutte's *VIe Armée* on the left flank of the Marne *poche*, to recapture Soissons and squeeze the Germans, forcing them to abandon the salient entirely. His level of relaxation about the situation was now so complete that when, upon his return to Paris, Foch received a call from General Berthelot reporting that the Germans were crossing the Marne, in reply the Generalissimo simply told Berthelot to "limit their progress". When he heard this, Clemenceau was furious, saying that Foch had lost the plot and threatening to sack him. Fortunately for Foch, Colonel Grasset, the French attaché to the Supreme War Council, cautioned patience, telling Clemenceau to hold off from making a hasty decision and see what happened in the next few days.[10]

The infantry battalions now forming the three brigades of 34th Division were all new to the division, having arrived in France from a variety of locations in the Mesopotamian and Egyptian theatres as well as East Africa. Although all of the battalions had plenty of battlefield experience and comprised experienced men who had spent most of the war overseas (with the location making home leave difficult), this had been learned during the Gallipoli campaign or in the Middle East, conditions which were very different from those they now encountered. Indeed, since they had only landed in France during May and June, their experience of trench warfare fighting on the Western Front was next to nothing.

---

8   Greenhalgh (2011), pp. 394-95.
9   Greenhalgh (2011), pp. 395-96.
10 Greenwood, pp. 89–90.

5.1 101st Brigade

The recently promoted Brigadier General Woodcock, DSO, commanded 101st Brigade.[11]

The 2/4th Battalion Queen's (Royal West Surrey) Regiment was formed at Croydon in August 1914 as a Second Line unit attached to 2nd Surrey Brigade in the 2nd Home Counties Division. On 24 April 1915, the 2/4th Queen's was brought up to full strength and moved to 160th (Welsh Border) Brigade in 53rd (Welsh) Division, and the following month 400 men were attached from 2/5th Battalion. In July 1915, it reported for service in the Mediterranean, sailing from Devonport on the 17th, bound for Alexandria. With the 53rd Division providing reinforcements for the Gallipoli campaign, the 2/4th Queen's landed in Suvla Bay on the night of 8/9 August. By the end of September it had been reduced by battle casualties and sickness to just half of its landing strength, and in October was forced to form into a composite battalion, being evacuated to Mudros on 13 December with just 14 officers and 224 other ranks.[12] From there it travelled to Alexandria as part of the Egyptian Expeditionary Force, spending considerable time resting and recuperating, before becoming involved in a number of actions during the Sinai and Palestine campaigns of 1917, including the capture of Jerusalem in December. With the success of the German Spring offensives of 1918, urgent reinforcements were required, the obvious place to look being the Middle East. Not only was the offensive action there now slowing with the onset of summer, but these were highly trained and experienced soldiers; a better option than combing out more men from the home front. The 2/4th Queen's sailed from Alexandria on 18 June on the HT *Malwa*, landing at Taranto in Italy three days later, then spending a week travelling north to Proven, where it transferred to 101st Brigade on 29 June, the battalion under the command of Lieutenant Colonel W.J.M. Hill DSO, who had joined as CO a month earlier.[13] Whilst morale was fine, the health of the battalion was noted as being poor due to the prevalence of pyrexia (fever), diarrhoea, septic sores, plus cases of malaria and dysentery. However, sickness appears not to have been a major problem, with only 3 percent of the men reporting sick during July.[14]

At the outbreak of war, the 1/4th Battalion Royal Sussex Regiment recruited eight companies from across Sussex and brought them together to form the 4th Battalion, part of the Home Counties Division Territorial Forces. In April 1915 it was posted to 160th Brigade, 53rd (Welsh) Division, becoming the 1/4th Battalion. On 17 July 1915, it embarked at Devonport on HMT *Ulysses* to join the Mediterranean Expeditionary Force (MEF), arriving at Alexandria 11 days later, then departing for Gallipoli on 4 August and arriving off Mudros Bay on the 7th. The 1/4th Battalion Royal Sussex Regiment, together with the 2/4th Queen's, landed at Suvla Bay, Gallipoli, on 8 August. With the rest of the MEF, it evacuated Gallipoli in December 1915 and returned to Egypt, where it remained until 1917, when the battalion moved into Palestine and took part in operations there, including the First, Second and Third Battles of Gaza, the capture of Beersheba and the capture of Jerusalem. In June 1918 the battalion left Palestine, arriving at Alexandria on the 17th, before sailing in convoy to Taranto on 22 June on the liner

---

11 TNA WO 95/2456: 101st Infantry Brigade Headquarters, June 1918.
12 Westlake, Ray, *British Regiments at Gallipoli* (Barnsley: Leo Cooper, 1996) p. 12.
13 Haswell, Jock, *Famous Regiments Series: The Queen's Royal Regiment (West Surrey)* (London: Hamish Hamilton, 1967).
14 TNA WO 95/2457: 2/4th Royal West Surrey, June 1918.

Ormonde, accompanied by several protective Japanese destroyers. Nearing their destination, one of the convoy, the P&O liner *Kaisar-i-Hind*, carrying 3,000 troops and 500 crew, was hit by a torpedo close to the engine room, but the torpedo failed to explode. The battalion then went via Marseilles to the Western Front. On 30 June, the 1/4th Royal Sussex, under the command of Lieutenant Colonel G.S. Constable, joined 101st Brigade in the 34th Division, with an effective strength of 29 officers and 941 other ranks.[15]

The 2nd Battalion Loyal North Lancashire Regiment was in Bangalore, India, at the outbreak of the war, and on 16 October 1914 it sailed from Mumbai as part of Indian Expeditionary Force (IEF) B under overall command of Major General A.E. Aitken, destined for the East African theatre. On 3 November it landed near the port of Tanga, German East Africa (now Tanzania), with 27th Indian Brigade, in concert with the invasion Force C near Longido to the north, with the 2nd Loyal North Lancs being the only British unit within the IEF. With several parallels to the later failed Gallipoli offensive of 1915, the plan to capture German East Africa turned out to be overly ambitious and was described as "the action of a lunatic". Commencing with a botched landing, General Aitken ordered his troops inland towards Tanga. Although the 2nd Loyal North Lancs were able to fight their way into the town over the next 36 hours, on 4 November, poor support and a stout defence by a tiny force of German Askaris under Lieutenant Colonel Paul von Lettow-Vorbeck forced the majority Indian forces back to the sea, leaving the 2nd Loyal North Lancs alone and exposed in the town against intense fire. In a bizarre twist of events, several nests of killer bees were disturbed during the fighting, causing the insects to attack the men, with one casualty stung a reported 50 times.[16] The force's eventual withdrawal and ignominious re-embarkation was described as a "sorry debacle", having suffered heavy losses of 817 men killed, wounded or missing during the attack, including 115 from the 2nd Loyal North Lancs, plus the loss of eight machine guns, 455 rifles and 500,000 rounds of ammunition.[17] The British Official History described the Battle of Tanga as "one of the most notable failures in British military history".[18]

For the next 18 months, the battalion was engaged in fighting small-scale actions on the frontier of Kenya and German East Africa, with skirmishes around Lake Victoria and the capture of the Kilamanjaro area, all of which were more akin to the Boer War than the Great War. Due to the battalion's isolation, it was unique in one aspect: in addition to its infantry role, it manned an improvised artillery battery and established mounted infantry and machine gun companies. In May 1916, the 2nd Loyal North Lancs moved to South Africa to recover from mass ill-health resulting from a number of tropical diseases, spending their time recovering, re-equipping and training. It moved to the somewhat healthier climate of Egypt, landing at Suez in January 1917 and by April was attached to 232nd Brigade in the 75th Division. The battalion was moved in rapid succession to 233rd and 234th brigades of the same division, and

---

15 Battlefields 14–18 <www.battlefields1418.50megs.com/4sussex.htm> TNA WO 95/2458: 4th Royal Sussex, 30 June 1918. Read, I.L. 'Dick', *Of Those we Loved* (Barnsley: Pen and Sword, 2013), p. 325.
16 *Western Front Association* <www.westernfrontassociation.com/media/3039/201611.pdf>
17 Loyal North Lancs <lancashireinfantrymuseum.org.uk/the-regiments-in-the-great-war-1914-18-3> *Lives of the First World War* <www.livesofthefirstworldwar.iwm.org.uk/community/5255> *Western Front Association* <www.westernfrontassociation.com/media/3039/201611.pdf>
18 Hordern, Charles, *Military Operations East Africa, August 1914-September 1916, Vol . I* (London: MacMillan and Co., 1941), p. 100.

then detached as a result of a medical board on 9 August 1917. It proceeded to Sidi Bashr and was then placed on Lines of Communication at Gaza.

In May 1918, the battalion sailed from Port Said on board the *Huntspill* to France, landing in Marseilles on 26 May. A week later, the 2nd Loyal North Lancs, under the command of Lieutenant Colonel Charles E.A. Jourdain, DSO, was attached to 94th Brigade in 31st Division, with 36 officers, one Medical Officer and 1,097 other ranks, together with 19 horses, 25 mules and various vehicles. It also reported having 320 trained Lewis gunners within its ranks, but sufficient guns and replacements only arrived in the middle of June. By this time, more than half of the men with the battalion had not had any furlough leave back to Britain for 18 months and morale was starting to be impacted, especially as they were now the closest they had been to home since the start of the war. For some it had been even longer, and those who had spent eight years away from home were the first to be sent on two weeks' home leave. After that, only four men per day were released on leave, meaning that it would take four months just to get through all those who had been away for over 18 months.

On top of this, between 50 and 160 men from the battalion were in hospital at any one time during June, with approximately 80 percent of cases suffering from an epidemic of influenza. By late June, influenza was reported to be rampant in the 2nd Loyal North Lancs, with many men suffering the effects but not yet sufficiently ill to be sent to hospital, and the battalion was reduced to 734 all ranks. Malaria was also having a significant impact, with the other two battalions in 94th Brigade reportedly unfit for action. The battalion was informed on 20 June that it would be transferred from Second to First Army, becoming part of 34th Division. General Nicholson visited the battalion on the 24th and informed Lieutenant Colonel Jourdain that the 2nd Loyal North Lancs were to be attached to 103rd Brigade for the present time, under Brigadier General Chaplin, but this was subsequently changed to 101st Brigade, commanded by Brigadier General Woodcock. As part of this order, the battalion was reduced to 900 other ranks, with the 150 men surplus to requirements transferred to other battalions. The battalion never saw action on the front line during June, although several officers did manage a single reconnaissance in readiness for deployment. Instead, the battalion spent the month training. On 30 June, Woodcock went on a week's home leave, with Jourdain taking over temporary command of 101st Brigade and Major C. Seabroke assuming command of the battalion until Woodcock's return on 4 July. By the start of the month, the first wave of the Spanish flu had begun to subside, with the number of men in hospital suffering from influenza declining steadily throughout early July, only nine men reported to be hospitalised by the 18th.[19]

The 101st Light Trench Mortar Battery (LTMB), like all of the 34th Division's trench mortar batteries, had been re-constituted with effect from 26 June 1918, and all were reconstituted by 2 July.[20]

---

19 TNA WO 95/2457: 2nd Loyal North Lancashire Regiment, June–July 1918. Lancashire Regiment <www.lancashireinfantrymuseum.org.uk/the-regiments-in-the-great-war-1914-18-3>
20 TNA WO 95/2436: General Staff, 34th Division, 2 July 1918. TNA WO 95/2439: Headquarters Adjutant and Quartermaster General, 34th Division, 2 July 1918. TNA WO 95/2448: 34th Divisional Trench Mortar Batteries, June 1918.

5.2 102nd Brigade

The famous Tyneside Scottish brigade, 102nd Brigade was under the command of the recently appointed Brigadier General E. Hilliam, CMG, DSO, who had assumed command on 21 May. Having been shorn of its Scottish battalions during the recent reorganisation, it, alongside all other BEF brigades, now comprised just three battalions instead of the previous stipulation of four.

The 4th Battalion Cheshire Regiment was commanded by Lieutenant Colonel Geoffrey Hillier Swindells in July 1918. It was formed as a Territorial Forces battalion from the Wirral, with headquarters in Birkenhead. By March 1915 it was in Bedford, making final preparations for embarkation to India, but on 15 July orders arrived for it to re-equip for the Mediterranean theatre. It landed at Suvla Bay in Gallipoli, suffering heavy losses during its time on the peninsula. By the time it was evacuated in December 1915, casualties and sickness had reduced it to just 15 percent of its strength. The 4th Cheshires then moved to Egypt, being involved in the three Battles of Gaza and the capture of Beersheba and Jerusalem. On 31 May 1918, the battalion left Egypt bound for France, where it joined the 34th Division in early July.[21]

The 7th Battalion Cheshire Regiment had its headquarters in Macclesfield, with companies from across the eastern part of the county. Both the Cheshires sailed from Devonport in July 1915, going via Alexandria to Gallipoli, where they landed on 9 August. In December 1915, the battalion was withdrawn from Gallipoli and moved to Egypt, where it remained until 31 May 1918. Sailing to France on 18 June, it arrived at Taranto without incident four days later. The following day, the battalion entrained, spending the next week travelling north and arriving at Proven on the afternoon of 30 June. A total of 81 men reported sick *en route* from Taranto to Proven, representing 10 percent of the strength of the battalion, many suffering from malaria and several with signs of having influenza. The 7th Cheshires were attached to 102nd Brigade on 1 July under the command of Lieutenant Colonel H.L. Moir, spending the next few days undergoing musketry and Lewis gun practice and several episodes of gas training. The battalion was ordered to carry out a practice occupation of trenches in the East Poperinghe defence line on 9 July, but this occupation lasted little more than 90 minutes before the battalion was withdrawn again, having apparently fulfilled its remit. Further musketry, firing range and bayonet training then took place, as well as practice in the use of small box respirators.[22]

Like the two Cheshire battalions, the 1st Battalion Herefordshire Regiment also landed at Gallipoli, with 25 officers and 750 other ranks wading ashore at 'C' beach, Suvla Bay, at 0720 hrs on 9 August 1915, immediately going into action. Their divisional artillery had been left behind in England under orders for France, and the division had no other wheeled transport and no horses. It too was evacuated on 12 December 1915, with casualties and illness reducing the battalion strength to below 100 all ranks, moving to Egypt alongside the rest of 53rd (Welsh) Division. After rest, reinforcement and retraining, it was involved in the defence of the Suez Canal and Egypt, taking part in the Battle of Rumani in July 1916 and General Allenby's Palestine campaign during 1917. The 1st Herefords fought in the three Battles of Gaza and at Beersheba and Khuweilfeh, helping to capture Jerusalem in December 1917. In the subsequent

---

21 Crookenden, Colonel A., *The History Of The Cheshire Regiment In The Great War* (Uckfield: Naval and Military Press, 1938).
22 TNA WO 95/2462: 7th Cheshires, June-July 1918.

advance in March 1918, the battalion took part in the Battle of Tel Asur. On 1 June 1918, the 1st Herefords departed the Palestine theatre, sailing from Alexandria on board HMT *Kaiser I Hand* on the 17th of that month. Despite being escorted by a Japanese destroyer, the battalion's ship narrowly missed being torpedoed *en route*, before finally landing safely at its destination of Taranto on 21 June. Two nights later, the battalion entrained, with two passenger carriages for the officers, but most of the men, equipment and horses travelling in one of the 29 filthy goods trucks. They spent seven long and uncomfortable days travelling through Italy and France before arriving at Proven on 30 June, where the battalion, commanded by Lieutenant Colonel H.M. Lawrence, DSO, joined 102nd Brigade.[23] During June, one in 50 of the strength of the battalion reported sick, further reducing its numbers.

The 102nd Light Trench Mortar Battery was only formed on 10 July 1918, from drafts from base and other divisions, meaning it had no prior experience of conditions on the Western Front, having spent only a couple of days at II Corps School prior to its move south.[24]

5.3 103rd Brigade

Under Brigadier General J.G. Chaplin, DSO, 103rd Brigade, now comprising three Scottish battalions, was no longer the Tyneside Irish brigade of previous years.

The 1/5th Battalion King's Own Scottish Borderers (KOSB) from Dumfries and Galloway was initially in 155th Brigade, part of the 52nd (Lowland) Division. The battalion sailed from Liverpool on 24 May 1915 for service at Gallipoli, landing on 6 June. In January 1916, it moved via Mudros to Egypt, where it remained until 17 April 1918, when it sailed from Alexandria for France on board the P&O steamship the *Kaisar-I-Hind*, having taken on replacements including battalion second-in-command Major P.S.L. Beaver, transferred from the Wiltshire Regiment, prior to sailing (Beaver transferred to the 4th RSF upon arrival in France, but returned to the battalion on 31 May). It too had a close escape, with a German submarine firing a torpedo that only narrowly missed the *Kaisar-I-Hind* and almost hit the SS *Caledonia*. The 5th KOSBs landed in a cold and wet Marseilles on the morning of 17 April for service in France. Travelling by rail for three days and nights, the lucky ones were able to bag a seat in one of the compartments, but many men were forced to endure a bitterly cold and thoroughly miserable journey in one of the trucks, each of which carried 37 men. To make matters worse, it started snowing during the journey, and many must have cursed their luck of leaving the warmth of the Palestinian theatre for a cold and wintry France. Finally detraining at Noyelle-sur-Mer, 10km from the Channel coast, just north of the Somme, the battalion underwent intensive training, including gas, bayonet and close order drill. Towards the end of April, the majority of men were issued with new clothing better suited to conditions on the Western Front than those they had hitherto been wearing, while 100 reinforcements were added to the battalion, giving it a strength of 34 officers and 870 other ranks. However, during May, several hundred men were transferred to other units. On 7 May, the 5th KOSBs were put into the front line for the first time when they relieved elements of the 7th Gordons and 7th Black Watch at Neuville-St-Vaast. During their stay at the front, they were involved in firing more than 700 gas projectors into German lines

---

23 *Herefordshire Regiment* <www.herefordshirelightinfantrymuseum.com> The history of Ewyas Lacy, <www.ewyaslacy.org.uk> and TNA WO 95/2462: 1st Herefords.
24 TNA WO 95/2461: 102nd Infantry Brigade Headquarters, 10-13 July 1918.

at Arleux, before being relieved on the 15th. A further period of front-line duty started on 24 May in the Vimy area, with the battalion being bombarded by approximately 1,500 mustard and phosgene gas shells on the 27th. A hot sun warmed the morning air, leading to a number of men becoming casualties from the re-vaporised gas, resulting in 36 men being taken to hospital. The following day, the inexperience of the battalion to the after-effects of a gas attack became evident, when more men were hospitalised after failing to wear their respirators in the vicinity of where the pervasive mustard gas had fallen. Two men were particularly unfortunate, suffering blistering of their skin after using a latrine seat over which some of the mustard gas (powder) must have been sprayed, whilst others began vomiting after exercising. The battalion had 49 other ranks hospitalised having been gassed during the latter part of May, and a total of three officers and 128 men reported sick over the month. At the end of May, the battalion had a strength of 37 officers and 831 other ranks, and on 2 June it once again took over a portion of the line, this time in Toast Sector, Vimy, being relieved on the 11th. On 6 June, Lieutenant Colonel R.N. Coulson left for leave in England, with Major Beaver taking temporary command of the battalion until his return on 23 June.

The 1/8th Battalion Scottish Rifles (Cameronians) was another unit with the 52nd (Lowland) Division, with all companies coming from Glasgow. It sailed from Liverpool on the same day as the 5th KOSBs, via Egypt to Gallipoli, arriving there on 14 June 1915. The battalion fought at Gully Ravine in late June and on 1 July, after taking heavy casualties, the 7th and 8th Battalions were temporarily merged (not resuming its own identity until February 1916). Further fighting took place at Achi Baba Nullah and Krithia Nullahs before the unit was withdrawn in December. In January 1916 it moved via Mudros to Egypt, where it took over a section of the Suez Canal defences at the start of March. Its involvement in the fighting in the Sinai and Palestine campaign ended in March 1918, when it departed Arsuf for France, sailing from Alexandria on 12 April on board HMT *Canberra* and landing at Marseilles on 17 April, where the 37 officers and 816 other ranks disembarked in the rain, weather which was to become all too familiar over the coming weeks. They were commanded by Lieutenant Colonel J.M. Findlay, DSO, who had returned to the battalion on 13 May after being thrown from his horse at the start of April, only to be given two weeks' home leave immediately on rejoining his battalion. The 52nd Division concentrated near Abbeville and the 8th Scottish Rifles briefly went into the line (albeit a quiet part of the line) opposite Arleux near Vimy on 15 May for a period of eight days, before being relieved by the 7th Royal Scots on the 23rd. The battalion sent out platoons to improve posts each night from 26 May until 2 June near Neuville-Saint-Vaast, gaining valuable knowledge of conditions on the Western Front. It spent a further 10 days in the line later that month undertaking wiring duties as well as reconnaissance and trench improvements. On 25 June, the battalion received information that the 52nd Division was to be reduced by one battalion per brigade, with the junior battalions (8th Scottish Rifles, 5th KOSB and 5th A&SH) transferred to 103rd Brigade of the 34th Division on 28 June. Findlay recounted that he felt grief at this decision, expressing some wariness of the venture into the unknown in the days ahead. Things didn't bode well when the battalion took over billets from the French which were described as "indescribably filthy", but Findlay could only hope that with time they would improve. A draft of 40 other ranks from the 14th Highland Light Infantry arrived on 11 July.[25]

The 1/5th Battalion Argyll & Sutherland Highlanders was initially with the 52nd (Lowland) Division, and on 1 June 1915 it sailed from Devonport for Gallipoli, via Egypt and Mudros, landing at Cape Helles on 3 July. By 8 January 1916, it was being evacuated from Gallipoli back to Mudros, arriving in Egypt in February, where it served until 11 April 1918, when the 52nd Division sailed for France on the *Kaiser-I-Hind* with 41 officers and 1,035 other ranks. The 5th Argylls arrived in Marseilles on 17 April, commanded by Lieutenant Colonel C.L. Barlow, DSO. They too had a rude awakening to life back on the continent, with heavy rain on the 18th and a failure of their rations to arrive on time, but a couple of days later they were on their way north, departing Marseilles in the early morning of the 20th. Like the 5th KOSBs, the 5th Argylls then spent several periods in the front line near Mont St Eloi during May, and then a longer spell in the Willerval sub-sector near Vimy in June, when they carried out their first trench raid on the 13th. The men also benefitted from leave back to the UK being opened up, with everyone eager to return and see their homes for the first time in three years. Those who stayed were involved in several training exercises, gas training, close order drill and inspections, and a number of officers and NCOs departed on courses, with almost 200 men detached during May. At the end of the month, the battalion had a fighting strength of 28 officers and 839 other ranks, but with influenza affecting a number of the men, those figures had been reduced to 24 officers and 760 other ranks by 21 June. On 25 June, the 5th Argylls received information that they were to join the 30th Division, but this was amended and they joined the 34th Division on the 28th, with a strength of 27 officers and 771 men. Lieutenant Colonel Barlow proceeded to Britain on leave on 2 July, only returning on the 29th.[26] The brigade also included the 103rd Light Trench Mortar Battery, all LTMBs having been reconstituted by 2 July.

In June 1918, 103rd Brigade reported zero casualties during the entire month, and the new brigade was inspected by General Sir Herbert Plumer, commanding Second Army, on 3 July.[27]

There were various other units within the 34th Division, including the 2/4th Battalion Somerset Light Infantry, under Lieutenant Colonel E.B. Powell, DSO, which was formed at Bath in September 1914 as a Second Line Territorial Force battalion before becoming part of 135th Brigade, 2nd Wessex Division. By the end of October 1914, recruitment had been so successful that the battalion was more than 1,000 strong. On 12 December 1914, the 2nd Wessex Division set off for India under Lord Kitchener's orders but was broken up on arrival in Bombay in early January, with some elements sent to Bangalore. From there it was involved in quelling an uprising by the local Moplah population.[28] In August 1915, the 2/4th Somersets were mobilised and moved to Madras upon rumours of further unrest, before sailing for the Andaman Islands, an archipelago in the Bay of Bengal, as a defensive force in case of German raids there. The battalion returned to Calcutta in January 1916, where it spent the next 18 months, suffering an outbreak of cholera in July 1916 and losing 800 men to the first line battalion in Mesopotamia

---

25   Findlay, Colonel James, *With the 8th Scottish Rifles 1914–1919* (London: Blockie, 1926), pp.154–56. TNA WO 95/2467: 8th Scottish Rifles.
26   TNA WO 95/2466: 5th Argyll & Sutherland Highlanders, April-July 1918. The diary is incomplete, missing the period from 8–28 July 1918.
27   TNA WO 95/2465: 103rd Infantry Brigade Headquarters.
28   Wryall, Everard, *The History of the Somerset Light Infantry* (London: Methuen, 1927).

as reinforcements during the year. On 25 September 1917, the battalion landed in Suez, Egypt, coming under orders of 232nd Brigade in 75th Division, part of General Sir Edmund Allenby's Egyptian Expeditionary Force. The battalion fought in the Third Battle of Gaza, the capture of Gaza, the capture of Junction Station, the Battle of Nebi Samwil in 1917 and the Battle of Tell'Asur in 1918. With the onset of summer making fighting in the theatre almost impossible, a decision was taken to transfer a number of battalions to bolster the forces on the Western Front. Thus, on 2 May 1918, the 2/4th Somerset Light Infantry left the 75th Division and embarked for France from Port Said on board HMT *Ormonde*, arriving at Marseilles on 1 June after an uneventful voyage. They joined the 34th Division at Berthen as the Pioneer Battalion on 19 June. By the end of the month, they had managed just 10 days of training in the new kind of warfare and were at Wylder, from where the battalion moved to Proven, with the fourth company, D Company, being disbanded and absorbed by the other three companies on 5 July.[29]

There was also the 34th Battalion MGC, which left the 34th Division on 7 May 1918, being transferred to Fourth Army, before returning to the parent division on 28 June under the command of Lieutenant Colonel E.H. Kendrick.[30] Unlike the infantry battalions, the machine gunners had been heavily involved in defending both of the German attacks during the Spring offensives, losing 11 officers and 158 other ranks in March and 15 officers and 356 other ranks during the fighting around Armentières in April. The battalion arrived in Proven from the Vadencourt area on 28 June, where it enjoyed a few days out of the line for the first time in what felt like months.

Other units within 34th Division were: 152nd Brigade Royal Field Artillery, under the command of Lieutenant Colonel Alcard, which only rejoined the division alongside 160 Brigade RFA on 5 July; 34th Divisional Ammunition Column (DAC), commanded by Colonel C.N. Simpson, DSO, who was granted two weeks' leave from 8–22 July 1918, with Captain A.W. Mollindinia assuming command of DAC operations until his return on the 23rd;[31] 207th, 208th and 209th Field Company, Royal Engineers; Assistant Director Medical Services, 34th Division; 102nd, 103rd and 104th Field Ambulance; the Divisional Signal Company; the Army Chaplain's Department; the Adjutant & Quartermaster Branch; and the 34th Divisional Ordnance Services, commanded by Major D. Strickland from 28 June 1917.

Shorn of its infantry experience, having lost the battalions of the Northumberland Fusiliers and Durham Light Infantry, the 34th Division was no longer the division of the Somme or Passchendaele. This hard-won infantry experience had been replaced by regiments pretty much straight off the boat from North Africa and the Middle East, with many of these containing officers borrowed or transferred from other regiments. The 5th KOSBs were fairly typical of the experiences of the newly arrived battalions, being expected to immediately assimilate all of the details of a completely new method of warfare involving new weapons of war and completely different tactics, together with armfuls of pamphlets and instructions. Nevertheless, the 5th KOSBs missed much of the heaviest fighting on the British front, having arrived after the Operation *Georgette* battle had petered out. They undertook training at Witte, especially gas

---

29 *The Long, Long Trail* <www.longlongtrail.co.uk> TNA WO 95/2451: 2/4th Somerset Light Infantry, May 1918. Unfortunately, the War Diary is very concise, with most days just a single line of comments and containing very little detail for each entry.
30 TNA WO 95/2436: General Staff, 34th Division, 7 May 1918; 28 June 1918.
31 TNA WO 95/2448: 34th Divisional Ammunition Column operations, 8 July 1918.

drill, before moving on 7 May to the ruined town of Neuville-Saint-Vaast, north of Arras, where the devastating impact of war – and especially the recent German offensive – confronted the men. Occupying half-flooded trenches a mile and a half from Vimy Ridge, being shelled with 1,500 phosgene and mustard gas shells on the night of 25/26 May resulted in 36 casualties when the gas vaporised the following morning. Battalion strength was 37 officers and 831 other ranks at the end of May. After being relieved, the 5th KOSBs moved to a rest camp at St Eloi, where a severe outbreak of influenza swept through the battalion during June, laying low large numbers of the men for much of the month; nine officers and 206 other ranks were sent to hospital, the majority suffering from influenza, which represented about a quarter of the battalion strength. Reinforcements of 21 officers and 218 other ranks then arrived, many of whom were aged only 18 or 19 with no combat experience, whilst others were transferred from other battalions to bring the KOSBs up to strength. Some also returned from hospital, and the battalion ended June with strength of 39 officers and 826 other ranks. Three officers even managed to attend a tank demonstration at Wavrans during late June. The battalion then spent a week of training and inspection, followed by a week of musketry drills. A further draft of 167 reinforcements arrived in the first half of July, including 67 noted to be of exceptional quality, with the battalion now at Cormette and Proven. Two of their number, however, were rejected as they were identified as Russians unable to speak English![32] On 1 July, Lieutenant Colonel Dooner, the 34th Division's GSO1 (responsible for training, intelligence, planning operations and directing the battle as it progressed) departed for a week's leave to England, and the following day the division marched from Herzeele to Proven for training and reorganisation.[33]

In one way, the 5th KOSB was much more fortunate than most of the other infantry battalions joining the 34th Division, since at least it had been able to spend a month training and equipping for fighting in France before it moved south. The division's Royal Artillery, 34th Battalion MGC, Signals, Royal Engineers etc. had vast experience serving with the 34th Division, having been based in France and Flanders for the duration of their service overseas, but all had been badly mauled during the German Spring offensives, suffering heavy casualties, and several were severely under-strength, tired and in need of further rest. Unfortunately for them, they were all now required to support the French efforts in the battle further south. What made matters worse was that virtually all of the infantry battalions, apart from the 5th KOSB, had had no opportunity to even taste conditions on the Western Front, apart from training and route marches, departing south almost as soon as they had arrived in Proven. The 2nd Loyal North Lancashires' only experience was two opportunities for a small number of officers to reconnoitre the front. The 4th Royal Sussex did not spend a single minute on the front line before they entrained from Proven, with the battalion second-in-command, adjutant, transport officer and several other subalterns all absent on leave back to England. Whilst this was clearly welcome for those officers lucky enough to be selected for leave – many of whom had not seen their homes or loved ones for two years, some for three – the Sussex was shorn of several of its most experienced officers for its first engagement on the Western Front. Matters worsened for the battalion when Lieutenant Colonel Constable was injured falling from his horse, requiring Captain Weekes to take charge. D Company of the 4th Royal Sussex, replete with several draftee

---

32 Scott Elliot, p. 236. TNA WO 95/2466: 5th KOSBs, June–July 1918.
33 TNA WO 95/2436: General Staff, 34th Division, 1 July 1918.

replacements, was now led by Lieutenant Boniface, with just two second lieutenants under him, the shortage of experienced officers seeming likely to hamper the battalion's effectiveness.[34]

The 1st Herefords had their first experience of gas and the opportunity to try out their small box respirators, with three companies successfully passing through the gas hut. With two days of potential training lost, one due to inclement weather on the 12th and the next day lost with the battalion being moved to St Omar, this was vital experience they could ill afford to lose. What little training it received was in basic musketry skills, something it had done much of in Palestine, rather than potentially focusing on anything more useful.[35] However as events unfolded, these fresh infantry battalions making up the newly formed 34th Division were ironically perhaps better prepared for the new style of mobile combat than they might have imagined.

---

34 Read, pp. 339-42. Lieutenant Colonel Constable only returned to 4th Royal Sussex on 3 August 1918.
35 TNA WO 95/2462: 1st Herefords and WO 95/2467: 4th Royal Sussex.

6

Operation *Marneschutz-Reims* – The Germans Decoy Operation *Friedensturm* (Peace Offensive)

6.1 Planning Operation *Friedensturm*

The 'Grippe' or Spanish flu was now rampant within the German Army, but the long pause since Operation *Georgette* had wound down had enabled the battalions of Army Group Crown Prince Rupprecht to recover and bring them up to parity with the French and British. However, for Army Group Crown Prince Wilhelm, the situation was very different. The effects of the *Grippe*, together with two months of almost continual fighting, was seriously compromising the ability of the army group to be an effective fighting force. Nevertheless, the German High Command still believed there was sufficient manpower to allow it to strike one final knockout blow and force the enemy to the peace table.

General Ludendorff, wanting an offensive which he believed would finally break the Entente, chose what he felt was the vulnerable British sector in Flanders for the attack, which he codenamed Operation *Hagen*. The plan was to use Army Group Crown Prince Rupprecht to push the British back to the sea and out of France, but believed that with recent replacements, the British were now numerically too strong around Ypres. To enable the Germans to launch Operation *Hagen*, they first had to weaken the Allies by forcing them to divert reserves away from Flanders. To do this, the Germans designated a diversionary attack along the front of the Seventeenth Army, codenamed Operation *Eckenbrecher* (*Corner Breaker*), using forces from Crown Prince Wilhelm's Eighteenth and Seventh Armies. Further east, things looked more promising, the sector between Château-Thierry and Verdun being weakly held by the French with some American support.

On paper, the plan looked deceptively simple. Codenamed Operation *Marneschutz-Reims* (*Marne Defence – Reims*), Document No.5 was issued by Ludendorff on 14 June 1918 and set out the details for the attack. The German Seventh Army would attack the Marne River area (the Marne defence element) around Mery, whilst the First and Third armies would attack east of Reims to Tahure, with 10 July earmarked for the start of the operation. Châlons-sur-Marne would be their principal objective. Colonel Bruchmüller would once again act as artillery advisor to Army Group Crown Prince Wilhelm. Within the plan, there was the belief that a successful exploitation of the junction between the two attacking groups in the direction of Epernay might yield great results. Critical to the success was the capture and retention of *Côte 204* (Hill 204), looming high above the west of the town of Château Thierry, in the south-west of the Marne sector. Immediately following the operation, Ludendorff planned to concentrate all available artillery, trench-mortars and squadrons on the Flanders front, ready to commence Operation *Hagen* a fortnight later.[1]

The OHL had to concede that an attack would have to be made chiefly by the same troops which had recently been engaged in the advance across the Chemin des Dames. Using these tired troops was a risk that they would have to take, as there was simply no alternative; Ludendorff wanted to rest the divisions of Army Group Crown Prince Rupprecht ready for the Flanders offensive. Ninth Army, newly arrived from Romania, relieved Seventh Army and was inserted into the line on both banks of the River Aisne, between the Oise and Ourcq.[2] Within the initial attack plan, Ludendorff added that it was vital for the Entente to continue to believe that the Germans intended to carry on their offensive operations toward Paris. There are two obvious conclusions to be drawn from Ludendorff's statement: firstly, that the Germans were not aiming to capture Paris during the attack; and secondly, that Ludendorff considered *Marneschutz-Reims* to be merely a diversionary attack in preparation for Operation *Hagen*, which would be the main thrust further north in Flanders. There is clear evidence that this focus on Operation *Hagen* coloured Ludendorff's planning, potentially blinding him to the growing threat posed by the Allies' impending attack on the Marne salient, with a number of localised French attacks taking place over the following days. On 28 June, an attack south of the Aisne involving large numbers of tanks and other armoured vehicles and combat planes pushed west of Soissons on the front of Group Staabs, advancing and occupying Cutry, the hills to the north and south, and Hignières. Villages well to the rear of the German lines, such as Vauxbuin, were also targeted by large-calibre artillery. The importance of these attacks should not be underestimated. Firstly, they permitted the Allies to assess the strength and fighting ability of German forces. Secondly, despite recent reverses where the French were being perceived as losing the will to fight, they gave a clear signal to the Germans that this wasn't the case and that the French were still fully committed to the battle and the war. Thirdly, because there were so many of these smaller localised attacks, when the 'big push' finally came, the enemy might underestimate the threat, giving the Allies a valuable element of surprise which might prove decisive.

One of the fundamental aspects of any German operation would be the immediate and violent *Gegenstoss*, or counterattack, to regain lost territory before the enemy had time to consolidate their position or move up reinforcements. However, the poor state of some of the units facing these local French attacks and raids, plus the need to avoid denuding the Marne attacking force, meant that the Germans decided not to counterattack. This change in behaviour didn't go unnoticed by the Allies, who concluded that the units around Soissons were of a lower fighting quality and therefore potentially vulnerable to an offensive of their own.

The war diary of the Seventh Army seems to dismiss any such concern, believing that the execution of *Straßenbau* (road widening) – the eventual name given to Operation *Marneschutz-Reims* – would have a direct relieving effect on the front at Soissons and that no reserves would be required, whilst acknowledging the need to materially reinforce its west front.[3] The four previous

---

1 Marne Source Book, pp. 11–12 and Ludendorff, Eric, *My War Memories 1914–1918, Vol.2* (London: Hutchinson & Co., 1919), pp. 249, 278, 306.
2 Ludendorff, pp. 307–08.
3 Marne Source Book, p. 221; Ludendorff, p. 317 and Zabecki, p. 107.

German offensives had many similarities, which gave the Entente a significant advantage when trying to anticipate the next German attack. The advance on day one of Operation *Blücher* had been 18km, and it was anticipated that the fifth of the Spring offensives would conquer a similar distance, bringing it to the vicinity of les Grandes Loges–Vadenay and possibly even crossing the Marne.[4] But the big difference here was the obstacle of the river itself. Whilst the River Aisne was 40–55 metres wide, with its widest part being around Soissons, the Marne was altogether a different magnitude. It was some 70–80 metres wide and 3–4 metres deep, the current averaging 50–75cm, with 1.5-metre-high firm banks and steep, mostly bare slopes on either side, the French holding the hills 170 metres above on the south bank, commanding a good view of the river valley. As such, it was much the biggest natural obstacle the Germans would face in any of their Spring offensives. Despite this clear disadvantage, most of the ground to the north of the river was covered by extensive woodland, affording good protection against observation for the Germans, which would be crucial during the preparations for the attack. Another feature of the area was the relative scarcity of roads, with most only narrow country lanes. This would inevitably have the effect of constraining the ability of the Germans to move men and supplies quickly towards the front. Given these difficulties, it is therefore surprising that the First Army set the day one objective of penetrating a distance of 23km, which was 5km further than had been achieved during the first day of Operation *Blücher-Yorck*.[5]

General Bruno von Mudra's Order 2510 of 16 June decreed that the assaulting troops of his First Army would be split into three parts, with the advance in the direction of Bouzy–Epernay to link up with the Seventh Army being the centre of gravity of the whole attack. Here, the Germans anticipated little in the way of resistance. The prerequisite for success would again be to surprise the enemy, so deception would play a key role over the next month.[6]

The Germans were in no doubt that the terrain immediately surrounding the river would be a difficult obstacle to overcome. The lack of any real cover close to the river bank would mean that bringing up crossing materials and the approach by troops would be easily spotted and therefore subject to hostile artillery, machine gun and infantry fire by troops positioned on the south bank. The defensive position was aided by a railroad embankment at the top of the slope, which afforded excellent protection to the French and would have to be overcome if the attack was to succeed. It would be essential to quickly gain possession of the ridge. But even more than the element of surprise, it would be overwhelming firepower in the initial phase that would play a decisive role in the battle.[7]

The scale of artillery preparation and support was set at a minimum of 14½ batteries per kilometre, totalling 600 batteries, comprising:

- 388 light batteries;
- 197 heavy batteries;
- 15 super heavy batteries.

---

4   Marne Source Book, p. 25.
5   Blanchard, p. 22 and Marne Source Book, pp. 25, 36.
6   Marne Source Book, p. 26.
7   Marne Source Book, p. 37: document No. 30, 17 June 1918.

With 90 light and 65 heavy batteries required for the attack but unavailable, this shortage of artillery was causing concern within OHL. General Max von Boehn, commanding Seventh Army, wrote to Army Group Headquarters on 30 June, stating that 54 light batteries and 18 heavy batteries would be required but were not currently available, and there were too few artillery pieces to go around. A fifth and sixth gun was issued to each battery from the reserve and split between Operations *Marneschutz-Reims* and *Hagen*, so would not be available to plug any gaps or exploit any success from the former if they were on the move to support the latter.[8]

6.2 Scope creep and conflicting objectives undermine Ludendorff's plans

General von Boehn calculated that preparations for the attack would be completed by the end of June, but that a further 12 days from 1 July would be required to move his Seventh Army troops and ammunition into the area and to prepare the woods and forests for the offensive. There were also significant logistical challenges in the salient. For example, the standard-gauge railway could only transport four trains a day, whilst the narrow-gauge lines could cope with just seven ammunition trains per day, hardly sufficient to supply the divisions in the *poche*.[9]

One of the key features of the proposed offensive was that its scope kept expanding, entirely the result of Ludendorff's continual meddling. On 18 June, in a telephone message to Crown Prince Wilhelm, Ludendorff requested the 'Reims' element of the attack be widened east as far as Wetterecke. The secret Order Ia – 797, also dated on the 18th, saw the advance across the Marne towards Epernay renamed from *Marneschutz* to *Straßenbau* (translated as 'road building').[10] By expanding the offensive beyond the original objective of capturing Reims and freeing up the railway line, the 39 divisions that Ludendorff intended to throw into the battle were now intended to result in a stunning and decisive victory for the German Army, collapsing French morale once and for all and causing the French to sue for peace, his so-called '*Friedensturm*' or *Peace* Offensive. But with the ever-expanding scope came yet another delay to the launch date: first to 14 July and finally to the 15th.

Crown Prince Wilhelm wrote to the commanders of his army group that the objectives should be fixed at the start and be a good distance, in order to prevent the troops stopping too quickly. Ludendorff approved the plan on 20 June, indicating that the main point was to weaken the enemy in men and materiel. Artillery commanders were asked to prepare a preliminary plan only up to the evening of the first day of attack, which seemed to hint at a more limited scope. A day later, Crown Prince Wilhelm confirmed that in spite of the expanded scope of the offensive, no additional regiments would be assigned to First Army for the attack. The next day, the objective was again amended and the new plan laid out the principal objective as being to cut off the hostile forces in the hilly forests around Reims. This constantly changing emphasis and conflicting objectives did little to inspire confidence in the efficacy of the plan.[11]

The plan for First Army, for the 'Reims' attack, comprised eight divisions in three army Korps: three divisions in Group Lindequist, two in Group Gontard and three in Group Langer,

---

8   Marne Source Book, p. 228 and Ludendorff, p. 278.
9   Marne Source Book, p. 39.
10 Marne Source Book, pp. 49, 57.
11 Marne Source Book, Order No. 2605, pp. 78, 86, 91, 111, 119.

plus two in the Army Reserve. The average strength of these divisions was 746 men.[12] There was consistency in one aspect though: the need for rapid execution of the attack in the initial phase, especially the first two days, and to capture as much territory as possible. Hostile divisions and artillery, together with any local reserves brought up, must be overrun and beaten on the first day.[13]

Towards the end of June, Army Group Crown Prince Wilhelm began to worry about developments around the vital rail hub of Soissons, in the north-west of the salient. Localised attacks by the French had pushed back the German front line towards Soissons, and a telephone call from Seventh Army Headquarters to the army group suggested the French might use the new, more favourable position as a jump-off line to attack and recapture Soissons. Several German divisions in line in the region of Soissons, including the 14th and 6th, were in desperate need of replacement by fresh troops, whilst the 47th Reserve Division was considered to be completely worn out and unfit for fighting. But the French were evidently not without problems of their own: prisoners captured from the *38e Division* stated that a large number of the replacements were the so-called 'class of 1918' or were munitions workers combed out from the factories.[14]

On 29 June, Army Group Crown Prince Wilhelm's Headquarters ordered a reduction of 30 batteries from the original planned total of 600.[15] Despite this, First Army would be able to call on almost 500 artillery guns and 300 *minenwerfer* (heavy mortars) for the attack which would fire without registration.[16]

At some point during June, OHL, recognising the challenges ahead, seriously considered abandoning the offensive and going over to the defensive. But Ludendorff believed that another attack might conceivably be decisive: territory would be gained, bringing Paris under direct threat; British reserves would have to move south, weakening forces in Flanders and increasing the chance of success there; and German morale would receive a further boost. It was clear to him that the recent victories had not yet been decisive.[17]

---

12   Marne Source Book, pp. 175–76.
13   Marne Source Book, p. 120.
14   Marne Source Book, pp. 205, 265.
15   Marne Source Book, p. 214.
16   Marne Source Book, pp. 252, 305.
17   Ludendorff, pp. 279–80.

7

Operation *Hagen* and Operation *Friedensturm*

Ludendorff began preparations for Operation *Hagen* on 22 June, aiming in the direction of Amiens and Paris, and the intention was to commence movement of artillery, trench mortars and divisions around the second half of July. On 10 July, Army Group Crown Prince Wilhelm wrote to the Operations Section of OHL warning that a simultaneous attack against both Amiens and Paris would make it difficult to maintain momentum, since it would require ever more divisions to be added as the front diverged during the advance. Consequently, a decision would have to be made by Ludendorff whether to attack Amiens or Paris, but not both, given that 50 divisions would be required for the one attack.[1]

7.1 Attack Particulars

Seventh Army's preparations for *Straßenbau* had been completed according to plan on 14 July, with the infantry assault due to start at 0200 hrs the next morning.

The first rounds of artillery fire started at 0200 hrs German time on 15 July from Soissons to Tahure, with the infantry attack commencing at 0450 hrs behind a rolling barrage on a front from Charteves, east of Château-Thierry, to Vrigny and from Prunay to Tahure. During the artillery preparation, engineers crossed the Marne and began erecting pontoon bridges and other means of crossing to the south bank. Hostile counterbattery fire was causing heavy casualties and slowing or disrupting attempts to cross the river, with field artillery units unable to get across on the flimsy pontoons.[2]

Elements from Corps Kathen, Wichura and Conta of the Seventh Army reached the south bank and pushed forward southwards towards the hills, against fierce resistance from well organised echeloned machine gun, artillery and infantry positions. Corps Schmettow, fighting north of the Marne, faced even more stubborn resistance, especially from dug-in machine guns, making little progress. Elsewhere, the First and Third armies were having more success, having overrun the first and many of the second positions and pushing on into the intermediate line, enabling supporting artillery and ammunition columns to follow up behind. By mid-afternoon, however, the attack had stalled, due in part to the difficulty of getting guns across the Marne

---

1 Marne Source Book, p. 346.
2 Marne Source Book, p. 539.

and into position south of the river to support the attacking troops; Army Group Crown Prince Wilhelm estimated that they would require at least a full day's preparation before the attack could proceed further. Ludendorff was forced to admit:

> It was now clear that the object of the Operation – to cut off the enemy in the Reims valley through a junction of the Seventh and First armies in the vicinity east of Epernay – could not be attained. We had to be satisfied with minor successes. … First Army and the right of Third Army were directed to continue the attack in the belief that the enemy had to be held on the front in order to certainly prevent him from noticing that the attack had stopped, [and to stop him from] sending his reserves against the Seventh Army. The conduct of the enemy was an excellent example of 'giving way', tactics that we had been more or less directed to pursue since the Battle of the Somme. The result of this first day of battle had again shown that decisive, apt leadership can readily evade any superior hostile attack by a 'mobile' defence.[3]

However, Von Boehn commanding Seventh Army continued to believe that the French had insufficient reserves to reinforce their front and that a continuation of the attack for a second day would result in further gains.[4] Not wanting to delay Operation *Hagen*, troops began moving north to Army Group Crown Prince Rupprecht on the 16th, resulting in the gravity of attack narrowing and falling largely on the German First Army.[5] Further north, near Longpont, Fritz von Below's Ninth Army had troubles of its own. French forces had been advancing in local attacks on the 15th and 16th in order to improve their positions, whilst Corps Kathen was confronted by French tanks making an attack on the villages of Moulins and Paroy. But the feeling within the OHL and Army Group Crown Prince was that these were nothing more sinister than localised attacks in response to *Marneschutz-Reims*. What they failed to appreciate was that they were in fact attempts to improve French jumping-off positions in advance of their own attack.[6]

Meanwhile, around 1900 hrs, a squadron of 60 French, British and American planes bombed the Marne valley crossings, causing considerable damage and a number of German casualties. German fighters sent to intercept them were reported to have shot down 25 of the enemy for the loss of just five of their own, and a further 25 Allied planes were reported shot down the next day.[7]

In places, German casualties had been horrendous. By the time they crossed back over the Marne, the 47th and 398th Infantry Regiments had a fighting strength of 400 men, whilst the 6th Grenadier Regiment was down to just 150 men. Other units losses were even worse, with some being reported to have been virtually wiped out.[8]

Army Group Crown Prince Wilhelm directed the cessation of attacks south of the Marne but a continuation of them north of the river against the wooded heights around Reims, and on

---

3   Marne Source Book, pp. 540–41.
4   Marne Source Book, pp. 544, 547.
5   Marne Source Book, Ic No. 9305, Secret, op, p. 544.
6   Marne Source Book, pp. 548, 566, 576.
7   Marne Source Book, p. 549.
8   Marne Source Book, pp. 551, 581.

the evening of 16 July issued new orders for First Army to make preparations to capture Fort Pompelle to the east of Reims. The latter were quickly altered to include an operation to capture the city itself, pushing First Army's right wing south and then turning in from the east.[9]

On the 17th, strong Allied counterattacks were continuing across large parts of the Marne battle front, pushing the Germans back in many places and recapturing a number of villages. Several villages had changed hands multiple times during the day. Fighting was especially fierce in the Corps Kathen and Wichura sectors south of the Marne, with heavy losses on both sides. That day, Corps Conta lost almost all of the terrain it had gained since the 15th, and bridges across the river continued to be destroyed faster than they could be built, worsening the logistics situation for the Germans. Seventh Army therefore sought an urgent answer from army group headquarters whether it needed to commence preparations to evacuate back north of the Marne on the night of the 17th. The immediate reply from the army group was that the position must be held in order to prevent any flanking of the attack on the hills of Fleury from the south bank. The war diary of Army Group Crown Prince Wilhelm concluded that the course of events, however, would soon demand a new decision.[10]

7.2 French preparations for the defence of the Marne

German preparations had been beset by problems and setbacks. Some were unavoidable, such as the shorter nights of July making night-time movements more difficult. Others were self-inflicted wounds, most notably a German engineer officer who had swum across the River Marne to reconnoitre the south bank but had been captured. In his possession was a complete set of plans for the attack, including the location of several ammunition dumps and assembly points, as well as battery positions; all vital information that could be used to disrupt German preparations. On top of that, a high-placed spy within German Crown Prince Wilhelm's staff reported that *Friedensturm* was the only offensive currently under consideration. This fact was passed to Colonel de Cointet, the French *2me Bureau* chief, to General Pétain and from him through to Foch, and they agreed that it was an absolutely critical piece of the jigsaw, since it meant that the French could focus all their efforts and reserves on the Marne *poche* instead of worrying about other German offensives.[11]

Unknown to the Germans, the French had begun detailed preparations to prevent the Germans crossing the Marne as early as 2 July, two weeks before the actual attack. The overall defence would be based on the new elastic defence in depth deployment laid out in Pétain's Directive No.4. The front line would be held by isolated strongpoints, to be garrisoned by platoons or sections, and three-quarters of the infantry strength was to be held back behind this thinly held first line. In the *IVe Armée* sector, General Gouraud had meticulously prepared his defences in depth, having occupied the same ground since the autumn of 1914, but to the west of Reims, the French had occupied these positions only since the end of May. General Berthelot, had been in command of *Ve Armée* for 10 days, and therefore had no time to order the construction of proper defences. Having said that, he was no fan of elastic defence and had

---

9 Marne Source Book, Order Ia 2672 Secret, pp. 562, 565, 585.
10 Marne Source Book, pp. 591–93
11 Greenhalgh (2011), p. 388. Cointet memoirs, p. 101, cited in Greenhalgh (2011), p. 388.

pretty well ignored the instruction by pushing the vast majority of his forces into front-line positions.

The French believed the vicinity of Mont-Saint-Père–Mézy-Moulins to be the most likely location for the Germans to try to cross the Marne, as it had good cover for working parties as well as cover in the rear for reserves moving up the line. The topography of the Marne river bank meant that the troops garrisoned on the front line were required to check and if possible repulse the German advance back into the river, rather than simply slowing it down. Troops would be available for an immediate counterattack if the Germans managed to get a foothold on the south bank, and small parties of Germans could be permitted to land, but with instructions to cut off their escape.

7.3 15 July – A bridge too far

Ludendorff clung to the belief that the attack was based on sound military principles and remained convinced that it would succeed. A total of 52 divisions from von Boehn's Seventh, von Mudra's First and von Eben's Ninth armies would attack along a 110km front, preceded by another massed artillery bombardment, set up once again by Colonel Bruchmüller. But the attack had started to go wrong even before a shot was fired by the Germans. At 2000 hrs on 14 July, French guns opened up on the German positions after receiving an alert, and continued for the next four hours.[12] With the French having uncovered the exact timing of the attack only hours before, starting at midnight they commenced a fierce counterbombardment on likely assembly positions, villages, roads and rear areas, 10 minutes before the Germans were due to commence artillery preparation; one battalion of the 47th Infantry was reported as having been completely routed by the bombardment.[13]

Whilst First Army attack units in Groups Lindequist, Gontard and Langer were able to move into position without trouble, when the offensive fire opened up at 0110 hrs German time (0010 hrs), in the 10th Division there was immediate disruption to all communications in the vicinity, with the division's Signal Officer reporting that all telephone communications had been completely shot to pieces by enemy shelling.[14] At 0510 hrs, the first reports appeared to suggest that elements of 398th Infantry had safely crossed the Marne, with the 2nd and 3rd Battalions reportedly across by 0522 hrs, but that all units were meeting with stiff resistance on the south bank of the river and making little headway. Connection had been lost with units on their left and right flanks, and with heavy casualties, reinforcements were urgently required.[15] Early reports from Seventh Army lacked detail, but they too suggested that elements had crossed the Marne against fierce resistance. Almost all of the existing bridges and other hastily constructed crossing points had been blown, and attacking units were having huge difficulty launching their boats, many failing to get across the river before being sunk or having their passengers killed.

By 0545 hrs, the 6th Grenadiers had passed beyond the villages of Mezy and Moulin and were working their way southwards. But by 0910 hrs, having been outflanked and counterattacked, they were driven back across the Marne, suffering heavy losses in killed and

---

12 Marne Source Book, p. 501.
13 Marne Source Book, p. 509. Ludendorff, p. 279.
14 Marne Source Book, p. 507.
15 Marne Source Book, p. 510.

captured. Immediately north-east of Mezy was the village of Chartèves, which sat just north of the river. Here the whole area was under heavy Allied bombardment, making the construction of pontoon bridges and crossing by boat impossible. Everywhere the infantry was requesting urgent artillery support. At 1030 hrs, the 2nd and 3rd Battalions, 47th Infantry, were ordered to attempt another crossing of the river. Where units did manage to get across, they almost always lacked heavy machine gun and trench mortar support, which were vital in consolidating their positions south of the river, so it was left to the infantry, supported by artillery, to push forward up the south bank.

At 1915 hrs, orders arrived that artillery (which had been due to be withdrawn ready to move to support the planned *Hagen* offensive) would instead remain in position temporarily to support the following day's renewed attack. In the 10th Division, this included elements of the 6th Bavarian Field Artillery and 100th Foot Artillery Battalions. Facing the stark reality of the complete failure of the attack in the 10th Division sector, at 1935 hrs Corps headquarters ordered 10th Division to withdraw back across the Marne overnight.[16]

Elsewhere, in spite of a fierce artillery barrage on the German lines and crossing points, the attackers were having more success. In First Army, Group Lindequist had taken Prunay and was north-east of Wez-Thuizy, and by 1020 hrs the Bavarian Ersatz Division was south-west of Dontrien. The early morning fog was lingering, preventing planes from getting airborne, frustrating both sides' attempts at aerial reconnaissance. The 36th Division was attempting to ascend the slope south of the river, but this was stubbornly defended by portions of the US 3rd Division and French *125e Division*. At Corps Wichura, everything was said to be progressing favourably, with two divisions reaching St Agnan and La Chapelle, while the 1st Guards were approaching Comblizy. Corps Conta was also seeing progress but was only able to get a small proportion of its artillery across the Marne on ferries.[17] To make matters worse, the Kaiser had arrived at the battlefield on the evening of 15 July, fully expecting to see German troops holding Reims. But the Kaiser would have to content himself with the limited gains made and that they had at least been able to cross the Marne in a few places, creating a bridgehead 14km long and 6km deep south of the river by the time night fell.

The French GQG's response to the unfolding events was somewhat confused, in the morning at least, with Pétain considering the situation serious enough to order Fayolle to suspend preparations for the counteroffensive planned for the 18th and transfer some of the forces from Mangin's *Xe Armée* to the bottom of the Marne *poche* in an attempt to repulse the German advance south of the river. When Foch arrived at Fayolle's headquarters later that morning, he spoke with the commander of the GAR, who explained Pétain's request. Driving back to Foch's headquarters at Mouchy-le-Châtel for a meeting with Haig, Colonel Desticker, Foch's Chief of Staff, telephoned General de Barescut from the French GQG's *3e Section* at 1300 hrs to countermand Pétain's order, with the *2e Corps de cavalerie* ordered to make an about-turn and return to *Xe Armée* for the attack on the 18th. Foch also decided to add another division to Mangin's forces, with *58e Division* inserted into the line between 15 and 17 July, but *168e Division* going the other way added to CAG's reserves. There could, he said, be absolutely no question of slowing down the preparations for the counteroffensive; it would be folly to take

---

16   Marne Source Book, p. 515.
17   Marne Source Book, p. 518.

any of the 22 divisions from Mangin's *Xe Armée*, which would spearhead the attack, for such a purpose as Pétain intended. With such an abundance of resources available to Mangin, he did concede that Pétain could – if absolutely necessary, and only after consulting with Foch beforehand – transfer some troops south to bolster the defence. He also agreed to postpone the attack by one day, to give the French a little more time to prepare. However, reports were arriving which indicated that the German attack was already beginning to stall and that the front was stabilising, especially in *IVe Armée*'s sector. Foch used this piece of positive news to instruct Pétain to move reserves from *IVe Armée* to *Xe Armée* instead and to allow Mangin to continue with his preparations unfettered. But events could still turn against the French, so Foch met with Haig later that day and requested that Haig release to him two additional divisions to support the defence on the Marne; the scale of the German attack indicated that it could not just be a feint, so the chance of the Germans attacking the British front had diminished. But just in case he was wrong and the Germans did attack, he ordered the two British divisions to disembark further to the west so that they could be returned more quickly in the unlikely event that they were needed.[18]

7.4 16 July

Third Army Headquarters telephoned Army Group Crown Prince Wilhelm at 1235 hrs on 16 July detailing the French elastic defence in depth system. First positions had been prepared as a foreground zone, with the second position being the main line of resistance and artillery deeply echeloned in the third position. The whole arrangement had only begun in the few days preceding the offensive, but nevertheless, all defensive positions were ready when the attack commenced.[19]

Recognising that the attack had been a failure, with numerous reports of heavy casualties, the German OHL realised that there was now little prospect of a breakthrough and was forced to issue orders by noon on the 16th for the suspension of the offensive by First and Third Armies, and to move to the defensive. According to Ludendorff, "we had to content ourselves with the improvement in our position brought about by regaining possession of the heights we had lost in the spring of 1917 and we had even secured a deep forward zone". Contradicted by the reality of the situation along the Marne, this was simply face-saving in an attempt to rationalise and excuse the failure of the offensive. It was abundantly clear that the German masterplan for a decisive offensive was now in complete tatters, and the *Friedensturm offensive* had been an absolute strategic, operational and tactical failure.[20]

According to the war diary of Army Group Crown Prince Wilhelm on the 16th, it was now clear that no further progress south of the Marne would be possible, with the only success on that day coming north of the river. The French defences opposing First and Third Army were just too well organised, whilst those opposite Seventh Army were of lower quality but were

---

18   Greenhalgh (2011), pp. 399–400. Greenwood, p. 88. Neiberg, p. 121. Woldike, Aage, *Report by the Field Marshal Commander-in-Chief of the French Armies of the North and Northeast on the Operations of 1918. The Offensive Campaign (18 July – 11 November). II Part. Château-Thierry–Soissons counter-offensive (18 July-6 August)* (2003), p. 18.
19   Marne Source Book, p. 550. Ludendorff, p. 310.
20   Ludendorff, p. 301.

aided by the terrain south of the Marne. The continuation of the advance and the anticipated sacrifice of men and materiel to gain these positions would not correspond to any probable gain. Only two attacks were contemplated: one an attack between Sermiers and Vrigny, which might force the French out of the Reims basin, and the other to take Fort Pompelle to the east of the city; Ludendorff ordered First and Third armies to move several divisions to support the latter attack, especially that to the west of Reims. Thus, orders were issued at 1945 hrs for Seventh, First and Third armies to halt the attack and prepare for defence. Two days of planning would be required for the next thrust around Reims, as well as the need to bring up additional artillery support, with the attack planned for 21 July, four days away. But by then, events to the west of the Marne salient would mean that it would be too late.[21]

7.5 17 July

On 17 July, the retirement was fixed for the night of the 20th/21st, but it would be imperative for German forces south of the Marne to hold out until then. New pontoons and crossing points would need to be constructed, since all existing ones had been destroyed. The OHL thought that a continuation of the attack up the Ardre valley might still result in the envelopment of Reims, and Ludendorff met General von Mudra and his Chief of Staff from First Army at Rethel on the 17th to discuss the plans. However, it was clear that preparation for even this local attack would take several days.[22] On the night of the 17th, Ludendorff travelled to Rupprecht's headquarters to reinspect the state of preparations by Fourth and Sixth armies for Operation *Hagen*; its objectives being possession of the heights between Poperinghe and Bailleul and the high ground about Hazebrouck.

21 Marne Source Book, p. 571.
22 Marne Source Book, p. 310 and Ludendorff, p. 311.

Operation Hagen and Operation Friedensturm 61

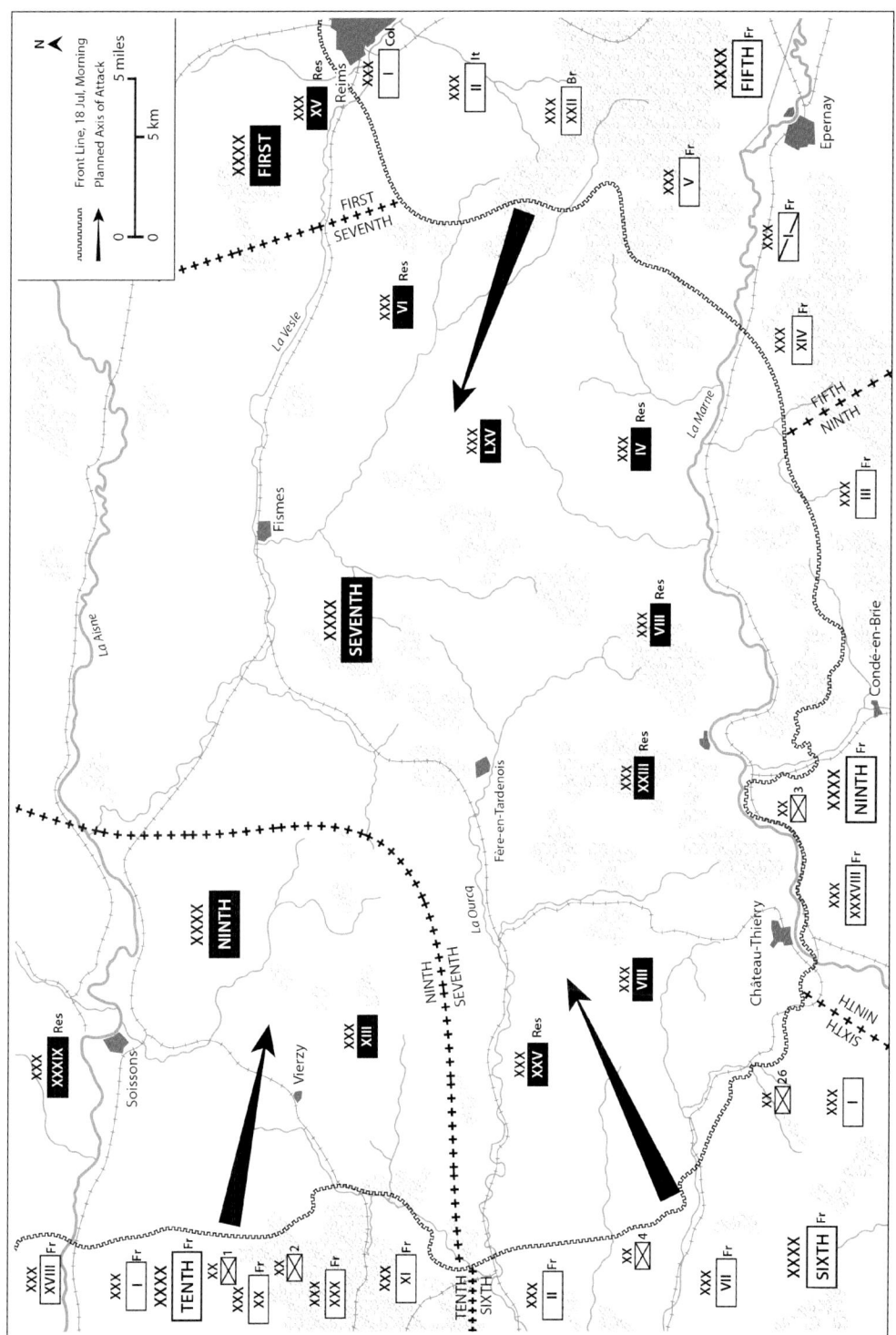

Map 1. Severing the German jugular vein – Order of Battle on 18 July 1918.

8

18 July – The Massive Allied Counteroffensive

Counteroffensive

Having decided to launch the major counteroffensive without the use of the usual preliminary barrage, Mangin aimed to achieve total surprise and to overrun the German front lines before they had time to react. This was possible due to the large number of tanks involved, replacing the artillery guns and taking the lead in the place of the artillery, with the artillery's role amended to be one of support, deploying a strong rolling barrage just in front of the infantry, who were ordered to advance as rapidly as possible, bypassing areas of resistance (in effect borrowing the German stormtrooper tactics). The chance of success had also been increased due to the phoney attacks that Mangin had carried out up and down his front in the days preceding the counteroffensive, with the Germans assuming it was just typical French activity rather than anything more significant. Mangin had cleverly used the localised attacks on the positions astride the Savières brook as an opportunity for his troops to get used to attacking without a preliminary barrage, as well as increasing their flexibility and learning to adapt their tactics in light of unfolding events.

The five French armies commenced their attack at 0435 hrs, led by Mangin's *Xe Armée*, spearheading the attack from the western flank of the *poche* with 18 divisions, including two American double-strength divisions rushed to the attack, together with 2,000 guns, 345 light tanks and 580 aircraft. Many of the attacking divisions only arrived shortly before the start of the operation, with their concentration in the *Forêt de Retz* near Villers-Cotterêts being an absolutely masterful display of concealment. Mangin had made an astute decision to continue to hold his front thinly rather than to reinforce and flood his front line, worried that it would alert the enemy to an impending attack, so held all additional troops back under cover of the dense canopy of the *Forêt de Retz* for as long as he could. This included three divisions (the *19e*, 38e and *153e*) as well as the entire *30e CA* which would be introduced between his two corps holding the front line. Degoutte's *VIe Armée* immediately south of Mangin and covering the south-west section of the salient between the Rivers Ourcq and Marne attacked with 10 divisions in three corps, which included I US Corps under Major General Hunter Liggett (the first time the Americans had fielded an entire corps in the front line), plus 1,000 guns, 145 tanks and 350 aircraft. Although this was a somewhat smaller effort with less frontage to attack than Mangin, the objective was a difficult one: capturing the high ground between the two rivers, a stiff test, especially for the untried Americans. To the south of the *poche*, the weakened and hard-pressed armies of de Mitry (*IXe*) and Berthelot (*Ve*) could only offer limited support, having been defending against the Germans' fierce *Marneschutz-Reims* offensive since the 15th. With far fewer tanks, they had been obliged to utilise a preliminary barrage prior to the infantry attack, and whilst this too had been largely successful, it had removed the element of surprise so vital to the success further north. At the very right extreme of the attack, Gouraud's *IVe Armée* east of Reims would make only a limited contribution, since it was still actively involved in repulsing the floundering German efforts, with Foch deciding to remove Gouraud's reserves and move them west to bolster Mangin's attacking forces spearheading the attack.[1]

The counteroffensive began on 18 July with the little-known Battle of Soissonais and The Ourcq. A masterstroke of Allied planning, it serves as the first instance of a large-scale combined arms battle. By the end of the first day, progress on parts of the front had been nothing short of spectacular, especially in *Xe Armée*'s sector along the western flank of the salient. It had, however, come at a heavy cost, with Entente casualties reportedly extremely high, estimated at 60–70 percent overall and up to 75 percent in Mangin's *Xe Armée* spearhead.[2] Even Mangin was concerned; worried that he would need urgent replacements in order to sustain the attack and exploit these remarkable gains.

The Germans' ability to defend the left flank of the salient facing *Xe Armée* had been undermined by several structural factors. The first was the total mismatch in the number of attackers versus the number of defenders, with the latter having an absolute dearth of high quality and well-trained manpower: just eight German divisions of varying quality facing 22 infantry divisions and three divisions of cavalry across Mangin's five corps, including two of the double-strength American divisions. Most of the German reserves were located near to Fère-en-Tardenois, which although relatively close to the western flank, was too far to the east and within range of the guns of Berthelot's *Ve Armée*, meaning that if *Ve Armée* attacked, then they would be pinned to the area and unable to move. Worse still, the Germans hadn't suspected an attack and had been totally surprised and wrong-footed, their front lines quickly overrun. Troops to the south might have been able to support and reinforce the German Ninth Army had they too not been engaged in resisting Degoutte's *VIe Armée* or facing south-east and therefore in the wrong direction, expecting to combat an attack by *IXe* or *Ve Armées*.[3]

As a meeting at Army Group Crown Prince Rupprecht's headquarters in Spa began, spirits were initially high. Ludendorff had gone to finalise preparations for Operation *Hagen* with Rupprecht, but any positivity quickly evaporated as news began to filter through that the French had deployed large numbers of tanks to pierce a line south-west of Soissons. Ludendorff immediately ordered two divisions to be sent to the battlefield: the 20th Division, which had been intended to advance up the Ardre valley, and the 5th Division, moving by rail via Laon. The latter's progress was hampered when shelling of the railway line forced the division to detrain and make an arduous march on foot. Meantime, the 20th Division had problems of its own. There was only sufficient capacity to transport the infantry in lorries. Everything else – all of the horses, vehicles and supplies – had to be broken up and transported separately.

---

1   Clayton, pp. 171-72 and Greenhalgh (2014), pp. 314-15.
2   Neiberg, p. 124 and Greenhalgh (2014), p. 316.
3   Neiberg, p. 126.

So upon arrival, the infantry regiments would be on their own until the support arrived.[4] A terrible feeling of being in the wrong place at the wrong time now beset the meeting, and Ludendorff instantly closed the conference in a state of great nervous tension. He returned to his headquarters at Avesnes, only arriving at 1400 hrs, when he was met by Hindenburg. Retiring to Ludendorff's office, the pair discussed the events of the day and their response, particularly the left wing of Ninth Army and right of the Seventh, which by then had become seriously threatened. Ludendorff later commented that the seriousness of events was only revealed to him in the early hours of the afternoon.[5]

Despite the abject and near total intelligence failure to identify the forthcoming Allied counterpunch, the German High Command quickly grasped the seriousness of the situation and the threat of the salient being cut off from both west and east. Yet as it had already deployed all available reserves to the west of the front around Soissons, it was powerless to give any further help.[6]

General von Winckler

4   Ludendorff, pp. 312-13.
5   Ludendorff, pp. 312-13.
6   Ludendorff, p. 314.

A decision to transfer forces back across to the north bank of the river now appeared to be urgently required, and the OHL duly issued orders for withdrawing these forces by echelon, commencing the night of 18/19 July. But in order to be able to evacuate the south bank safely, it would be necessary to prolong the occupation of the sector west of Château-Thierry for as long as possible. Furthermore, it would be essential for German forces to make a stand south-west of Soissons and on the Ardre in order to prevent the entire salient collapsing.[7]

Fresh orders were issued to organise a new defensive line along the line Soissons–Belleu–Noyant–Hartennes–Le Plessir-Heleu–Grand Menil–Latilly–Spaux–hills north of Château-Thierry. Three divisions were made available to Third Army to construct the position, but the army was to fall back on this line only in case of utter necessity and a second defensive position was simultaneously being fixed further to the rear, running from the north bank of the River Aisne–Bucy-le-Long–hills west of Acy–Droizy–Beugneux–Nanteuil–Notre Dame–Coincy–Epieds–Charteves.[8] At this point, Group Boehn was moved from Seventh to First Army, whilst Groups Watter and Winckler – which had borne the brunt of the attack – were to receive the 10th and 19th Reserve divisions, plus any other troops and heavy artillery which could be assembled and sent to the area in order to counterattack.

---

7 Marne Source Book, Ia 1039 secret; Army Group Ia 2678 sec, mob. II Aug. Mob. Archives, p. 614. This date contradicts some of the earlier text.
8 Marne Source Book, pp. 614-15.

9

July 1918 – The Danger Remains

On 1 July, Foch wrote to both the French and British commanders-in-chief, outlining his own plans for future operations. Directive No.4 laid out in stark terms the threat that they were facing, with the enemy halted just 18 miles from Dunkirk, 15 miles from Châlons and 36 miles from Paris, adding that an advance of 24 miles towards Abbeville would sever the line between the British and French, resulting in very serious consequences for the Allies. Foch therefore prioritised the protection of Paris and Abbeville at all costs, with the concentration of defensive organisation in the area from Lens to Château-Thierry. Reserves would be organised into a corps or army and be placed in front of both Paris and Abbeville, with Foch assuring that mutual support would be immediately deployed if one or the other were attacked. Field Marshal Haig responded to Foch that his reserves, XXII Corps – comprising three divisions and a motor machine gun battalion – were already located on the Somme near Amiens, ready to move north or south to wherever the threat developed, and that the Canadian Corps plus three other divisions and the Cavalry Corps in general reserve could follow XXII Corps if so required, with XXII Corps put on high alert to move to protect the vulnerable boundary between the French and British armies. Pétain also replied to Foch, indicating that eight French divisions (two of which were tired), a cavalry corps of three divisions and two American divisions were north of the River Oise, while a further 10 French divisions and one American division were between the River Oise and the Marne. Further east, he could also call on seven infantry and three cavalry divisions.[1]

It was true that neither Foch nor Pétain liked each other very much. Whilst both respected the other leader, they were very different characters and Foch was not above criticising his Commander-in-Chief, even before Foch had become Generalissimo in April. At a conference of Allied leaders at Pétain's headquarters in Compiègne on 24 January 1918, Foch and the British Chief of the Imperial General Staff (CIGS), General William Robertson, citing the French counteroffensive at Verdun, had stated that the best method to halt the expected German offensive was to go on the counteroffensive themselves. But Pétain openly disagreed

---

1   Edmonds, Brigadier General Sir James, *Military Operations France and Belgium, 1918. May–July: The German diversion offensives and the first Allied counter-offensive* (London: MacMillan and Co., 1939), pp. 217-19 and Kinloch, Terry, *Godley: the Man Behind the Myth* (Dunedin: Exisle Publishing, 2018), p. 193.

with their conclusion, stating that the reality of the situation in 1918 was very different, with the Germans having moved numerous divisions from the Eastern to the Western Front, and due to their superior numbers they could attack in multiple locations simultaneously. Whilst he was in favour of making plans, he added that the sheer lack of a sizeable Allied reserve would likely scupper any chance of such counteroffensives. In an unusual example of Entente solidarity, both Haig and Robertson agreed with Pétain, saying the British, due to the difficult battles of late 1917, were both exhausted and depleted and they had almost no reserves available. So whilst it was sensible to make offensive plans for the coming year, neither could see where the reserves would come from to launch them. This was not the first time that Pétain's pragmatic stance had annoyed Foch, but on this occasion he had to admit that the French Commander-in-Chief had read the situation correctly.[2]

Foch had also been critical of Pétain in a meeting with Clemenceau, saying that Pétain was too defensive in his mindset, and repeated this again to government leaders in early 1918 in the hope of getting Pétain sacked and replaced by General Fayolle, whom Foch saw as being easier to deal with. Fayolle was to some extent in a difficult, sometimes impossible position, caught between the very different characters of the Generalissimo in overall charge of Allied operations and Pétain, Commander-in-Chief of the French Army.[3] Pétain was seen as a realist with a dry, sardonic appraisal of the military situation; a man who took his job extremely seriously, weighing up every decision, in stark contrast to Foch and his more ebullient 'will to victory' demeanour, who never seemed to get anxious and always appeared positive. Foch was also extremely ambitious, believing he was destined for the highest office, something that never seemed to concern or interest Pétain, relying instead on his performance to speak for itself. This, some claimed, suggested that he lacked ambition, even that he'd fallen into the role of Commander-in-Chief by accident. Certainly he had never been the most accomplished 'people-person', holding some unorthodox views and never fearing of making critical comments about his peers and superiors if he felt it was right to do so. However, he was consistent on one major topic: believing that politics and military matters should stay well away from one another, and that politicians had no place anywhere near the battlefield, detesting every time a politician was seen at the front. But equally, he believed military men should not engage in politics, himself included.[4] One other factor was important: Foch (like Fayolle) was a devout Catholic, which he believed had given him a high level of inner strength and natural self-confidence, and the French Commander-in-Chief was very suspicious of this fact throughout their relationship, recognising that hope and faith would be no use in winning the war.[5]

At the meeting of the Supreme War Council in Versailles from 2–4 July, General Foch, when challenged on why he only made a general statement about the impending German offensive and what the Allies plan and response would be, answered those assembled by striking out three rapid blows with his right, then his left and again with his right, followed by launching a vigorous kick to demonstrate that he, unlike Ludendorff, regarded war as an art, not a science. He also demonstrated the French belief that unlike the Germans, who had been forced to have intervals between their offensives, to regroup and move artillery and reinforcements to the

2   Ryan, p. 156.
3   Greenhalgh (2011), p. 335.
4   Atkin, pp. 6-8, 22.
5   Fayolle, pp. 251-57 and Ryan, pp. 153-54.

attack front, they would attempt to make a more or less continuous attack, giving the enemy no respite or time to recover.[6]

Foch wanted to be in a position to crush the now imminent German offensive and turn to the counteroffensive as quickly as possible, and by attacking in a different part of the front, he anticipated that he would throw the enemy off balance. The request from Foch required four divisions to be sent south to support the French, and Haig decided to send XXII Corps under Lieutenant General Sir Alex Godley, with 51st (Highland) and 62nd (West Riding) Divisions, which had been south-west of Amiens in the Somme area since June, ideally located to make the move south. To it he added the 15th (Scottish) Division from First Army and the 34th Division from Second Army, giving XXII Corps four divisions, all of which were as close to full strength as any in the summer of 1918, with a steady stream of drafts and replacements arriving during June and early July.

General Godley was an extremely experienced officer, having joined the British Army in 1885 and served during the Boer War. He had many vital skills, including being very well respected for his organisational and planning abilities, regarding smartness, obedience and musketry high amongst his priorities. Unfortunately, his skills did not extend to combat command, and he was a poor battlefield leader. Indeed, he was not well-liked by his men, who saw him as distant, aloof and uncaring. Unusually, he took his wife, Luisa, with him to the theatres in which he served, and she often worked in one of the convalescent hospitals close by his headquarters. He had commanded the Australian and New Zealand Division at Gallipoli in 1915, with mixed success, with the New Zealand Minister of Defence writing to Major General Andrew Russell to suggest that someone other than Godley be placed in command of the Kiwi forces. This first taste of battlefield command was not without controversy, and the events surrounding the slaughter of several Australian light horse units during successive charges resulted in it being called 'Godley's abattoir'. Some saw him as being too rigid and failing to take changed circumstances into account in his orders. The following year he resurfaced in France, commanding the New Zealand Division, and in June 1917 II ANZAC Corps was involved in the successful capture of the Messines Ridge, but some argued that the attack could have been even more successful had Godley better co-ordinated the follow-up attacks. He was severely criticised for his leadership and battlefield command of the ANZAC troops at Passchendaele in October 1917 and blamed by many for the heavy casualties suffered by his men during the fighting, with his artillery failing to provide the cover that the infantry required. His planning and preparation for II ANZAC Corps received particular criticism, being overall considered inadequate. He was also censured having previously been challenged about overstating the gains and underplaying the losses in the New Zealand Division to James Allen, the New Zealand Minister of Defence.[7] But Godley pressed Haig not to postpone the attack and ordered a third attack on 12 October, which became a costly failure, resulting in heavy casualties which surpassed 2,700 and the date remains New Zealand's single worst day for losses during its history. He was severely criticised

---

6   Maurice, Major-General Sir Frederick, *The Last Four Months: How the War was Won* (Boston: Little Brown & Co, 1919), pp. 82-83 and Goya, Michel, *Flesh and Steel during the Great War* (Barnsley: Pen and Sword, 2004), p. 252.
7   Macdonald, Andrew, *Passchendaele: The Anatomy of a Tragedy* (Auckland: Harper Collins, 2013), p. 235 and Harper, Glyn, *Dark Journey: Three Key New Zealand Battles of the Western Front* (Auckland: Harper Collins, 2007), pp. 101-02.

for his decision to make a third attack after days of heavy rain, with waist-deep mud that engulfed the battlefield – making the bringing up of guns and reinforcements almost impossible – and the inability to cut the wire resulting in almost no ground gained. The impossible ground conditions meant that many casualties had to be abandoned to die in the mud and rain, and this has been seen by many Kiwis as Godley's biggest command failure.[8]

9.1 Payback time and learning to co-operate, but is it too late?

Now expecting an imminent attack on the front between Château-Thierry and Reims, General Foch requested additional aerial support for the French forces on 10 July and Field Marshal Haig ordered nine squadrons from IX Brigade RAF to fly south, departing on the 14th. The previous day, Foch had telegraphed Haig requesting that four divisions, in two groups of two, be sent to the French *IVe Armée* area near Châlons, and shortly after another telegram was sent requesting a corps headquarters be immediately despatched and a further four divisions be made ready to follow the first four. With Haig away in London, he requested a delay to the despatch until he had had the chance to meet with Foch on the 15th, and warned his Chief of the General Staff, Lieutenant General Sir Herbert Lawrence, of the dangers of complying with Foch's request. Haig also composed a letter, to be passed on to Foch during the meeting, which related his surprise at the change in plan from the meeting at Versailles earlier that month. In it he wrote:

> I beg that you will inform me definitely of the reasons which have led you to change your view of the general situation and to depart from the strategical plan laid down in your Directive Generale No.4 of 1st July for the guidance of the several Commanders-in-Chief of the Allied Armies … The British front is threatened just as much as when the Directive was issued … and that consequently the British reserves should only be engaged to support the French Armies *si l'ennemi concentre décidément se masses dans la direction de Paris* [if the enemy is decidedly concentrating and massing in the direction of Paris]. Such a situation has not yet arisen.[9]

That night, a telephone message was relayed to Haig, in which the British War Cabinet urged him to exercise his judgement under the Beauvais agreement and block the removal of his reserves if he felt the threat merited it. As he pondered his response, Haig remarked that if things went well, the War Cabinet and the Generalissimo would take the credit, but if they went badly, then he himself would be the scapegoat. Despite his clear reservations, Haig felt obliged to comply with Foch's request, and XXII Corps under Lieutenant General Sir Alex Godley was despatched to the French front.[10]

It was to be the first right hook to the German western flank of the salient described by Foch that the 34th Division was now sent. On 10 July it was placed in GHQ Reserve and held ready to move at short notice, and the following day the division was relieved by the US 30th Division,

---

8 Takle, pp. 126–27 and Grover. Alex Godley profile <https://teara.govt.nz/en/biographies/3g12/godley-alexander-john>
9 Edmonds, p. 225.
10 Edmonds, pp. 225-26.

nicknamed the 'Old Hickory' Division, with men drawn from North Carolina, South Carolina, Virginia and Tennessee, in the defence of the East Poperinghe line. The Old Hickory too was new to the Western Front, having only sailed from the United States in May. Further training and organisation of the reconstituted 34th Division was planned for the forthcoming period, with special focus on its entirely new infantry, but events further south meant plans were revised after just three days, hardly sufficient time for acquaintances to be made let alone any significant military endeavour. On 12 July, 34th Division received its provisional orders for entrainment south.[11]

With the Germans attacking east and west of Reims on the morning of 15 July, this changed the situation for the Generalissimo, since he believed that the Germans didn't have sufficient strength to attack on two fronts at once, meaning the risk of attack on the Somme or in Flanders had virtually evaporated overnight. Whilst Haig didn't share Foch's view, believing that an attack on the Lys salient was still possible, he too had to concede the likelihood had now reduced markedly. Foch concluded that whilst he agreed with Haig's prognosis, his first priority was to deal with the battle in play; he only required the British reserves in case of necessity, and they would be returned at once if the British front was threatened. With the locus of the attack moving west from the original intelligence, Foch therefore changed the destination of the British from Châlons to Provins, 60 miles behind Ninth Army's front.[12] A back-and-forth between Pétain and Foch then ensued, with the former requesting that the 15th (Scottish) and 34th Divisions be handed over to him as reserves, but Foch declined the request, deciding to keep them at his disposal. Weygand, issuing the order on behalf of Foch on the 18th, stated that they were to remain in reserve for the time being, but he was moving them to Villers-Cotterêts to exploit the results already obtained. Pétain also asked Foch for four British divisions – the 29th, 56th (1st London), 57th (2nd West Lancashire) and 61st (2nd South Midland) – to be made immediately available to him to follow the four divisions of XXII Corps into battle. At 1300 hours on 15 July, a warning order was received for the 34th Division to transfer from II Corps in Second Army to XXII Corps, moving by strategical train to the French front, "destination unknown".[13]

The omnibus-type train comprised one first-class coach with a capacity for 32 officers and 30 covered trucks, each of which could carry 40 men or between six and eight horses. A further 17 flat trucks would carry the artillery. Unused as they were to French train travel, A&Q (Adjutant and Quartermaster) branch issued guidance on the use of the strategical train, which included several instructions that were to make the journey even more arduous than it might have been. Top of the list was a total ban on any alcohol on board, and no one was allowed to leave the train unless it was at an authorised stop, and then only to relieve themselves. Anyone found contravening this order would be severely dealt with. Each train was designed to carry a battalion of up to 750 men, with additional troops and a field kitchen travelling in the next available train.[14] While on the move, orders were received from the French GQG that the corps headquarters, arriving

---

11 TNA WO 95/2441: Headquarters Royal Artillery, 34th Division.
12 Edmonds, pp. 226-27.
13 Letter No. 20.871, 17 July 1918, cited in Woldike, p. 104. Letter No.2.178, 18th July 1918, cited in Woldike, p. 109. Several battalions entrained on 17 July to "destination unknown", including the 7th Cheshires.
14 TNA WO 95/2439: Adjutant and Quarter-Master General, 34th Division, 14 July 1918.

later that afternoon, was to be at Romilly-sur-Seine. However, the advance party didn't receive their instructions in time and failed to make the detour to the new location, so when General Godley arrived they were nowhere to be found and nothing was ready for him.[15] Well known as someone who would never pass the opportunity for a bit of social climbing and courting of potential patrons, Godley was rather irked by the decision to change the destination of his headquarters from Vitry-le-François to Romilly-sur-Seine, as it had potentially robbed him of the chance to meet with Foch at his Reserve headquarters. He did, however, get to meet General Pétain on the 17th. The 34th Division's Advanced Divisional Headquarters made immediate plans to move by rail from Proven, arriving at Louvres on the 17th and proceeding to Senlis by road, where the Divisional Headquarters was established, the destination being changed whilst some of the division was already en-route.[16]

Further orders required 101st Brigade to depart from Proven station, just north-west of Poperinghe, at 1800 hrs, and this was completed by 1400 hrs the following day.[17] A Sergeant Colley of the 1st Herefords described the intriguing, almost chaotic incident in his diary:

> Suddenly one day came the order to move; mysterious places were mentioned and even after we had entrained no one appeared to know quite where we were going. We travelled for more than 24 hours passing to the south of Paris, arriving at our destination at night and immediately set out on a 14-mile march. Great was our satisfaction when we eventually arrived at our destination weary, tired but happy to discover that we were going into good billets.[18]

Both the 15th (Scottish) and 34th divisions thus had their destination changed mid-journey as a result of Foch's decision on the 16th not to attach them to the French *Groupe d'armées du Centre* (GAC), believing that they had sufficient reserves to ride out the current German offensive, but instead to send them to the GAR, where they were to be ready to go into action: either offensively in support of *Xe* or *VIe Armée*, or defensively in support of *IIIe Armée* to the west of Compiègne.[19] So instead of heading east towards Reims to join the 51st (Highland) and 62nd (West Riding) divisions, upon arrival at Pontoise in the northern suburbs of Paris, the 34th Division was directed towards Chantilly, north of the capital. After a train journey lasting 26 hours, they detrained at Chantilly at 1930 hrs on 17 July. The move to *XXII Corps'* area further east was confirmed postponed and the division was placed under the command of General Émile Fayolle, as part of *Groupe d'armées de Réserve*, the French Reserve. Most of the division detrained at Senlis, midway between Paris and Compiègne, on 18 July. At 2100 hrs that evening, orders were received that 34th Division was to come under the command of the French *Xe Armée*, and it was told to move at 0500 hrs on the 19th – dismounted personnel by

---

15 TNA WO 95/9742, XXII Corps General Staff, 15 July 1918.
16 TNA WO 95/2436: General Staff, 34th Division, 16–17 July 1918. Edmonds, pp. 234–35. Grover.
17 TNA WO 95/2456: 101st Infantry Brigade Headquarters, Order No. 210, 14 July 1918, 15–16 July 1918.
18 Diary of Sergeant Colley, 1st Herefords, cited in 'Herefordshire Regiment, Their First World War Story', *Herefordshire Light Infantry Museum* <https://herefordshirelightinfantrymuseum.com/>
19 Foch, letter No. 2111, 16 July 1918 cited in Woldike, p. 26.

bus and lorry, mounted personnel by road.[20] This at least allowed the men to get some sleep after their long and tiring train journey. The *Xe Armée* had been commanded since 10 June by the vastly experienced General Charles Mangin, in his third spell in charge of an army, having been sacked twice previously. Colonel Hergault, his *Chef d'État-Major* (Chief of Staff), was similarly experienced, and between them they sought to push their five corps into battle, with the two British divisions to be used to consolidate or exploit any gains.

After an overnight stop on 18 July, bivouacking in the open, the 4th Royal Sussex departed Chantilly the following morning on board a series of French trucks. However, the dust, heat and petrol fumes, combined with the uncomfortable ride, made the journey almost unbearable, and everyone was relieved when they arrived mid-afternoon at their destination of Vauciennes.[21] The 5th KOSBs were due to entrain at 1800 hrs on the 16th from Waayenburg, but due to an accident on the line, this was delayed until 0415 hrs the following morning and they arrived at Senlis at 1000 hrs on the 18th. The 1st Herefords at least were able to spend some time that afternoon bathing and cleaning up after their travels.[22] The 34th Divisional Artillery entrained at Proven on the 16th, travelling via Dunkirque, Calais, Boulogne, Noyelles, Chars and Pontoise, before detraining at Chantilly and marching to Senlis on 17 July, and from there to the area of Longavesnes and Vivières, 8km north of Villers-Cotterêts, on the 20th.[23]

9.2 Offensive action orders issued to the GAR and GAC on 12 July

On 12 July, Pétain gave the much-anticipated order for the GAR and GAC to commence preparations to move from the defensive to the offensive, to reduce the enemy salient at Château-Thierry by executing two lateral thrusts towards the plateaux located north of Fère-en-Tardenois to break the enemy front.[24] By exploitation and with the maximum of speed, *Xe Armée* would attack in the direction of Oulchy-le-Château, *VIe Armée* towards Breny–Armentières-sur-Ourcq and *Ve Armée* from south of the Vesle in the direction of Arcis-le-Ponsart. The plan envisaged the three armies together driving towards the strategically important town of Fère-en-Tardenois, with the clear instruction from Pétain that the principal effort would come from Mangin's *Xe Armée* on the western hinge.[25] Coincidentally, *Abteilung IIIb*, the Imperial German military intelligence branch, issued an intelligence report on 13 July, containing information from captured French reports which showed that General Mangin had succeeded General Maistre in command of the French *Xe Armée*. The profile described Mangin as an infantry officer who was very active in the French general staff. He was said to be relatively unknown, having been appointed to command the 155th Division in October 1916 after General de Laporte d'Hust had been killed. He was reported to have been the commanding general of *1er Corps* since January 1918 and had been behind the successful action in May and June north-east of Montdidier.[26]

---

20 TNA WO 95/2436: General Staff, 34th Division, Narrative of Operations with X French Army, 16–18 July 1918.
21 Read, pp. 342-43.
22 Scott Elliot, p. 237 and TNA WO 95/2462: 1st Herefords.
23 TNA WO 95/2442: Headquarters Royal Artillery, 16–17 July 1918.
24 Pétain, 3rd Section, No.14546 of 7/12, Annex No.42, cited in Woldike, p. 5
25 Pétain, p. 5. Personal and Secret Instruction No.14546 of 12 July 1918, Annex No.42, Woldike, p. 5.
26 Marne Sourcebook, pp. 406-07.

General Mangin had impressive resources at his disposal for the attack, by far the largest force of the five armies involved in the counteroffensive, totalling 17 divisions across his four corps:[27]

- *1er Corps d'armée* (*1er CA*) comprising five divisions, with three in the first line (*72e*, *11e* and *153e*) south of the River Aisne, *162e* north of the river plus *69e* in Corps Reserve.
- *20e Corps*, with three divisions in the first line (US 1st, *1re DIM* and US 2nd) and two in Corps Reserve (*58e* and *87e*).
- *30e Corps*, with two divisions in the first line (*48e* and *38e*) and two more in Reserve (*19e* and *1er*).
- *11e Corps*, with two divisions in the first line (*128e* and *41e*) and *5e Division* in Corps Reserve.

Xe Armée would make its main effort in the centre toward the Chaudun plateau and the Villers-Hélon crest in the direction of Oulchy-le-Château with 13 divisions (of which eight would come from GHQ and the GAR), plus *2e Corps de Cavalerie* (*2e CC*). *Xe Armée*'s firepower was also bolstered by the largest amount of tanks: *301e régiment* of light tanks and five groups of Schneider and Saint-Chaumond heavy tanks, plus considerable artillery reinforcements.[28] *VIe Armée* was tasked with attacking astride the River Ardre towards Brenzy–Armentières-sur-Ourcq, but would only receive one regiment of light tanks and possibly one or two divisions as reinforcements, whilst *Ve Armée*, attacking towards Arcis-le-Ponsart, would receive one regiment of light tanks, the *1er CC* and potentially two or three extra divisions. The challenge for *Ve Armée* was a stiff one, being tasked with passing from its defensive order of battle over to attack in just one night.[29]

An intelligence report from the French *2me Bureau* on 16 July laid out the situation of German divisions along the Western Front, a total of 207. Amongst them were 145 divisions on the front line and a further 62 in the rear of the front, with 15 placed between the River Oise and Château-Thierry and 36 from Château-Thierry to Massiges. Some 179 divisions had been engaged since 21 March, the majority of those having been in action two or three times.[30] Haig received a letter from Foch requesting that the British supply him with any information they had explaining the location of this imminent threat. It also warned him that if Foch had to move reserves up to Flanders, then it would be better to do this sooner rather than later, in order to "nip the enemy attack in the bud". Moreover, this would require the withdrawal of troops from the fronts which were not threatened for the benefit of those in danger, a clear indication that Foch did not consider the British front to be where the main threat existed. After considering the matter, Haig decided to sign the letter, but instructed General du Cane, the British liaison officer to Foch, that he should verbally advise Foch that if British troops were needed to exploit the success, then they should of course be used. This indicated that he didn't want them to be used for defensive purposes, but rather in attack, and is supported by the letter

---

27 Woldike, p. 9.
28 Woldike, p. 6.
29 Woldike, p. 6.
30 No. 9.263/2, 17th July 1918, cited in Woldike, p. 95.

that Godley sent to General Sir Herbert Lawrence on the 17th. In it he told General Pétain that Haig had forbidden XXII Corps from being used except in the case of absolute necessity. Godley ended the letter by saying that he had received no such order from army commander General Berthelot; his only instruction had been one from Foch signed by General Weygand, placing XXII Corps under Pétain's orders.[31] In his defence, Major General Sir John Davidson, Haig's intelligence chief, had written to Godley on the night of 15 July and confirmed that he was only to take orders from Foch or his Chief of Staff, Weygand. According to Edmonds, Foch was delighted with the first part of the message, confirming that he saw no immediate threat to the British front. On the contrary, he felt the Germans would be fully pressed defending the counteroffensive he was about to launch, and it would be futile to recall XXII Corps now, since their return to Flanders would take six to eight days to complete.[32]

The 51st (Highland) and 62nd (West) divisions, now part of General Berthelot's French *Ve Armée*, also had XXII Corps headquarters in the area, with General Godley taking little or no part in events for either 15th (Scottish) or 34th divisions, leaving Generals Reed and Nicholson to their own devices during their time in Mangin's *Xe Armée*. To some, the absence of your corps commander might feel like a major hindrance, especially when you were under direct French command, but Godley is not regarded as one of the war's great generals. His memoirs of this period talk in great detail about whom he met and dined with and where he visited but lack any insights into his military thinking or about the events of July 1918. Whilst it is only speculation, the absence of General Godley may have been seen by both Nicholson and Reed, as something of a blessing in disguise. His reputation was not helped as, according to one staff officer, Godley was poorly suited to working with the French, since his grasp of the language was "quite hopeless"; although he did speak a little French, he was by no means fluent, yet baulked at the suggestion of using an interpreter.[33]

From Senlis, the majority of 34th Division marched the 38km to Largny, just west of Villers-Cotterêts, on 19 July, then a further 10km through the Vivières–Puiseux–Soucy–Longavesne area, where it concentrated on the following night, coming under the command of General Hippolyte-Alphonse Penet's *30e Corps*, the centre corps of Mangin's *Xe Armée*. During the march, the division crossed the same ground fought over by 4th Guards Brigade during the First Battle of the Marne in August and September 1914, and within a couple of kilometres of the location of the Guards grave honouring those who had fallen. The 5th KOSBs endured a hot, dusty and slow bus journey of 19 miles, followed by a trying three-and-a-half hour march with frequent forced halts, before they reached their final destination of Feigneux, 14km west of Villers-Cotterêts. During one halt, a violent thunderstorm lasting half an hour drenched the remainder of the division waiting to move off. Standing shivering in their cold and wet uniforms, the spirits of the men were undoubtedly dampened by the thunderstorm, but were restored the following day, which was spent resting and cleaning equipment in sunnier weather.[34] The following day, the transport section of the 5th KOSBs had an exhausting 40km march from Feigneux through Senlis, Baron and Nanteuil to Crepy, which lasted all day, only arriving

---

31 Letter to Lieutenant General Sir Henry Lawrence, 17 July 1918 in TNA WO 95/9742: XXII Corps War Diary.
32 Edmonds, p. 238.
33 Kinloch, p. 193.
34 Scott Elliot, p. 237.

at 2130 hrs. On the night of 20/21 July, the battalion marched all night, a distance of 25km on heavy roads to Soucy. Lieutenant Colonel Coulson described it as one of the most trying the battalion ever experienced, with many of the new drafts struggling with conditions and falling out until the following morning, march discipline described as being very poor and in need of significant improvement. For the 8th Scottish Rifles, the transport arrangements were nothing short of farcical. The French liaison officer arrived at Lieutenant Colonel Findlay's billets at 0655 hrs to deliver the order for the battalion to embus a mile away at 0700 hrs, only to find that the CO was still in bed and completely unaware of the order. The hastily arranged departure commenced immediately, with many of the men still breakfasting.[35] With the heavy traffic congestion, this further movement was not completed until 0900 on the 21st, with the divisional headquarters at Vivières. To add to the general state of confusion, the division was now in the area of the French *20e Corps*, whilst being assigned to *30e Corps*, making its logistical arrangements even more challenging. But General Nicholson need not have worried, since both *20e CA* and *30e CA* were considered to be elite formations, containing vast amounts of hard-earned experience across its divisions, and it was unlikely that having another foreign division would have phased *30e Corps*' staffs.[36]

Despite the arrival of the two British divisions with the French *Xe Armée*, there were none of the normal arrangements for handover and relief that the British were used to. This was especially the case for the medical services, with Colonel E.W. Bliss, ADMS (Assistant Director Medical Services), 34th Division, worrying that nothing was yet in place with sanitation around his headquarters reported to be appalling. Neither were any of the usual evacuation routes set up, with trains having to go via Paris to evacuate the wounded towards the British hospitals at Rouen or to the French coast. He met with the Deputy Director Medical Services GHQ South on the 18th and with his counterpart from 15th (Scottish) Division the following day, when the two discussed arrangements for the evacuation of British troops, which he expected to be fraught with problems, given the location of the two divisions embedded within the French Army as well as their isolation from other BEF forces. The *Directeur du Service de Santé*, his equivalent in the French *30e Corps*, then arrived, disrupting his plans and requesting to send ambulances to assist with the evacuation of French casualties to Crepy.[37]

A first conference was held on the 19th, with Lieutenant Boniface of the 4th Royal Sussex only told very scant and patchy information, which he then had to relay to his company commanders. It was summarised as, "We're part of 30 Corps, 10th French Army, now in action on front Soissons–Villers-Cotterêts–Oulchy-le-Château", with only a hastily sketched map to provide orientation. Things were not made any easier because all of the French maps needed interpretation, which slowed everything down and made communications through the chain of command problematic. Having never met the other battalions in the brigade, these were confirmed to Boniface and he in turn informed the other officers of the battalion, saying: "We're part of 101st Brigade with 2/4th Queens and 2nd Loyal North Lancs – got that? 102nd Brigade – 4th Cheshires, 1st Herefords and some Somersets. 103rd Brigade – all Jocks and Argyll and Sutherlands and KOSBs … I missed it – I couldn't write fast enough."[38] If he'd had

---

35 Findlay, p. 160 and TNA WO 95/2466: 5th KOSBs, 19 July 1918.
36 Neiberg, p. 121.
37 TNA WO 95/2443: Assistant Director Medical Services, July 1918.
38 Read, p. 347.

difficulty keeping up with the basic composition of the division, then what hope did they have in capturing the critical detail necessary to mount the attack?

A divisional depot was established at both Largny and Vez to the west of Villers-Cotterêts on 21 July. Orders were received for a night march in order to relieve a French division on the front line near Parcy-Tigny on the night of the 22nd/23rd,[39] but heavy rain began to fall as they paraded ready to march. The rain quickly intensified into a torrential summer downpour, thoroughly drenching the men waiting patiently to move off. A further delay of three wet hours later, to an accompaniment of thunder and lightning, completely soaking the men, they finally moved off, for the first time in France in full 'battle order', carrying all of their kit and equipment. Their now sodden and heavy greatcoats, carried *en banderole* round the haversack on

General Penet

their back, caused significant discomfort to the marching men. Arriving at a crossroads at Pont Due, their passage was blocked by a column of artillery and a halt was called, the men having no option but to sit down in the mud and wait for the guns to pass. Whilst this uncomfortable wait might not have bothered many of the more seasoned Western Front soldiers, these infantry were

---

39 Wryall; TNA WO 95/2456: 101st Infantry Brigade Headquarters, Administrative Instructions, No.54, 20 July 1918.

entirely new to the conditions; it must have felt a long way from Egypt and Palestine. Colonel Findlay described the rain and mud during the march as "about as unhappy [an] experience in the wet we ever put in".[40] Unfortunately for the men, things didn't get any easier, with heavy traffic churning up the wet roads into an appalling state, the surface described as spongy mud with foot-deep ruts in the road.[41] By the time the battalion arrived at the ruined village of Soucy at 0800 hrs on the 21st – footsore, tired and hungry after an arduous 16-mile march – no billets were available and the men were forced to bivouac in the woods just outside the village in their soaking wet clothes. With the rain finally relenting, the exhausted men were at least able to get some sleep in comparatively dry conditions.[42] Incredibly, two loads of mail then arrived for the men of the 8th Scottish Rifles, considerably contributing to a lifting of their spirits.[43]

Scott Elliot describes the 52-year-old General Mangin, commanding *Xe Armée*, as "one of those military geniuses which only a great war reveals",[44] but does not expand on this statement. Nor does he suggest whether Mangin was simply the right man in the right place at the right time. Originally from Sarrebourg in the region of Lorraine, the square-jawed general with piercing blue eyes detested the Germans with undimmed fury, largely attributed to their occupation of Alsace-Lorraine after the Franco-Prussian War of 1871, with his family forced to flee their home. Like Gouraud to the east, Mangin was always keen to visit front-line positions, but had a lucky escape when he was shot in the chest during the Second Battle of Champagne in September 1915. He was fortunate that the wound was not more serious, being able to return to duty just 10 days later.[45]

Mangin was about to get another big dose of good luck and a final chance to redeem himself. Both Clemenceau and Foch had identified 'The Butcher' as being the man they wanted, with Foch recalling him to a field command for the third time and Clemenceau duly issuing the order. The wily Prime Minister and charismatic Generalissimo understood the character of Mangin perfectly, with Foch in particular having complete faith in him, admiring his aggressive streak and seemingly endless supply of energy, firmly believing that Mangin was ideally suited to fighting an aggressive offensive campaign when it was time to do so.[46] Whilst the two French leaders saw his undoubted attacking qualities, many of Mangin's peers disliked him intensely; he was well known for his regular bouts of insubordination to most of the commanders senior to him. This dislike included his immediate superior, General Émile Fayolle, commander of the GAR, who called him "a devil of a man" and quipped that whilst General Degoutte, his other army commander, waged war for France, Mangin only waged war for himself.[47] The ill-feeling was invariably mutual, with Mangin in particular nursing an animosity towards Pétain which bordered on outright hatred, while the relationship between Mangin and both Fayolle and Pétain can be characterised as testy, with the former constantly pushing the boundaries of his superiors. For his part, Fayolle also believed that Mangin suffered from megalomania. As for

---

40 Findlay, p. 161.
41 Scott Elliot, p. 238.
42 Scott Elliot, pp. 237–38 and Greenhalgh (2011), p. 377.
43 Findlay, p. 162.
44 Scott Elliot, p. 240.
45 Keegan, John, *The First World War* (Bodley Head, 1998), p. 203 and Lloyd, pp. 75–76.
46 Neiberg, pp. 71, 198; (2003), p. 74.
47 Fayolle, pp. 297, 121.

Pétain, Fayolle viewed him as being "timorous", not exactly the characteristic required for a Commander-in-Chief in the middle of a crisis.[48]

Whatever the reason for his reappointment to command *Xe Armée*, General Mangin was perhaps at the zenith of his career, although he did not know it at the time. A voracious attacker, his character was in stark contrast to that of XXII Corps' General Godley; the two men could not have been more different. Whilst it can only be speculation – since there is no evidence that either men ever met the other – it is unlikely that in this case opposites attracted. Mangin was a combat commander, a fighting general, used to leading from the front, with a very strong opinion on how his men should fight, whilst Godley seemed content to be a *château* general, leading from the rear and apparently more interested in his status and social climbing than anything happening on the battlefield itself. Indeed, at one point Godley was billeted in an actual *château*, the luxurious home of the Comte de Chandon.[49] Mangin's reputation would certainly have preceded him by this point in the war, and perhaps Godley felt that his contribution would be better received by General Berthelot than Mangin? One other fact is clear though, as demonstrated in the war diary of XXII Corps Headquarters. Virtually all of the entries relate to the two divisions serving in *Ve Armée* (the 51st and 62nd), and you have to search hard to find anything relating to either the 15th (Scottish) or 34th divisions. That fact alone clearly demonstrates that General Godley and his staff were much more involved in supporting the two divisions to the east than those in *Xe Armée*, and that most of the organisation and decisions were left to Generals Reed and Nicholson. Although the situation was by no means ideal for Godley, with XXII Corps split into two – fighting on different fronts as part of two different armies – and the decision having been taken out of his control, he should have provided greater support to the two divisions further from his headquarters, unfamiliar as they were with the terrain and fighting under foreign command, rather than leaving them largely to fend for themselves. Despite the fact that the 15th (Scottish) Division was under the command of the French *20e Corps* and 34th Division under *30e Corps*, Godley should still have been involved in some capacity supporting the two British divisions.

It is approximately 55km from Soissons to Reims and from Reims to Château-Thierry, and 39km from Soissons in the north to Château-Thierry in the south. Nelson describes the landscape perfectly: narrow and ancient roads slicing across an impossibly flat tableland of ripening wheat fields, before twisting and winding through the deep ravines of Missy and Ploisy and picturesque villages – Missy-aux-Bois, Ploisy, Chazelle and Berzy-le-Sec.[50] The near-flat plateau made it almost impossible to move undetected by the enemy, making the task for the attacking forces especially problematic. German artillery was concealed beyond observation, deep in the ravines and valleys. Further east, a series of ridges were occupied by German forces in strength.

In essence, virtually every advantage was with the defenders. The narrow roads, whilst few in number, stood out like white ribbons against the dull greens or browns of the plain and were easily registered for artillery fire, which made their use a dangerous occupation. In July 1918, most of the fields contained waist-high wheat, ready for harvest. Where woodland existed, it was generally found in small copses (*bois*) located on hillsides and in valleys where arable farming

---

48 Ryan, p. 155 and Fayolle, pp. 123–25.
49 Neiberg, p. 130.
50 Nelson, p. 165.

was not practical. The attacking artillery had the added problem that it would have to occupy this open flat plain, offering very little concealment and an obvious target to the Germans. But if the Allies could advance rapidly and occupy the ravines, just as the Germans had done at the end of May, then they could turn the situation on its head and to their distinct advantage.[51]

The topography of the valleys presented formidable obstacles to any attacker. The majority of valleys ran in a rough south–north direction, meaning the attackers would have to cross them from west to east. Whilst some of the valleys were only a few hundred yards wide, many were much more significant, averaging 3,000–4,000 yards across and hundreds of feet deep. They were also steep, with the most precipitous sections usually in the valley bottom closest to the streams running through them, and the shape of the slope was often convex, meaning that defenders could conceal themselves in the bottom unobserved. The steep-sided ravines would present an insurmountable obstacle for the many tanks, especially the less mobile Saint-Chamond and Schneider models. At the bottom of the valleys ran small streams, often accompanied by marshland and bog.[52] The villages of the area contained buildings of solid masonry, which the Germans had rapidly converted into strongpoints, and between most of the villages there were large isolated farmhouses, which had also been fortified.[53] But the defenders did not have everything in their favour. There had been signs of apprehension within the German commanders on the Ourcq front, who sensed a build-up in enemy forces. Unfortunately for the defenders, their protests largely fell on deaf ears, with several reserve divisions withdrawn to help with the attacks on the Marne and in the Champagne.[54]

The Allies' knife thrust at the north-west edge of the pocket would "aim for the jugular", while the divisions still holding the line further south, at the bulging southern limit, would "pummel the body".[55] Foch's plan was to slice east across the salient just south of Soissons and breach the German supply lines, forcing the Germans to retreat. It would be a bold thrust eastwards, moving as rapidly as possible, with the aim of cutting off the German forces and preventing them from retreating.

After eight days in the Cantigny sector, the US 1st Division was relieved on 7 July and moved to the village of Breteuil, 16km behind the front line. Almost immediately, rumours began to circulate that the 1st Division would be leaving France. Perhaps, the men thought, it would be returning to the USA to promote Liberty Loans or was being transferred to the Italian front or even to intervene in the fighting in Russia. However, these rumours seemed unfounded when the division moved 70km south to Plailly, just outside the French capital, for further rest and refitting on the 13th.[56]

---

51   Brady, Frances, *Study of the Physical Geography of the Soissons, Crepy, Château-Thierry, Rheims Area* (1931), p. 2.
52   Brady, pp. 3-4.
53   Brady, p. 5.
54   Michelin, p. 22
55   Johnson, Douglas and Hillman, Rolfe, *Soissons 1918* (College Station: Texas A&M University Press, 1999).
56   Nelson, p. 168.

9.3 Leadership and staff disruption on the eve of the attack

On the eve of the offensive, and with one eye on finally establishing an American army in France, General Pershing ordered several significant changes to the command structure within the US 1st Division. Most of the changes only occurred on 17 July, a mere 16 hours before the intended attack, resulting in a huge amount of upheaval and disruption for the division's staff. General Robert Lee Bullard, the divisional commander, was promoted to command III Corps and replaced by General Charles P, Summerall, previously 1st Division's artillery commander. Other changes included Brigadier General Hanson Ely, who moved from command of the 28th Infantry to a brigade command in 2nd Division under General James Harbord, whilst Ely's position at the head of the 28th was given to Colonel Conrad S. Babcock, who arrived with no combat experience at all. He was going to have a steep introduction to battlefield command, and he wasn't the only one.[57]

What the 1st Division needed most of all was experience gained in battle. Although it had fought successfully in Cantigny on 28 May, the attack itself had been very brief, lasting only a matter of minutes. Moreover, it involved barely 4,000 men from the division, augmented by French artillery, aircraft, trench mortars, tanks and flamethrowers. Once the initial attack was over, 1st Division had spent much of the time in the line, sheltering from near-constant German shelling and from several concerted counterattacks. That represented scant experience for the battle ahead.

The same limitation could be applied for the US 2nd Division, but for different reasons. It had successfully captured the *Bois de Belleau* the previous June, but this had quickly developed into an attritional battle, where artillery eventually played the decisive role in turning the tide in favour of the raw doughboys and Marines. It had taken the division almost a month of intense fighting to advance 2,000 yards and clear the wood, suffering 8,251 casualties, almost one-third of its entire fighting strength. Its final units were relieved by the US 26th (Yankee) Division on the 7 July, although they remained close by as a precaution against further German counterattacks.[58] The losses were predominantly among the marines, infantry and machine gunners, with casualties rapidly replaced by untried draftees from other divisions. Worse was the loss of experienced officers, either as casualties or transferred to other divisions in order to impart their new-found battlefield knowledge. An episode of 'musical chairs' resulted in near wholesale change at the top of the 2nd Division. Major General Omar Bundy, considered by Pershing to be a weak commander, was replaced on 15 July by Brigadier General James G. Harbord, who was elevated in rank to major general (Harbord had arrived in France with General Pershing in May 1917 as his Chief of Staff, but had begged the Commander-in-Chief for a battlefield command, being given charge of 4th Marine Brigade in June and elevated to command 2nd Division on 15 July), and Lieutenant Colonel George Herbst superseded Colonel Arthur L. Conger. Colonel Harry Lee now commanded 4th Brigade, Lieutenant Colonel Thomas Holcombe assumed command of the 6th Marines and Colonel Logan Feland the 5th Marines. Lee's second-in-command, Lieutenant Colonel Bearss, was in hospital, and Colonel James F. McIndoe had been promoted to IV Corps' engineers, with Colonel William

---

57   Nelson, p. 172.
58   Clark, George B., *The Second Infantry Division in World War I* (Jefferson: McFarland & Co., 2007), p. 91.

A. Mitchell now commanding the 2nd Engineers. The 2nd Division was put at the disposal of *Xe Armée* on 14 July.[59]

9.4 A god-awful traffic jam and a logistics nightmare

Early on the morning of the 16 July, elements of the US 1st Division began to arrive in their assembly area, bivouacking under cover of the thick Compiègne Forest canopy. However, the main road leading to and within the forest was completely jammed with traffic: infantry, horses, artillery, tanks and trucks containing ammunition and supplies. At 2100 hrs on the 17th, the majority of 1st Division left Mortefontaine, moving in an easterly direction towards their jumping-off positions, and was immediately drenched by a most violent thunderstorm, which turned the roads into a quagmire and made progress along the slippery routes painfully slow, with some parts almost impassable. The sky turned pitch black and the "darkness became so intense that it was impossible to see the man in front. It was necessary therefore to close the units and have the men hang on to the equipment of the man immediately in front. In the inky darkness, many of the men struggled to keep their footing, stumbling and falling on the uneven, rutted, muddy and slippery surface, further slowing the overall progress of the Division."[60] If there were a positive from this difficult situation, at least enemy aircraft could not get airborne, meaning that the Americans were able to move unobserved by the Germans.

Each company was assigned a French guide to direct them towards the front line. However, many of the guides were poor, either failing to turn up at the agreed location or time, or if they did arrive, several of them proceeding to get lost *en route* to the front. One guide even led 26th Infantry's H Company west instead of east, before being corrected by an officer.[61] The delay and general difficulties experienced in getting into position had two major side-effects: there was a major shortage of maps amongst both the US 1st and 2nd divisions, and few if any of the officers had time to reconnoitre the ground they were attacking. In effect, they would be going in 'blind', a situation which was far from ideal, but one for which they had little alternative.

Many 1st Division units arrived at the agreed positions with little time to spare. The long march had been exhausting and the men were soaking wet from the heavy rainstorm overnight. Nevertheless, many took the opportunity to catch what sleep they could. According to Captain Caldwell, leading M Company, "they were just all in",[62] while Sergeant Gerald V. Stamm of H Company described the men as "muddy, sodden scarecrows with not enough stuff left in them to break up a quilting party", let alone attack the Germans in a few hours' time. Both the 26th and 28th Infantry Regiments reported that they were without grenades; their ammunition carriers were out of contact, stuck in the traffic jam, when the attack commenced.[63]

But that was nothing compared to the difficulties experienced by US 2nd Division, and it was this late-arriving formation which was "to pay the lion's share of the butcher's bill".[64] Having received its orders on 14 July, the divisional artillery had several sets of instructions, including

---

59   Clark, pp. 95-96.
60   Major Clarence Huebner cited in Nelson, p. 171.
61   Nelson, p. 172.
62   Captain Edgar N. Caldwell, cited in Nelson, p. 173.
63   Sergeant Gerald V. Stamm cited in Nelson, p. 173.
64   Johnson and Hillman, pp. 42-43.

some to detach itself from the infantry. It then spent much of the next two days moving 24km first north towards Betz, then south back towards its original destination, and finally another 19km march towards Villers-Cotterêts. Such was the level of disruption caused to the artillery that it took them more than a day to travel that 19km through heavily congested roads.[65] At 2030 hrs on the evening of the 15th, a French staff officer arrived at 2nd Division's headquarters at Chamigny with orders for the division to move yet failed to specify where the move was to be or when it would commence. All they knew was that the headquarters was to open at 1000 hrs on 17 July at Carrefour de Nemours, headquarters of *Xe Armée*. Dissatisfied with the evident disorganisation, Harbord and his Chief-of-Staff, Colonel Preston Brown, arrived at *Xe Armée* headquarters to find Mangin away touring the front lines. Unfortunately, it proved a futile first visit, since no one else at Mangin's headquarters could furnish Harbord with more detailed orders, other than that they were now part of Major General Pierre Berdoulat's *20e CA*; they could say absolutely nothing about the attack itself.[66] Harbord and Brown then motored to *20e CA*'s headquarters at Rétheuil, where they finally got hold of a copy of the attack order. Later that evening, they travelled to the headquarters of the newly formed American I Corps at Taillefontaine, giving the orders to the corps and divisional staff, who spent the night of 16/17 July writing the attack plan for the division. An offer of assistance from staff officers and the G1 of the *1re DIM*, the division sandwiched between the two American divisions, was surprisingly turned down, despite the French formation already being in the line and, having fought there since May, being intimately familiar with the territory that the Americans were to attack.[67] It is not known who instigated the rebuttal, but Harbord seems the most likely candidate to blame, certainly according to Johnson and Hillman. They cite that he was unaccustomed to being palmed off and kept in the dark, so perhaps he was angered by the seeming shambolic organisation at the French *20e CA* level and the delay in getting hold of the attack order. But similarly, hubris, pettiness and a complete overconfidence in the ability of 2nd Division to make a successful attack seem to be the main reasons why the Americans turned down the offer. It was to prove a costly mistake. A more mature, reasoned and frankly sane commander, completely new in the job – with a division only just out of the line after being badly mauled during its first battle, having suffered huge casualties and having replacements who had seen no fighting – might seek out the knowledge and experience of a division already in the line, who knew the terrain and – more importantly – the state of the enemy which it was to attack in a little over 24 hours. But not Harbord, nor any other staff officer from the 2nd Division. Worse, by doing so, they had no way of knowing how the Moroccans would attack on the left flank or the *38e Division* on their right, so co-ordination between divisional boundaries would be nigh on impossible. Even if his staff officers or Chief of Staff were apprehensive of approaching one of Pershing's 'favourites', they should have had the wherewithal to challenge the decision and make the case that they should accept the French offer of help. The rejection represents a major failure of I Corps' and 2nd Division's staff work.

Much time had already been wasted, and even though the infantry eventually managed to receive some rudimentary orders, they were still several kilometres away under the canopy of the *Forêt de Retz*. The men of 3rd Brigade had a slightly easier journey as they were closer to the

65 Clark, p. 95.
66 Clark, pp. 96-97.
67 Johnson and Hillman, p. 59.

front than 4th Brigade, who were almost 20km behind the line, but all troops had to contend with a monstrous traffic jam ahead of them as they approached the front on foot in terrible weather, soaked to the skin by the thunderstorm.

The 5th Marines on the left boundary of the division lacked virtually any maps, resulting in them jumping-off from the wrong location and creating a gap in the attacking line. They had a particularly difficult sector to traverse, with few natural landscape features (at least in the early part of the attack), and their challenge was exacerbated due to their late arrival so they had no opportunity for any reconnaissance, which meant they would have to attack 'blind'. Only the 9th Infantry was in place when the barrage rolled forward, but this didn't stop criticism from Brigadier General Ely, who regarded the 9th's CO, Colonel LeRoy Upton, as an inadequate commander. Severe congestion hindered the 23rd Infantry, led by Colonel Paul B. Malone, causing them to have to run the final couple of kilometres or so, which was not ideal when they were about to enter battle. Even worse, the 23rd Infantry had been forced to ditch most of their auxiliary weapons and ammunition because of their weight, including machine guns, 37mm 1-pdrs, Stokes mortars, hand grenades and rifle grenades. Some of the machine guns didn't arrive at the front until the 19th. This more than anything else was to prove a fatal error. The 5th Marines were late arriving, enduring a horrible journey to the front lasting almost two days, marching much of the 24km to their jumping-off positions and double-timing the final 1km.[68]

9.5 0435 hrs – Battle commences

With no preceding artillery bombardment, a creeping barrage rolled forward at 0435 hrs, signalling the start of the counteroffensive. Within minutes, several German guns responded with their own barrage, resulting in heavy American Expeditionary Forces casualties.[69]

The first wave advanced at a steady walking pace, attempting to keep up with the rolling barrage through the waist-high wheat and chest-high maize. According to Nelson, the Germans had spent the past few weeks strengthening their defences, digging pits several feet deep on the eastern edges of the lanes that afforded them some protection from artillery shelling.[70] When the barrage rolled past, they climbed their ladders and took up positions waiting for the attackers to make themselves visible. With the sun having now risen and the wheat offering little in the way of protection for the attackers, the doughboys made good targets for the waiting German machine gun crews, resulting in further heavy casualties.

Early in the attack, 1st Division's 28th Regiment became pinned down 200 metres in front of the German's front line by machine gun and automatic rifle fire coming from the Râperie Ferme strongpoint, located 1.5km from their jump-off position. A platoon was despatched to outflank the Germans, whilst another from H Company simultaneously made a frontal assault on the position with fixed bayonets, capturing five heavy machine guns and 100 Germans.[71] For many involved in the attack, this was their first experience of combat, and the capture of the strongpoint and the German prisoners being marshalled towards captivity signalled a noticeable change in morale within the ranks. The next strongpoint to be attacked was

---

68   Clark, pp. 99-102 and Johnson and Hillman, p. 73.
69   Nelson, p. 176.
70   Nelson, p. 177.
71   Nelson, p. 178.

Ferme de St Anand, which was beyond 1st Division's northern boundary, in the French *153e Division*'s sector. However, the French were struggling to make progress and the Germans were enfilading 1st Division's left flank with 77mm artillery, machine guns and trench mortars from their fortified position at the farm, causing a number of casualties. A squad from G Company, together with a contingent of French, captured the farm, taking another 100 or so German prisoners in hand-to-hand fighting.[72] The attack on Ferme de St Anand was one of many such actions that first morning, and units quickly became intermingled in the chaos. Men from rival squads and regiments would criss-cross each other's sectors instead of moving along in parallel formation. Casualties were also mounting and many attacking units found themselves without officers to lead the attack, meaning inexperienced NCOs were thrust into leadership roles or tasked with organising assaults. The hasty nature of the assembly, poor co-ordination, absence of maps and in many cases written orders meant that virtually none of the NCOs had any information about the objectives of the attack, other than a need to continue to drive eastwards. That in itself was not unusual. However, the extent of the information void up and down the front was a circumstance that the Americans in particular had not encountered before, and this inexperience in coping with such a situation would play a part in reducing their effectiveness on the 18th.

9.6 French cavalry finally get into action

As early as 0930 hrs, General Fayolle had become doubtful that a breakthrough could be made that day. The lack of cavalry support was a significant failure, caused by the traffic congestion on all approach roads, with the cavalry confined to using the snarled-up roads to move forward.[73] The *2e Corps de cavalerie* (2e CC) under General Robillot had arrived at Meaux on 14 July, but this was almost 43km from Villers-Cotterêts and even further from the actual front line. With the commencement of the German offensive on the 15th, Robillot had been ordered to move his cavalry east, away from *Xe Armée* and placed at the disposal of the GAC, but this was later reversed and Robillot and the men under his command could be forgiven for not knowing what they were meant to be doing or where they should be. Once they arrived at Villers-Cotterêts, they found it almost impossible to debouch from the *Forêt de Retz* since it was crowded with troops and transport. When they did arrive, the fighting was too intense and the German resistance still too strong to allow the cavalry to come into action. A few squadrons attempted to force their way forward by fighting dismounted between *20e* and *30e Corps*, but even this proved futile and defeated the reason for deploying the cavalry in the first place: their speed of movement and opportunity to exploit any gaps in the line. Fayolle wrote to General Mangin telling him that using the cavalry as dismounted infantry was a mistake and that "it was essential that this Cavalry Corps be preserved for more profitable use later".[74] As subsequently reported: "About 6:00pm French Cavalry were seen approaching from the west along the Coeuvres-et-Valsery road and they continued to pass the bivouac area for two hours. It presented an enthralling sight to those who saw it. From whence this cavalry came, or where it went, no one ever knew, for we

---

72 Nelson, p. 182.
73 Fayolle, p. 123.
74 Woldike, pp. 15–18, 42, 113.

never saw it again."⁷⁵ During the afternoon, Major Austin would also recall that the French put "large bodies" of cavalry on reconnaissance and that "the Boche went after them pretty hard".⁷⁶ Another man from 1st Division, Captain Senay, witnessed a charge by French cavalry towards a gap in the German line late in the day on the 18th, but the attack rapidly disintegrated after being enfiladed by intense German machine gun fire. The few survivors dashed back off the field and Senay characterised it as a "complete disaster for an outmoded weapon of war".⁷⁷ According to Nelson, the French cuirassiers, having spent much of the previous day creating a massive traffic jam in the rear of the AEF, impeded the ability of men, artillery and supplies to follow up the day's breakout.⁷⁸ But the *coup de grace* came from American III Corps commander General Bullard, who simply wrote: "I was perfectly sure they [the French cavalry] would do no good, and they did none."⁷⁹

9.7 Mangin makes an audacious decision

On the evening of the 18th, Lieutenant Colonel Hellé telephoned Colonel Hergault, Mangin's Deputy Chief of Staff, to say that Generals Pétain and Fayolle had arrived at his headquarters and were on their way to see Mangin at his command post at Bonneuil. They had already told Hellé that they had no reserve divisions to feed into the battle and that Mangin would have to stop, being content with the great success already achieved. Hellé concluded the call saying that Pétain had described the day as being "Beautiful, it's very beautiful … it's almost too beautiful … but you have to stop." At about 1800 hrs, Pétain and Fayolle arrived at the PC close to *Côte 255*, where Mangin gave them a summary of the situation, the results of the day and explained some of the difficulties encountered, using a large map on a table at the foot of a beech tree next to Mangin's observatory. Pétain reiterated that it had indeed been a very great success, beyond what even he had hoped for, but that he did not have another division to give to *Xe Armée*. Upon hearing this, General Mangin protested but Pétain stuck to his guns, exclaiming: "I have none; I know you are a seducer, but this time I am very strong, for, having absolutely nothing myself, I can give you nothing."

Mangin remonstrated once more, believing that he must not stop such a large attack when it could bring decisive results and that it would have been better not to start it in the first place. Pétain repeated that he had nothing to give, adding that he was obliged to consider the other divisions fighting south of the Marne. That was his immediate focus and he wanted to prevent the situation there getting worse. He concluded that *Xe Armée* should commence adopting defence in depth and strengthening the current front line. But despite the intervention of Pétain, Mangin persisted, stressing that it was easier to force the Germans to abandon south of the Marne and even the *poche* of Château-Thierry by continuing the pressure on *his* front than it was by resuming a direct attack south of the Marne. As he was leaving with Fayolle, a clearly

---

75 Huntington FW, Operations of Co. G, 18th Infantry, 1st Division, in the Aisne–Marne offensive, July 18–23 1918, in Nelson, p. 193.
76 Austin Raymond B, World War I veterans survey collection, US Military History Institute, Carlisle, Pennsylvania, in Nelson, p. 194.
77 Senay Charles T, From Shavetail to Captain, in Nelson, p. 194. Senay, Operations of the 28th Infantry 18–23 July, 1918, Combined Arms Research Library, Fort Leavenworth, Kansas, in Nelson, p. 194.
78 Nelson, pp. 193–94.
79 Bullard, R.T. (1925), 'Personalities and reminiscences of war', cited in Nelson, p. 194.

exasperated Pétain repeated that he had no reserves and therefore could offer no divisions to Mangin.

After his departure, Mangin thought for a moment before telling his Chief of Staff: "Basically General Pétain told me he would not give me anything, but he did not give me the order to stop the attack. Therefore we will continue with what we have and will resume the attack tomorrow." Deciding it was better to ask for forgiveness than ask for permission, he summoned Commandant de Suzannet, Foch's liaison officer, and recounted his conversation with Pétain, before asking him to contact the Generalissimo immediately, saying:

> I am putting myself in a very difficult position with no reserves made available to me but I agree with the instructions of General Foch to continue the attack tomorrow and I will issue the order accordingly. This evening I shall receive an order of operations from General Fayolle which will conform to the instructions which General Pétain has given to General Fayolle and I shall be obliged to stop. I am going to ignore that instruction and continue the offensive with the means available to me.[80]

It was clearly a risky policy to interpret Pétain's guidance so loosely, and there was a good chance that the French Commander-in-Chief would not look kindly on Mangin's actions, with the likely result that he would be sacked. But he firmly believed that he was right and that it was the correct decision to continue with the attack the following morning.

Foch indeed disagreed with Pétain's interpretation, siding with Mangin and agreeing to immediately release four divisions from general reserve in order that the battle could be continued with the utmost vigour, with Foch planning to give the Germans no respite from the Allies. For his part, Mangin was absolutely thrilled with how the battle had panned out so far. There had been smaller operations at Malmaison and Verdun in the autumn of 1917, and Mangin's hastily improvised counterattack on the Matz in June, but this had been on an altogether different scale and to 'The Butcher' a spectacular success. In an Order of the Day, he told his men that they had "removed the stain of the new barbarian occupation from the cradle of France and had assured not just the safety of France, but the entire Île de France region".[81]

The Allied counteroffensive on 18 July had indeed been a stunning success, especially in *Xe Armée*'s sector of operations, with the prize for the largest advance going to the *1re DIM* sandwiched between the US 1st and 2nd divisions of *20e CA*. In total, the five attacking armies had captured 20,000 prisoners of war, 518 artillery pieces, 300 *minenwerfer* and a massive haul of more than 3,000 German machine guns, with *Xe Armée* alone accounting for 10,000–12,000 of the prisoners and 250 of the guns. Neiberg comments that this haul was even larger than the later more celebrated first day of the Battle of Amiens on 8 August 1918, when 17,000 Germans surrendered.[82] The huge number of prisoners captured during 18 July indicates both the speed of advance – overrunning German positions and not giving the enemy the time to respond – as well as the low morale of the ordinary German soldier, who was keen to surrender at the earliest opportunity rather than resist, defend and fight. It is also testament to Mangin's tactics of not

---

80 Mangin (1950), pp. 279–82. AFGG, 30e Corps, 18 Juillet 1918.
81 Mangin (1920), pp. 196–98. Neiberg, p. 129.
82 Neiberg, p. 130. Fayolle wrote on the evening of the 18th that *Xe Armée* had captured 10,000 prisoners that day, No. 39/O.P. Woldike, p. 113.

deploying any artillery preparation before the surprise attack, since many of the Germans would probably have been either killed or wounded during the bombardment; because this did not take place, large numbers of prisoners were captured instead.

According to Major Huebner, the night of 18/19 July passed fairly quietly, with little in the way of shelling by either side, giving the exhausted men of *Xe Armée* the opportunity to get some much-needed rest.[83] However, both sides knew the fighting would resume again at first light. The Germans brought up the 34th Division to bolster their forces, inserting it to the right of the 28th Division in front of Ploisy, about a mile east of Missy-aux-Bois, with the German front line being halfway between the two villages, straddling a large wheat field.[84] The Germans were still holding a key hilltop strongpoint across the Paris–Soissons road to the north-east, known as the Vauxbuin position, which had been captured from the French during their last advance and significantly fortified by the Germans. It was from this elevated position that the Germans would be firing into the US 1st Division and French positions on the 19th.

9.8 0400 hrs, 19 July – The battle recommences

The attack on 19 July followed the same plan as the previous day, starting with a rolling barrage but no preliminary bombardment. But the Germans would not be so surprised a second time, and all units were alert and ready. As the men formed up for the attack in the semi-darkness of dawn, there were few indications of the horrors of the day ahead. As the barrage rolled forward on time at 0400 hrs, 35 minutes earlier than the day before, the men followed closely behind. Through the fog and smoke, they were able to advance barely 100 yards before scores of repositioned German machine guns, supported by artillery, opened up with withering fire, forcing them back to the starting point with heavy casualties. According to Sergeant Gerald Stamm: "[I]t was plain that Fritz was in an ugly mood, and that there would be hell to pay."[85]

M Company, which the previous day had accepted the surrender of several hundred Germans in the cave near Missy-aux-Bois, became disoriented in the confusion, fog and smoke of the battlefield. The company veered too far left when crossing the Paris–Soissons road to the north of its intended route and outside 1st Division's sector. As it crossed to the east side of the road it came under heavy fire from the Vauxbuin position, wiping out all but five men from the company.[86] Spotting a break in the American line, German units began to form up for an immediate counterattack, but this was broken up by a battalion of 75mm guns from 7th Field Artillery under the command of Colonel L.T. Holbrook, which raced into position, fired on and dispersed the Germans before they could commence their counterattack.

The attacks on the 19th yielded yet more prisoners, with another 7,000 captured that day, as well as 240 guns in just two days of the counteroffensive.[87] After the initial successes including the recapture of Château-Thierry and the Germans abandoning their positions south of the river and crossing back to the north bank of the Marne the following day, there had been dogged and determined rearguard resistance by the defending Germans, now totalling 40 divisions,

---

83 Huebner, Clarence, cited in Nelson, p. 194.
84 Nelson, p. 195.
85 Stamm G, cited in Nelson, p. 196.
86 Nelson, p. 196.
87 Woldike, No.67-O.P., p. 119.

reinforcements having been pushed urgently into the fight, with additional field and heavy batteries brought to the front.[88] A series of limited German counterattacks, combined with exhausted and depleted ranks of Franco-American troops, had meant the attack had begun to stall, and little progress east was made between 21 and 23 July. The fresh German 5th Division recaptured some lost ground, including the village of Le Plessier-Huleu. Three more German divisions, supported by a small number of tanks, also made a powerful counterattack.[89] On top of the determined German resistance, they had begun to construct two fortified lines in the rear, one running north–south close to the Soissons–Château-Thierry road and the other 3–5 miles further east, utilising a section of the abandoned *ligne du Gouvernement Militaire de Paris* (GMP) trench line, but also utilising the terrain and in particular two sets of ridges which overlooked the ground to the west. Although it was claimed to be virtually impenetrable, with interlocking fields of machine gun fire, this new line was hastily constructed and is more accurately described as a major obstacle. Nevertheless, it would still have to be overcome in order for the counteroffensive to proceed.

Everyone in the French chain of command recognised that Mangin's first thrust was now exhausted and that their *grande offensive* risked failure if it was allowed to peter out. An urgent injection of fresh new troops was needed to give it the impetus it desperately needed in order to maintain the momentum. Even Pétain, not best known as a natural optimist, recognised that the opportunity must not be squandered at this critical juncture and both he and Foch acknowledged that the opportunity to sever the jugular vein and trap the Germans in the *poche* was slipping from their grasp, with the Boche able to retreat in an orderly manner, albeit pursued as they went. For Foch, it was essential that they keep up the pressure on the Germans, and he hand-delivered a letter to the French GQG on the 23rd pointing out that the Germans were being allowed to retire in good order. Foch argued that the best option was a renewed attack using Mangin's Xe Armée to make a strong flanking advance using a concentrated force of troops.[90]

Pétain, however, was absolutely determined to avoid the mistakes of his predecessor, Robert Nivelle, who had continued his attacks in the spring of 1917, with disastrous consequences, when all evidence indicated that he should have called a halt to the offensive rather than risk yet more unnecessary casualties. Pétain now faced a major dilemma, and at a crucial moment he paused to consider the right path. Some have claimed that he hesitated, his characteristic caution getting the better of him whilst he wrestled with the options and tried to decide on the correct course of action. Could he, by reinforcing the neck, still sever the jugular of the *poche*, and if so which side of the salient would give him the best chance of success? Or should he throw more divisions to the south of the salient and accelerate the push northwards? He didn't have the reserves to play with, and whichever option he chose, there would be criticism from several of his army commanders that he had made the wrong choice.

Pétain had done much to restore morale in the French Army since his appointment as General-in-Chief in May 1917, commanding the armies of the north and north-east. Initially appointed as Nivelle's Chief of Staff on the 29 April 1917, Nivelle had been urged to resign but refused to go. A farcical fortnight ensued, Pétain being appointed to replace Nivelle on 15

---

88 According to Scott Elliot, p. 240. Edmonds, p. 254
89 Michelin (1919), p. 29.
90 Greenhalgh (2011), p. 403.

May, with Foch as his Chief of Staff, but for three days – and in spite of his replacement now giving the orders – Nivelle still flatly refused to resign. Finally, on 19 May, amidst chaotic and acrimonious scenes at the French headquarters, Nivelle was forced to accept the inevitable and departed, albeit reluctantly and after hurling one final insult that he had been betrayed. Foch would act as a technical advisor to the French government and a foil to Pétain's more cautious strategic and organisational control of the French armies.[91]

The new Commander-in-Chief had an expert understanding of the relationship between artillery and infantry, but even before his appointment he also had a willingness to disagree with his superiors.[92] Now, as leader of the French Army, he would have to stand behind his beliefs. At the very outset of his tenure, Pétain set out a new operational doctrine, issuing a series of pamphlets which emphasised the need to increase both the amount of materiel and its mobility, with a strong focus on tanks and aircraft. For his part, Foch fully supported his Commander-in-Chief and began to oversee the acquisition of large stockpiles of materiel for use in 1918. This was followed by another pamphlet which explained Pétain's offensive philosophy. Put simply, he would absorb the enemy reserves with repeated attacks on different fronts, and once he had built up sufficient materiel strength (as opposed to manpower), he would make a more general push.[93]

Every decision that Pétain made was influenced by his primary goal of limiting French casualties during battle. Only that way could he sustain his effort towards victory. He would use firepower, air power, tanks, indeed any means at his disposal to spare the infantry and minimise unnecessary casualties. Many French regiments were still chronically understrength and men were being combed out from the home front, but still in insufficient numbers to cover the losses. Pétain had been a champion of the massive rollout of tanks, believing they could do much of the work of the infantry at a significantly lower human cost, and the French Army of 1918 was the most modernised of all nations at that time, with Doughty believing it to be "the arsenal of the Entente".[94] Much of the groundwork had been done by Nivelle, who had seen the benefit of utilising tanks to support the infantry, but so too had Pétain, who decided to massively speed up their production as soon as he became Commander-in-Chief. He was aided by the mercurial General Jean Estienne, who had commanded the *22e Régiment d'artillerie* under Pétain during the Battle of the Marne in 1914. Estienne is considered by many in France to be the *Père des Chars* (Father of the Tank).[95] As commander of the *Artillerie Spéciale*, France's tank arm, he had overseen its development from a fledgling unit, putting early prototypes into battle, and by the summer of 1918 it had become a major constituent of the combined arms attacking force, acting as mobile artillery and using speed to break through the enemy's lines without the need to 'soften up' the enemy with preparatory bombardments. Estienne's motto was "To accomplish anything entails consciously resigning yourself to doing less-than-perfect work", believing it was better and quicker to build imperfect tanks that could use the battlefield experience and be modified accordingly, rather than developing a series of prototypes that might never see action. He favoured the lighter and more nimble two-man Renault FT-17 light tanks over the slower and lumbering Schneider and Saint-Chamonds, ordering vast numbers of the former to

---

91 Neiberg (2003), p. 53.
92 Doughty, pp. 355-59.
93 Clayton, p. 140 and Goya, p. 230.
94 Goya, p. xiv. Doughty, p. 511.
95 Estienne-Mondet, A, *Le général J.B. Estienne, père des chars* (Paris: L'Harmattan, 2010), pp. 177-79.

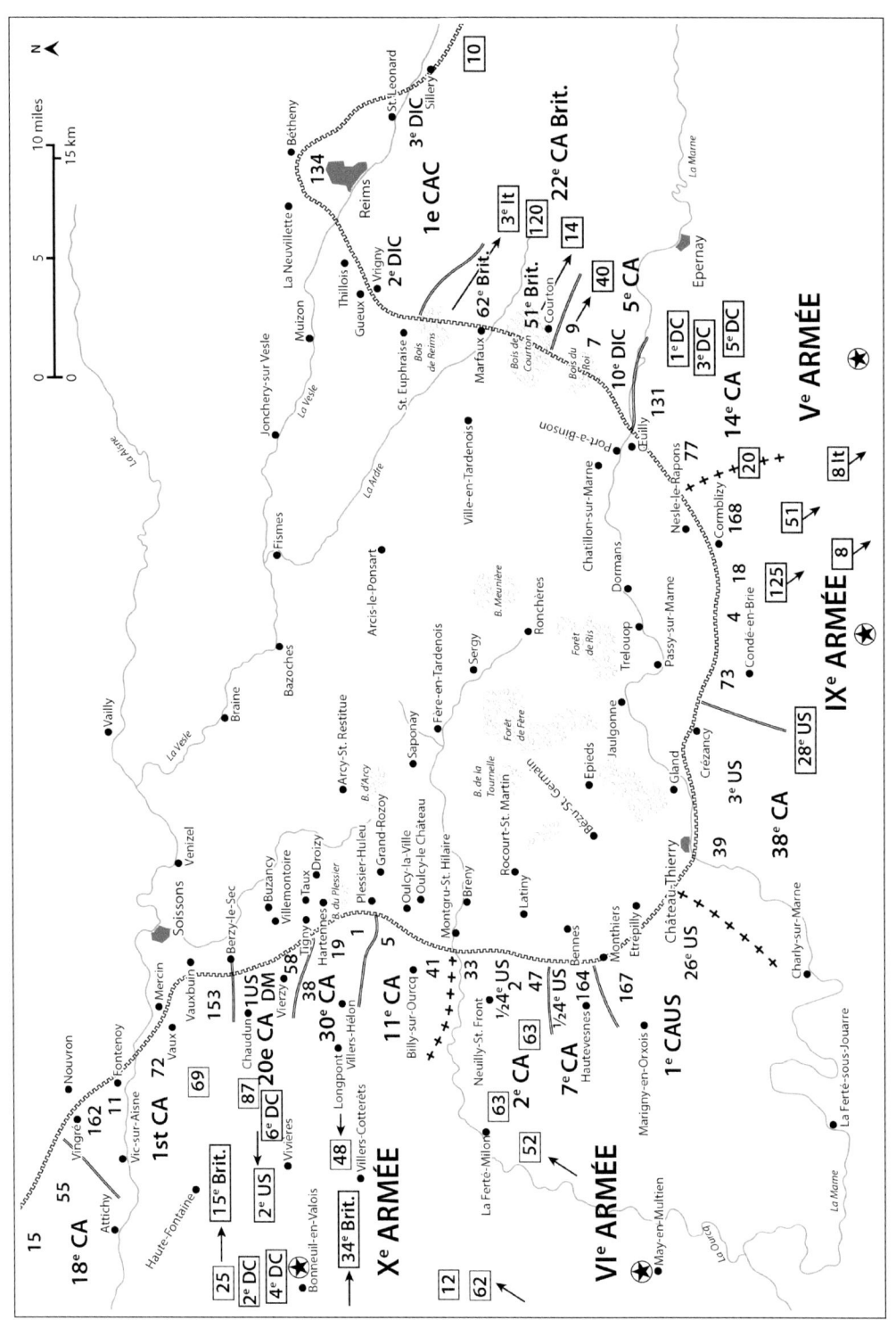

Map 2. Marne Salient on 20 July 1918.

be constructed in the belief that they would be far superior for exploiting a breakthrough or for undertaking reconnaissance missions. The six-man Schneider weighed 13.5 tonnes, whilst the nine-man Saint-Chamond weighed in at a massive 24 tonnes, and neither could move at more than walking pace. This was in stark contrast to the lightweight Renault tank, with its two-man crew and innovative rotating turret, able to travel up to 8 miles per hour. They were, however, notoriously unreliable, with large numbers breaking down before they arrived at the start line.[96] It was not just on the ground that Pétain was a revolutionary; he also had his eyes set skywards, intending to create a mass of aviation in order to decisively gain air superiority and mastery over the Germans above the battlefield, both for fighters and bombers. He created the *Division aérienne* (Air Division), headed by Colonel Duva, Head of Aviation at the French GQG 1, for the task.[97]

Pétain's doctrine was evolving with him, but still faced critics at home and abroad, threatening to resign at a meeting of the War Committee in December 1917 if they could find a better alternative to conduct the war. British Prime Minister Lloyd George had gone over Pétain's head, complaining directly to President Poincaré about the apparent French military inactivity, with no signs of major Allied offensives being planned for the first time in the war, and the British unnerved by the prospect of such a major change in French strategy. According to Pétain, the French would be entirely on the defensive for the first part of the year at least. This paints a rather unflattering picture of the French Commander-in-Chief as being the pessimist extraordinaire. The plans he developed in the winter of 1917, for limited-objective attacks, were a recognition that the offensive prowess of the French Army was still somewhat uncertain and he dared not risk being too over-ambitious. However, attacks were planned; he envisaged the French attacking in two or three sectors simultaneously, with the British doing likewise further north, feeling strongly that the Germans would not be able to counter two points of friction at once.[98]

In the period from his appointment until the spring of 1918, Pétain dominated the army and was highly regarded by both officers and *poilus*, with most men believing that he cared deeply and sincerely for his soldiers and that his actions went beyond talk, demonstrating that he would not waste their lives and limbs.[99] Nor was he as defensively minded as many people believe; he was not at all opposed to going over to the offensive, having no intention of remaining solely on the defensive.[100] He understood perfectly well that a war could never be won by being solely defensive in approach, and that at some point someone was going to have to get up out of the trenches and break the deadlock on the Western Front. But Pétain's beliefs opposed the notion of *l'attaque à l'outrance* (the all-out attack), and to underscore this he coined the phrase '*la feu tue*' (firepower kills), with attacks to be undertaken with all necessary caution and planning, always accompanied by superior firepower.[101] First mentioned during the Battle of Verdun, it is an apt interpretation of his philosophy, since in his view such a tactic was much more likely to be

---

96   Goya, pp. 207-10.
97   Greenhalgh (2014), p. 290.
98   Ryan, p. 150.
99   Doughty, pp. 360–61.
100 Atkin, pp. 8–9. Doughty, pp. 356-57.
101 Atkin, p. 9.

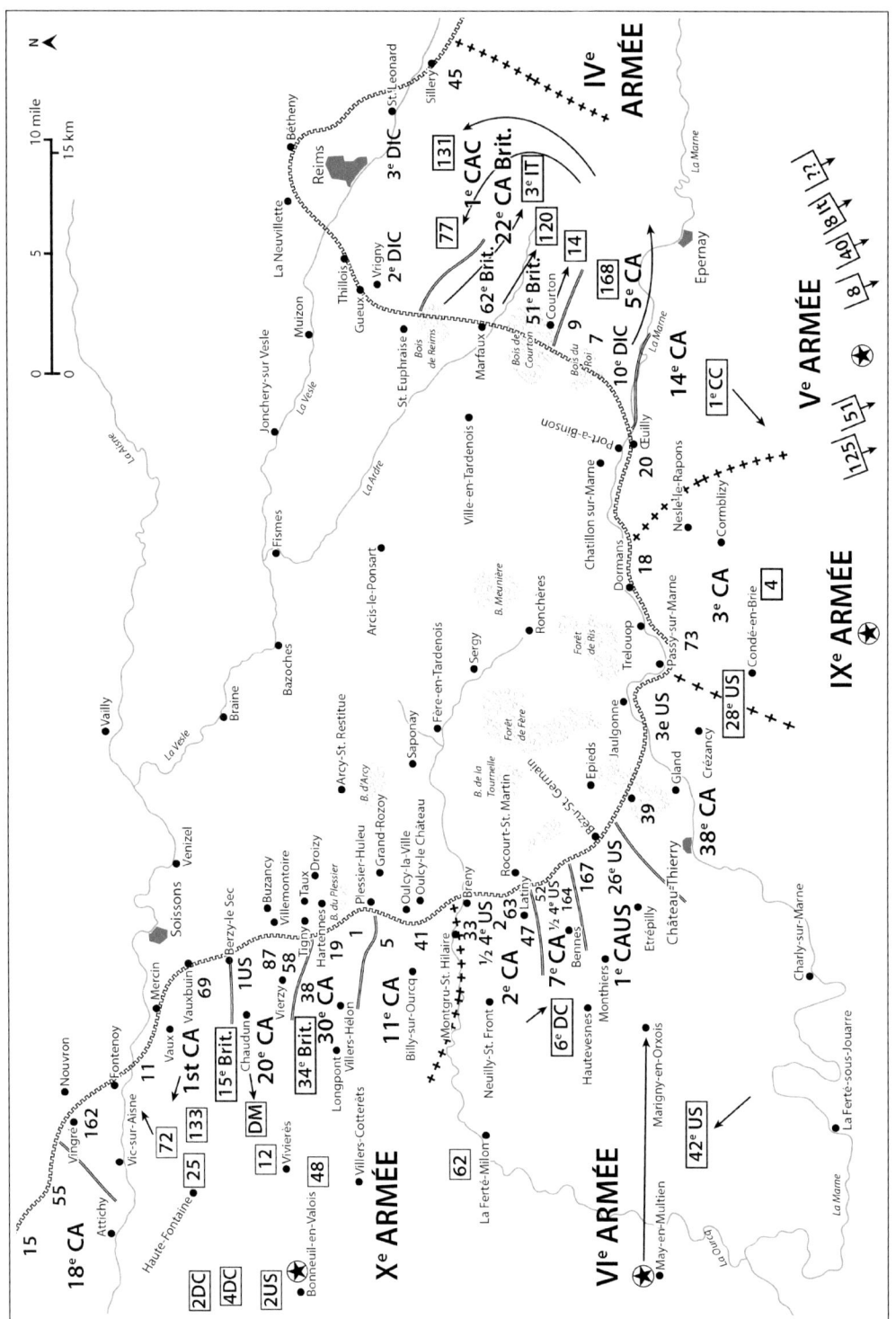

Map 3. The Marne Salient on 22 July 1918.

effective, whilst at the same time minimising the infantry casualties.[102] In spite of the worrying news coming from the Eastern Front, Pétain refused to cave in to pressure from Paris to launch a large offensive, believing it would do nothing to keep the Russians in the war. Instead, he supported Haig's decision in the autumn to take on the main burden of fighting by launching a British offensive in Flanders, even if it was only temporary.[103]

A few days earlier, he had published Directive No. 5, which built on some of the previous directives he had issued. One of the key changes was to move the thinking and aspiration from gaining limited objectives to somewhat more distant ones, since he believed that the morale of the army was improving and they could stomach a little more adventurous attacks. But he was certain that the ordinary *poilus* and their infantry commanders would never agree to the massive offensives favoured by his predecessor. To help to persuade the troops that he was serious about restricting casualties, precise and concise orders were preferred to plans, and the importance of subordinates using their initiative on the ground was emphasised. Artillery preparation, were it to be needed, was to be brief but violent, aiming to neutralise rather than destroy the enemy, and the expectation of 'manoeuvre' and a return to a war of movement featured once again, after being absent from French doctrine for several years. In a broad sense, he was thus well aligned with Mangin's most famous quote: *Quoi qu'on fasse, on perd beaucoup de monde* ("whatever we do, we lose a lot of people"). This phrase has, however, often been taken out of context to depict Mangin as an uncaring commander, even a 'Butcher of men', the very antithesis in character to Pétain.[104] Mangin's actual quote is contained in a letter to his wife on 8 May 1916:

> Civilian or military people who say in Paris – that I have too many people killed are ill-informed. We wouldn't dare say it here. Indeed, the bombardment is appalling and the shelters almost zero: whatever we do, we lose a lot of people. If the two infantry mix in the fight, less is lost by cannon and more by rifle and grenade. But the loss figure is roughly constant, with some exceptions. Example: my division lost 3,000 men in a fortnight (it had lost 4,000 men to Vimy from September 25 to October 8), I cannot find these losses exaggerated. The division which had preceded it on the ground had also lost 3,000 men, but it held out for a shorter time and had also lost a great deal of ground, which mine regained entirely. A neighbouring division on the right lost 5,000 men to also cede a lot of ground. On my left, the 6th Division lost 3,500 men in twenty-four days: it neither attacked nor suffered major attacks, it was only the bombardment. The conclusion of General Nivelle and mine, that of General Pétain then, after experience, is that in the battle of Verdun (in the current phase of this battle at least), stagnation does not prevent losses; if you are attacked, you have to counter-attack by force: you lose fewer people than by allowing yourself to be done. As far as I'm concerned, you can say that I lost a little less people than the others, and that I have moved forward. No one here is against it.

Even the brilliant success of the very limited attack at Le Hamel had resulted in casualties. Pétain had previous form for halting an operation, having stopped the attack at La Malmaison on 1

---

102 Tournoux, Jean, *Pétain and de Gaulle* (London: Heinemann, 1966), p. 23.
103 Doughty, p. 375.
104 Mangin (1950), p. 112.

November 1917 after the Germans had retreated from their positions, like a cautious gambler quitting when ahead. He was content with his gains, managing to take German positions in eight days which Nivelle had failed to take in weeks.[105]

His limited objective offensives were proving to be a winning formula, and more importantly to Pétain, resulted in fewer casualties incurred than for the defenders. The French had advanced up to 6km in places during La Malmaison, making it one of their largest gains since 1914, at a cost of just 2,241 killed, 8,162 wounded and 1,460 missing, one-tenth the losses of Nivelle's offensive and vastly favourable in comparison with the costly British offensive at Passchendaele. In addition to the advance of 6km, they had captured 11,000 German prisoners, 200 guns, 220 *minenwerfer* and 700 machine guns.[106] The attack had not been without risk, being the largest operation since the mutinies of earlier in the year but is a good example of how Pétain's character has been incorrectly portrayed as being negative or pessimistic. In reality he was much more a pragmatist and realist, instinctively knowing where and when to attack and when was the right moment to call a halt and consolidate. It was important for another reason too: the ordinary *poilu* had seen that the French commanders could mount an operation that was successful, restrained and resulted in limited casualties, and this had heartened the French and provided a significant boost to morale and improvement in discipline, in effect resuscitating the entire French Army. Casualty levels had indeed dropped, from an average of 80,000 a month to just 36,000 a month during his tenure, but despite this decline, many regiments were still severely understrength and just like the British, Pétain was forced to thin his divisions on the Western Front. He managed to maintain 108 divisions in the field, but each one was reduced from 12 to nine battalions, with barely 9,000 men per division.[107] But thanks to Pétain's pre-emptive and far-sighted actions, the French Army was rested, better trained and better equipped when the German Spring offensives began on 21 March 1918 than it had been even a few months earlier. The well-regarded General Fayolle had returned from Italy to take charge of France's reserve force, the reconstituted *Groupe d'armées de reserve* (GAR), that Pétain had refused to hand over to inter-Allied control as part of a general reserve earlier in the year, meaning that it could be moved to wherever it was needed whilst maintaining the greatest level of protection to the French front. But Franco-British planning had been fraught with problems, with neither commander yet willing to supply divisions to a general reserve.[108]

Pétain was also aware that he could rely on few if any reserves and that continuing the offensive was very much an 'all in' gamble, a last throw of the dice, contrary to his sometimes prudent nature. Ultimately though, the decision to continue the attack was made for him, with Foch deciding on 20 July that now was the time to press their advantage by putting whatever additional divisions he could muster into the fight and to reinforce Mangin's *Xe Armée* and the left of Degoutte's *VIe Armée*, to try and sever the jugular at the vulnerable neck of the *poche*. Foch saw things more clearly (and arguably more simply) than Pétain, sensing the Germans were rapidly weakening and believing that the odds were in their favour. Continuing the attack was a sure bet, with now being the perfect time to strike the fatal blow. He therefore added the remaining reserves to the left hinge of the salient: the US 32nd and 42nd Divisions to *VI*

---

105 Ryan, p. 140.
106 Doughty, p. 389.
107 Ryan, p. 145. Doughty, p. 387.
108 Greenhalgh (2014), pp. 270-72.

Armée and French *12e* and *25e divisions* to Mangin's *Xe Arm*ée. Importantly, both the latter divisions were well rested: *12e Division* had been recuperating in Lorraine since early April and *25e Division* near Verdun had not been in action for almost a year. He also recognised that the US 1st Division and French *58e Division* were all but spent forces, both having suffered horrific casualties, especially the Americans, so agreed to relieve them in favour of two fresher divisions, with the French *153e* and *1st Moroccan* divisions also in the process of being relieved by the French *69e* and *87e divisions*.[109]

Despite the clear tensions emerging and whilst Foch held the balance of power, Pétain still commanded the French Army and was therefore able to direct his troops to where *he* believed they might be most effective. Sending a long and detailed telegram to the five army commanders and General Fayolle commanding the *Groupe d'armées de reserve*, he instructed them on the next phase of operations. *Ve Armée* (Berthelot) would march on Fismes from both banks of the River Ardre, whilst *IX Armée* (de Mitry), with only a small contingent left south of the Marne, would push most of its forces north of the river. In the centre, Degoutte's *VIe Armée* would attack and capture Fère-en-Tardenois and Mareuil, and *Xe Armée* would make its main thrust towards Braine on either side of the River Vesle. The telegram ended with Pétain stressing that "everyone will understand that no respite must be allowed to the enemy until the objectives have been attained". Fayolle added his own commentary to the order, stating that "it is not merely a matter of driving the enemy from the Château-Thierry pocket, but also of cutting off his retreat to the north and capturing the bulk of his forces" with the role of *Xe Armée* firmly securing the left flank and repulsing any German counterattacks were they to develop, being particularly important.[110] Foch wrote to Pétain the following day, stressing the importance of pushing *Xe Armée* to its "ultimate limit" in order to reap the benefits from the current battle, but to also reorganise any spent divisions urgently.[111] The French report into events of 22 July admitted that neither the *Xe* nor *Ve Armées* had been able to gain any successes that day, and that the enemy attached a very special importance to the retention of the plateaux south-west of Soissons and the heights north-east of Vrigny as the two key hinges on which Von Boehn's army must be pressed and forced to draw back. Moreover, the Germans still had the benefit of air superiority, which although rapidly dwindling, would necessitate all movements being made at night.[112]

On 22 July, *Xe Armée*'s front extended for 45km from Fontenoy on the River Aisne south towards Belleau, north-west of Château-Thierry, and Foch believed that this location offered the best chance for positive exploitation. But it was already evident that the nature of the battle had evolved, with the Germans having brought up substantial numbers of reinforcements and the French shorn of the majority of their tank force. Mangin therefore would be obliged to throw in additional infantry to the fighting, but with the additional German reinforcements, this would provide a stiff test for the attackers. Whilst Mangin was eager to press the enemy, the French Commander-in-Chief was less keen. Having diverted the two British divisions to the sector, together with the US 32nd 'Red Arrow' Division under Major General W.G. Haan,

---

109 Edmonds, p. 254.
110 Edmonds, pp. 249-50 and Fayolle, Instruction to Sixth and Tenth Armies, No. 89, 7pm on 20 July 1918 cited in Woldike, p. 130.
111 Foch, General Directions, No.2257, 1pm on 21 July 1918, cited in Woldike, p. 135.
112 Edmonds, p. 257.

ordered up from Alsace,[113] in support and having few other options available to him, Foch now ordered Mangin to utilise the two British divisions which had been put at Foch's disposal. There was still the prospect that Haig might recall the two formations at any time, so Foch desired to use them before they were sent back, and like Mangin he wanted to inject fresh impetus into the offensive by adding the relatively rested British troops into battle and trying to force the enemy from their new defensive positions. He also recognised other factors that were key to his decision. Firstly, by continuing to attack himself along *Xe Armée*'s front to the west of the salient, if he could breach the Soissons–Château-Thierry road and the railway line, this would prevent the Germans from resupplying their troops in the salient. Secondly, by continuing the offensive, it would prevent the Boche from moving any troops away from the sector, which would reduce the risk of any new attack on the British further north. Finally, he calculated (correctly) that Haig would not try to recall the divisions whilst they were actively deployed during the first few days of operations. Foch judged that in the unlikely event of the Germans commencing an attack in Flanders, requiring Haig to recall the British troops, then at least he would be able to gainfully employ them for a few days.[114]

Although Foch ordered Mangin to deploy the two British divisions, he remained concerned about Mangin's reputation for impetuousness and impatience, fearing that he might throw them into the fighting too early and without sufficient preparation. Also noting the lack of tanks now available to press the attack, he therefore wrote a personal note to Mangin in which he said: "The attention of the *Xe Armée* is called to the advantage which may accrue if, without checking the offensive for long, it prepares further operations with the new divisions which are reaching the Army every day, so as to produce strong combined action at the moment when the Army wishes to inflict a serious reverse on the enemy." In effect he was telling him not to throw the divisions in too soon and waste a fantastic opportunity for a decisive victory. Understanding how Mangin thought and operated, Foch's handwritten letter played to Mangin's undoubted ego, emphasising the larger battle unfolding and that a little patience would increase his chance of making *the* major contribution to the inevitable victory.[115]

There was more localised but still bitter fighting on 22 July, focused on Oulchy-le-Château, where the Germans repulsed a combined infantry, artillery and tank attack on the town. According to the diary of Max von Boehn's Seventh Army, the Germans now considered the immediate crisis to be over and the danger of envelopment and annihilation of Seventh Army no longer imminent, with it able to make an orderly withdrawal north. There was even speculative talk about launching a counterattack of their own against Mangin's left flank, but this was found to be unfeasible, with Soissons under heavy fire, the railway capacity inadequate to supply any attack and insufficient troops available to launch it. Frankly, given events unfolding it was simply a fantasy for the Germans to consider anything except stout, resolute defence. Cracks

---

113 The US 32nd Division was formed from Army National Guard units from Wisconsin and Michigan, but had only been in France since February 1918, being the sixth US division to disembark on the European continent. This was its first real combat experience, having served its period of front-line training in a quiet sector in Alsace. It would arrive on the evening of 29 July, serving in the French *38e Corps*, part of *VI Armée*. American Battle Monuments Commission (ABMC), *32d Division. Summary of Operations in the World War* (Washington, DC: US Government Printing Office, 1943), p. 7.
114 Gale, p. 145.
115 Edmonds, pp.259–60.

were beginning to show in the disjointed and dysfunctional German OHL. On 21 July, Crown Prince Wilhelm proposed the withdrawal of the line between Soissons and Reims, in order to shorten the front, provide forces for attack and regain the initiative for Germany. Whilst the plan had merit, especially given the desperate German manpower situation, it would mean abandoning all of the territory gained during Operation *Blücher-Yorck* in May and Ludendorff was not at all keen on the plan. However, the following day he ordered the Chiefs of Staff of Seventh and First armies to make the necessary preparations for a retirement and the three centre corps of Wichura, Schoeler and Kathen to make another withdrawal north.[116] A sudden and speedy strike across the main Soissons–Château-Thierry road and the loss of Le Plessier-Huleu had forced the hand of Group Etzel, which was left with little option but to pull back.[117] On the back of this development, General Mangin issued the order on the 22nd for General Penet's *30e Corps*, comprising the French *1er* and *19e* and British 34th divisions, and General Berdoulat's *20e Corps* – *58e*, *87e* and British 15th (Scottish) divisions – to make the principal attack at 0500 hrs and reach the objective of the line the *Orme du Grand Rozoy*–Taux–Buzancy, whilst *11e Corps* under the newly installed General Prax would attack the oval-shaped *Butte Chalmont*[118] and render whatever assistance it could to *30e Corps*. The *20e Corps* would be supplied with 37 tanks from the reorganised *Groupements Chanoine* and *Herlaut*, with *30e Corps* having 62 at its disposal. After the briefest of intense hurricane bombardments lasting just five minutes, the *19e Division* and part of *1er Division* were to turn the *Bois de St Jean* from the south. The *87e* and 15th (Scottish) divisions, benefitting from a longer artillery bombardment lasting 40 minutes, were to capture Villemontoire, Buzancy and the fortified farmstead of Chivry Ferme, pushing on to the *Bois d'Hartennes* woods beyond. With this successfully completed, a signal would be sent indicating that the *58e* and British 34th divisions, in the centre of the line and connecting the two corps, could commence their own attack, linking the fighting into a broader offensive.[119] But this linking movement, with the British acting as the hinge, was complicated and not without its risks, not least the fact that the 34th Division's infantry had no experience of making such a movement and they would have to conduct the move flanked by foreign troops on either side. The French *58e Division* fighting in the centre alongside 34th Division had been formed at the outset of the war, with units from Bourges, Nevers, Chalon-sur-Saône, Mâcon, Autun, Cosne and Dijon in eastern France, and was commanded by Brigadier General Priou. Its most recent action had been the fierce fighting near Matz during Operation *Gneisenau* in June, where it had lost 4,270 men killed, wounded or missing. From 10 June – 16 July it had been resting, refitting and training in a quiet sector until it had been called on to move by camions to Vivières, and four days later to move to Vierzy and into the line, where it relieved the *38e Division*.[120]

There is a degree of irony that in spite of German efforts to pull enemy divisions away from their front to defend against the various offensives that they had launched since the spring, it was they who now were being forced to do this and defend the western hinge of the Marne salient.

---

116 Edmonds, pp. 259–61.
117 Greenwood, p. 123.
118 French maps of 1918 refer to it as the *Butte Chalmont*.
119 Edmonds, p. 264. Hergault on behalf of Mangin, Operations Order No.274, No.780, 22 July 1918, cited in Woldike, p. 139.
120 Armées Françaises dans la Grande Guerre (AFGG) <www.memoiredeshommes.sga.defense.gouv.fr>

The German jackboot was very definitely on the other foot, with Ludendorff's hand having been forced, and he grudgingly decided to suspend further planning for Operation *Hagen* and to focus instead on the matter at hand: preventing the French from severing the jugular and saving the Marne salient from being entirely cut off. This gave Foch what he considered to be a fabulous opportunity of mounting a series of offensives of his own on some of the more thinly held parts of the German lines, including recapturing Mount Kemmel, attacking around Festubert and a joint Anglo-French operation at Amiens. But both Foch and Ludendorff recognised that their first priority was to win the battle still underway, with control of the flanks of the *poche* being where the battle would be won or lost. Pétain had added whatever reserves he could, as had Ludendorff; the only difference being that the German ones were low-grade trench divisions and understrength. Foch firmly believed that he had the upper hand and that a breakthrough was still possible; that he could tighten the noose despite all of the evidence pointing to the contrary, with the Germans already slipping away to the north in an orderly manner. The Germans were destroying everything they could not take with them, and in his view there was still insufficient harassment of the retreating enemy. Although they had captured 20,000 prisoners and over 400 guns, he concluded that the Germans were not yet decisively beaten.[121] Foch wrote to Mangin saying that the fresh new divisions had been given to him, not the other armies in the salient, and that he must now make "a strong unified action" against the enemy. If Mangin could crush the hinge of the *poche*, Foch added, then they would trap the Germans inside and Foch still firmly believed this was possible, writing to Pétain on the 23rd and visiting him later that day at his headquarters in Provins. Foch proposed that cavalry units be used for attacks along the River Ourcq towards Fère-en-Tardenois, the original target of 18 July, and urged Pétain to maintain the pressure on both flanks of the salient, saying that it was necessary to rupture one of his flanks, with the obvious choice being the right wing of Mangin's *Xe Armée* and left wing of Degoutte's *VIe Armée*.[122]

---

121 Fayolle, p. 123.
122 Greenwood, pp. 127, 133.

10

Relieving the Exhausted French *38e Division*

10.1 Prelude

Pétain had somewhat reluctantly finally conceded to Foch, ordering the two British divisions to support Mangin's *Xe Armée*. But despite his concern, Pétain must have known that if anyone would use additional troops for an attack, then it would be Mangin. Quite simply, defence was just not part of the DNA of 'The Butcher'. In fact, the same stipulation applied to two French divisions, the *12e* and *25e*, which although by no means fresh, were also only to be used for attacking purposes.[1]

At noon on the 21st, 34th Division commander General Nicholson held a conference of his three brigade commanders at his headquarters in Vivières, to the north of Villers-Cotterêts, where he outlined what little he knew about the deployment of the division in the forthcoming operations. The division, now at the disposal of Foch as part of his inter-Allied reserve, would be placed under the orders of the French *30e Corps*, commanded by General Penet, on the 22nd, and whilst he expected this to happen, relations between the allies were at a particularly low point. Nicholson was disappointed at having his newly reconstituted division subordinated to the French, believing that this might reduce his freedom and blunt its effectiveness. Once the conference had broken up mid-afternoon, Lieutenant Colonel Dooner and the brigade majors left to reconnoitre the line and Captain R.J. Cash, the 101st's Brigade Major, proceeded to Longpont, the headquarters of the French *38e Division* in order to liaise with the French and keep abreast of the situation at the front, where he was verbally informed of the details for the relief of *the 8e Régiment de marche de tirailleurs* by 101st Brigade. Written orders were received by 34th Division on the following day that it was to relieve the *38e Division*, commanded by General Guyot d'Asnières de Salins since 1916 and comprising the *76e Brigade* and *4e Brigade marocaine*.

Within the ranks of *38e Division* was the *Régiment Infanterie Coloniale du Maroc* (RICM), the most decorated regiment in the French Army.[2] It was said to be one of Mangin's favourites and was in the vanguard of the attack from 18–22 July. The veteran French division had defended

---

1 Greenwood, p. 123.
2 Gale, p. 13.

Côte 304 for three months during the Battle of Verdun and its very strong reputation was well merited, with it being committed to action on at least 15 occasions during the war and considered to be one of France's supreme assault divisions, with superior men, equipment and training compared to many other formations.[3] It had advanced alongside the two American divisions on the 18th, capturing the village of Longpont within just 45 minutes, advancing another 4km and capturing Montrambœuf Ferme the next day, then seizing Parcy-et-Tigny the next. It was positioned on the left of *30e Corps*' line, holding a 2km front from Parcy Tigny to the *Bois du Plessier-Huleu*, opposite the village of Hartennes-et-Taux.[4] To its left was the *58e Division* (the right-most division of *20e Corps*), with *38e Division* holding the left part of the corps and *19e Division* (under the newly appointed General Giraud) on the right of the British.[5] With their orders firmly established for 101st Brigade to take over the right sector and 102nd Brigade the left, divisional headquarters was established in a cave close to Chavigny Ferme.[6]

The 34th Division's Operation Order No.229, issued at 2200 hrs on the 21st, outlined the main elements of the plan: the British, now part of the French *30e Corps*, would relieve the *38e Division*, to be completed before dawn on the 23rd. All told, *30e Corps* held a line between the villages of Coutremain and Parcy-et-Tigny, a distance of 2,200 metres, with French *58e Division* (*20e Corps*) to the left of 34th Division and *19e Division* forming the right half of *30e Corps*.

The *38e Division*'s commander, General de Salins, made what he believed were adequate arrangements for the relief operation, but these flattered to deceive. The *38e Division* had moved from a period of rest to occupy a sector towards the Chavigny and Saint-Pierre-Aigle on 15 July, and on the 18th it had been fighting through Longpont and Chavigny Ferme and from there up to Tigny and on towards Hartennes. But with the British having not yet set eyes on the terrain, de Salins organised French guides to meet the British close to *30e Corps*' ammunition dump at La Grille Ferme and from there to conduct them to their preliminary positions. Despite handing over draft orders personally to General Nicholson and imparting his knowledge of the ground, the Operation Order omitted several key details which would require urgent clarification, whilst other information such as the objectives and details of enemy strength were entirely missing. The division could only hope that this vital additional information would arrive before the men went into action, otherwise they would be attacking in an entirely new theatre virtually blind.[7]

Once issued, the relief plan was intentionally simple, and thankfully for the British contained much of the detail missing from the previous day's orders. After it had relieved *38e Division* in line, the 34th Division would become the left division of *30e Corps*, inserted between two vastly experienced French divisions. To its right (south) was the *71RI* of *19e Division* and to its left (north) the *11e Tirailleurs* of *58e Division*, which formed the southern part of the neighbouring *20e Corps* – with the 15th (Scottish) Division now part of *20e Corps* too). The order contained the

---

3   Goya, p. 236.
4   After the war, de Salins was one of the founders of the Scouting movement in France. TNA WO 95/2456: 101st Infantry Brigade Headquarters, 20–21 July 1918.
5   TNA WO 95/2465: 103rd Infantry Brigade Headquarters, Order No. 221, 21 July 1918.
6   TNA WO 95/2436: General Staff, 34th Division, Narrative of Operations with Xe French Army, 21–23 July 1918.
7   TNA WO 95/2436: General Staff, 34th Division, Operation Order No. 229, 21 July 1918 and Edmonds, p. 265. JMO.

boundaries for each division as well as the jumping-off positions the brigades would take. The 101st Brigade would be the right brigade, relieving four battalions of *Groupement Dufoulin*, with 102nd Brigade taking the left section and relieving three battalions of *Groupement D'Homme* 600 yards north-east of Montrambœuf Ferme. This ground was almost entirely flat, with the only cover being from standing crops and the only protection some recently dug slit trenches occupied by the French. Finally, 103rd Brigade would be in Divisional Reserve and its orders were to relieve two battalions of the *4e Zouaves* at a quarry 300 yards south-east of the same farm. In reality, the quarry was a series of caves built into the side of a small track running east–west and the position of the caves afforded a good deal of protection for the men sheltering within from enemy shelling which might fall in their vicinity. Whilst the caves were reasonably sizeable, they would be crammed with men from several different battalions and headquarters staff, including 34th Battalion Machine Gun Corps. So whilst they offered better protection than for the men exposed on the fields just to the north of Montrambœuf Ferme, any German shells landing there could do serious damage to the divisional leadership. (On the evening of the 23rd, a German barrage did indeed cause some casualties, mainly to men who were already wounded and on their way to the dressing station in the caves, and another shell fell close to the entrance on the 25th, killing several men from the Motor Ambulance Column who had been unlucky to simply be standing outside when the shell landed).[8] In the Operation Order there is just a single sentence discussing one critical element of the plan: all units were to take over maps, documents, aerial photographs (if any) and any signalling apparatus from units which they relieved. With the division being wholly new to the area, they had no prior experience of seeing the terrain they were to fight on, from which they could draw upon. Under normal circumstances this would make fighting more difficult, but when added to the fact that the 34th Division's infantry was entirely new and had never fought on the Western Front, they needed every advantage and bit of luck they could gain.

Marching to La Grille Ferme, 103rd Brigade was met by French guides from *38e Division*, who would escort them to the front-line positions. The 2/4th Somersets left Vivières at 1000 hrs on 22 July and marched into position at Moulin (mill) de Villers-Hélon, before moving again at 0900 hrs on the 23rd to caves 300 yards south of Montrambœuf Ferme, where it remained in Divisional Reserve until the 26th, moving to a new position in the *Bois de Nadon* at 2130 hrs on the 27th.[9] Much of the 22nd was spent by 101st Brigade marching the 15km from Puiseux en Retz to Montrambœuf Ferme, with their progress much slowed by having to march through the woods, leaving the roads free for vehicles passing towards the front. Having been settled in the woods near Puiseux since the morning of 20 July, 102nd Brigade marched via Longpont to just north of Moulin de Villers-Hélon, from where they sent their battalion commanders

---

8   TNA WO 95/2436: General Staff, 34th Division, Operation Order No. 230, 22 July 1918; WO 95/2451: 34th Battalion, Machine Gun Corps, 23 July 1918 and WO 95/2443: Assistant Director Medical Services, 1830 hrs, 23 July 1918; 25 July 1918.

9   Wyrall. TNA WO 95/2451: 2/4th Somerset Light Infantry, 22–27 July 1918. Montrambœuf Ferme was one of the largest stone-built farms in the area, with an 8ft-high stone wall giving it adequate protection. Within 300 yards of the farm was a series of south-facing caves, which had been mined for their limestone and offered excellent protection from enemy shelling. The caves were sufficiently large to accommodate 100 stretcher cases under the care of Major F.S. McMenamin, RAMC. TNA WO 95/2443: Assistant Director Medical Services, 23 July 1918. TNA WO 95/2453: 103rd Field Ambulance, 0720 hrs on 23 July 1918.

to a brigade conference that afternoon.[10] The 4th Royal Sussex, accompanied by a sole guide, managed to navigate their way through open fields in the darkness, picking up the French front line with little trouble, with French troops from *38e Division* wishing their British comrades "bon chance" as they departed.[11]

Lieutenant Colonel Swindells, the commander of the 4th Cheshires, along with his company commander, intelligence officer and interpreter, left Puiseux at 0730 hrs on the 22nd to reconnoitre the ground to be taken over that night, meeting with General Nicholson and the other battalion commanders for a conference at Montrambœuf Ferme. After it broke up, Swindells and his intelligence officer reconnoitred the line and worked through the final details of the relief.[12] The Advanced Division headquarters also moved to Chavigny Ferme on the 22nd, coming under the orders of French *30e Corps*. Although the division was still nominally part of British XXII Corps, this was largely confined to routine administrative matters. Anything relating to issues of ammunition and supplies, ordnance and the despatch of wounded men was instead referred directly back to British GHQ 'Q' (South) branch at Creil, 13km north-west of Senlis. Unfortunately, these arrangements very quickly broke down, especially the supply of artillery shells, which were found to be totally insufficient for the planned attack.

Finally in possession of more detailed orders and at least some maps from *30e Corps* (even if most were the less useful 1:80,000 scale editions which gave little detail of the battlefield), General Nicholson held a second conference with his brigade commanders and GOC Royal Artillery at 1530 hrs on the 22nd at Montrambœuf Ferme, where he gave further details of the proposed attack to take place on a two-brigade frontage at 0900 hrs the following morning between *Bois de Ourjenne* and Hartennes-et-Taux, in conjunction with the French *19e Division* on the right and *58e* on the left, to capture enemy positions between Tigny and Le Plessier-Huleu, supported by just three French Saint-Chamond tanks. The 34th Division's objective was two spurs south of *Côtes 137* and *133*, on a line between Hartennes and the Château-Thierry road. The 160 Brigade RFA, under orders of the French *38e* Divisional Artillery, would move into position to cover the 34th Division's attack.[13] There was an indication that the terrain would be difficult to traverse, with the preliminary instruction requiring the men to cross the exposed open ground to the north of the spur in small numbers only, in order to avoid undue casualties. However, it was also stressed that the objective was not to be considered as final and they were to push on as far as possible, with enemy resistance and their own casualties being the limiting factor.

Within the instruction there were strong indications that the supply problems affecting the division were still evident, especially relating to a lack of artillery shells. With the exception of the 15th (Scottish) Division 10 miles to the north, the nearest British units were 50km away near Reims and the closest railhead was in Villers-Cotterêts. French shells and ammunition, whilst in copious supply, were incompatible with British guns, since they operated at different calibres, meaning the British would have to be totally self-sufficient. Only two guns per battalion of the 101st Trench Mortar Battery were able to accompany 2/4th Queens and 2nd Loyal North Lancs but were instructed to support the infantry only if ammunition became

10 TNA WO 95/2461: 102nd Infantry Brigade Headquarters, 20-22 July 1918.
11 Read, p. 352.
12 TNA WO 95/2462: 4th Cheshires, Brief account of Operations from 22 July to 2 August 1918.
13 TNA WO 95/2442: Headquarters Royal Artillery, 22 July 1918.

available, whilst the divisional artillery was to co-operate with the attack but with due respect to expenditure of ammunition, and only one of the two brigades of Royal Field Artillery was to be involved in the attack. At least the machine guns would be able to support the attack in number, since they operated with the same .303 calibre bullets as the infantry, with two sections of four machine guns per battalion being ordered to assist the assault. But with some of the artillery still arriving, the firepower seemed hardly sufficient for the attack and a decision was made to augment the single group from the division's field artillery with three groups of French 75mm field guns.[14] For success to be possible, it would be vital for the artillery and infantry to co-operate closely, but here the lack of opportunity for them to work with each other previously, as well as their lateness in arrival and the evident challenges of being under French command, caused significant discomfort and inconvenience for all involved.

Three hours later, the orders were cancelled by General Penet, with Brigadier General Chaplin travelling to divisional headquarters for fresh instructions, which were given verbally to Nicholson. These were broadly the same orders as those issued earlier, with headquarters and two battalions of 103rd Brigade (8th Scottish Rifles and 5th A&SH) to move to Blanzy to be attached and under the orders of the French *19e Division* as a Corps Reserve, while the 5th KOSBs and 2/4 Somersets in Divisional Reserve.[15] However, before these orders could be carried out, a further new order was received from *30e Corps* that the 34th Division was to attack early on the 23rd.

There is no commentary in the 103rd Brigade war diary, or that of any of the battalions, about their subordination to the French, but with Franco-British relations at an all-time low, it was unlikely to have been a popular decision, even for a division whose infantry was new to fighting in France. In the memorandum of the 22nd, General Nicholson made it clear that the plan of attack had been drawn up for him by the staff of the French *38e Division*, due to their knowledge of the country and experience gained in previous attacks. He indicated that he was none too happy with some of the detail, stating that modifications to it were possible if so approved by brigade commanders and suggesting "a possible but not desirable modification for 101st Brigade to attack on a front of two Battalions" (instead of two battalions behind each other as was the order from the French), with the two rear companies leapfrogging the leading battalions through to the first objective.[16] This tactic had been first used by the French in October 1917 during the Battle of La Malmaison, proving successful in maintaining momentum and in gaining territory, but with events since the turn of the year being almost exclusively defensive, it had taken until now to have another opportunity to deploy the tactic.

At this precise moment, the German Ninth and Seventh armies held much of the higher ground on the front, along a line running north–south from the River Aisne below Courmelle as far as Buzancy and Villemontoire. From there it snaked slightly south-west through Saint-Rèmy-Blanzy–Tigny–Coutremain and the western edge of *Bois de Plessier* to Le Plessier-Huleu and Billy-Sur-Ourcq, with the fresh 19th (Royal Saxon) Ersatz Division going into the line on the 21st, relieving the exhausted and decimated 51st Reserve Division. The front then passed into the line held by *VIe Armée* through Nanteuil-sur-Ourcq, Sommenlans and then eastwards

---

14   TNA WO 95/2456: 101st Infantry Brigade Headquarters, Preliminary Instruction No.1, 22 July 1918.
15   TNA WO 95/2465: 103rd Infantry Brigade Headquarters and WO 95/2456: 101st Infantry Brigade Headquarters, 21 July 1918; Preliminary Instruction No. 1, 22 July 1918.
16   TNA WO 95/2436: General Staff, 34th Division, G. 23, 22 July 1918.

towards Courchamps.[17] The 19th Ersatz Division was considered no better than a third-class division, but it had the advantage of being fresh, having served in a quiet sector until 30 June and completing two weeks of training thereafter.[18] The attacks from 18 July onwards had forced the Germans progressively eastwards, but by the 22nd Groups Etzel, Winckler, Schoeler and Watter were defending well-prepared and equipped defensive positions, with the advantage of high ground to their rear; any further Allied advance would be an attritional slog, taking ground yard by yard.

Colonel Fritz von Lossberg, Fourth Army's Chief of Staff and a major proponent of defence in depth, visited Army Group von Boehn's headquarters that afternoon, reporting back to OHL that morale in Seventh and Ninth armies was still holding up well. Nevertheless, they recognised the difficult position they were in, with the defenders under extreme pressure, and after some discussion ordered preparations made for the withdrawal of the line to new defensive positions. The decision was not without risk, however, since it meant extending the line somewhat, with six fresh divisions required to defend it. The only problem was that the OHL could only provide four of the six required, with even these barely strong enough for the task. At the Army Group staff meeting that evening, von Boehn reported that he was entirely satisfied with how the day had gone, saying that his troops had inflicted severe casualties on the enemy, with many tanks destroyed in front of the German lines. Unfortunately this was no more than bluster, and he was only fooling himself and his staff that it was anything other than an enormously costly reversal. Arriving back at Crown Prince Wilhelm's headquarters, von Lossberg had to report that things were not good on the western flank of the Marne salient. The reserves had been used up and the men were exhausted from the fierce fighting since 18 July, with some companies reduced to just 20 or 30 men. The artillery, vital to the defence, was no better: it too was exhausted, with the guns worn out from the constant firing, and lacking men, horses and critically shells.[19]

The official history of the 34th Division has the following to say about the division's move to the front line:

> Under the most favourable circumstances this [relief] would have been difficult for any troops, but for a newly constituted Division, composed of infantry troops which had not yet been in action in France, and which had just completed a trying move by rail, bus and route march, it was a very severe test. There was no time for reconnaissance. The country was entirely new; there were no organised trench systems on either side. The enemy's positions were never accurately known till they had been captured. To all these difficulties there were added those inseparable from acting for the first time with foreign troops. … As much reconnaissance as possible was carried out, but naturally it was not much, and the artillery had no opportunity of registering.

17   Takle, p. 233. Greenwood, p. 119.
18   United States Army, *Histories of two hundred and fifty-one Divisions of the German Army which participated in the war (1914-1918)* (Washington, DC: War Department, 1920), p. 305.
19   Greenwood, pp. 122–24.

It goes on in a rather understated way to observe: "The whole proceeding was rather unsatisfactory, but the state of affairs was such that a very little might induce the Hun to retire again, and it was worth risking a good deal."[20]

The evidence to support a lack of reconnaissance is by no means conclusive, and not all battalions fared so badly. Battalion commanders and company officers from 101st Brigade made a reconnaissance of the front of the *8e Régiment de marche de tirailleurs* at 0900 hrs on 22 July, with the CO and company commanders of the 2/4th Queens able to utilise the view from the church tower in Villers-Hélon. The Divisional Signal Officer went round communications with his counterpart from the French *38e Division*. The orders for 101st Brigade were for it to relieve the French, under Lieutenant Colonel Dufoullin, by 0400 hrs on the 23rd, with the 2/4th Queens on the left and 2nd Loyal North Lancs on the right.[21] At 1100 hrs, guides were obtained for the battalion commander and machine gun officers from the 34th Battalion MGC for the reconnaissance, with no more permitted to reconnoitre, there being no trench system or other means of concealed approach.[22] Likewise, the CO and the three company commanders of 5th KOSBs were able to reconnoitre their positions at Montrambœuf Ferme, with the battalion arriving at Chavigny Ferme at 1930 hrs, having travelled through the woods and avoided the main roads. Under cover of darkness, it advanced, finding shelter in a huge cave near Villers-Hélon. A day after the debacle of the march to Soucy, march discipline had improved markedly: perhaps the result of the sounds of warfare and the threat of going into imminent action focusing their minds.

Meanwhile, the CO and two company commanders from the 8th Scottish Rifles rose at dawn on the 22nd to reconnoitre their front near Parcy-Tigny. Going forward with their French intelligence officer guide, they were unable to see much, but were at least able to locate the key villages and woods ahead, returning to a cave in the *Bois de Maulay*, established as the French *Quartier-General* (brigade headquarters) for lunch.[23] In Divisional Reserve, 103rd Brigade moved its headquarters up to the vicinity of Montrambœuf Ferme, with Brigadier General Chaplin able to reconnoitre the line and country in front and the Divisional Report Centre set up in buildings at the farm.[24] Lieutenant Colonel Moir of the 7th Cheshires proceeded alone to reconnoitre his sector, which turned out to consist of the Paris Trench (GMP Line) extending from the north-east and east of Parcy-Tigny, south-east to where the road from the village to Hartennes-et-Taux cut the trench line, which was currently occupied by French troops from the *38RI*.[25] For the 1st Herefords, their night march commenced at 2100 hrs from their position in a wood near Mont de Villers-Hélon up to and across the Paris Trench, which stretched north-west to south-east in this sector and on to Parcy-Tigny, arriving at the front line two hours later,

---

20 Shakespear, pp. 254-55.
21 TNA WO 95/2457: 2/4th Royal West Surrey, 22 July 1918; WO 95/2456: War Diary, 101st Infantry Brigade Headquarters, 22 July 1918; Brigade Order No.215, 22 July and WO 95/2450: 34th Divisional Signals Company, 22 July 1918.
22 TNA WO 95/2451: 34th Battalion, Machine Gun Corps, B Company, 22 July 1918.
23 Findlay, pp. 162–63.
24 TNA WO 95/2465: 103rd Infantry Brigade Headquarters, 22 July 1918.
25 TNA WO 95/2462: 7th Cheshires, Report on the Operations extending from 22 July 1918 to 2 August 1918.

completing the relief of the French *38e Division* within a scarcely plausible 50 minutes.[26] There is evidence that some maps had been issued on the 21st, meaning that even if reconnaissance was less than comprehensive, they would at least know some of the ground they would be attacking. However, most of those issued were the French 1:80,000 scale, with the small scale making them of limited value. With French guides organised to assist with the relief, all further maps and aerial photographs would be passed on once the troops arrived.[27] The 4th Royal Sussex received maps on the 21st and were impressed by the detail they contained.[28] Despite the opportunity to reconnoitre the line by a number of officers and many only had a brief look at the front before returning to their battalions.

The account by divisional historian Lieutenant Colonel Shakespear of the period immediately leading up to the 34th Division's entry into the line is an almost exact repetition of what had happened to the US 1st and US 2nd divisions and the 15th (Scottish) Division before them. It thus begs the question of whether the problem was that the French were poor at planning ahead and slow in issuing written orders from corps to division, that the back areas were then still suffering from severe traffic congestion five days into the offensive, or that the issue was simply cultural due to language differences with the French relying less on written orders and more on localised initiative compared to the British or Americans? There is no doubt that the need to translate orders from French into English and vice versa added complexity (and consequent delay) to the situation, and also that communication was never as easy when both parties spoke a different language and used incompatible telegraphy systems. However, the French Army of summer 1918 was by now vastly experienced in translating orders into English for the AEF, having done so for the last year or so. Whatever the cause, all four of the American and British divisions fighting for 'The Butcher' found their experiences of receiving orders from above, and especially of relief, ranging from unsatisfactory to downright reckless.

The plan of attack prepared by *38e Division*'s *Chef d'État-Major* (Chief of Staff) was issued to 34th Division on the afternoon of 22 July and was based on the French experience from their previous attacks; General Nicholson was determined to adopt it, believing it was the best chance of success. In reality, he had little option, since there was simply no time for him to propose an alternative, and neither had he or almost all of his subordinate commanders had made any meaningful reconnaissance of the territory they were about to attack.

The French had advanced to high ground on a ridge between Coutremain and Tigny, but with every wood and copse bristling with enemy machine gun nests, further progress proved impossible. Intense flanking fire and a German counterattack had forced the French back, recapturing Longpont, but they had been held up in a wood just west of the village, directly in front of where the 5th KOSBs were now positioned.[29] The new plan laid out before the division was that *20e Corps* to the left (north) of *30e Corps* would attack and capture the villages of Tigny, Villemontoire and Taux, while *20e Corps* would then turn the wood north of Hartennes-et-Taux, with *19e Division* on the right of *30e Corps* advancing through Le Plessier-Huleu towards

---

26   Scott Elliot, p. 240 and Diary of Captain Edward Wilmot, 1st Herefords, cited in 'Herefordshire Regiment, Their First World War Story'.
27   TNA WO 95/2456: 101st Infantry Brigade Headquarters, Brigade Order No. 215, issued at 1715 hrs on 22 July 1918 and Edmonds, p. 259.
28   Read, p. 349.
29   Scott Elliot, pp. 240–41.

the *Orme du Grand Rozoy*, a large elm 1,500 metres north of Grand Rozoy and halfway to the hamlet of Courdoux, which being on virtually the highest point of the ridge above the village would act as a focal point for the attack. The *19e Division* would turn the *Bois du Plessier* and *Bois de St Jean*, and the role of the three divisions (*58e* of *20e Corps* and the 34th and *19e* of *30e Corps*) was to form the connection between the northern and southern wheeling movements and advance due east to high ground east of the Soissons–Château-Thierry road in the direction of Launoy.

The ultimate objective was the *Bois d'Arcy*, which lay 9km to the east of the Soissons–Château-Thierry road. An objective so distant does not seem to indicate the 'bite and hold' limited objective tactics favoured by the British from 1917 onwards, nor the French tactics under the supposedly defensive Pétain. Neither does it indicate a lack of confidence in the hitherto inexperienced British infantry from the French planners at *Xe Armée* headquarters. In some ways the plans are more closely aligned towards the open warfare 'fire and manoeuvre' tactics favoured by the American Commander-in-Chief, General Pershing, for which he has received much criticism. But with the inexperienced Americans of 1st and 2nd divisions and the vastly experienced 1st Moroccan Division sandwiched in between being able to progress 10km on their first day of fighting on the 18th, it is possible that both General Mangin and *30e Corps* commander General Penet believed it necessary to give a more distant objective in the event that the British were able to emulate the previously successful deep penetration, and that the *Bois d'Arcy* was the logical objective for the attack; the 3km-long wood was a sizeable obstacle which lay directly in the path of the attack and would take time to clear.

Eighty-five tanks would also be available for the attack, scattered amongst Mangin's *Xe Armée*.[30] This was of course only a fraction of what had been available on 18 July, but the losses that day and over the next 48 hours had been nothing short of spectacular. *Xe Armée* had started out with 238 tanks, but almost three-quarters had been knocked out, either by enemy fire or through mechanical failure. Things were a little better elsewhere, with *VIe Armée* losing 11 of its 100 Renault FT-17s and *Ve* and *IXe Armées* losing 25 of their 104 tanks.[31] A hasty reorganisation, brought about as a result of the recent heavy losses, meant that the French *20e Corps* now had a *groupement de marche* of 34 medium tanks, cobbled together from four different *groupements*, with *30e Corps* having 49 tanks to call on, mainly Renault FT-17s plus a smattering of Saint-Chamonds. In reality, whilst 85 tanks might notionally be available, far fewer would make it to the start line and their overall contribution was likely to be somewhat limited; nowhere near enough to be able to use them *en masse*. They would need all of the help they could get, Mangin issuing orders that "a great deal of smoke shells" were to be used to conceal the progress of the tanks.[32]

The 34th Division headquarters war diary described a material alteration to the general plan which was only added later in the day by *30e Corps* headquarters and not received by 34th Division until the evening of the 22nd, well after they had settled on their plan of attack. The revised order stressed that it was crucial that 34th Division must only advance once *20e Corps* on its left had crossed the road from Soissons to Château-Thierry.[33] As a result of this last-minute

---

30   Edmonds, p. 261.
31   Gale, p. 224.
32   Gale, p. 145.
33   Shakespear, pp. 254–55.

change, with the attack due to go in at dawn, the division's General Staff frantically worked through the night to adjust the timings of artillery and infantry instructions. The unfortunate consequence was that they were relayed to the front lines either just in time, or in one case too late to be acted upon.[34]

Within the plan, General Penet had decided to supplement the two brigades of British artillery (152nd and 160th Royal Field Artillery) with additional French firepower left in position from the recent fighting: *32e* and *41e Régiments d'artillerie*, each of three *groupes*, together with a heavy group of a dozen 155mm howitzers under Colonel Beranger of *32e Régiment d'artillerie*. This change, under the overall command of Brigadier General E. Walthall, CMG, DSO, from his headquarters at Chavigny Ferme, was made particularly difficult since the French guns only arrived at the very last minute. Additionally, the two sets of artillery would have to be self-sufficient. Whilst several officers spoke the other's language, crucially including Brigadier General Walthall, there was little time to develop any coherent joint plan and co-ordination. Besides these challenges, the French operated on metric, whilst the British used Imperial measurement, making their guns incompatible; and even if they did speak each other's language, they couldn't communicate easily, since the two telephony systems were also incompatible. Almost everything the British came across which originated from the French needed translation or conversion, with even seemingly benign items such as temperature having to be converted from celsius to fahrenheit and back again. Observation posts were all manned by French: Balloon 87 by Captain de Vertus at Beaurepaire Ferme and *52e reconnaissance Escadron* under Lieutenant Redon at Russy-Bemont.[35] Commandant Sutterlin was attached as liaison officer for Group North (*Groupement Nord*) under Lieutenant Colonel Saville, DSO, covering 102nd Brigade, whilst Lieutenant Colonel Thouvenot was attached as liaison officer for Group South (Lieutenant Colonel Warburton), covering 101st Brigade and supported by *41e Regiment d'artillerie*. Whilst these factors on their own might not be a major issue given sufficient time to overcome them, time was a luxury they simply did not have. It was a dangerous combination of risks which could have huge implications for the attacking infantry, not least the creeping barrage, which was due to launch in the next few hours. But there was precious little that Walthall could do about it, and with few other options he simply pressed on as best he could. The infantry, both French and British, were going to need all of the artillery support they could get.[36]

By 0145 hrs on 23 July, 102nd Brigade was installed in its front-line positions 2,000 yards due west of the *Bois de Reugny*, with the 1st Herefords on the left by the road from Tigny to Montramboeuf Ferme and the 7th Cheshires on the right, near the road from Parcy-Tigny to Coutremain. To its left was the largely untried French *11e Régiment de marche de tirailleurs Algériens*, which, not unlike the British, had limited battle experience fighting on the Western Front, having only been formed in January 1918.[37]

---

34 TNA WO 95/2436: General Staff, 34th Division, Narrative of Operations with *Xe* French Army, 23 July 1918.
35 TNA WO 95/2442: 34th Divisional Headquarters Royal Artillery, Artillery Defence Scheme, 23 July 1918; G/643 and Edmonds, p. 265.
36 Gale, p. 145.
37 "A magnificent regiment, although of recent formation, under the command of its modest and heroic leader, Lieutenant Colonel Charles-Roux, attacked relentlessly on the 20, 21 & July 23, 1918, in front

The 101st Brigade Order No.213, only issued at 0320 hrs – barely 90 minutes before the attack was due to go in – gives a good indication of the dynamic nature of the fighting and the challenges of translating orders into English so they could be understood by the 34th Division. It stated that the principal attack of the entire *30e Corps* would be made due east through Plessier-Huleu towards its ultimate objective of the *Bois d'Arcy*. Whether this is an interpretation of 101st Brigade's role or a clear instruction from corps headquarters is unknown. Whatever the case, 101st Brigade was left in no doubt that the success (or otherwise) of its attack would be central to the overall events of the 23rd. With the 2nd Loyal North Lancs on the right and 2/4th Queens on the left, 101st Brigade was holding a frontage from a small copse 500 yards north of Coutremain to Parcy-Tigny, with *19e Division* to the right (south). To its left, 102nd Brigade would form the northern boundary for *30e Corps*, with the 34th Division attacking on the front between the *Bois de Curjenne* and Hartennes-et-Taux, 1km south, towards its ultimate objective of the line between the *Bois d'Anciens* and the large farm at Neuville-Saint-Jean, a distance of 4km. The *20e Corps* to the left, under General Berdoulat, had the ultimate objective of Maast-et-Violaine, almost 10km distant. There were no buildings barring its progress, potentially making its task somewhat easier than that of the British, who faced a number of difficult defensive obstacles which they would have to overcome.[38] The 2nd Loyal North Lancs would lead the attack alongside the French *19e Division* to the right and would capture the first objectives of the *Bois de Chanois* and the woods to the north, establishing itself in a sunken road running north–south just beyond the wood. The 4th Royal Sussex would then pass through the 2nd Loyal North Lancs and capture the second objective, pushing out patrols to the *Bois d'Encens*. In a further leapfrogging movement, the 2/4th Queens would form a link between 101st and 102nd brigades and provide fire support in order to break up any potential enemy counterattacks, pushing on to the Soissons road, where it could cover the advancing troops from a ditch alongside the road.[39] As part of their instructions, the men were ordered to carry forward as many tools as possible to assist in consolidation of captured ground. This burden, however, would inevitably slow the men down, when it was rapid progress that was needed in order to seize the initiative. Unfortunately for the 2nd Loyal North Lancs, they arrived at the front with just 19 officers, one medical officer and 677 other ranks. Worse still, several of their more experienced officers on leave in Britain, meaning they would have to fight their first engagement on the Western Front under-strength and lacking many of their senior officers.[40]

---

of Tigny and the Bois d'Hartennes always with the same enthusiasm, the same spirit of sacrifice and dedication, despite very heavy losses, despite the disorganization of its cadres, taking prisoners, taking machine guns and clinging to the conquered ground"; Note No.21586 GHQ on 17 December 1918 mentioning the Tenth Army fighting of 20-23 July 1918..

38   TNA WO 95/2456: 101st Infantry Brigade Headquarters, Brigade Orders No. 213, 0320 hrs, 23 July 1918. No.228, 23 July 1918.
39   TNA WO 95/2456: 101st Infantry Brigade Headquarters, Brigade Order No. 213, 0320 hrs, 23 July 1918.
40   TNA WO 95/2457: 2nd Loyal North Lancashire, 21 July 1918.

10.2 Attack Order of Battle

The attack order of battle was as follows:

- 101st Brigade would attack on a front of 500 yards and capture the *Bois de Chanois* and the woods to the north and establish itself in the sunken road which ran north–south just east of the woods.
- The 1st Herefords, leading 102nd Brigade, which was operating on a front of 300 yards, would advance in close touch with the French *58e Division* on its left and encircle and capture the *Bois de Reugny*.
- The 7th Cheshires would then move up in support of the Herefords, with both moving forward to capture the first objective, mopping up any enemy combatants in the village and organising against counterattack.
- The 4th Cheshire's would advance and pass through the 1st Herefords and 7th Cheshires on the first objective, then attack and capture the second objective. Once completed, they would consolidate the line.
- 102nd Brigade on the left would attack with three battalions in echelon on a front of 300 yards and capture the *Bois de Reugny* by encircling it north and south. The 2nd Battalion was to move up on the southern flank of this movement and advance to the first objective, with both mopping up the village and organising it against counterattack.
- The 1st Cheshires and the third battalion of 102nd Brigade, would pass through and attack the second objective.
- From here, orders would be issued to advance on the ultimate objective of the *Bois d'Encens* and the plateau of Neuville-Saint-Jean.
- Four machine guns per battalion would support the attack and all battalions would attack in depth.[41]
- 103rd Brigade was to be detached and sent to Blanzy to act as Corps Reserve, with 5th KOSBs and the pioneers as Nicholson's Divisional Reserve.

The instructions for the artillery barrage were issued at 2200 hrs the night before the attack; very late in the day, giving little time to make the necessary preparations. A 10-minute hurricane bombardment would commence at 0740 hrs, with the main attack commencing at 0750 hrs, but no preliminary bombardment would occur. Mangin was a big fan of this style of attack, having seen it work effectively before. However, it is almost certain that by the 23rd (after five

---

41 TNA WO 95/2461: 102nd Infantry Brigade Headquarters, Brigade Order No.228, 23 July 1918, mentions four guns per battalion, which is supported by TNA WO 95/2451, 34th Battalion, Machine Gun Corps, 23 July 1918. A section contained four Vickers guns, and the diary states that No.1 Section, A Company was on the right with 2nd LNL, No.2 Section, C Company, on the left with 2/4th Queens and No.1 Section, C Company, with 4th Royal Sussex. However, B Company, 34th Battalion, Machine Gun Corps, lists eight heavy machine guns to support each battalion. Four guns would go over with the assaulting infantry battalions, the other four being kept in close support to occupy positions vacated by lead sections on moving forward. Eight guns held back in reserve from B Company were kept packed onto four fighting limbers in a sunken road 2,000 yards from the front line, ready to move forward should a breakthrough be effected.

days of attacking in a similar manner), the Germans were well aware of *Xe Armée* not using a preliminary barrage and would be alert for any increase in shelling, so the element of surprise, whilst helpful, would no longer have been decisive. That said, the varied timing of the attacks since 18 July helped wrong-foot the Germans, and the later start would not have hindered the prospect of success. After 10 minutes, the artillery would then pause for three minutes, in the hope of luring the defenders back to their positions, before reopening fire on the initial barrage line for a further three minutes. From there a rolling barrage would begin, which would lift 100 yards every three minutes to 300 yards east of the first objective. It would remain on this position for just 10 minutes, before lifting again, at a rate of 100 yards every four minutes.[42]

The machine gunners had been able to borrow 10 infantrymen per section to assist as carrying parties, but many of these would become casualties as the morning wore on.[43]

The French *20e Corps*, containing the 15th (Scottish) Division, attacked to the north of Tigny at 0500 hrs, and by 0615 hrs reports were received from *58e Division* that the attack was progressing favourably. Fifteen minutes later, Nicholson issued a warning order to 101st and 102nd brigades to be ready to attack at short notice, with the Executive Order sent by *30e Corps* staff received by him at 0715 hrs. Despite being in frequent contact with the staff of the French *58e Division*, Nicholson had been unable to assume command of his portion of the line until 0700 hrs, only a matter of minutes before the order to attack was received from General Penet's headquarters. The order was transmitted at 0720 hrs, by telephone, wireless and rocket signals of red flares. But with all of the telephone wires cut due to heavy shelling and all of the runners becoming casualties, there was a delay in communicating 'zero hour' of 0740 hrs to the rocket stations and the attacking units.[44] Somehow, 101st Brigade received its message in time and immediately advanced, but 102nd Brigade did not, having not seen the rockets due to heavy mist and smoke coverage, and the battalions only started to advance at 0755 hrs, five minutes late. It must have been a surreal experience for many of the men, attacking in the cold of the early morning, especially those of the 2nd Loyal North Lancs, who had seen little action since the fighting in Tanga, German East Africa, in November 1914.

No sooner had they started than things immediately began to go wrong, only some of which had been caused by the delay and ensuing confusion. The artillery had commenced counterbattery fire promptly at 0720 hrs, but the hurricane bombardment – which was never intended to knock out the German artillery, only to force them to take shelter and cause whatever disruption it could – was too weak and too brief, leaving most of the German guns untouched. So when the bombardment rolled forward at 0740 hrs, it allowed the enemy artillerymen to quickly regain their composure and start firing back, with a fierce German response coming within minutes, firing onto the front line and into Parcy-Tigny. The German machine gunners, many of whom remained untouched by the feeble artillery barrage, also got their guns into action and began firing on the advancing British, holding up much of the attack and preventing further progress in several locations. The war diary of the 34th Battalion MGC leaves us in no doubt that it was

---

42   TNA WO 95/2436: General Staff, 34th Division, G.25, 2200 hrs, 22 July 1918 and WO 95/2457: 2nd Loyal North Lancs states the attack was due to commence at 0620 hrs with red rockets signalling its start.
43   Shakespear, pp. 255–56.
44   TNA WO 95/2436: General Staff, 34th Division, Narrative of Operations with *Xe* French Army, Action of 23 July 1918 and WO 95/2456: 101st Infantry Brigade Headquarters, 0735 hrs, 23 July 1918.

the German artillery doing most of the damage and causing the majority of casualties at this time, firing on unprotected infantry attempting to advance from their front-line positions. The first and second waves suffered heavy losses with the third wave not able to move forward at all.[45] Likewise, the *58e Division* to the left was unable to make any progress eastwards and had failed to cross the Soissons–Château-Thierry road (the signal for the 34th Division to advance), with Shakespear doubtful that this happened at all on the 23rd.[46] The British were in no doubt that by issuing the order, General Penet was fully convinced that *58e Division* would be successful almost immediately in capturing its objective. However, it was also plainly obvious that since they had yet to actually cross the road, events were not going according to *30e Corps*' plan, which left Nicholson in something of a quandary. With the late arrival of his orders from *30e Corps* and the non-appearance of *58e Division*, things were starting to go awry even before his own attack had commenced. How long would it be before the *58e Division* reached their objective; and should he wait until they did so, or should he attack at the allotted time in the hope the French would be able to catch up during the day?

10.3 102nd Brigade makes good progress but 101st Brigade is stalled

The 7th Cheshires on the right and 1st Herefords on the left from 102nd Brigade, together with eight guns of the 34th Machine Gun Battalion attached to each battalion, were able to make some progress, advancing steadily through high-standing cornfields for 400 yards, which although they gave little protection, allowed at least a small degree of concealment, for which the men were thankful. Lieutenant Colonel Moir was wounded in this action, but not seriously enough to be evacuated and he remained on duty for the rest of the day.[47] Sergeant Colley of the 1st Herefords recalled: "Few who were there and live will ever forget that advance through the cornfield. We experienced our first taste of gas shells and suffered heavily from this cause."[48] In spite of heavy German machine gun fire from Tigny, the *Bois de Reugny* and the *Bois de Chanois*, the 1st Herefords reported that they had been able to advance their line 1,200 yards and were digging in 300 yards west of the *Bois de Reugny*, with the 7th Cheshires ordered to bring up their left to conform with the Herefords and to keep their right in touch with 101st Brigade on the Paris Defence Line, where it crossed the Parcy-Tigny–Coutremain road. Their advance was halted when the intensity of machine gun fire enfilading them became too fierce, with German defensive positions having not been captured by the French *25e Division*. The men dug in on the *Ligne du Gouvernement Militaire de Paris* (GMP Line)[49] and, waiting for troops on either flank to arrive, pushed out a defensive flank facing Tigny to try to gain touch with the right of

---

45   TNA WO 95/2451: B Company, 34th Battalion, Machine Gun Corps, 23 July 1918.
46   Shakespear, p. 256.
47   TNA WO 95/2462: 7th Cheshires, report on the operations extending from 22 July 1918 to 2 August 1918, says the 7th Cheshires advanced perhaps as far as 1,000 yards, suffering 180 casualties.
48   Diary of Sergeant Colley, 1st Herefords, cited in 'Herefordshire Regiment, Their First World War Story'.
49   Also called the Paris Defence Line, the GMP Line had been constructed in 1914 as one of the lines of defence for the French capital but had been abandoned and was in a poor state of repair when the British arrived, with wire entanglements consisting of nothing more than a single line of plain fencing wire, rather than the more effective barbed variety. Neither was the trench very deep, offering only limited protection from hostile shelling overnight.

58e Division, which was still 400 yards west of Parcy-Tigny. The right regiment of *58e Division* had, according to the Herefordshire war diary, been unable to advance against the village due to heavy enemy machine gun fire and showed no appetite to do so. This comment is perhaps unfair, since it seeks to paint the French as lacking the impetus to attack. Just like 102nd Brigade, they were pinned down by hostile machine gun fire, yet the war diary seeks to explain away the lack of British progress whilst not giving the same explanation for their French comrades.[50] To the rear, the 4th Cheshires had arrived at their positions in a gully by 0810 hrs, where they remained for the next 30 minutes, being heavily shelled the entire time. Moving forward, C Company on the right advanced into Parcy-Tigny around 0930 hrs, but was held up by enemy machine gun fire and dropped into the protection of a sunken road. Despite C Company being held up, A and D Companies on the left continued their advance towards the *Bois de Reugny*, but they too came under heavy machine gun fire from Tigny, forcing them to find shelter in a small patch of dead ground, where they held their position awaiting further orders and desperately searching for any signs of the French to their left. To the right, B Company advanced to some trenches just east of Parcy-Tigny, but having spotted that the other companies were held up, they too halted. The 4th Cheshires weren't the only ones under the mistaken impression that Tigny had fallen to the French: the reserve battalion of machine gunners in their limbered waggons moved into the open approaching the village, only to be fired on by hostile artillery, losing one horse killed. Pinned down by German machine gun and heavy artillery fire, the 4th Cheshires were unable to move forward for the next nine hours, when dusk brought the very welcome cover of darkness. At 2100 hrs, an order was received for their line to be advanced a little and this was carried out without incident; it was consolidated and patrols pushed out overnight.[51] Meanwhile, the 7th Cheshires and 1st Herefords of 102nd Brigade were having more success and had followed closely behind the barrage, advancing to a line 1,200 yards beyond their starting point, but with both flanks now exposed, they too were stopped by intense machine gun fire from three sides.

The apparent success of 102nd Brigade, and the *19e Division*, having reached the railway line south of *Bois du Plessier* by noon, contrasts starkly with that of 101st Brigade. The message to attack was only despatched to the 2nd Loyal North Lancs at 0737 hrs, a mere three minutes prior to the intended start time, giving the battalion no time to relay the order to the front line. Their commander, Lieutenant Colonel Jourdain, immediately went up to the support line to verbally pass on the order to commence the attack, but despite his efforts, C and D Companies in the front line were only able to commence their attack at around 0800 hrs, 20 minutes late, enabling the surviving German machine gunners to return to their guns and get ready to intercept the attack. Despite the efforts of the four guns of No.1 Section of A Company, 34th Battalion MGC – which went over with the third wave of the 2nd Loyal North Lancs – neither were able to make any headway and the 16 machine guns from A Company were ordered to take up defensive positions covering the Loyal North Lancs, where they remained until they

---

50   TNA WO 95/2436: General Staff, 34th Division, Narrative of Operations with *Xe* French Army, Action of 23 July 1918 and WO 95/2461: 102nd Infantry Brigade Headquarters, 0720 hrs, 23 July 1918, has it as an advance of 1,000 yards.
51   TNA WO 95/2462: 4th Cheshires, 23 July 1918. Brief account of operations from 22 July to 2 August 1918 and WO 95/2451: 34th Battalion, Machine Gun Corps, 23 July 1918.

were relieved by the French on the night of 27/28 July.[52] Despite Jourdain countermanding the order to advance, the first wave consisting of No.12 Platoon, C Company, never received it and was practically wiped out in the cornfields, advancing no more than 50 yards before being forced back under heavy machine gun fire and an artillery barrage from the *Bois de Chanois* and Coutremain, with the *19e Division* likewise pinned down. This immediate setback forced Jourdain to halt the advance entirely in order to avoid further unnecessary casualties, ordering a withdrawal back to their starting line in the GMP around 1030 hrs. To the left of C Company, D Company of the 2nd Loyal North Lancs and B Company of the 2/4th Queens, under Second Lieutenant R.M. Lessells, managed to cross the Coutremain–Tigny road by around 0930 hrs, in what was described as no more than a "strong raid". They advanced around 1,000 yards to within 600 yards of the Hartennes–Château-Thierry road, with guns of B Company, 34th MGC, silencing a couple of troublesome German machine gun posts which had been firing on the attackers from the direction of the *Bois de Reugny* and a quarry south-east of Tigny, but they too were immediately counterattacked and forced back to their starting point. D Company, 2nd Loyal North Lancs, having suffered 60 casualties – including Second Lieutenant J.R.T. Jones killed and every officer wounded – were forced to leave a third of their wounded men behind in the cornfield.[53] The half-company of eight Vickers machine guns, having been able to get forward, then came into action from their positions in an attempt to stop any further German counterattacks. To the right, the French reported that they too were being held up by intense machine gun fire from Coutremain.[54] At this point, yet another example of the incompatibility of equipment arose at the very worst possible moment. With some of the barrage shells falling short and hitting the infantry of 101st Brigade, signal lights were brought out to warn the artillery to lengthen their range. However, despite frantic efforts, these lights were found to be inoperable, since they could not be fired from British Lee Enfield rifles due to the different calibre of the French Lebel rifle.[55]

Whilst 102nd Brigade was busy pushing out a defensive flank on both sides, neither 101st Brigade nor the French *58e Division* had been able to make progress, with both withdrawing to their starting positions and leaving 102nd Brigade ahead but dangerously exposed. The 2/4th Queens later reported that had their flank been supported, they could have captured Hartennes-et-Taux, as the Germans were spotted retiring from the village, abandoning guns and machine guns. However, the enfilade fire was so severe that no progress could be made. To the immediate rear, the 4th Royal Sussex, without any instructions, orders or information for several hours,

---

52   TNA WO 95/2451: 34th Battalion, Machine Gun Corps, Report on operations of A Company, 34th Battalion, Machine Gun Corps, from 22 July to 2 August 1918.

53   Shakespear, p. 257. Edmonds, p. 266. Three companies from the 4th Royal Sussex were sent up to support the Loyal North Lancs in their attack but were not required and returned to their bivouacs. The only casualties the Sussex suffered were during a German bombardment on their bivouacs early on in the day, which resulted in 15 killed and 48 wounded. TNA WO 95/2458: 4th Royal Sussex, 23 July 1918; WO 95/2457: 2nd Loyal North Lancs, Record of operations of the 2nd Battalion, Loyal North Lancashire Regiment, from 23 July to 4 August, 1918 and WO 95/2451: 34th Battalion, Machine Gun Corps, 23 July 1918.

54   Shakespear, pp. 256–57 and TNA WO 95/2456: 101st Infantry Brigade Headquarters, 0930 hrs, 23 July 1918.

55   Edmonds, p. 267.

simply had to improvise as they went, driving forward in support of the 2/4th Queens and 2nd Loyal North Lancs.[56]

By 1100 hrs, the attack was beginning to flounder and the situation, clearly hampered by the lack of information, becoming increasingly grave. Casualties were mounting and neither the 2nd Loyal North Lancs, the 2/4th Queens, nor the French able to make any progress, having been held up by machine gun fire. With the attack failing, the forward guns of the Field Artillery had been unable to move forward, although they were still available to cover the front and hold off any German counterattacks were these to develop. What is clear, though, is that the artillery was too weak to make a telling contribution beyond the hurricane bombardment in the morning, suffering as it did from a shortage of shells. This made it incapable of providing sufficient targeted supporting fire to subdue the enemy, with its efforts further undermined by not being able to reconnoitre enemy positions or to register its guns prior to the attack commencing. By late morning, German artillery and *minenwerfer* began shelling the wood 500 yards north of Coutremain, where remnants of the 2nd Loyal North Lancs were sheltering, causing 70 casualties to the battalion and leaving it perilously short of effectives. This forced the hand of Jourdain, who ordered C and D Companies to be withdrawn a safe distance.[57]

Orders were given for 102nd Brigade to prepare another attack on the *Bois de Reugny* in the afternoon in conjunction with the right regiment of *58e Division* to its left, but by noon it was clear that the attack was not going to succeed, with *58e Division* heavily counterattacked and suffering severe casualties, in no condition to mount a further attack. The order was subsequently cancelled. At 1230 hrs, fresh orders were received for 101st and 102nd brigades to dig in and consolidate the present line, although they were instructed that they could fall back to the original front line if their hand was forced by a German counterattack. With the attack of 102nd Brigade held up, 16 guns from the Machine Gun Battalion took up defensive positions in two groups.

Reports sent back by 102nd Brigade headquarters indicated that although it was the only brigade to make any clear movement forward, it had suffered very heavy casualties during the morning's largely fruitless action: an estimated 17 officers and 520 other ranks. Across the 34th Division as a whole, it had suffered almost 1,300 casualties, with almost nothing to show for its efforts. For 101st Brigade, the 2nd Loyal North Lancs was the only battalion to make any noticeable advance, but it too reluctantly complied with the latest orders, falling back to its start line but maintaining outposts beyond and crucially holding the front line lightly and disposing in depth. The 102nd Brigade, which had started the day 300 yards to the rear of 101st Brigade's line, managed to hold on to some of its gains, consolidating its new line 250 yards in advance of the left flank of 101st Brigade. An order was issued at 1800 hrs for a renewal of the attack, but with casualty levels high and battalions having pretty much fallen back to their starting line, this too was cancelled and that night the 1st Herefords were relieved by the 4th Cheshires.[58] Intelligence reports the following day indicated that 102nd Brigade had managed to advance about 1,000 yards and that it was the Germans' effective defence and a failure of the flanks to

---

56   Edmonds, pp. 266–67 and Read, p. 354.
57   TNA WO 95/2457: 2nd Loyal North Lancs, Record of Operations of the 2nd Battalion, Loyal North Lancashire Regiment, from 23 July to 4 August 1918.
58   TNA WO 95/2456: 101st Infantry Brigade Headquarters, 23 July 1918; 102nd Brigade, 23 July 1918.

progress, rather than any counterattack, which held up the British.[59] There is no mention in any of the war diaries of any of the 100 tanks operating in *Xe Armée*, and it is unlikely that any of them played a significant part in support of the British efforts.

The account in the 1st Herefordshire war diary, whilst brief, is instructive of the difficulties encountered during their first attack:

> 04:45 – Preliminary attack orders received. Attack commenced at 07:40; Final order: B & C [Companies] – Firing Line, D – Support, B – Left Flank, A – Reserve. 07:40 – Very heavy shell fire experienced immediately move commenced. High standing corn found difficult to move through and making control impossible. Casualties from enemy machine guns occurred before attack progressed many yards. Attack held up at 1,200 yards from point of deployment owing mainly to units on either flank failing to advance at all. Battalion maintained ground gained until after nightfall when relieved by 4th Cheshires on right and 7th Cheshires on left. Casualties heavy; approximately 8 officers and 230 soldiers. Continuous shelling of whole line during night making search for and evacuation of wounded difficult. Gas shells experienced by Battalion for first time during this attack.[60]

For the 4th Cheshires, their first forays into action had proven equally taxing, with casualties totalling four officers and 273 other ranks, two-thirds of whom had been gassed at the edge of Parcy-Tigny, their respirators giving little protection against the mustard gas fired into their positions. A further 19 men were sent to hospital on the 24th having developed painful large water blisters all over their bodies and legs from exposure to mustard gas the previous day, their inexperience contributing to the high casualty levels.[61]

Casualties, 22–28 July[62]	Officers	Other Ranks	**Total**
Killed	2	128	**130**
Wounded	43	1,095	**1,138**
Missing		26	**26**
Total	45	1,249	**1,294**

Thus, within a few minutes of the attack commencing, the losses had been so severe that both the 7th Cheshires and 1st Herefords had been reduced to the extent of becoming combat ineffective, with the 1st Herefords obliged to reorganise into just two composite companies, under Captain Poulson and Lieutenant Fraser.[63] The two dozen Vickers heavy machine guns

---

59 TNA WO 95/2436: General Staff, 34th Division, summary of operations and intelligence, 23 and 24 July 1918 and Takle, p. 232.
60 TNA WO 95/2462: 1st Herefords, 23 July 1918.
61 TNA WO 95/2462: 4th Cheshires, 23 July 1918, and Brief account of Operations from 22 July to 2 August 1918.
62 Shakespear, p. 266.
63 TNA WO 95/2462: 1st Herefordshire War Diary.

of the 34th Battalion MGC had proved insufficient, whilst ammunition supply problems had meant that the 101st and 102nd Trench Mortar Batteries had played little or no part in the fighting. The ADMS counted casualties totalling 26 officers and 892 other ranks, including 200 gas cases, between the 23rd and 25th.[64]

It is worth noting, however, that whilst casualties were especially high for 102nd Brigade,[65] the 1,200 yards of advance probably represented the greatest distance the brigade had covered in a single burst during their entire war to date. It had made nowhere near that progress on 1 July 1916 on the Somme, nor in Arras or Passchendaele during 1917, and during the 1918 German Spring offensives it had largely been retiring rather than going forward. So it is surprising to see that this undoubted and immediate success is not more widely recognised within the 34th Division, since it involved completely new (untried and untested) infantry battalions, none of which had fought on the Western Front previously, and Shakespear correctly concluded: "All things considered, the new troops had done very well."[66] Unhappy with how events had unfolded, that evening General Nicholson ordered a thorough overhaul of communications, with special attention to be paid with regards to liaison with the French on their flanks.[67]

Although held in reserve during 23 July, the 5th KOSBs had several casualties, notably from gas shelling, which lingered in the dense woods. The KOSBs' Adjutant, Captain T.D. Craig, was also wounded when hit in the calf by a fragment of shell. Although not initially seriously hurt, Craig had to be evacuated and his leg was subsequently amputated.[68] During the night of 23/24 July, a single battalion, the 4th Cheshires, relieved the remnants of both the 7th Cheshires and 1st Herefords in the line, and the following morning corps commander General Penet arrived at 34th Division's headquarters with expressions of sympathy for Nicholson's losses and pleasant messages from General Mangin.[69] Nicholson's response to these messages is not known and can only be imagined, but no doubt they included robust questions about the French failure and lack of progress on either flank, not to mention Penet's premature order for *30e Corps* to advance without confirmation that the corps to the north had been successful. That said, the day was not a total failure. North of the River Ourcq, the French also advanced beyond Le Plessier-Huleu and reached the western edge of the hamlet of Oulchy-la-Ville, as well as capturing Montgru, whilst to the south, the Franco-American troops were 1,000 metres east of the Château-Thierry road, occupying Rocourt and most of the *Bois de Chatelet*.[70] But the men of the 4th Royal Sussex were unaware of any of these other successes as they settled down to sleep in a recently abandoned German camp, amongst the detritus and filth left behind.

If there was one positive to come out of the events of the 23rd, it was that the hastily organised medical facilities – and particularly the excellent co-operation between French, British and American medical staff – proved to be extremely effective. A number of French *poilus* as well

64　TNA WO 95/2436: General Staff, 34th Division, Summary of operations and intelligence, 23 July 1918. TNA WO 95/2443: Assistant Director Medical Services, 0300 hrs, 24 July 1918; 25 July 1918.
65　Casualties for the 7th Cheshires totalled 180 and for the 1st Herefords the count was eight officers and 230 other ranks.
66　Shakespear, p. 258.
67　TNA WO 95/2436: General Staff, 34th Division, Operation Order No.232, 2040 hrs, 23 July 1918.
68　Scott Elliot, p. 241.
69　Shakespear, pp. 257–58.
70　TNA WO 95/2436: General Staff, 34th Division, summary of operations and intelligence, 24 July 1918.

as several wounded German prisoners began arriving at the 34th Division's Walking Wounded Collecting Station and were treated by the British medical staff, with wounds dressed there. By that evening, around 100 gas cases had arrived, both British and French, who were evacuated by a convoy of American ambulances to the Main Dressing Station of the 104th Field Ambulance. Additionally, the 103rd Field Ambulance had leant a number of medical orderlies and stretcher bearers to the American hospital at Crepy, which had been overwhelmed by casualties, and unlike the infantry or artillery, medical spares such as stetchers, blankets and even tetanus shots were provided by the French for 34th Division.[71] But overall, it is impossible to conclude that the attack on 23 July was anything other than a costly failure. This was largely the result of four days of relative quiet that the Germans used to reinforce their lines, recognising the vital importance of the Soissons–Château-Thierry road to supply its army in the Marne salient and that retention of the road was key to holding onto the salient. The road rose steeply from Château-Thierry, running north–south skirting a ridge and flanked by spurs and ravines, which gave the defenders extremely good cover for any strongpoints and interlocking lines of defence.[72] The overall lack of success and the losses of tanks engaged in the action on the 23rd had persuaded Mangin not to throw his reserve tanks into the throng, preferring to retain them for use another day, when more might be available. However, whilst more tanks might become available to replace the 39 he had lost, he was worried that there might be no one to drive them, having suffered 128 casualties on top of the previous day's heavy losses. On the evening of 23 July, he therefore decided to withdraw the exhausted tank units from *Xe Armée*'s sector, which had been in constant action for six days.[73] The final comment on the day's events must be given to the war diary entry from Headquarters Royal Artillery 34th Division, which simply stated: "160th Brigade RFA supported a minor attack by the 34th Division."[74] Having seen much action on the Western Front and clearly benefitting from its vast experience, this does perhaps give a more truthful perspective to the events of 23 July.

During the afternoon of the 23rd, Foch visited Pétain at Provins, where the two generals discussed the current situation. The battle was still raging along the western flank, but with limited success, yet Foch remained convinced that the Allies had gained the upper hand and he gave his host a letter, in which he urged a renewed effort to regain momentum. French intelligence reported that the Germans had 205 divisions on the Western Front, with 163 in the front line and 42 in reserve. This was identical in number to the picture on 16 July, but their distribution was significantly different and the vast majority of additional reserves had been pushed into the front line between the River Oise and Château-Thierry, which had seen a doubling of divisions from 15 to 32.[75] Foch added that Pétain should still aim to break one of the German flanks of the salient and to push on with vigour, but to beware of spreading his forces too thinly along the line, instead concentrating them ready to carry out a powerful attack. The western flank near Soissons was the flank to be broken by all available means of fresh divisions (although he currently had none), artillery and tanks allotted to Mangin's *Xe Armée* and the

71 TNA WO 95/2453: 104th Field Ambulance, 23 July 1918.
72 Greenwood, p. 128.
73 Gale, p. 146.
74 TNA WO 95/2442: Commander Royal Artillery, 34th Division, 23 July 1918.
75 Distribution of German divisions on the Western Front as of 23 July 1918. No.9471/2, 24 July 1918, cited in Woldike, p. 145.

left of *VIe Armée*. Ordered to prepare to execute the attack towards Fère-en-Tardenois once more, *Ve Armée* on the eastern flank would be reduced in its combatant resources but would act by successive concentrations. What this amounted to was an instruction by Foch for Pétain to exploit the successes achieved, akin to the German infiltration tactics whereby they reinforced success and bypassed resistance, but on a massive scale. In a slightly surreal turn of events, Foch, upon leaving the meeting with Pétain, then informed Sir Douglas Haig that he no longer required the two British divisions that he had requested on 12 July. It is a puzzling situation, since there were no other reserves on which Pétain could call to make his renewed attack, yet Foch had just urged him to throw in whatever reserves he could collect. For Foch simply to relinquish two available and fresh British divisions just doesn't seem logical. Evidently, Pétain must have convinced Foch that he had sufficient resources available to him or close at hand in order to press on with the attack, but it is a most surprising reversal of character for the two men.[76]

Late that evening, Pétain wrote to General Maistre's *Groupe d'armées du Centre* and to General Fayolle commanding *Groupe d'armées de Reserve* emphasising the points made by Foch. Each Army Group was to make one principal attack with the maximum of force. A focused blow would in his view, and that of the Generalissimo, have the best chance of success. The GAR, with the whole of *Xe Armée* and the left of VIe *Armée*, was to drive eastwards towards the north of Fère-en-Tardenois instead of south-eastwards towards Braine, between the upper Crise and the Longpont–Fère-en-Tardenois road.[77] The orders were duly passed on by GAR to *Xe Armée* and down the chain of command, but in reality they caused little in the way of disruption to the existing orders already distributed.

---

76   Edmonds, pp. 267–68. Pétain was able to transfer two reserve divisions and prepare three more to GAR, together with releasing the Italian II Corps to *IIe Armée*. Foch letter to Pétain, No. 2233, 23 July 1918 cited in Woldike, p. 141.
77   Edmonds, p. 268.

11

24-27 July
All Quiet on (this part of) the Western Front

11.1 Pétain and Mangin

The 23rd had been a frustrating day, and to Pétain it was clear that the results had been unsatisfactory. In order to make more progress, he decided to undertake a rapid reorganisation and regrouping, temporarily taking personal control of the GAC. He also instructed Fayolle and Maistre to ensure that the next attacks were carried out with the maximum of force and determination, and to keep up the pressure on the entire front. As part of Pétain's reorganisation, the *58e Division* was moved by car and truck behind *Xe Armée*'s front, which would allow the *12e Division* to push forward into the *20e Corps* line, the intention being that it would leapfrog *12e Division* and capture the vital heights of the *Butte Chalmont*. Other divisions would also attack on either side, capturing the *Orme du Grand* Rozoy and Arcy-Sainte-Restitue plateau, which would allow them to attack the important Bazoches-sur-Vesles region. Naturally, Mangin was keen to commence the attack, but Pétain had once again to warn him that he needed to protect his left flank, with the Commander-in-Chief ordering him to leave two divisions guarding his left wing.[1] A lull in the fighting on the 24th along *Xe Armée*'s front allowed Foch time to meet with the three Allied leaders – Pétain, Haig and Pershing – at his headquarters in Bombon to discuss the next phase of operations that he had planned. This was a momentous occasion, since the three national commanders rarely met together during the entire war and was made even more significant with recent events.

Foch's Chief-of-Staff, Maxime Weygand, read out a statement at the meeting, laying out the current situation:

> The Allied armies have therefore reached the turning point of the road. For the first time, because of the number of divisions the Germans have been forced to commit, we have a superiority of reserves; and, because [of] the number of battle-worn divisions the Germans have had to pull out of the line, we also have more fresh reserves … and

---

1   Greenwood, pp. 136–37. Telegram No. 1.067 – 1.063/M. Personal and Secret Instruction from Pétain to Fayolle and Maistre, No. 30.879, 23 July 1918, cited in Woldike, p. 143.

more than this, we have superiority in equipment, in aeroplanes, tanks and now behind us stands a powerful force of Americans, increasing at the rate of 250,000 men each month ... In our favour we have material superiority and much better morale due to the fact that the enemy has not, in spite of unprecedented efforts, produced the decisive result that is vital to him.[2]

Whilst the Marne victory might not produce outright victory, Foch hoped that it would allow the Allies to strike again and again at the Germans across a wide front. It was essential, therefore, to offer the enemy absolutely no respite; the moment had come to abandon the attitude of general defence and to move over to the offensive.

So rather than a single decisive knockout blow, which Foch believed was doomed to failure, the Allied strategy would entail co-ordinated attacks to knock the Germans off guard and prevent them from reinforcing the attacked location, commencing with an Anglo-French attack on Amiens and Montdidier, pencilled in for 8 August. By attacking at multiple points at the same time across the front, it was hoped that this would enable the Entente forces to progressively push the Germans back towards their own border. There was no doubt that it was a risky policy, since it required the initial attacks to cross the scarred battlefields from which they had retreated in the spring of 1918, which would be no mean feat if it could be achieved. The three national commanders argued that it would be fraught with problems, but Foch reiterated that he believed the Germans were on the verge of cracking and urged them to consider the prospect that the war might be won in 1918. He also stressed that whilst the entry of the British had seen modest gains on the 23rd, the relatively inexperienced US divisions had made a major impact on the battle already underway and demonstrated the clear benefits of co-ordinated and combined endeavours. By persuasion and force of character, Foch got his way and the three commanders departed with a clear plan for their operations ahead, with the information they needed to alert their respective headquarters.[3]

Strong and determined German resistance allowed them some vital respite on the night of the 23rd/24th, allowing them to make a further orderly retirement in the centre of the Marne salient. Corps Schoeler, Kathen and Wichura fell back northwards to newly prepared defensive positions, with little apparent interference. It also gave them a period with which to plan their next steps. With the front shrinking, the sector held by General von Kathen's corps was handed over to General Wichura.[4] Likewise, the French *IXe Armée*'s front had also disappeared, having been progressively shrunk as the Germans fell back, so Foch decided to withdraw *IXe Armée* entirely, with *3e Corps* remaining in line and transferred to *Ve Armée* at noon on 25 July.[5]

The focus returned to the front of *Xe Armée* on the 25th, with the principal effort centred on the heights dominating the Ourcq valley from the *Orme du Grand Rozoy* to the *Butte Chalmont*, with the hope of opening the road to Arcy-Sainte-Restitue and allowing *VIe Armée* to push on towards Fère-en-Tardenois.[6] On the 25th, the French *41e* and *5e divisions* commenced a brilliant pincer movement around the important town of Oulchy-le-Château, situated on the road from

2 Greenwood, pp. 143-44.
3 Takle, p. 261.
4 Edmonds, pp. 268-69.
5 Code Telegraph from General Buat to Maistre, No. 1229/M, 24 July 1918 cited in Woldike, p. 147.
6 Woldike, p. 51.

Soissons to Château-Thierry, capturing it by midday and advancing to the outskirts of Cugny, with elements of *11e Corps* gaining a footing on the slopes of *Butte Chalmont*. Oulchy-le-Château was a vital obstacle for the French to capture, the largest settlement between Soissons and Château-Thierry, laying almost midway between the two. Alongside *41e Division*, *5e Division* had by-passed the hamlet of Oulchy-la-Ville and started to clear the kilometre-long *Bois de la Baillette* which lay between Oulchy-la-Ville and the Soissons–Château-Thierry road, with Oulchy-le-Château beyond. With *11e Corps'* attacks having been completely successful, the Germans were forced to retire once more, losing important positions astride the River Ourcq. This successful advance, however, presented something of a dilemma for Fayolle, since he had decided to transfer both of the divisions (*41e* and *5e*), together with their artillery from Mangin's *11e CA*, to Degoutte's *VIe Armée* in the hope that this would facilitate an even more rapid retreat by the Germans as they pushed on the western hinge of the salient.[7] Whilst this news would have delighted Degoutte, there is no doubt that Mangin saw it differently. He wrote to his wife saying that he had protested both to Pétain and Poincaré when they had visited his headquarters, with the French Premier being impressed by the amount of captured German materiel on show. In typically forceful language, Mangin told Pétain that he believed the plan was absurd and that it completely prevented him from moving forward. Once Poincaré departed back to Paris, Pétain calmly confirmed the contents of his third letter to Mangin on the subject and chastised him, calling him to order, concluding the conversation by saying that the execution of his orders would not involve any further comment.[8] Even after being told by Pétain that his decision was final, he still attempted to argue his case, in the firm belief that it was his duty to push himself to the very limit. But it was a dangerous game to play and he risked being sacked once more for gross insubordination. On 26 July, Pétain wrote to Foch, laying out how he had been forced to reiterate the instructions to Mangin once again, making sure that both Foch and Fayolle thoroughly understood the necessity of launching a powerful and vigorous attack and ensuring that it was prepared properly.[9]

In Mangin's concluding comments to his wife that evening, he said that he complained that Pétain and the GQG had bullied him into making a climb down and that he had no other option than to protest. But there is a good deal of irony in his view, since he had never baulked at using exactly the same tactics with his own commanders to get his own way, doing so time and again. Furthermore, his penchant for self-promotion was becoming increasingly unpopular with some of his superiors, especially Fayolle. Fayolle simply replied that of course he could do more because he'd just been given five fresh divisions![10] In his defence, his combative style and direct pleadings seem to have been effective, with Pétain agreeing to return the *11e CA* to Mangin the next day.[11] But it is more likely that the success of the *11e CA* on the 25th, together with other advances within *Xe Armée*, meant that it was no longer necessary to transfer the formation to *VIe Armée*, although Mangin may also have influenced Pétain to reverse his decision.

Von Boehn was under extreme pressure around Soissons: Group Endres lost Villemontoire to the fresh and newly arrived French *12e Division*, and the centre of *Xe Armée* captured the

7   Greenwood, pp. 146-47.
8   Mangin (1950), p. 283.
9   Letter from Pétain to Foch, No.35.173, 26 July 1918 cited in Woldike, p. 158.
10 Fayolle, p. 123.
11 Mangin (1950), p. 283.

entire area from Oulchy-la-Ville to Côte 200 east of Coincy, putting the *Butte Chalmont* under imminent threat.[12] The French *20e Corps* was also successful in forcing its way right into the grounds of the *château* at Buzancy, led by an audacious attack from the 15th (Scottish) Division, but was unable to hold its gains and was pushed back out of the village later in the day. The only reinforcements arriving was *12e Division*, but with no more as yet appearing, further offensive action could not recommence, including attacking the *Butte Chalmont*. But all of this was about to change, with Mangin already planning how he would deploy the *68e*, *25e*, *127e* and *38e divisions*, as well as the relatively fresh British. In agreement with Fayolle, Mangin decided that he would *add 68e Division* to *11e CA* once it had been returned to him, and *127e Division* would replace the American divisions which had been ordered to join the newly formed American First Army. So in all, Mangin had received six fresh divisions – the British 15th (Scottish) and 34th divisions and the French *12e*, *25e*, *68e* and *127e divisions*, with two more (*17e* and *56e*) on their way and due to arrive shortly. The French tank force was now virtually back up to near full strength too, which might aid future plans Mangin had in mind, with his close friend Estienne still fully supportive of utilising the tanks in sufficient masses to make their number count. Casualties since 18 July had been heavy and the units were said to still be disorganised, and it was taking time to bring in replacements to fill the void left by those losses. But Foch had other ideas and ordered them to be withdrawn pending completion of the reorganisation, which he believed would take at least a month to complete, meaning that they would play little part in any immediate events.[13]

As the pocket progressively shrunk, hundreds of artillery pieces began to be transferred to new positions to support attacks on the flanks of the salient, clogging up the roads, most of which were wholly inadequate for the volume of traffic passing along them. Pétain also ordered what remained of *3e CA* to move further east, to Berthelot's *Ve Armée* at the base of the salient, rather than west to support Mangin. Indeed, the manpower situation appeared to be improving rapidly, with Foch already releasing back to Haig the two British divisions in XXII Corps under French control south of Amiens. Two American divisions were close to arriving at Château-Thierry and three French divisions, part of GAR, were also on their way to reinforce the left flank. Although there was relatively little that Mangin could do to change how his forces were deployed, he had a fresh division available, ordering it into line on the right of *20e CA*. Despite having to wait for further reserves to arrive, he remained determined to continue pressing the enemy as strongly as his available forces would allow, *Xe Armée* therefore issuing the order for a slight revision to its objectives:

- *1er CA* was to attack the *Montagne de Paris* to the west of Soissons and the plateau south of Vauxbuin;
- *20e CA* would attack and capture Villemontoire and Tigny;
- *30e CA* was to aim for the *Orme du Grand Rozoy* and the high plateau north of Beugneux;
- *11e CA* would seize the *Butte Chalmont*.

---

12 Greenwood, pp. 146-47.
13 Letter No. 33620 from General Buat, 2245 hrs on 25 July 1918 cited in Woldike, pp. 154–55. Greenwood, pp. 147-48.

This required a degree of rejigging of both divisions and corps, and for the 34th Division on the right of *30e CA* to pull out of the line and move closer to its new objective. It was a clever move by Mangin, who had identified that the right portion of his front was perhaps a little weaker and that by shortening the front of the right flank (by extending the left flank south), he could attack with concentrated power with the intention of forcing a rupture in the German line. From there he intended to deploy the cavalry to move rapidly north towards the River Ourcq, cutting off the retreating Boche.[14] Whilst it was a relatively quieter day on Mangin's *Xe Armée* front, with *11e CA* failing to capture the heavily held *Butte Chalmont* (although *41e Division* did gain a foothold on the hill), Fayolle urged Degoutte to assist *Xe Armée* by capturing more ground along the Ourcq towards Fère-en-Tardenois and ordering up cavalry from *6e Corps de Cavalerie* to act as spearhead. The French GQG hoped that it would be able to move at speed through *8e CA* positions to attack the German line held by Groups Winkler and Wichura, throwing the enemy into disarray and creating a breach. Three divisions of *1er Corps de Cavalerie* were placed ready to join the attack, aiming to capture the plateaux of Branges, Lesges and Serches towards Fismes. If successful, the German defenders would be forced to withdraw east, releasing the right of *Xe Armée* to advance towards Fère-en-Tardenois and maybe even retaking the area between the Vesle and Aisne rivers.[15]

Over in the German OHL, the situation was starting to unravel. Despite all of the evidence facing him, Ludendorff simply could not bring himself to issue the order to retreat from the Marne salient, clinging to any piece of even partially good news. These, however, were few and far between, and his mood steadily darkened during the day as he wrestled with the intractable problem facing him which sooner or later he would be forced to make. He met with Graf von Schwerin, head of *Herresgruppe Schulz*, who discussed the decisions he had made when faced with a similar situation in Sofia. Schwerin urged Ludendorff not to wait too long to withdraw because if he faltered, then the Entente forces would simply press him back anyway; it was much better to retire in an orderly manner than to do so under pressure, disorganised and harassed. One option was to withdraw to the new 'Beugneux Line' from Oulchy-le-Château to Fère-en-Tardenois and from there to Bligny, or he could hold out on their current positions until the 26th. But the western German flank (opposing Mangin and Degoutte) was deteriorating rapidly and it was doubtful that it could be held much longer. In spite of Schwerin's advice, Ludendorff seemed unable to make the decision, with some at the German headquarters fearing that he was having a mental breakdown. Several options were still under active consideration, with nothing as yet ruled in or out. Ludendorff wrestled with the decision late into the night, but eventually he called a Staff meeting just before midnight to announce that he'd settled on withdrawing his forces to the *Blücher Stellung* from the River Aisne to the River Vesle, with all troops in front of the line to be evacuated. Both First and Seventh armies were to withdraw to these new bridgeheads, linking up with Ninth Army.[16] For Ludendorff, it was indeed a bitter pill to swallow, being a personal humiliation that his much-vaunted *Friedensturm* was in complete tatters and that he was now staring at the distinct prospect of defeat. How had it come to this, having thrown his last knockout punch, that the fate of the war should turn so quickly against

---

14   Greenwood, pp. 139-51; Les armées françaises dans la Grande guerre (AFGG); Tome X. 10,1/ Ministère de la guerre, état-major de l'armée, service historique, pp. 469-71.
15   Greenwood, pp. 141, 154.
16   Greenwood, pp. 149-50.

the German nation? He was at once furious, then utterly dejected, then apoplectic with rage, railing against everyone and everything before finally retiring to bed in a spiral of self-pity.

11.2 24 July: Minor adjustments to the line

French aircraft were especially active in the early morning of 24 July, taking advantage of a break in the weather to launch reconnaissance patrols.[17] During the day, a French aircraft crashed very close to the 1st Herefords' positions and a patrol by the 7th Cheshires brought in a wounded German. The line remained held by 101st and 102nd brigades, disposed in considerable depth to limit the impact of any enemy shelling. Despite these arrangements, German bombardments containing blue cross and yellow cross gas shells resulted in around 30 casualties on the 24th. That night, 152nd Brigade RFA went into action in relief of the *32e Regiment d'artillerie* and the centre of the line advanced to straighten out the re-entrant.[18] After being under French command since the 23rd, Brigadier General Walthall, the Commander Royal Artillery (CRA), assumed command of the artillery covering the 34th Division, which comprised:[19]

- 152nd Brigade RFA;
- 160th Brigade RFA;
- *41e Regiment d'artillerie* (French);
- *5e Groupe du 100e d'artillerie* (French).

Although the British artillery had previously liaised and co-ordinated attacks alongside its French counterparts, this was the first time a British Commander Royal Artillery had been in command of any French artillery units, and it would require clear and precise communication between the two. The language barrier was relatively simple to overcome since several of the artillery officers spoke passable French, and the French artillery liaison officer spoke good English.

Troops from the German 9th Division, from Silesia, were identified as being opposite the British, but this formation was relieved on the night of the 27th, having suffered heavy casualties.[20] On the night of 24/25 July, the defences of the section of line held by the 2nd Loyal North Lancs was strengthened, with additional wire being thrown out in front of their positions. However, they were unable to dig their trenches deeper, the ground being too rocky, forcing them to abandon their trenches entirely overnight.[21] During the afternoon of the 25th, an artillery bombardment set off an explosion at an ammunition dump, burning uncontrollably throughout the night. However, part of the artillery bombardment fell short, with several shells landing on the front and support lines of the 4th Cheshires, causing several casualties. The

---

17   TNA WO 95/2436: General Staff, 34th Division, summary of operations and intelligence, 24 July 1918.
18   TNA WO 95/2462: 1st Herefords, 25 July and TNA WO 95/2436: General Staff, 34th Division, Narrative of Operations with *Xe* French Army, 24-28 July 1918.
19   TNA WO 95/2442: Commander Royal Artillery, 34th Division, 25 July 1918.
20   Takle, pp. 233–34.
21   TNA WO 95/2457: 2nd Loyal North Lancs, Record of Operations of the 2nd Battalion, Loyal North Lancashire Regiment, from 23 July to 4 August 1918. TNA WO 95/2462: 4th Cheshire's, Brief account of Operations from 22 July to 2 August 1918.

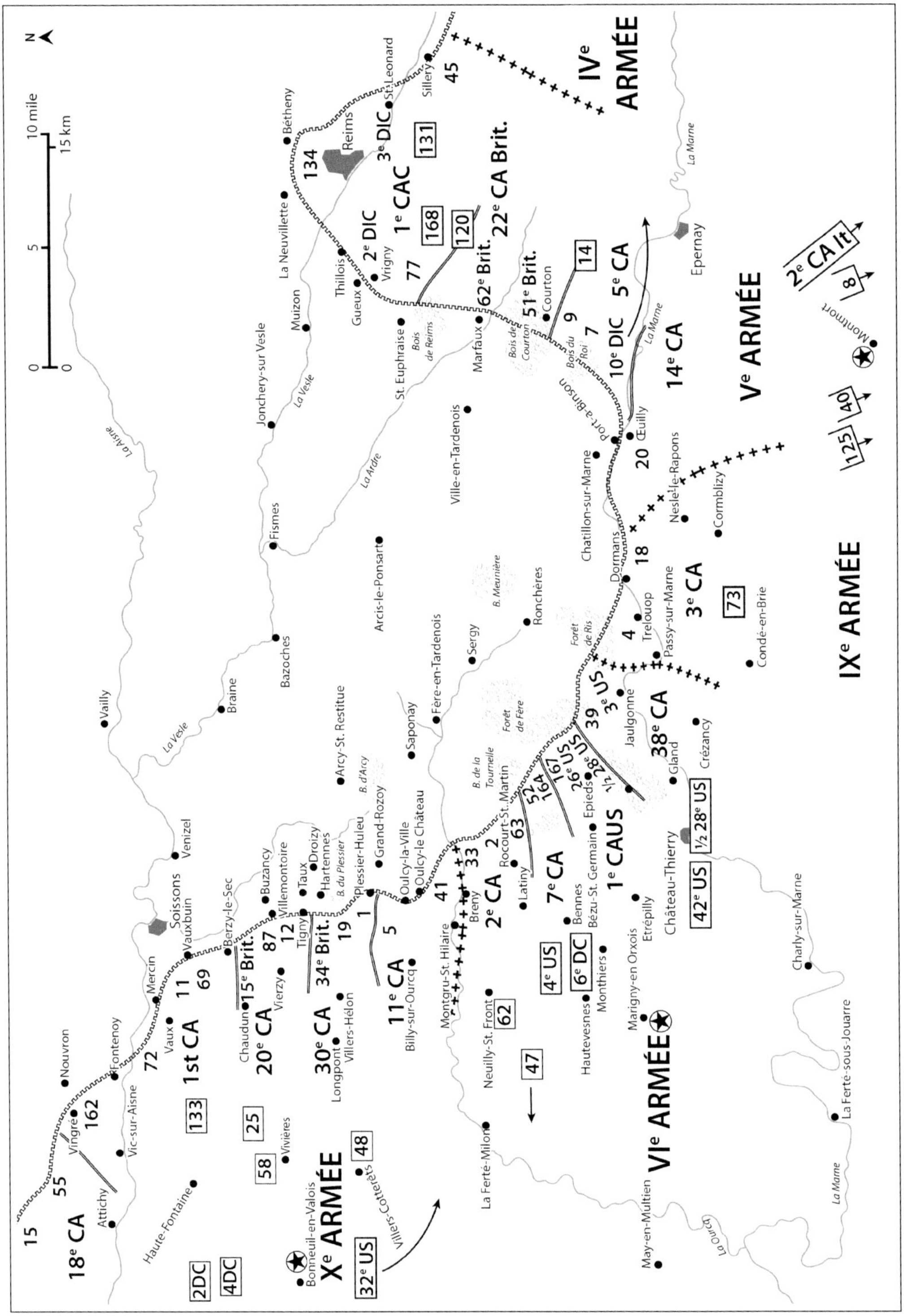

126 Fighting for the Butcher

Map 4. Marne Salient on 25 July 1918.

following day, a large explosion and fire east of Hartennes was observed.²² The 207th Company, Royal Engineers busied themselves repairing roads in forward area, screening crossroads near Montramboeuf Ferme and bridging a swampy area near the brigade headquarters. The 208th Company cleared fallen trees from the road between Montramboeuf Ferme and Tigny that the Germans had laid across it to block Allied progress. However, with the road being freely observed by the enemy, it was only possible to work after nightfall.²³

With the attacks to the south-west making progress, there was mounting evidence that the Germans facing the 34th Division might be forced into a tactical retreat. As a result, Fayolle and Mangin deemed it sensible to organise two advanced groups, charged with pursuing the retreating enemy. The right group, under Brigadier General Woodcock and comprising 101st Brigade, B Battery of 160th Brigade RFA, 207th Company RE, A Company 34th Battalion MGC and a section of 103rd Field Ambulance, would be augmented by one *sous officier* and six men from the French *3e Dragoons*. The left group, having a similar makeup under Brigadier General Hilliam, was also boosted by the two platoons of cavalry from *3e Dragoons*. The artillery not involved would move independently to advanced positions, ready to fire. This meant that pretty much the entire division in line would be in close pursuit of the Germans, and new, more distant objectives were set accordingly, with high ground between Droizy and Courdoux selected as an obvious location for the Germans to halt and make a stand. However, if the retreat continued beyond even this point, then they were instructed to closely follow up the enemy, harassing them strongly, and it was hoped that the positive tone would help to improve the men's spirits after the difficulties of the 23rd.²⁴

Ordered by Mangin to withdraw from the front, 34th Division took the opportunity to rest and regroup, being relieved on the night of 27/28 July by the French *19e Division* on the right and the *12e Division* on the left (which had replaced the *58e Division* in line), extending their flanks inwards. This time they were ably guided by French *poilu* and 34th Division concentrated in the *Bois de Nadon* and *Bois du Bœuf*, just west of Saint Rémy-Blanzy, with the tree canopy providing very welcome additional cover.²⁵ A period of better weather was particularly fortunate for the 5th KOSBs, who were without blankets or waterproof sheets during this time.²⁶ With the divisional artillery also withdrawn to the west of the infantry that night into the cover of woods south of Villers-Hélon, the entire division was now able to grab some much-needed respite after five days in the line. Unfortunately for the men, the wood bristled with French howitzers and their regular firing throughout the night made getting any proper sleep almost impossible. The 8th Scottish Rifles, still in Corps Reserve, reconnoitred the high ground at *Bois-de-la-Tuilerie*

---

22 TNA WO 95/2436: General Staff, 34th Division, summary of operations and intelligence, 25 July 1918.
23 TNA WO 95/2449: 207th Field Companies, Royal Engineers, and TNA WO 95/2449: 208th Field Companies, Royal Engineers, 24–29 July 1918.
24 TNA WO 95/2436: General Staff, 34th Division, GS286/26, 25 July 1918.
25 Read, p. 355.
26 TNA WO 95/2436: General Staff, 34th Division, narrative of operations with *Xe* French Army, 24-28 July 1918. Scott Elliot, p. 241 and TNA WO 95/2462: 1st Herefords on 27 July simply states: "Received orders from brigade that we were to be relieved by French battalions; these people did not turn up according to brigade orders; eventually relieved by French at midnight." TNA WO 95/2456: 101st Infantry Brigade Headquarters says the division was relieved by regiments from the French *19e* and *12e divisions*; Brigade Order No.218, 27 July.

in case of German counterattacks.²⁷ After being relieved by the French on the 27th, the night march by the 1st Herefords on 28/29 July was just as tricky as when they entered the line on the 23rd, with roads crammed with vehicles holding up their progress several times. In an all too familiar tale, the French guide accompanying the battalion lost his way, requiring them to find their own way through unknown country in pitch-black conditions.²⁸ Despite several days of reduced fighting, the 4th Cheshires had continued to take casualties, totalling almost 50 men wounded between the 24th and 27th. It was relieved at 2340 hrs on the 27th by the *56e Division* and moved to the *Bois de Nadon*, where it suffered a further 70 casualties between 28 and 31 July.²⁹ Over the period, about a quarter of their losses were men suffering the after-effects from being gassed, and the quality and duration of their gas training and overall preparedness was rightly called into question by both brigade and divisional staff. The 4th Cheshires had lost more than 40 percent of their strength since the start of the month, with the 53 replacements nowhere near sufficient to cover losses:

4th Battalion, Cheshire Regiment³⁰	Officers	Other ranks	Total
1 July	**30**	**904**	**934**
On strength From hospital From base From UK Total	 3 1 **4**	 18 31 **49**	 18 34 1 **53**
Off strength To hospital To TMB Casualties Total	 7 **7**	 46 1 389 **436**	 46 1 396 **443**
Decrease	3	387	390
31 July	**27**	**517**	**544**

Fighting resumed on the afternoon of the 25th, with the French capturing Oulchy-la-Ville and pushing on towards the neighbouring town of Oulchy-le-Château. Nanteuil-Notre-Dame and Coincy were also captured, pushing the line forward around 2,000 yards. The following evening they captured Villemontoire after heavy fighting and occupied Oulchy-le-Château, capturing four German guns and 700 prisoners.³¹ Those passing into captivity of the British 34th Division between the 23rd and 29th were from six infantry and one artillery regiments.³²

---

27   Findlay, p. 165.
28   TNA WO 95/2462:1st Herefords, 28-29 July 1918.
29   TNA WO 95/2462: 4th Cheshires, 24-31 July 1918.
30   TNA WO 95/2462: 4th Cheshires casualty return, month ending 31 July 1918.
31   TNA WO 95/2436: General Staff, 34th Division, summary of operations and intelligence, 25 July 1918.
32   They were 7th Guard IR (Guard Ersatz Div.), 18th Bavarian RIR (Bavarian Ersatz Div.), 234th and 236th RIR (51st Reserve Div.), 24th and 23rd Ersatz IR (19th Ersatz Div.) and 47th Ersatz Field

Facing the British, the Germans had, from north to south, the 236th RIR (Reserve Infantry Regiment) and 234th RIR of the 51st Reserve Division and the 18th Bavarian RIR from the Bavarian Ersatz Division, with the Guards Ersatz Division holding the line from Courdoux to Beugneux, having been in the line since 24 July.[33] On 27 July, Crown Prince Wilhelm directed that a new defensive line, the *Blücher Stellung*, be constructed behind the River Vesle to the confluence with the Aisne. Six of the German divisions from von Boehn's Seventh and von Below's Ninth armies, exhausted from the recent fighting and denuded by casualties, were withdrawn and tasked with constructing the defences, with an intermediate position (*Ziethen*, or small bridgehead) 4 miles south of the Vesle. But the Operations Staff at the OHL remained unconvinced of the need to withdraw and Ludendorff postponed the date for the retirement, wanting to see how events developed and even whether he could regain the initiative by attacking himself. Consequently, he ordered the OHL to prepare an attack from Osly, 5 miles north-west of Soissons, on a front of 12 miles, with the aim of outflanking the French and crossing the Aisne southwards.[34] But with few signs of the Allied counteroffensive slowing down, even less of it petering out as the Germans' *Friedensturm* had, the Germans were faced with a stark reality. One division had lasted just two days of fighting before casualties forced von Boehn to pull them out again.[35] There now ensued a brief but acrimonious stand-off between Ludendorff and the German Crown Prince, with the latter convinced of the need for an immediate retirement behind the Vesle and the Aisne, telegraphing the OHL to state his case:

> If the battle is to be fought out in the area south of the Aisne and Vesle, the despatch of fresh forces of all arms, including the general artillery reserve, is necessary. It can be expected with all certainty that the enemy will continue the battle. He has sufficient forces at his disposal. In these circumstances the Group of Armies does not believe that it is expedient to fight the struggle out south of the Vesle. A large part of the Armies and of the transportation service would be destroyed and wasted. The Group of Armies therefore proposes to withdraw the Ninth, Seventh and First Armies step by step behind the Aisne and Vesle. The Group of Armies will examine whether it would be advisable to retain an advanced position south of the Aisne and Vesle. The shoulders of the movement, the right wing of the Ninth Army (Soissons area) and the Reims area in particular, will have to be strengthened. The reconnaissance is in hand; the material preparations can be begun without delay directly a decision has been made. As soon as the enemy recognises our intentions he will no doubt proceed to further action. It is therefore of great importance to anticipate this by attacking on our own account.[36]

There were thus two camps completely at odds with one another, fundamentally disagreeing on the correct course of action, all as a result of the relentless pressure being exerted by the Allies since 18 July right across the Marne salient. The German Crown Prince, commanding his own

Artillery Regiment (19th Ersatz Div.).
33 TNA WO 95/2436: General Staff, 34th Division, summary of operations and intelligence, 27 July 1918.
34 Edmonds, pp. 289-90.
35 Greenwood, p. 142.
36 Edmonds, p. 290.

army group (*Heeresgruppe Deutscher Kronprinz*), was urging the German High Command to make an immediate withdrawal to hastily prepared defences in order to buy him some time before renewing their attacks, whilst the OHL itself, and Ludendorff in particular, vigorously opposed giving up any territory voluntarily, and if that was necessary, fighting to the last man. Von Below, commanding Ninth Army, demanded five fresh 'attack' divisions and 10 'position' divisions, plus numerous additional batteries of heavy artillery, but no attack could start for at least another fortnight. Frankly, he might as well have asked for 100 fresh divisions as for five, because he had the same chance of securing them as he had those he requested. They simply did not exist and were not available for the OHL. Despite this, the OHL replied that it would do what it could, even if this was not sufficient for the task, and that Ninth Army should make preparations for the counterattack. Ceding to pressure from both within and without, the OHL instructed Seventh Army and the right wing of First Army to retire to the *Blücher Stellung* on the night of 26/27 July, with von Boehn instructing four of his five corps (Schmettow, Conta, Wichura and Schoeler) in the centre to withdraw, but to hold onto the strategically important *Butte Chalmont* position, which overlooked Oulchy-le-Château and much of the surrounding countryside. It is clear that whilst the authority of the OHL was not exactly starting to ebb away, its ability to influence events was diminishing almost by the hour, the result of the reversal of fortune and complete loss of the initiative to the Allies. Moreover, the increasingly erratic, cantankerous and unreasonable Ludendorff was making the situation dangerously volatile, with decisions made on a whim and many within the OHL fearful of even approaching the First Quartermaster General, for fear of his latest outburst and the tongue-lashing involved.

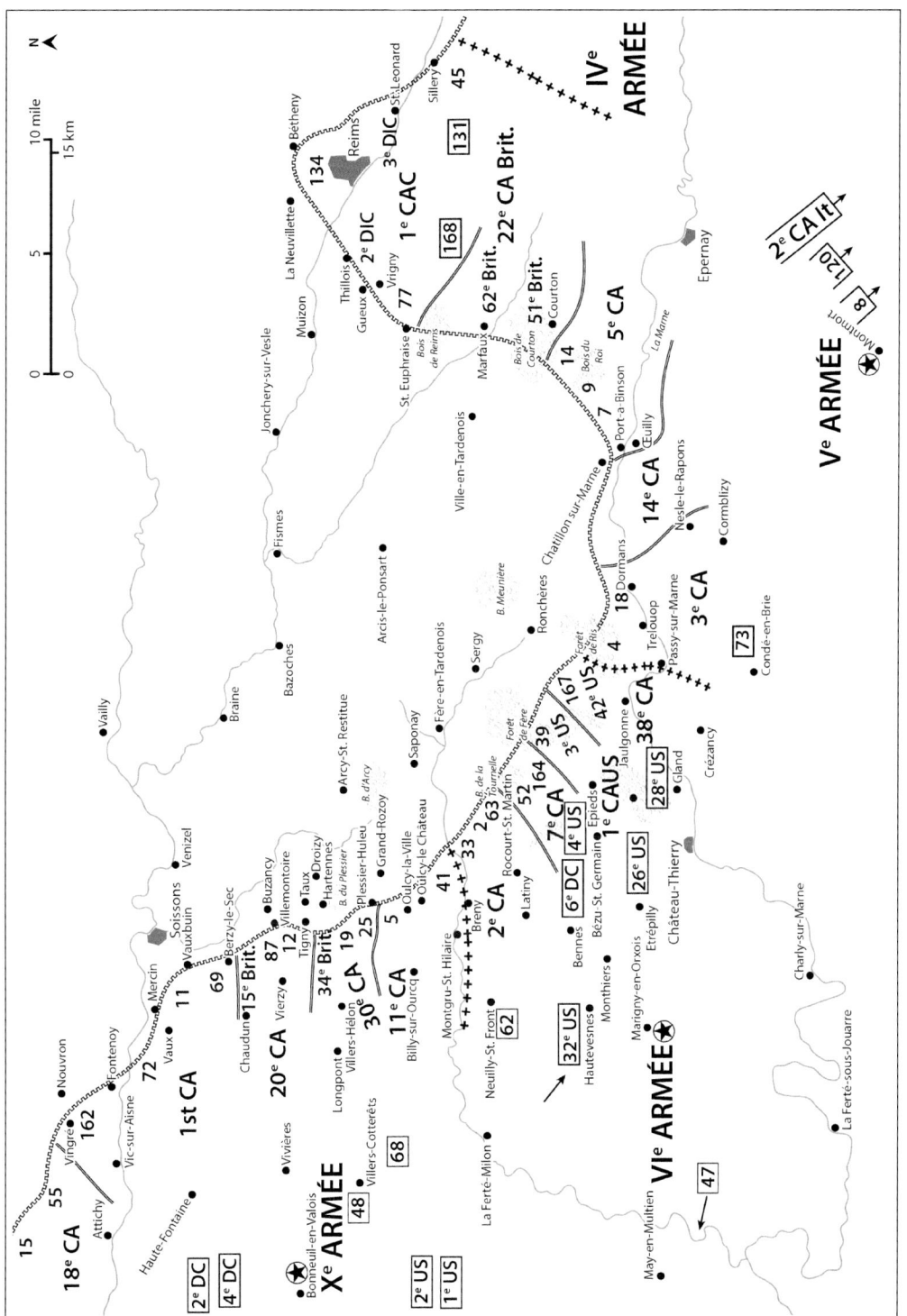

Map 5. Marne Salient on 27 July 1918.

12

Aftermath of the Battle of Soissonais and the Ourcq

12.1 Marne pocket reduced

The Battle of Soissonais and the Ourcq had commenced in the early morning mists on 18 July and had raged for 10 long, exhausting days. The fighting had been ferocious, no more so than along *Xe Armée*'s front, and the German resistance along the western hinge of the Marne salient had been stubborn and determined, assisted by the terrain which had aided the defenders. Casualties had been enormous for both the attackers and those defending their positions, but the incessant pressure had eventually led to the Germans being progressively forced to retire, driven back by attacks right along the line. This had the effect of gradually shrinking the Marne pocket, allowing Pétain to reorganise all five armies for the next phase. However, the momentum of the early part of the battle, which had been nothing short of astonishing, had now slowed to such an extent that a new plan was needed, and whilst the risk of the Germans opening up a new offensive in Flanders had by now evaporated, there would be no new injection of any significant number of fresh troops into the battle, with 11 fresh divisions already having been added to the attack. Additional reserve troops, were they to become available, would instead be routed north towards Amiens for the forthcoming Anglo-French offensive planned for early August, which aimed to clear the Paris–Amiens railway line. The British clearly would not be sending any more divisions south to support the current offensive, nor would the Americans be directing any more troops towards the salient, at least not in the short term. Mangin too was shorn of some of his most experienced divisions, exhausted and weakened by casualties. The *Marocaine* (*1re DIM*) and *153e divisions* were withdrawn back to the GAR and then sent north towards Amiens, with the *128e* and *58e divisions* moving north to join *IIIe Armée*, whilst the US 1st and 2nd divisions departed and were sent to join up with the AEF forces in the east.[1]

In reality, this next phase was just a continuation of the Allied counteroffensive with revised objectives, focusing on finally capturing the hub of Fère-en-Tardenois, the original objective set out for 18 July. Although the French and Americans were now threatening the town, they had yet to enter it or to remove the enemy from within. Pétain thus ordered the commencement of a new phase of the battle, known as the Battle of Tardenois, with the withdrawal of *IXe*

---

1   Woldike, pp. 38-39.

Armée allowing *VIe* and *Ve Armées* to link up once more, creating a firm junction between the GAC and GAR and pressing on in an organised and methodical manner northwards with the intention of forcing the Germans back to the River Aisne and completely closing the Marne pocket. Although Mangin had been reasonably happy with how some of the events had gone, he worried about the stiff German resistance, the enemy still holding open the door to the salient which he was trying to close.[2]

Distribution of German Divisions on the Western Front

	Front Line	Reserve	**Total**	Russian Front	River Oise to Château-Thierry	Château-Thierry to Massiges
16 July	145	62	**207**	36	15	36
23 July	163	42	**205**	37	32	39
28 July	155	50	**205**	37	River Oise to Reims = 68	
5 August	130	67	**205**	38	River Oise to Reims = 35	

How often each German division had been engaged since 21 March[3]

	16 July	23 July	28 July	6 August
Once	47	33	30	28
Twice	70	66	71	72
Three times	52	62	62	63
Four times	8	17	15	15
Five times	2	3	4	4
Total engagements	385	434	438	441

By 27 July, Ludendorff had made the decision and the OHL had provisionally fixed the date for the orderly retirement to the new *Blücher Stellung* in several stages, which was to take place on the night of 1/2 August. But whatever happened, the defences would not be ready until the 1st at the very earliest. Ludendorff hoped that they might be able to hold out longer, depending on how well they could defend their current positions and how long it took them to evacuate their stores and supply dumps back across the River Vesle and the Chemin des Dames. The plan was subsequently altered, with Ninth Army ordered to retire in a single bound back to the River Aisne but required to retain Soissons, to allow First Army to retire in several orderly steps. Only then would Soissons be finally evacuated.[4] However, Ludendorff's plans were beset with logistical problems from the outset, brought about due to an inadequate road and rail network to move the massive amounts of men and materiel. Yet these were the very same inadequate roads

---

2   Woldike, p. 32. Mangin (1950), p. 284.
3   Woldike, pp. 95, 145, 164.
4   Edmonds, p. 291. Greenwood, p. 152.

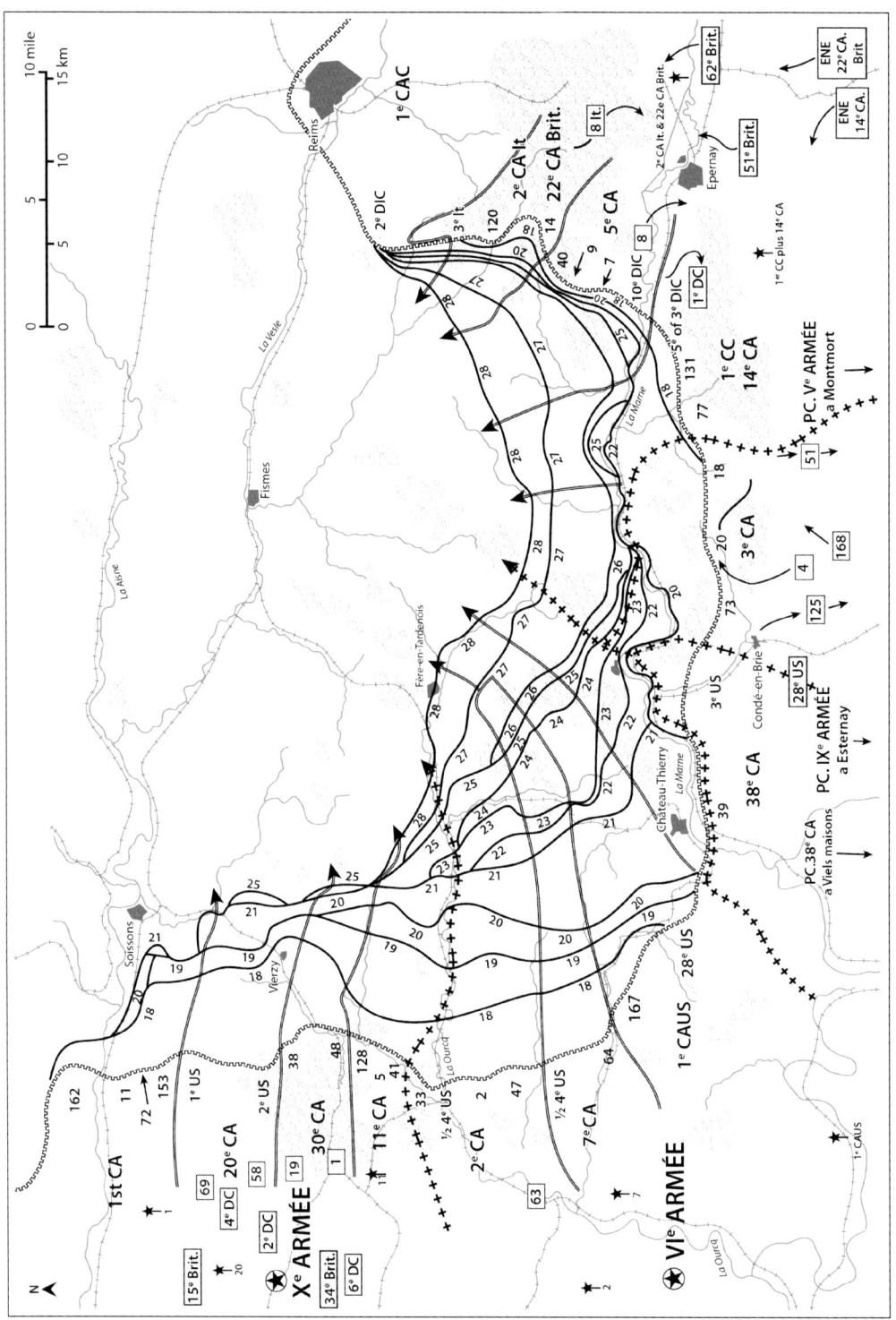

Map 6. The shrinking 'poche' during the Battle of Soissonais and the Ourcq, 18-28 July 1918.

and railway line over which the Germans had advanced so quickly at the end of May towards the River Marne. Ludendorff was not without advice; he must have felt that everyone seemed to be weighing in with their own opinion, but some were clearly more important voices than others. The Kaiser spoke with Hindenburg at his headquarters in Spa, Belgium, and expressed his concern at the situation and that the much hoped-for *Peace* Offensive had turned into a humiliating reversal, with the Germans on the back foot retreating, having suffered very heavy casualties. The Kaiser was worried that the losses had been so severe that they were beginning to rival those of Verdun, the Somme and Passchendaele; what should he report to the politicians back in Berlin?[5]

On the opposite side of the front, despite the progress evident along the line, Foch too was dissatisfied, complaining that the advance had not been uniform across *Xe* and *VIe Armées*' front and they were beginning to lose momentum once again. In spite of Pétain already having brought the number of tanks back up to strength, Foch wrote to the Commander-in-Chief on the 27th urging him to break the stalemate with renewed forceful attacks involving massed tanks. Fayolle replied that there was evidence that the German retirement was taking place where the *Xe* and *VIe Armée* sectors met and that additional focus should be placed in this area which might pay dividends. Responding to Fayolle's 'guidance', Mangin decided to move one of his fresher divisions to the area to exploit the opportunity, selecting the British 34th Division for the task, since they had only been involved in one day of heavy fighting since their arrival in his army.[6]

12.2 34th Division Order of Battle, 29 July 1918

At 0400 hrs on 27 July, there was a 20-minute German bombardment of high explosive shells and trench mortars, followed by an enemy patrol of a dozen Germans disguised in French helmets, who shot and wounded a sentry and captured three men from the 2nd Loyal North Lancs, taking them prisoner and leaving two of the helmets behind. Fortunately for the men captured, none was in possession of information about the impending attack. In retaliation, the battalion attacked a German strongpoint 150 yards in front of their lines the following afternoon, with support from artillery and a section of the 101st Light Trench Mortar Battery shelling the German positions, having earlier gained fire superiority from several snipers posted in trees, who had killed two German snipers. The mortar rounds were particularly effective in destroying the strongpoint and driving away enemy sentries.[7]

On the previous afternoon, General Nicholson had held a conference of his brigadiers to outline the scheme passed down to him by General Penet for a probable move south, where the division, in conjunction with the French on either flank, would attack the village of Beugneux and high ground north-east of it on the early morning of 29 July. Two days later he fleshed out the plan, delivering detailed instructions to the battalion COs from his headquarters in the *Bois du Bœuf*. The focus of effort for the attack was to be mainly confined to the right of *Xe Armée*,

---

5 Greenwood, p. 157.
6 Greenwood, pp. 152, 155-56.
7 TNA WO 95/2457: 2nd Loyal North Lancs, record of operations of the 2nd Battalion, Loyal North Lancashire Regiment, from 23 July to 4 August 1918 and WO 95/2436: General Staff, 34th Division, summary of operations and intelligence, 27 July 1918.

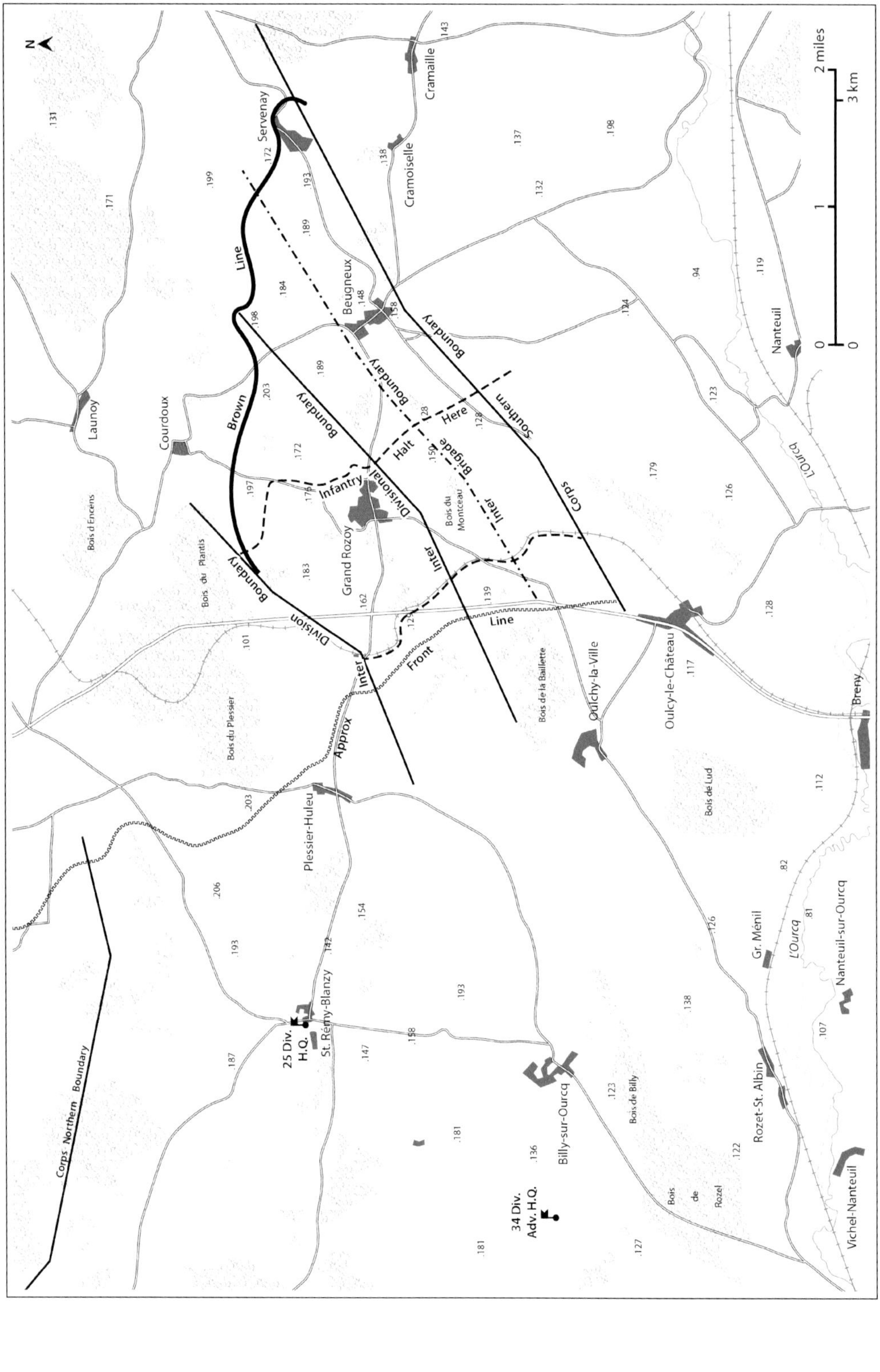

Map 7. Attack plan for 30 CA on 29 July 1918

with *30e Corps* making the principal attack, meaning that the 34th Division would bear a good deal of the burden. Meanwhile, *11e Corps* coming up on the right and *20e Corps* – containing 15th (Scottish) Division – and *I Corps* covering the left would do their utmost to push forward in support of *30e Corps*. The *9e Corps*, containing the freshly arrived *68e Division* and the all but exhausted *41e Division* in line from the Gare du Grand Rozoy to the River Ourcq, would guard and reinforce *30e Corps*' right flank, advancing towards Cramaille and the *Bois d'Arcy*.

Having had nearly six days to recover from the arduous fighting on the 23rd, Mangin believed that the 34th Division was up to the task, alongside the French *19e* and *25e divisions*. Less positively, Mangin had still not received the reinforcements promised to him, with *127e* and *17e divisions* yet to arrive from Verdun, but they were on their way and would arrive imminently (although probably too late to take part in the fighting). With the British still concerned about the shortage of artillery and infantry ammunition, an instruction was issued that all small arms ammunition should be taken from dead and wounded men during the forthcoming operation. In spite of this obvious difficulty, Nicholson issued a firm rallying cry:

> "[T]he operations in which the Division is about to take part, will, if successful, have a great and possibly decisive effect in this area … The Divisional Commander therefore relies upon all ranks doing their duty thoroughly and gallantly to the utmost of their power in order to defeat the enemy and uphold the honour of the British Army. Every advance must be made with dash, every position taken must be held at all costs and every success must be exploited to the utmost."[8]

Verbal orders were received at 1100 hrs and the full attack plan issued at 1330 hrs on 28 July, and for the first (and for the British the only) time it contained very specific and detailed instruction for the fighting, together with key information on boundaries, objectives and liaison with the French on both flanks. Most significantly, there were several pages on the plan of attack itself, including details of each phase. But first they would have to contend with yet another move to territory as yet unseen, concentrating 5 miles to the south-east near the *Bois de la Baillette* during the night. This would allow *30e Corps* to attack in the direction of Beugneux and Grand Rozoy on the morning of the 29th.[9]

The British were still smarting from the failure of the attack on the 23rd, both with their inability to move the line forward and their heavy casualties, as well as the apparent lack of progress by the French on their flanks. Whilst there is no definitive reason why the level of detail should suddenly improve, it is possible that Nicholson had directed to the French that the failure of the 23 July attack was partly due to the lack of information and detail provided (plus the complete absence of meaningful reconnaissance), and that further attacks risked the same outcome unless he was given more information with which to prepare his attack. Whilst his infantry was new to fighting, the rest of his units were seasoned Western Front veterans. He knew and they knew that Franco-British relations were as poor as they had been during the entire war; perhaps this was a sort of guarantee, that if Nicholson was to lose more men then he

---

8   TNA WO 95/2436: General Staff, 34th Division, GS286/50, 27 July 1918. Edmonds, pp. 287–88.
9   Edmonds, p. 268.

wanted to be assured the French on both flank would be making the same amount of effort that he was, and that he had evidence the French had planned the attack thoroughly.

The plan of attack was certainly comprehensive, running to a little over four pages of detailed instructions and supporting information, and the additional details left little open to interpretation, which would give the British the best opportunity of success.[10]

12.3 General scheme

As per issued attack orders, "The [34th] Division will carry out an attack on the enemy at an early date in conjunction with troops of the 11e French Corps on the right and the 25e French Division with seven battalions on the left (also part of 30e Corps) to capture the high ridge north of the Grand Rozoy–Beugneux–Cramaille road, which if successful, is calculated to compel the enemy's withdrawal from his present positions along the Château-Thierry to Soissons road north of Grand Rozoy. If the Division can reach its objective, the advance would exceed two miles." The assault, which was originally ordered for the 30th, had been explained to the Divisional Commander on the afternoon of the 27th. It was subsequently advanced by one day owing to the success of *11e Corps*, which, having driven off a rearguard of Germans on from the *Butte Chalmont*, which overlooked Oulchy-le-Château on the 28th, whilst the American I Corps, featuring the US 26th Division and French *167e Division*, had occupied Trugny on the 28th and was advancing on the main objective, Fère-en-Tardenois. The decision to bring the attack forward by one day was finally settled when aerial reconnaissance reported that the Germans were making preparations to abandon the salient altogether.[11] The French *25e Division* on the left of 34th Division would capture the *Bois de la Terre à l'Or*, the crest of the l'Orme du Grand Rozoy and Mamelon 205 (1km north of Beugnuex), with a heavy artillery bombardment to neutralise the village of Grand Rozoy from H to H + 1 hour and 20 minutes in order to prevent enfilade fire on the British from the west.[12] According to Edmonds, the sector was only held by German rearguards, but the vital nature of the location required a much stronger defensive capability and troop strength. Admittedly, the Germans had been reduced by both casualties and continued outbreaks of influenza, but they appreciated the significance of the challenge and would not rely on mere rearguards to protect it. So on this count, Edmonds underplays the level of German resistance. Bringing the attack forward to 29 July only made the move from the *Bois de Bœuf* and *Bois de Nadon* to the *Bois de la Baillette* more difficult, since the division would have to cram the two moves into a single night, with a night-time march of 10 miles over unknown country. But this time, guides from the French *5e Division* accompanied them and ensured they made the journey without incident. The divisional artillery was less fortunate, having difficulty moving their guns along the narrow tracks, and was only able to get one gun per battery into position and register it before the allotted time.[13]

---

10 TNA WO 95/2436: General Staff, 34th Division, narrative of operations with *Xe* French Army, events of 28/29 July 1918.
11 Takle, p. 234.
12 Ordre Operations No.35, 3ieme Bureau, 30e Corps in TNA WO 95/2442: Commander Royal Artillery, 34th Division, 26 July 1918; Read, p. 355 and Edmonds, p. 275.
13 Takle, pp. 234-35.

Troops

"The attack will be carried out by the 103rd Infantry Brigade plus one Company of 34th Battalion Machine Gun Corps on the right and the 101st Infantry Brigade plus 'A' Company of 34th Battalion Machine Gun Corps on the left." From right to left, the battalions lining up were the French *11e Corps* on the extreme right, with 34th Division taking the right half of *30e Corps*, comprising the 8th Scottish Rifles, 5th KOSBs, 2/4th Queens and 4th Royal Sussex from right to left, and the French *25e Division* taking the left half of the corps' line. The 2nd Loyal North Lancs would be in support of 101st Brigade.[14] "The 102nd Infantry Brigade (less one Battalion), 2/4th Somerset Light Infantry, 207th, 208th and 209th Field Companies RE and 34th Battalion MGC less two Companies will form a Divisional Reserve. The three Field Companies RE and 2/4th Somerset Light Infantry (Pioneers) will be under the command of the CRE. 4th Cheshires of the 102nd Infantry Brigade will be detailed as Corps Reserve and will be in position in the ravine at the north-west corner of the Bois de la Baillette. … The Artillery of the 34th Division is to be supplemented by two Regiments of French Field Artillery (total 108 field guns and 56 howitzers) supplemented by Heavy Artillery, [which] will support the attack."

Starting line, boundaries and objectives

"The approximate line from which the attack will start is shown in dotted Blue on the attached map. The actual line will depend on the result of an operation which will be carried out by the French 11e Corps on H minus 1 day with the object of capturing the Butte Chalmont. The limits of the front of the Division are shown in Blue and the dividing line between brigades in Blue Dotted Chain." Edmonds notes that by advancing the attack by one day massively disadvantaged the 34th Division, since it meant that once again it was unable to do any meaningful reconnaissance and everyone knew only too well how events had unfolded on the 23rd under very similar circumstances. They could only hope and pray that things would turn out differently this time![15]

The first objective is shown in Brown. With reference to this line it should be understood that the line is only intended to show approximately the line which has to be reached and on which a main line of resistance should be formed. A second objective will be ordered as and when circumstances permit. To reach its objective, it would have to advance across the flat ground in front, then through Beugneux and up the hill beyond before crossing the plateau of high ground above the village, marked by Côte 189 and the Orme du Grand Rozoy, a total distance of just over a mile (2,000 yards). The 34th Division's front line would be in the valley of a small stream, but upon arriving there, neither the valley nor the stream really deserved their name. The area was almost totally flat and devoid of any cover, save the standing crops in the fields, and the stream was no more than an unremarkable drainage ditch 6ft wide and only 3ft deep, with a small trickle of water running through it. The ditch denoted the boundary between two fields, and the men were able to step across it with relative ease.

14 Takle, p. 235.
15 Edmonds, p. 288.

Action of troops on flanks

"The 25e French Division from 30e Corps will attack on the left of the 34th Division. The line from which its attack will start is approximately from the north-east corner of the Bois de la Baillette along the ravine running through Point 148 (1km south-east of Martinpré Ferme). This Division, keeping touch on its right with the 34th Division, will attack with its left on the general line:- station of Plessier-Huleu–Bois de la Terre à l'Or–Orme du Grand Rozoy. It will take as much advantage of ground as possible to avoid enfilade fire from the Bois du Plessier. It will skirt Grand Rozoy on the north and mop up the village when the line of advance has reached a line to the north of the village. The first objective of this Division is to gain the line:- Bois de la Terre à l'Or–Orme du Grand Rozoy–Point 203–the northern boundary of the 34th Division zone on the eastern end of the feature 203. A second objective will be ordered according to circumstances. The French 11e Corps on the right of 34th Division, will attack from the Butte Chalmont, with its left in touch with the 34th Division and will establish itself on the line Wallée (1,500 yards east of the Butte Chalmont)–Beugneux (exclusive)."

Plan of Attack

"The Infantry of the 101st and 103rd Brigades and the 32 guns of the two Machine Gun Companies attached to them will be assembled during the night of the H minus 1/H day in their attack formations with the leading wave as close to the existing front line East and South of the Bois de la Baillette as possible. The position of assembly for the Divisional Reserve will be in the Bois de la Baillette.

The Artillery action will be as follows:-

a. 1st Phase – the barrage will open at H hour on the line of the railway East of the Bois de la Baillette. It will lift from that line at H plus N minutes. (The number of minutes represented by N depends upon the distance of the front line from the railway.)

The barrage will advance by lifts of 100 yards every 4 minutes and will continue at this rate until the leading waves of Infantry have reached the line shown GREEN on the map.

The barrage will remain East of that line until H plus 2 hours 10 minutes when it will cease.

During this pause of the barrage at least 2 Batteries of field guns and 2 sections of field howitzers (British) will move forward to advanced positions, which must be previously reconnoitred. This artillery will then come under the command of GOC 101st and 103rd Infantry Brigades, 1 Battery field guns and 1 Section of howitzers to each Brigade.

b. 2nd Phase – The Infantry will continue their advance at H plus 2 hours 10 minutes and the role of the field artillery will then be to cover and assist the advance of the Infantry, Batteries being moved forward as opportunity offers under orders from Divisional Headquarters."

For the attack, artillery from *11e Corps* would assist those of *30e Corps*, with 108 field guns and 56 howitzers earmarked:

- 12 Groups of 75mm/77mm guns:
- 3 Groups of British 77mm guns;
- 3 Groups of French 75s from *41e Régiment d'artillerie de campagne portés* (RACP);
- 3 Groups of French 75s from the *1e RACP*;
- 3 Groups of French 75s.
- 3 Batteries of 105 British Howitzers.
- 2 Groups of 155 Schneiders.
- To the left, the French *25e Division* had a similar number of French 75s and four groups of Schneiders.[16]

Special effort was to be made to neutralise enemy positions in the *Bois de Plessier* with gas and smoke. Crucially, the attack was to commence without artillery preparation. Whilst this was a risk, there had been a lull in the fighting for a few days, which might allow some element of surprise when the attack began. The guns would fire four rounds per gun per minute for the first eight minutes, then one round per gun per minute thereafter, with the creeping barrage consisting of high explosive and shrapnel. All batteries would send one gun forward to register from their new positions on the afternoon of the 28th. This would allow them to pinpoint the bombardment when the attack commenced, but by only registering a single gun, would not *necessarily* alert the Germans to a change in battery positions.

Once again, the artillery would be commanded by Brigadier General Walthall, with Colonel Beranger acting as his French counterpart and liaison. Group North (*Groupement Nord*) comprised 160th Brigade RFA under Colonel Warburton and Lieutenant Colonel Monod commanding *5e RAC* and would support the attack of 101st Brigade. Group South (*Groupement Sud*) comprised 152nd Brigade RFA under Colonel Saville and the French Commandant Sutterlin commanding *32e RAC* and would support 103rd Brigade. Additionally, the French *224e RAC* would be supplemented into the attack.[17] The creeping barrage would commence at 0444 hrs and the rate of fire would vary:[18]

- H-1 to H+8 = 4 rounds per gun per minute (rpgpm);
- H+8 to H+28 = 2 rpgpm;
- H+28 to H+32 = 4 rpgpm;
- H+32 to H+46 = 2 rpgpm;
- H+46 to H+150 = 1/2 rpgpm.

The Infantry actions will be as described below:-

---

16 Ordre Operations No.35, 3ieme Bureau, 30e Corps, in TNA WO 95/2442: Commander Royal Artillery, 34th Division, 26 July 1918.
17 Plan d'Emploi, 34e Division Artillerie in TNA WO 95/2442: Commander Royal Artillery, 34th Division, 28 July 1918.
18 Operation Order No.11, 31 July 1918 in TNA WO 95/2442: Commander Royal Artillery, 34th Division, 31 July 1918. Narrative of 34th Divisional Artillery, 22 July to 2 August 1918.

a. The disposition of Battalions is left to Brigadiers but troops should be disposed in depth, the principle that each Commander has a Reserve under his hand being observed. The density of the leading waves must depend upon the amount of opposition met with. These waves must be fed from those in rear.
b. 1st Phase
   i. The advance will commence at H hour, troops passing through the Infantry holding the line. The leading waves will follow the barrage, which will consist high explosive and shrapnel, as closely as possible.
   ii. Special parties must be told off beforehand to mop up the trench line which runs Southwards from Grand Rozoy and which the leading waves must pass over without pause.
   iii. Grand Rozoy is inclusive to the 25th French Division. It will be neutralised by Heavy Artillery throughout the advance and will be encircled and attacked by that Division from the North. The GOC 101st Infantry Brigade will, however, detail a flank guard to deal with any attack debouching from the village on the left flank. This flank guard must keep well away from the village to avoid the neutralising fire.
   iv. On reaching the line marked GREEN on the map the leading waves will halt and all Units will re-organise under the cover of the protective barrage which will remain down for about 50 minutes. During this pause every effort must be made to replenish supplies of ammunition and push forward machine guns. The neutralising fire on Grand Rozoy will probably continue during this phase and all troops must be warned that this is our fire and not that of the enemy even though it may be behind them.
c. 2nd Phase
   i. The advance will be resumed at H plus 2 hours 10 minutes and will proceed as before but without the creeping barrage. It is during this period that the closest liaison should be maintained between Infantry and Artillery Commanders so that full use may be made of the available artillery support.
   ii. The village of Beugneux and the woods to the West of it constitute the most formidable positions in this phase. *Frontal attacks on these positions must be avoided.* The GOC 103rd Infantry Brigade will detail a special party to occupy the Hill 158 at the southern end of the village either by the West using the copse running south from the road as a screen for the movement, or by both flanks using Hill 158 as a pivot of manoeuvre for movement SE of the village. The 101st Infantry Brigade will manoeuvre to turn the western flank of the woods.
d. 3rd Phase
   i. On reaching approximately the line marked BROWN upon the map a defensive position will be selected and consolidated as quickly as possible. At the same time GOC 103rd Infantry Brigade will push out a strong advance guard in the direction of the Bois d'Arcy and Point 192 south of Servenay. The GOC 101st Infantry Brigade will similarly push out advanced guards in the direction of Point 199 and the Bucy le Bras Ferme and also along the spur running north-east from Point 198.

On reaching this objective, 101st and 103rd brigades would consolidate on the line from Servenay to Point 199 and *Côte 205* to the divisional boundary, with 101st Brigade pushing an advanced guard towards Bucy le Bras Ferme and being ready to proceed north to Ferme d'Arson northeast of Maast-et-Violaine a further 5km north. The French 25e Division to the left would continue its advance north in the direction of Muret-et-Crouttes and Maast-et-Violaine.[19]

"The action of the Divisional Reserve cannot be accurately forecasted. It will be moved into the Bois de la Baillette and subsequently to the line of the road Beugneux–Grand Rozoy. There it will be held in readiness to capture the village of Servenay, to resist counter-attack or exploit success. The 2/4th Somerset Light Infantry will be held in readiness to be attached to the 102nd Infantry Brigade instead of the Battalion detailed as Corps Reserve. The Battalion of the 102nd Infantry Brigade detailed as Corps Reserve will be placed in the rear of the Left of the Division but will not pass the Soissons–Château-Thierry road without orders from the Corps Commander which will be issued through Divisional Headquarters."

"The 34th Battalion Machine Gun Corps less the two Companies attached to the 101st and 103rd Infantry brigades will be handled as opportunity offers. These Companies may be used during the pause between the 1st and 2nd phases to deal with counter-attack during the pause and with hostile opposition as soon as the Infantry advance is resumed. In the 3rd phase a proportion of guns may be detailed to occupy defensive positions to cover the line consolidated. It must be borne in mind that the ammunition supply will be difficult and that every gun must be brought as far forward as possible before it is brought into action throughout." [The ammunition supply problem persisted, with DADOS (the Deputy Assistant Director Ordnance Services) reporting a shortage of Vickers machine guns, a supply of replacement weapons and spare parts failing to arrive at the railhead on the 27th.][20]

Later that day, Instruction No.1 was accompanied by a further detailed plan, containing important updates concerning brigade and divisional boundaries and the direction of attack. It detailed that the enemy had been pushed back across the River Ourcq at Fère-en-Tardenois and along the *Butte Chalmont* to the GMP line of trenches. The Allied line now ran along these trenches to *Côte 125* and from there along the stream to Point 122 south of the railway station 1km south-west of Grand Rozoy. Beugneux was reported to be strongly held by the Germans. The French *25e Division* on the left of *30e Corps*, together with *11e Corps* to the right of the British, would attack according to the plan detailed in Instruction No.1. To the left of 101st Brigade, a company of the 2nd Battalion, *16e RI*, with an English-speaking officer, would maintain close liaison with the British.

The line of attack was to be the line of the stream from where it cut the southern divisional boundary to where it met the railway at Point 122, and from there along the railway line to the northern divisional boundary which ran broadly north-west–south-east. Troops were to be formed up in their attack formation by 0100 hrs the following morning, with 101st Infantry Brigade on the left and 103rd Infantry Brigade on the right, each containing one machine gun company, ready to attack in a north-easterly direction through Beugneux to the ridge beyond. Supplemented by the 2/4th Somersets, 102nd Brigade would be in the western end of the *Bois del Baillette*, with the Field Companies RE on the reverse slope west of Giroménil Ferme, with

---

19 TNA WO 95/2442: Commander Royal Artillery, 34th Division, 29 July 1918.
20 TNA WO 95/2444: Deputy Assistant Director Ordnance Services, 27 July 1918.

the farm serving as the battlepost for the division. The routes the attacking units were to take prior to the attack were also confirmed, with each brigade taking a separate route, so as to limit congestion, especially as the French would be withdrawing along these same narrow roads immediately prior to the British arrival. Additional to the troops of 34th Division, two troops of French dragoons (*3e Régiment de dragons*) and *l'Escadrille Nr 52* of the French Flying Corps would be placed at the disposal of the British to assist in the attack.

The planned deployment of French cavalry to support the exploitation of the attack and drive home any advantage is interesting. It suggests that the French were still thinking that gaps might appear in the German front line, allowing the cavalry to play a part in the attack and perhaps even open up the front.

The line of the initial barrage 150 metres east of the starting line required pinpoint accuracy, since any stray shells falling short were certain to fall on their own lines. Once the barrage lifted, the infantry were to keep as close to the barrage as possible. It is worth pointing out that whilst the infantry were all new to fighting on the Western Front, the artillery were veterans; a creeping barrage would have been second nature by the summer of 1918. The left flank of 101st Brigade was to get no closer than 300 metres to the south of Grand Rozoy, which might afford it a little protection in the event that the French were unable to take and hold the village, with one company of *2e Battalion 16eRI* attacking it from the south.

The Advanced Dressing Station would be established in Billy-sur-Ourcq, with the Main Dressing Station and Walking Wounded Collecting Post both in Chouy, whilst the Advanced Divisional Headquarters opened at Edrollle Ferme and an Advanced Report Centre at Giroménil Ferme. The distance from the front line to Billy-sur-Ourcq was almost 10km, with congestion expected *en route*, meaning that evacuation of casualties would be a slow process. Horse transport would take a circular route running Route du Pendu–Route Longpont–Corcy–Route de la Vallee de Nadon–Ferme Nadon–Fontaine Alix, whilst motor transport would take a different route to minimise any congestion: Villers-Cotterêts–Corcy–Longpont–Carrefour Montgobert.[21] Once the planning conference had finished, the remainder of the morning was spent reconnoitring assembly positions and the routes to them, as well as all of the vital forward areas, with the senior officers returning at noon for a second conference with General Nicholson, where he explained in more detail the action to be taken by the 34th Division.[22]

Prior to this, 34th Division would have to move south, and officers from *12e Division* arrived to reconnoitre the line with a view to relieving it that night and at 0200 hrs on 28 July, 102nd Brigade was relieved by 350eRI.[23] The 7th Cheshires were relieved by the *Battalion de Nouaillan*, the 4th Cheshires by *Battalion de Costeur* and the 1st Herefords by *Battalion de Tarle*, with eight machine guns per battalion going into the front line, with two British guides for each French company arranged and in place. The British would of course have to remove all of the SAA ammunition from the front line, since it was incompatible with the French Lebel rifles or Chauchat machine guns.

---

21 TNA WO 95/2436: General Staff, 34th Division, Instruction No.2, issued at 1330 hrs, 28 July 1918; Operation Order No.237, issued at 1900 hrs, 28 July 1918.
22 TNA WO 95/2436: General Staff, 34th Division, narrative of operations with *Xe* French Army, events of 28/29 July 1918.
23 TNA WO 95/2461: 102nd Infantry Brigade Headquarters, 0200 hrs, 28 July 1918. Order No. 229, 27 July 1918.

At 2100 hrs on the 28th, 34th Division began to move forward and reached the assembly position west of the railway without further incident. The Order of Battle was:

103rd Brigade and one company 34th Battalion MGC, on the right, with each assaulting battalion in two lines:
- 8th Scottish Rifles on the right;
- 5th King's Own Scottish Borderers on the left;
- 5th Argyll and Sutherland Highlanders in reserve.

101st Brigade and one company 34th Battalion MGC on the left, with each assaulting battalion disposed on a two-company front in four lines:
- 4th Royal Sussex on the right;
- 2/4th Queens on the left;
- 2nd Loyal North Lancs in reserve.

Both brigades had their headquarters on the western edge of the *Bois de la B*aillette, as was the Divisional Reserve, which consisted of:

- 102nd Brigade (less one battalion in Corps Reserve at the ravine in the north-west corner of the *Bois de la Baillette*);
- Headquarters and two companies of the 34th Battalion Machine Gun Corps;
- 2/4th Somerset Light Infantry;
- three Field Companies, Royal Engineers – disposed west of Giroménil Ferme.

Zero hour was fixed for 0410 hrs.

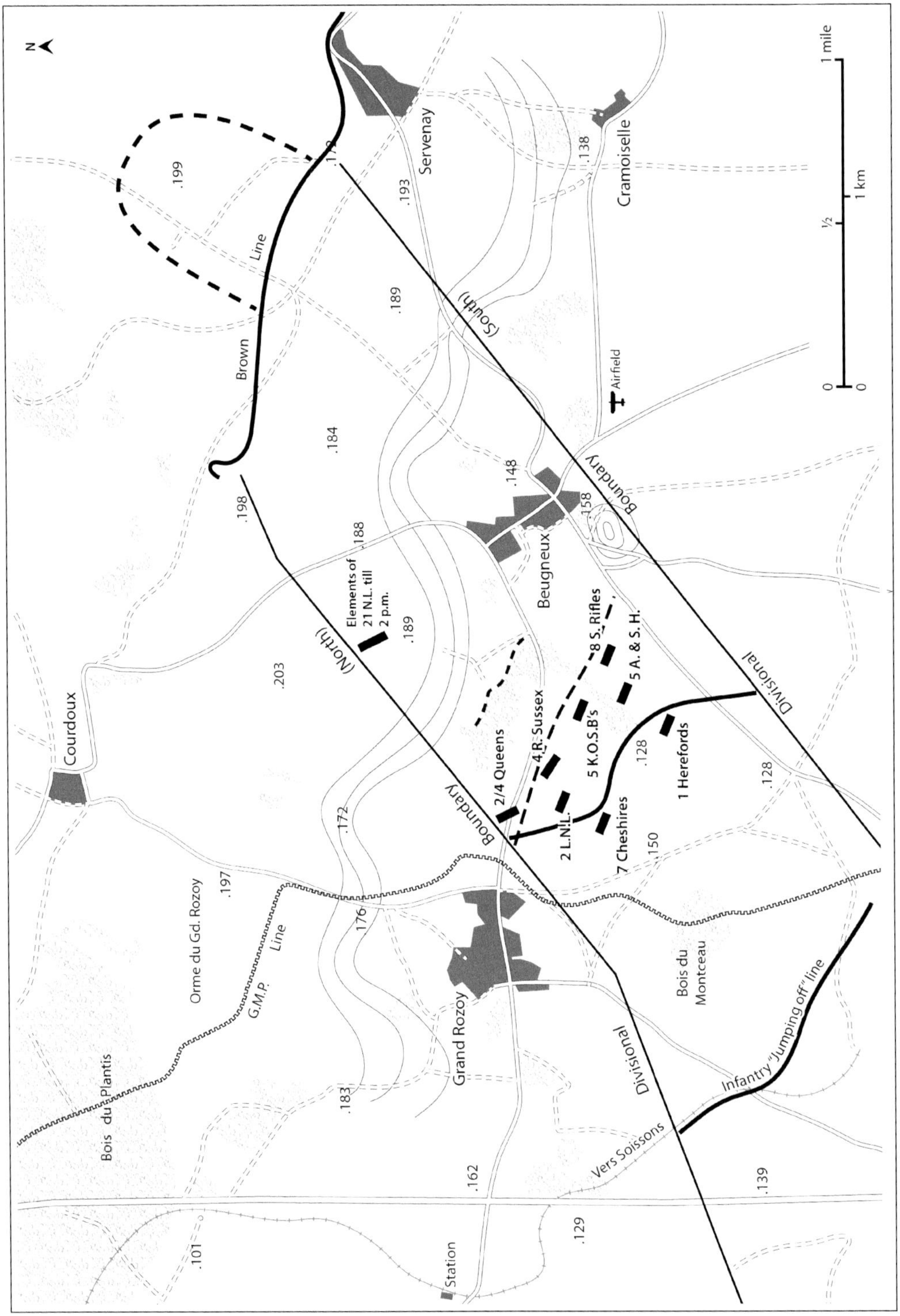

Map 8. 34th Division objectives, 29 July 1918.

13

Rolling the Dice and Pushing for a Decisive Victory

13.1 Halt or gamble?

During the morning of the 27th, the French had pushed the Germans back along the *Butte Chalmont* as far as the Paris Defence Line (or GMP Line) of trenches. According to the Germans, they had planned to withdraw from the *butte* anyway on the night of the 27th/28th, so it is perhaps debatable how heavily the Germans fought over this position.[1] Whatever the circumstances, the *Butte Chalmont* presented an excellent position for the French inasmuch as it commanded a wide flat valley to the north and was a very useful position for the French batteries to fire from. To the south, the right of *30e Corps* and the left of *VIe Armée*, there was growing evidence that the Germans were preparing to abandon their positions there too, with the French entering Fère-en-Tardenois and crossing the River Ourcq. To the north of the French, 34th Division occupied the GMP Line as far as Point 123 and from there along a stream to Point 122, south of the railway station, south-west of Grand Rozoy.

It had taken the combined efforts of the French, Americans, Italians and now the British a full 10 days of offensive action to finally clear Fère-en-Tardenois, the ultimate objective of the attack on 18 July. With the capture taking 10 arduous and costly days of fighting, would Mangin, Fayolle, Pétain and ultimately Foch decide now was the point at which to call a halt, or would they gamble, keep the pressure on the enemy and press their advantage? Fayolle in particular felt that things had not gone as well as he had hoped. In a moment of reflection, he wondered what might have happened if only he'd had four or five additional divisions available to *Xe Armée*; then the German defeat might have been turned into a German disaster and the success of the counteroffensive would be solely down to Foch's strategic genius.[2] With the opportunity to 'sever the jugular' and capture the Marne salient now long-since passed, with the Germans able to withdraw north, was it the right time to halt and consolidate? What would further attacks achieve except more heavy casualties, and for what? But to those in command, it was clear that despite now reaching the objective, the battle had not run its course and thus

---

1 Edmonds, p. 291.
2 Fayolle, p. 124.

renewed attacks were still necessary in order to drive the enemy back from his new positions and out of the salient entirely.

13.2 Into action again

A temporary brigade headquarters was set up at Ferme Bellevue, with 102nd Brigade reaching the *Bois de Nadon* in the early hours of 28 July and all units into their bivouacs by 0600 hrs, allowing them to get some much-needed rest. Later that day, the troops were ordered to march 8 miles overnight to new positions south of the *Bois de la Baillette*, a 2,000-yard-long wood which ran between Oulchy-la-Ville and the Soissons–Château-Thierry road. This time they were accompanied by French guides from *5e Division* along the route from St Remy-Blanzy to the Ferme de Frontenay and the *Bois de la Baillette*, one per platoon, personally arranged by Nicholson and his French liaison officer, Captain Beauchamp from *30e Corps*' staff.[3] The French guides from *5e Division* had the added advantage that they had been holding that section of the line for several days and were therefore familiar with the terrain. More importantly, they were able to indicate the positions of enemy machine guns and artillery, which would avoid the British accidentally stumbling into the enemy. Scott Elliot described that part of France as being extremely beautiful, the country consisting of undulating cornfields, with wheat standing 4ft high, dotted with woods and edged by low hills and irregular ridges, which rose some 150–190 metres above them. Tracks not much more than dirt paths, muddy and in a poor state of repair, criss-crossed the area.[4] The state of the tracks was made immeasurably worse by the heavy rain and the passage of countless pairs of boots during the preceding days. Despite the difficult conditions underfoot, most of the allotted French guides did their job effectively, the relief being completed without trouble. At 2100 hrs on the 27th, the 5th KOSBs marched via *Bois de Molloy* and Blanzy to bivouac in the *Bois de Bœuf*, arriving just before midnight. Despite the wood containing Scots firs and heather, giving the Scottish contingent at least a small taste of home, the night was notably cold and the men, still unaccustomed to the French climate and without blankets or waterproof sheets, struggled to sleep. The battalion commander and three company commanders proceeded to the *Bois de la Baillette* via Oulchy-la-Ville to reconnoitre the ground towards Beugneux. This, however, proved futile, since a low ridge in front of them meant that they could not see Beugneux, or much of the attack front from their positions. Yet again, a battalion would have to attack knowing little of what lay ahead. Lieutenant Colonel Findlay of the 8th Scottish Rifles and his Intelligence Officer, Captain Miller, also in the *Bois de la Baillette*, almost became casualties when the position they were reconnoitring was hit by German shellfire, requiring them to fling themselves into a nearby trench for protection and narrowly escaping serious injury.[5]

The 4th Royal Sussex received orders to proceed to a point of assembly along the railway line southwest of the *Bois du Montceau*, a lozenge-shaped wood 600 yards south of Grand Rozoy, which offered a degree of cover from which the men could debouche and advance at 0410 hrs on the 29th under a creeping barrage. They were aiming for a point 300 yards south of the Grand Rozoy–Beugneux road, where a halt was to be made until 0600 hrs before continuing

---

3   Shakespear, p. 258.
4   Scott Elliot, p. 241.
5   Findlay, p. 165.

the advance to the final objective, a line running between Courdoux and Servenay. Marching to their point of assembly, their French guide managed to completely lose his way, resulting in the men arriving late after yet another unnecessary detour and delay.[6] The 2/4th Queens were equally annoyed when their guide also failed to arrive and their one borrowed from the 4th Royal Sussex lost his way in darkness of the *Bois de la Baillette*.

General Nicholson explained the general plan of attack to his brigade and battalion commanders at a conference at 103rd Brigade headquarters in the *Bois de Bœuf* at 1700 hrs on the 28th, and an hour later these same orders were verbally relayed to all officers. The thrust of the operation involved the French *58e Division* from *20e Corps* advancing to the north to capture the villages of Tigny, Villemontoire and Taux and turning the wood north of Hartennes-et-Taux, whilst *30e Corps*, with the French *25e Division* on the left and British 34th Division on the right, moved through Le-Plessier-Huleu towards the Orme du Grand Rozoy and turning the *Bois du Plessier* and *Bois de St Jean*, attacking in conjunction with *11e Corps* to its right, immediately south of 34th Division. Maintaining close and constant liaison between the British and French to the immediate left of 101st Brigade was essential, with a company from *2e Battalion, 16eRI*, together with an English-speaking officer, designated for the task. Additionally, an amendment to the order instructed the 1st Herefords and 7th Cheshires of 102nd Brigade, currently in divisional reserve, to follow the attacking brigades; once the objectives had been reached, they were to pass through the attackers and occupy high ground south of Bucy Le Bras Ferme and at Le Mont Jour. The 4th Cheshires, whilst being in Corps Reserve, were positioned along the Vers–Soissons railway, just west of the main Soissons–Château-Thierry road which ran north–south, ready to resist any enemy counterattack from the north.[7] At 1000 hrs, the 7th Cheshires, 1st Herefords and the division's pioneer battalion, the 2/4th Somerset Light Infantry, moved forward to positions along the railway line and from there to the Paris (GMP) Line between Grand Rozoy and the Oulchy-le-Château–Beugneux road.

The French *25e* and *58e divisions* and the British 34th Division would form the hinge between the northern and southern turning movements, advancing due east to high ground east of the Soissons–Château-Thierry road. Nicholson stressed that success depended on the 34th Division not moving until *20e Corps* on its left had crossed the road.[8] For the 34th Division, the attack would be carried out with 103rd Brigade on the right and 101st Brigade on the left, each supported by a company of 16 guns of the 34th MGC. The 8th Scottish Rifles would be on the right of 103rd Brigade, the 5th KOSBs taking up positions to their right, with each battalion having one machine gun section of four guns and a pair of light trench mortars attached. The rolling barrage would commence just 200 yards beyond the front line and roll forward at a rate of 100 yards every four minutes, with the British passing through French lines at zero + four minutes. The barrage would halt on the Green Line at zero + one hour and 50 minutes to allow

---

6   TNA WO 95/2458: 4th Royal Sussex, 28 July 1918 describes the Courdoux–Servenay road. However, there is no road connecting these two hamlets and they are separated by gently undulating ground.
7   TNA WO 95/2461: 102nd Infantry Brigade Headquarters, 0450 hrs, 29 July 1918 and WO 95/2466: 5th KOSBs, 28 July 1918.
8   Findlay, pp. 165-66 and TNA WO 95/2465: 103rd Infantry Brigade Headquarters, Operational Order No.237, 28 July 1918.

the infantry to catch up and reorganise and would then cease firing. Its role would then change to one of supporting the infantry and cover any consolidation.[9]

General Penet, again recognising that the number of British guns was too light to ensure success, therefore decided to supplement the 34th Division with two regiments of French field artillery and heavy artillery.[10] It is noticeable that there was additional French artillery firepower added to each of the attacks made by 34th Division, and it should be acknowledged that it was the French and not the British who were the true masters of using artillery to suppress the enemy during the initial phases of an attack, deploying significantly more guns than the British.

A further Operational Order No.238, issued at 1330 hrs, explained the plan for the resumption of the attack at 1430 hrs (which of course assumed everything had gone according to plan earlier in the day). To capture the first objective of Beugneux, 103rd Brigade and a company of the machine gun battalion were used on the right and 102nd Brigade to its left, in the centre of the sector. The leading troops were ordered to be on the starting line by 1426 hrs, four minutes before the barrage commenced, which would begin 150 yards beyond the starting line, the infantry expected to be holding the line on positions from the northern border of the wood west of Beugneux to two houses on the road south-west of the village when it rolled forward. The barrage would halt along a line running north-west–south-east at position 203.194, close to the south-west corner of Servenay. Then 102nd Brigade would push through to take Beugneux from the south-west, with only one or two companies detailed to attack the village from the north-west, whilst 103rd Brigade would envelop and turn Beugneux from the south and push through to its own objective. All of the available heavy guns would already be pounding enemy positions and would then move on to other targets once the attack commenced. The 101st Brigade and 4th Cheshires would be made ready in the *Bois du Montceau*, available to support the attack if required.[11] Yet another order issued by Penet stressed that these advances were to be separate and distinct operations, only undertaken once the previous phase had been successful and a new line established, following one upon the other as soon as possible.[12]

With the Germans holding the higher ground to the north and east in force, notably *Côte 203* and *Côte 189* north-west of Beugneux (both of which dominated the surrounding country), this allowed them to observe any movement and to bring down an immediate reply. Although on a map the land appears to be almost flat, in fact it gently undulates, with the plain rising steadily north from Oulchy-le-Château towards Beugneux and Grand Rozoy, with the high points of *Côte 203* and *Côte 189* beyond. Between the two villages, halfway up the ridge on the forward slope, was another elongated wood, stretching 1,000 metres and containing a large number of German machine guns. More guns were located in Beugneux and in a detached wood on a small circular hillock, *Côte 158*, just south of the village, which provided good all-round protection for

---

9   TNA WO 95/2465: 103rd Infantry Brigade Headquarters, Order No.225, 28 July 1918; Operational Order No. 237, 28 July 1918.
10 TNA WO 95/2465: 103rd Infantry Brigade Headquarters, Order No. 219, 28 July 1918.
11 TNA WO 95/2436: General Staff, 34th Division, Operation Order No. 238, 1330 hrs, 29 July and WO 95/2465: 103rd Infantry Brigade Headquarters, Order No.238, 29 July 1918 (there is a misprint in the date and this is overwritten in pencil in the GS War Diary).
12 TNA WO 95/2465: 103rd Infantry Brigade Headquarters, Reference Order GS 286/70, 29 July 1918.

the village from every direction. With the village and surrounds amply protected, the sensible decision was made to outflank it from left and right, rather than make a frontal attack.[13]

Forming up for the attack at 0100 hrs, 101st Brigade and one machine gun company was the left portion of the attack, with 103rd Brigade taking their first forays into the action on the right, also with a machine gun company in support. A Company of 34th Battalion MGC had managed to move its guns to new positions on high ground near *Côte 189* overnight in readiness for the attack, which provided a better field of fire to support the infantry. However, Second Lieutenant Culy was wounded on the ridge and his position taken by a sergeant.[14] The 103rd Brigade therefore held a line from Fontaine Alix Ferme–Point 181–Point 174–Billy sur Ourcq–Point 185 east of Géromenil Ferme–southern end of Oulchy-la-Ville, with 101st Brigade in a line from St Remy-Blanzy–Point 142–Ferme de Fronteny–Point 180–northern end of Oulchy-la-Ville.

Significantly, the objective of the French *41e Division* to the right of 34th Division was a line running due south from Beugneux, rather than beyond it. Not only were there no significant obstacles facing the French attackers, but their objective was almost a mile short of the British objective of the Brown Line on top of the Beugneux ridge. On the face of it, this seems a somewhat puzzling decision by General Penet – why would he choose such different objectives for the two divisions fighting next to each other which might cause them to lose contact? Firstly, it would be essential that the British clear well beyond the village, to protect against the anticipated immediate German counterattack, hence their objective 1 mile to the northeast. But surely the French should conform to the British advance, rather than leaving their right flank exposed? With the ridge running east–west and *11e Corps* having further to travel (but unlike the British, facing no obvious obstacles), maybe he believed *11e Corps* might be able to reach the heights, but felt they would be unable to hold it due to German enfilade fire and potential reinforcements from Arcy-Sainte-Restitue, further to the north-east. Perhaps he also felt the British were fresher than his countrymen, having only recently arrived in the region, whilst *41e Division* had been involved in the fighting for 11 long and arduous days, but it was also possible to see that the task facing the British was an especially challenging one. However, the answer probably lies in both the condition of the troops and the geography. The hamlet of Cramaille lay just beyond the furthest point of *11e Corps'* objective and Penet must have believed that the French would not be able to capture the village, as this would require them to push on beyond it to secure the area and prevent a German counterattack. It was much better to hold a position which they could defend than risk over-extending themselves and losing what they gained. Each battalion had two companies in the front line, which were further split into two lines, one 150 yards behind the other in extended formation, with the remainder in artillery formation.[15]

---

13 Scott Elliot, pp. 242-43.
14 TNA WO 95/2451: 34th Battalion, Machine Gun Corps, 29 July 1918.
15 TNA WO 95/2465: 103rd Infantry Brigade Headquarters, 29 July 1918.

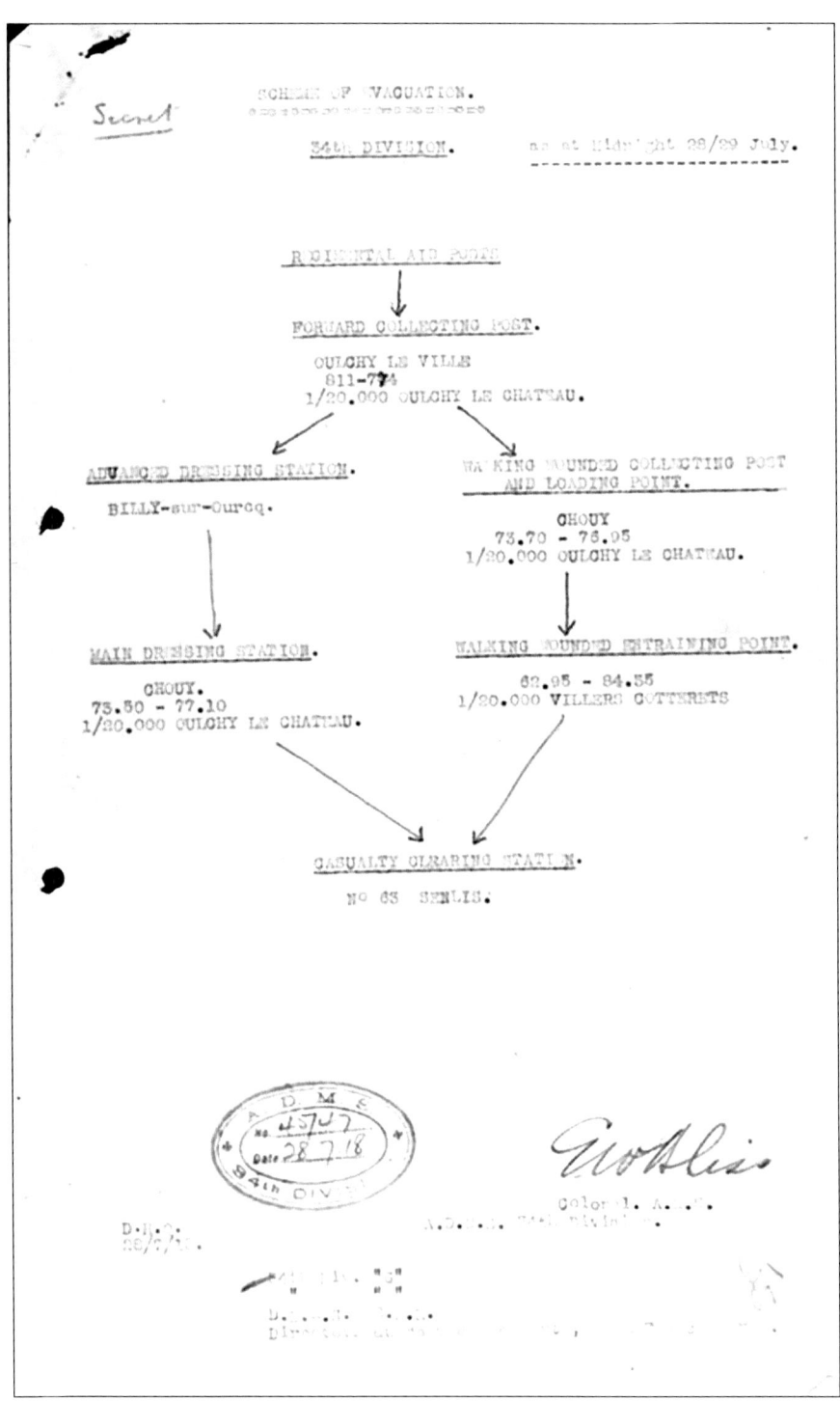

ADMS evacuation route. (TNA WO 95/2443)

13.3 103rd Brigade enters the fray

The 5th KOSBs moved from the *Bois de Bœuf* to Billy-Sur-Ourcq, through the hamlet of Oulchy-la-Ville, passing into their assembly positions in the *Bois de la Baillette* by 1550 hrs, more than 12 hours ahead of zero hour at 0410 hrs. As they moved through the *Bois de la Baillette* towards the front line, enemy shelling by German 5.9in guns resulted in heavy casualties for the battalion. Despite having been given five French guides, most of the battalion managed to lose touch during the shelling, becoming divided in the wood in the darkness, with only the headquarters and half of the leading company emerging intact at the eastern edge of the wood. The battalion commander, Lieutenant Colonel Coulson, perhaps fearing he might have lost much of his unit to the shelling, had a crucial decision to make: should he wait for the remaining companies to catch up and risk being late arriving at their attack positions, or should he push on towards the front line, believing the French guides would be able to direct his troops to the correct location in time? In the event, he made the only decision possible and returned to search for the missing companies in the wood. He also ordered runners to find the 5th Argylls and request that they come up to replace the missing KOSBs. The men finally arrived and he was able to move off at 0300 hrs towards the front line and cross the Soissons–Château-Thierry road, only a little over an hour before the attack was due to start. It is unlikely that Coulson would have been able to locate the stragglers, since the men had been mistakenly ordered to lie down in the dense forest during the enemy shelling.[16] Lieutenant Dunn, in charge of battalion transport, passing through the *Bois de la Baillette en route* to the front line, located the missing companies. In spite of having suffered a number of casualties to both men and mules, Dunn took charge of the situation and the men resumed their march east. By now much time had been lost and the men were hurried forward, arriving at their jumping-off positions as the clock struck 0400 hrs, just 10 minutes before zero hour.

The 4th Royal Sussex marched through the villages of St Remy and Blanzy, meeting their French *23e Division* guides at Ferme Montrambœuf. Moving forward again, they were subjected to a flurry of German gas shells fired close to their positions, but fortuitously these were inaccurate and the men didn't need to wear their respirators. Passing a heavily shelled narrow-gauge railway line which ran from Soissons–Château-Thierry, they crossed a cornfield and were able to take over the 250-yard portion of the line from the French Senegalese troops without incident. The first objective, a wood 800 yards distant [Bois de Montceau], could just about be made out in the moonlight and relief was completed by 0200 hrs. Shortly after, a German 5.9in shell landed right in the track where the Sussex men were assembling for the attack, killing the acting CO, Captain A.N.H. Weekes, and Regimental Sergeant Major John Simmons and wounding the Padre, Reverend W.H. Aglionby, CFMC, whilst Captain S.K. Reid, MC, was wounded by further shellfire at 0300 hrs.[17] Hailing from the village of Hurstpierpoint in Sussex, 29-year-old Arthur Nelson Hampton Weekes had been a pupil at Harrow School before joining the 4th Royal Sussex in 1908 as a Territorial soldier. Weekes' commanding officer, Lieutenant Colonel Constable, wrote to his father: "He was not only one of my best friends, but was also one of the best Officers I have ever known, thoroughly efficient and

---

16   Scott Elliot, pp. 243–44 and TNA WO 95/2466: 5th KOSBs, 28-29 July 1918.
17   Read, p. 356.

thoroughly brave. It is something great to feel that you have had such a son and to know what splendid work he has done and how much he was loved by all." Brigadier General Woodcock, commanding 101st Brigade, also wrote to Weekes' father:

> Your son had only been in my Brigade a month, but that was quite time enough for me to discover not only his high ability as a soldier but also his great personal charm. Believe me when I say that I feel that I have indeed lost a friend as well as an excellent Officer. As you know, at the time of his death he was commanding his Battalion, and the papers have told you how brilliantly the Division behaved. His Battalion was foremost in every attack, and it is the exact truth to say he fell at the moment of victory.

Captain R.C.G. Middleton, MC, took command of the battalion, with Captain J.C. Peskett, MC, as the new second in command and Adjutant.[18] For the 2nd Loyal North Lancs, whilst their passage to the front was less lethal, it was no less challenging. Half of the battalion lost touch on the way, owing to their French guides having disappeared *en route*, leaving the remaining A and C Companies to move off on their own.[19]

With but a moment to catch its collective breath, the attack went in promptly at 0404 hrs,[20] Lieutenant Colonel Coulson giving the order for 5th KOSBs to advance in extended order and push forward up the left incline, with both companies and platoons in artillery formation.[21] The ground they crossed during the initial stages of the attack, with breast-high fields of ripe wheat, was unlike anything they had experienced before. Almost immediately, they began to take prisoners, first in dribs and drabs, then in bigger groups, and the men's spirits were lifted by the general lack of resistance they encountered. As they passed into the darkness of the *Bois de Montceau*, however, this was about to change.[22]

It is important to state that the individual war diaries gave very differing (and often contradictory) accounts of events on 29 July, and it has been essential to analyse them individually to piece together the actual accounts of the day. Whilst the 34th Division war diary is by no means a work of fiction; it does seem to portray the division in a more positive light than most of the battalion diaries. It shows a fascinating relationship between the battalions and divisional headquarters, each with slightly different interpretations of events. It is entirely possible that Nicholson had instructed his Staff to paint the action in a positive light in order to demonstrate to General Godley that whilst the division was newly reconstituted, it had quickly become an effective fighting force and had been successful under very difficult circumstances. It would be the divisional war diary rather than any battalion diaries which was more likely to make its way

---

18   Warner, Philip L., *Harrow Memorials of the Great War, Vol. 6*. Shakespear, p. 259, records that Weekes was in command of 4th Royal Sussex with Major G.S. Constable MC promoted to the temporary rank of lieutenant colonel whilst away on leave and returning on 4 August 1918. Major Constable reverted to second in command on 14 August when Lieutenant Colonel W.R. Campion joined the battalion and assumed command. Read, p. 357, suggests that Captain Peskett was put in temporary command of the battalion.
19   TNA WO 95/2457: 2nd Loyal North Lancs, record of operations of the 2nd Battalion, Loyal North Lancashire Regiment, from 23 July to 4 August 1918.
20   Findlay states the attack went in promptly 10 minutes earlier at 0400 hrs.
21   Scott Elliot, p. 244.
22   Read, p. 358 and Edmonds, p. 284.

to Godley's desk. Furthermore, being one step removed from the fighting, the headquarters Staff was able to take a more 'considered' view of events, removing some of the more emotive narrative from the fighting battalions and perhaps even polishing the account a little. Nicholson was no fool, and neither were his experienced Staff, who knew their role was to support the division whilst still being true to events.

The divisional General Staff entry of events of 28/29 July reported that both assaulting battalions, preceded by a heavy rolling barrage containing high explosive, advanced without difficulty to the Green Line objective 1,600 metres from the jumping-off positions, where a halt was made until 0600 hrs according to programme and the men sheltered in the protection of the GMP Line. According to the 2nd Loyal North Lancs, the Green Line was 3,000 metres beyond their starting line and was reached by 0520 hrs with only slight losses. A and C Companies, 2nd Loyal North Lancs, consolidated in a sunken road running north-west–south-east from *Côte 150*. Unfortunately, neither of these distances is accurate: the Green Line was roughly 1,000 metres from the jumping-off line and the Brown Line 1,500 metres further on.[23]

The division formed up under a dense fog, mingling with the mist and smoke, close behind the rolling barrage, with the Queens and 4th Royal Sussex of 101st Brigade and the 5th KOSBs and 8th Scottish Rifles from 103rd Brigade in line from left to right, each accompanied by a section of machine guns. French 75mm shells from the creeping barrage were falling short and onto the cart track where two platoons were awaiting the order to advance, resulting in a number of casualties to the 4th Royal Sussex, with a quarter of D Company out of action before the attack had even started.[24] In the confusion and having had no time to confirm orders, the 5th KOSB's Reserve Company went over with the main attack. Y and Z Companies, 8th Scottish Rifles, advanced in two lines 100 yards apart, with X Company in support, whilst W Company advanced in artillery formation to the rear, the fog making keeping direction extremely difficult for the Scots.[25] They quickly encountered a belt of German tear gas, which whilst uncomfortable, did not cause the attack to slow. B and D Companies and the Battalion HQ of the 2nd Loyal North Lancs, unable to catch up and make contact with the two leading companies, instead decided to swing left to support the attack made by the 2/4th Queens but encountered considerable opposition from enemy machine guns located in the western part of the *Bois de Beugneux* and Grand Rozoy, with a dangerous gap developing between the left of 34th Division and the right of *25e Division*. A and D Companies, 2nd Loyal North Lancs, were by now well beyond the Green Line, having overshot their consolidation line an hour before the appointed time and they, alongside the advanced companies of the 4th Royal Sussex, began to take casualties as a result of walking into the barrage, before quickly retiring a safe distance back to the Green Line.[26]

The advance was continued at 0600 hrs towards the second objective, the Brown Line running north-west–south-east along the ridge 800 metres north of Beugneux and through *Côte 205*. This was confirmed by the war diary of 103rd Brigade, which stated that "the advance

---

23 TNA WO 95/2457: 2nd Loyal North Lancs record of operations of the 2nd Battalion, Loyal North Lancashire Regiment, from 23 July to 4 August 1918.
24 Read, pp. 357–58.
25 TNA WO 95/2467: 8th Scottish Rifles, 0414 hrs, 29 July 1918 and Scott Elliot, p. 244.
26 TNA WO 95/2457: 2nd Loyal North Lancs, record of operations of the 2nd Battalion, Loyal North Lancashire Regiment, from 23 July to 4 August 1918.

progressed without check and reached their first objective, the Green Line, well up to time, keeping in touch in spite of mist and smoke. Battalions reorganised and pushed on with great dash."[27] A report to 152nd Brigade RFA headquarters at Ferme d'Endrolle supporting 103rd Brigade's attack suggested that 103rd Brigade had captured their objective around 0600 hrs but were warned not to move the supporting battery until the situation had become clearer. It took another 75 minutes before confirmation arrived from 103rd Brigade that it had reached its objective and was re-forming, having captured 60-70 prisoners.[28] There is some criticism that the halt to reorganise from 0600-0700 hrs was much too long, allowing the Germans time to recover, but this is probably a little harsh, given the men were attacking unknown and unseen ground and would naturally require additional time to gather their forces and prepare to push on to the Brown Line. Moreover, they would have known that the Germans were experts in rapid recovery, so it is unlikely they would have waited for longer than absolutely necessary before pressing on.[29]

The 5th KOSBs and 8th Scottish Rifles made good progress towards Beugneux but were brought to a standstill by machine gun fire, causing some casualties, before the latter was able to neutralise the gun and reach the foot of *Côte 158*. Meanwhile, 101st Brigade advanced as far as the wood west of Beugneux, where it too was temporarily held up by enemy machine guns firing from the wood. By 0700 hrs, the north-east edge of the wood had been reached but very severe machine gun fire was encountered on both flanks, resulting in many casualties, including all of the runners from the 5th KOSBs, meaning no messages got back to battalion headquarters for the first three hours of the attack. The advance continued to about *Côte 189* just north-west of Beugneux, during which Lieutenant Colonel Charles Jourdain, commanding the 2nd Loyal North Lancs, was killed by enemy shellfire at around 0830 hrs, with Captain G.P. Atkinson, MC, taking command of the battalion two hours later as soon as he was located. The son of the Vicar of Ashbourne and Rector of Mapleton in Derbyshire, Jourdain had joined the British Army in 1888, initially with the 1st Battalion, Loyal North Lancs, before being promoted to command of 2nd Battalion in December 1913, choosing to extend his command beyond the four years normally expected. At the time of his death, he was the longest-surviving CO of any Regular battalion during the war. He had been one of only two officers who never reported sick during the East Africa campaign and had served almost 30 years with the regiment, being awarded the French *Croix de Guerre* posthumously.[30] Shortly after 0930 hrs, two platoons of the 5th KOSBs under Second Lieutenants Carmichael and Robinson arrived to reinforce A Company, 2nd Loyal North Lancs. Second Lieutenant Robinson was particularly unfortunate as he was killed around midday, with his brother Frederick having been killed in action on 8 June 1917 and another brother a prisoner of war.[31]

---

27 TNA WO 95/2465: 103rd Infantry Brigade Headquarters, 29 July 1918.
28 TNA WO 95/2442: Commander Royal Artillery, 34th Division, 29 July 1918.
29 Takle, p. 235.
30 TNA WO 95/2436: General Staff, 34th Division, narrative of operations with *Xe* French Army, events of 28–29 July 1918; Takle, p. 235; Hodgkinson, p. 19; Creagh, Sir O'Moore and Humphris, E.M., *The VC and DSO* (1923), p. 194
31 TNA WO 95/2457: 2nd Loyal North Lancs, record of operations of the 2nd Battalion Loyal North Lancashire Regiment from 23 July to 4 August 1918. The war diary spells his name incorrectly as Robertson, but there are no casualties matching this information for the 5th KOSBs at this time.

Conditions and progress had been extremely difficult, especially for the 8th Scottish Rifles, who got no further than 200 metres before shelling by the 47th Ersatz Field Artillery Regiment, with shrapnel and tear gas, temporarily stopped further progress east.[32] As dawn broke, they resumed the advance through a thick mist and quickly reached the light railway line, pushing out 50 yards beyond it and capturing a dozen German prisoners in the process. White lights, the French signal that their objective had been reached, were observed by the artillery on both the left and right flanks, with 100 prisoners reported passing the British battery positions on their way to captivity in the rear. The 5th KOSBs managed to force its way through the *Bois de la Baillette* to the south-west corner of Beugneux, with D Company reaching the north-west of the villages and the foot of the slope on the north side of it. They managed to hold on to their positions for four hours, before being shelled out and forced to withdraw to the road running south-west to Oulchy-le-Château, where German machine guns stationed in the south-east corner of Beugneux enfiladed their new positions.

The *Bois du Montceau* was cleared with little opposition and an advance of almost 2,000 metres was completed in short order. The 4th Royal Sussex crossed the unoccupied GMP Line, which many felt surprising, since the trench line offered some of the best defensive protection in the area. However, upon inspecting the dilapidated state of the defences and the small amount of rusting wire, it was clear that the Germans had never really occupied the line, other than as a temporary position.[33]

In stark contrast to the shell-filled terrain and fields of barbed wire which faced attackers elsewhere in France and Flanders, the high-standing corn proved no obstacle to their forward movement and initial progress overall was remarkably rapid. Apart from the Boche artillery and some of their own artillery shells falling short, and even though the cornfields offered no protection from enemy bullet or shell, the going had been comparatively trouble-free, with little in the way of infantry opposition.[34] By 0620 hrs, the 5th KOSBs were reported to be on the Green Line, just south-west of Beugneux, followed a quarter of an hour later by the 4th Royal Sussex and 2/4th Queens. But as they crossed the railway track, enemy machine guns situated on the rising ground of *Côte 158* began to cause a number of casualties, with the French to their right nowhere to be seen. Sensing the imminent danger, German artillery fire also increased markedly in intensity, but still too weak and short-lived to significantly impede the division's progress.[35]

13.4 Phase II – Advancing towards the Brown Line objective

So far, so good. Although casualties had been high, excellent progress had been made towards the objectives. But just as the fighting was hotting up, so too was the weather, making combat unpleasant for those not used to the heat. Fortuitously for the infantry of the 34th Division

---

Commonwealth War Graves Commission <https://www.cwgc.org/find-records/find-war-dead> records his date of death as 1 August 1918, not 29 July.
32   TNA WO 95/2467: 8th Scottish Rifles, 29 July 1918.
33   Read, p. 358.
34   Findlay, pp. 166–67 and TNA WO 95/2456: 101st Infantry Brigade Headquarters, 0550 hrs, 29 July 1918.
35   TNA WO 95/2456: 101st Infantry Brigade Headquarters, 0550 hrs, 29 July 1918.

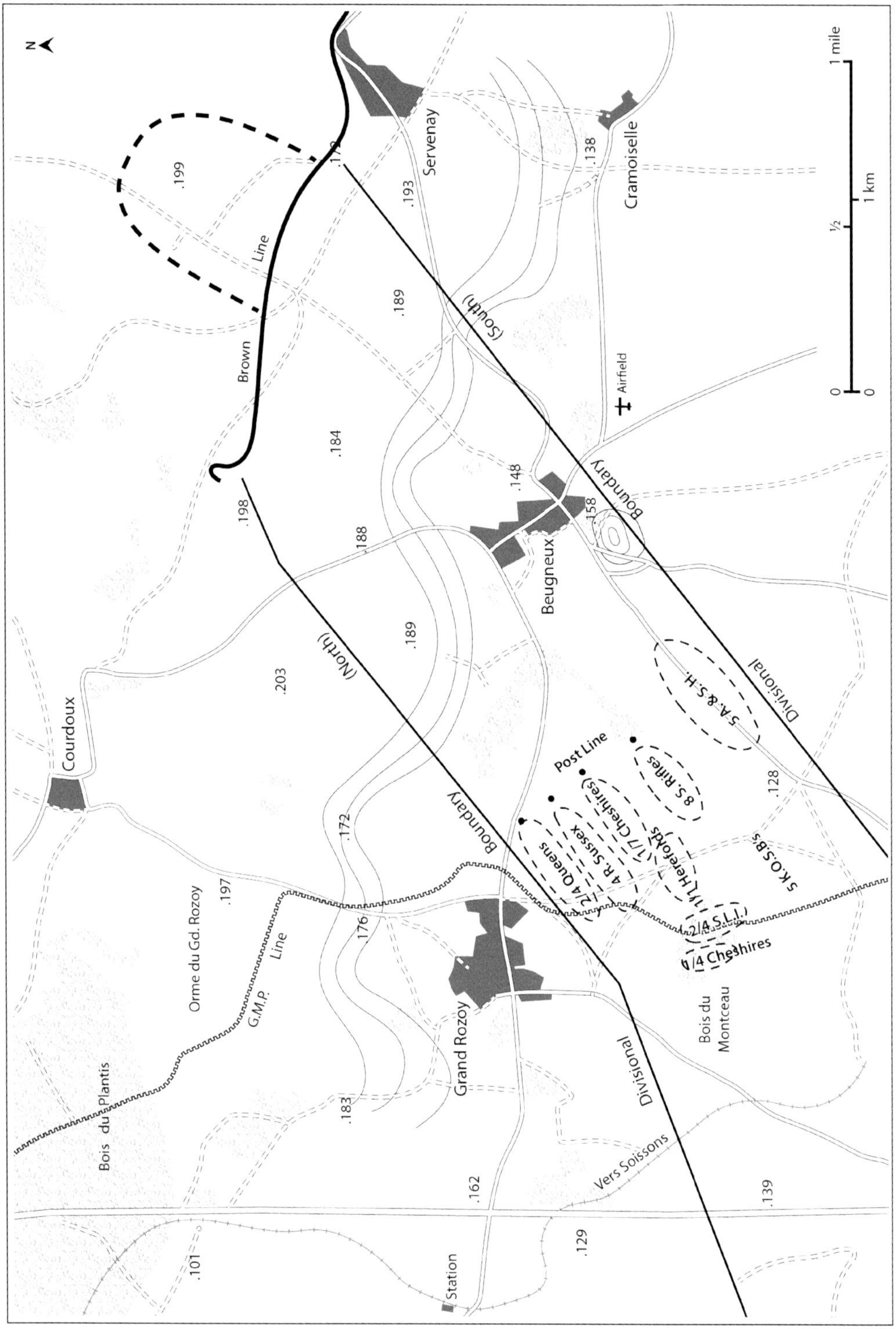

Map 9. Situation at 21:00 on 29 July 1918.

(apart from any replacements), they had of course recently arrived from Egypt and Palestine, so were very used to these sorts of conditions. The machine guns up alongside the infantry were able to provide supporting fire, passing first the Soissons railway line, then the GMP Line and forward to Point 136.[36] Battalions halted on the Green Line 250 metres shy of the Grand Rozoy–Beugneux road, according to programme, in order to consolidate. Their luck had lasted thus far, with the Germans' forward positions thinly held, but the next objective of the wooded slope to the west of Beugneux, bristling with enemy machine guns, was going to be an altogether tougher nut to crack. Having suffered relatively few casualties, progress was once again rapid, with the division crossing the east–west-running Grand Rozoy–Beugneux road at 0700 hrs across 100 yards of open ground towards the *Bois de Beugneux* on the slope beyond. German machine guns fired on the advancing Royal Sussex, resulted in a number of casualties and pinning them down. The first German counterattack commenced at 0730 hrs, preventing both the British and the French *25e Division* from advancing. Temporarily held up, a rethink was needed.

Second Lieutenant Read of the 4th Royal Sussex found a potential solution: a drainage ditch marking the boundary between two fields which led towards the wood, which might provide sufficient cover for him to get close enough to rush the machine guns. Taking three men with him, he crawled along the dry ditch to the edge of the wood and rushed a German machine gun, with Read shooting the gunner and Private Funnel, Read's batman, shooting the man supplying the ammunition.[37] Read was then joined by the remainder of his company, who carefully picked their way through the wood and up to the cornfield on the ridge above. Halting at the top of the ridge, he was able to observe the gently undulating plateau stretching for several kilometres in front of him, rising slightly in a northerly direction to a reverse slope beyond. He could see several groups of the Queens and French *poilus* to his immediate left making steady progress through the cornfields, but further ahead he spotted groups of Germans moving forward from a copse carrying heavy weapons. Unable to summon sufficient reinforcements to attack the enemy, the Germans were able to mount a counterattack with trench mortars, machine guns and heavy artillery, forcing the French, the Queens and the 4th Royal Sussex off the ridge and driving them down the hill and back across the road to the cover of an embankment, gathering wounded as they went. The casualties for the Royal Sussex had been severe, with the battalion now reduced to just six officers. Matters were made worse by the lack of ammunition, with Lewis gun pans in particularly short supply. But eventually they were able to cobble together eight Lewis guns, together with a captured German heavy machine gun and ammunition, to protect against further counterattacks. The troops from the French *25e Division* were now back on the wrong side of Grand Rozoy, forced out by the same German counterattack and joined by the Queens, who retired alongside them back to the GMP Line.[38]

At the same time to the east, Y Company of the 8th Scottish Rifles was 500 yards short of the railway station, where they were being held up by intense machine gun fire from *Côte 158*, taking heavy casualties and fearing that they would be unable to support the attack unless they could find a way to clear these enemy guns from the wooded hillock.[39] Some artillery support

---

36 TNA WO 95/2451: 34th Battalion, Machine Gun Corps, 29 July 1918.
37 Read, pp. 359-60.
38 Read, pp. 361-63.
39 Findlay, pp. 167-69.

arrived belatedly, firing on German machine gun positions in Beugneux and *Côte 158* for 40 minutes just after 0800 hrs, allowing the Scots to enter the village an hour or so later, where fierce street fighting ensued, with other elements of the battalion pushed up to the foot of *Côte 158* to attack the Germans dug in on the hill.

By 0915 hrs, 101st Brigade was reported to be holding a line north-west from Beugneux through *Côte 189*, with Grand Rozoy confirmed as having been captured by the French, the leading battalions having advanced more than a mile in short order. However, whilst *25e Division* had taken Grand Rozoy to the left around 1020 hrs, French troops from *11e Corps* to the right were nowhere to be seen; it emerged later that they did not commence their own attack until 0600 hrs, almost two hours late. The cause of this delay is not known and can only be speculated upon, but the result was that the line now ran from Grand Rozoy south-eastwards rather than west-to-east direction. An hour later, elements of the 2/4th Queens, 4th Royal Sussex, 2nd Loyal North Lancs and A Company, Machine Gun Battalion, were all attempting to hold a rather flimsy defensive flank 100 yards east of the Green Line, with outposts in front.[40] With the infantry still unable to communicate with the artillery to the rear, having fired off all of their Very lights by 0800 hrs, they could not call for additional artillery support to subdue the remaining enemy machine guns, which, despite every effort, still seemed to be active everywhere. The remaining German machine guns in the rear of the wood between the villages, in Beugneux itself and on *Côte 158* to the north began to take a severe toll on the attackers from both flanks, with B and D Companies and the Battalion HQ of 2nd Loyal North Lancs traversing left to support the faltering Queens, making an improvised flanking attack on both sides of *Côte 158* alongside the 8th Scottish Rifles. Runners from 2nd Loyal North Lancs would have to go back 3km across open country under constant fire to the Advanced Brigade Report Centre to pass on the message to lengthen the artillery range. It was decided that whilst they would give the order, the risks were high for the runners and Battalion HQ was not going to wait and see if they arrived at the artillery headquarters.

With his fellow battalion OC, Lieutenant Colonel Jourdain of the 2nd Loyal North Lancs, having been killed, Lieutenant Colonel E. Hill of 2/4th Queens was ordered to reorganise all troops in his vicinity and hold onto their present positions at all costs. Somewhat optimistically given his predicament, he was even told to prepare to counterattack the Germans should the opportunity arise.[41] Captain G.P. Atkinson, now in overall command of the 2nd Loyal North Lancs (although not informed of this until later), led a group of men through the woods in support of the Royal Sussex, clearing it and seizing the strategic crest of *Côte 189* north-west of Beugneux around 0740 hrs.[42] His task was made especially challenging, since it was the first time the men had made an attack whilst wearing their respirators, with tear gas lingering in the dense woodland. *Côte 189* was *the* key position along the attack front, since the ridge commanded the whole area as far as the heights of the Butte Chalmont to the south, the Germans having orders to hold both positions to the last.[43] With Beugneux and *Côte 158* being battered by heavy

---

40   TNA WO 95/2456: 101st Infantry Brigade Headquarters, 0915 and 1025 hrs, 29 July 1918.
41   TNA WO 95/2456: 101st Infantry Brigade Headquarters, 1100 hrs, 29 July 1918.
42   Shakespear, pp. 259-60.
43   The Butte Chalmont is the site of the *Les Fantômes*, a memorial sculpture by Paul Landowski unveiled in 1935, which faces north overlooking the battlefield. Landowski is most famous for his sculpture of Christ the Redeemer in Rio de Janeiro.

shelling, this allowed the Royal Sussex to penetrate as far as the road which ran north from Beugneux to Courdoux, but they too could get no further without additional much-needed artillery support. Exposed on the hilltop to severe enfilading German machine gun fire from the east, the Royal Sussex had little choice but to withdraw to the north-east edge of the wood. The Queens, meanwhile, could only advance part way up the slope north of the Beugneux woods, their line becoming dangerously overextended and in the wrong general direction (up the slope instead of across it). Just to the left (west), the remaining machine guns of D Company, 34th Battalion MGC, had been able to get forward quite successfully and were busy attempting to lay down suppressing fire from a cornfield 500 yards west of *Côte 158*, between 101st Brigade, 103rd Brigade and a line of unoccupied black huts. But the machine guns apart, it seemed that none of the infantry battalions were in contact with anyone to their left or right flanks: the Queens had been in brief contact with the Royal Sussex, but neither were in contact with the 2nd Loyal North Lancs on their right or the *25e Division* on their left, the French being bogged down attacking the heavily defended Grand Rozoy, contradicting earlier reports that it had been captured.[44] To the right of 103rd Brigade, the French *41e Division* was similarly struggling to make headway up the slope, enfiladed from both left and right and heavily shelled.

The 101st Brigade headquarters was back in the village of Oulchy-la-Ville, almost three miles behind the action and with little in the way of cover from enemy observation, making communication between headquarters and the front line both difficult and extremely dangerous. Worst of all, the distance between the two meant that it was too far and therefore too slow to get messages back quickly, especially those relating to the additional artillery support needed at this time or to request changes to the barrage, which had begun to go awry, shells falling onto their own front line.

When Lieutenant Colonel Findlay eventually managed to get a message back to the artillery, it was some time before the guns were ready to fire on the new targets. Nevertheless, the artillery eventually got underway, firing on the enemy defences and allowing the 8th Scottish Rifles to press forward and attack *Côte 158*. However, as soon as they did, it became evident that the barrage had been ineffective, with a number of enemy machine guns still active and causing Scottish casualties. Sensing the futility of further action, Findlay called a halt to the advance and ordered his men to take whatever cover they could find. Shortly after giving the order to hold their positions, a German *minenwerfer* shell hit his Command Post, killing his Intelligence Officer Lieutenant Johnnie Miller and badly wounding his Adjutant, Innes.[45] Findlay spotted the Argylls moving up to support his Scottish Rifles, but believing that reinforcement of the line (which was already held up) was the wrong course of action, he urged a different tack. He felt that a flanking movement to the north or south of Beugneux to turn the village was more likely to succeed. In order to instigate this, he needed to be in contact with the *41e Division* on his right, but the French were nowhere to be seen. In spite of the absence of the French, mounting casualties and being under heavy machine gun fire, units of the 8th Scottish Rifles managed to force their way to the foot of the hill, with the 5th KOSBs to their left passing round the north-west of the village of Beugneux, up through the woods and well up the slope of

---

44 Shakespear, p. 260; TNA WO 95/2467: 4th Royal Sussex, reported withdrawing to the edge of the wood around 0700 hrs. See also TNA WO 95/2451: 34th Battalion, Machine Gun Corps, 29 July 1918.
45 Findlay, p. 169.

Côte 189, gaining touch with parts of A and C Companies, 2nd Loyal North Lancs, and three companies of the 5th Argylls sent to reinforce the firing line between the wood and the village, and the other company dispatched up the west end of the *Bois de Beugneux* itself.[46]

To the left, the *25e Division* finally captured Grand Rozoy by 1020 hrs, but any efforts to capture Beugneux itself had faltered, 101st Brigade barely managing to hold a defensive line 100 yards east of the Green Line, with a few posts of 2nd Loyal North Lancs under the command of Captain Atkinson pushed forward on high ground north of the wood west of Beugneux. Upon being informed that Lieutenant Colonel Jourdain had been killed, Atkinson went back to get a first-hand situation report and be briefed on the dispositions of his remaining forces.

By mid-morning, General Nicholson began to sense that the attack was on a knife-edge, precariously poised between gaining his objectives and the disaster of being forced back by a German counterattack, with the advance currently at a standstill. Troops from 103rd Brigade were inside Beugneux attempting to clear the village; there was information that 101st Brigade held the wood to the west of the village and it was consolidating on the GMP Line, but the men were now badly bunched up into pockets of infantry, rather than in extended lines, with problems aplenty of keeping in contact with their left and right and some even facing in the wrong direction. Some infantry were observed retreating, which added to the confusion, and No.3 Section, A Company, Machine Gun Corps was sent forward under Second Lieutenant Pugh to a new position just left of the *Bois de Montceau* to cover any retirement.[47] By 1050 hrs, the attack was almost at a dead stop, with the line extending from the Grand Rozoy–Beugneux road to two houses on the south-west edge of Beugneux, the division having a tenuous fingerhold in the village itself. Ten minutes later, Nicholson issued orders to the divisional reserves (102nd Brigade plus the 2/4th Somersets and No.3 and 4 Sections of B Company, Machine Gun Corps) to occupy the Vers–Soissons railway defence line and reinforce and reinvigorate the attack by outflanking Beugneux by the west and taking it from west and north-west, before pushing on towards the Brown Line. The Machine Gun Corps was already moving forward in artillery formation towards the rear of the attacking infantry of 102nd Brigade and arrived in the GMP Line just after noon, with orders to consolidate and prepare to support the attack, whilst also being ready to withstand any German counterattacks that might develop. The Section Commander of No.3 Section, B Company, was killed whilst moving into position, with the section's sergeant put in charge.

If Nicholson reinforced the attack with additional infantry, he might still force the enemy to retire, meaning that a breakthrough was still possible and he would carry the day. Weighing up the various options available to him, which included consolidating the gains made on the current positions, he decided that it was the right time to gamble and thus ordered 102nd Brigade, the 2/4th Somersets and a company of 16 machine guns into battle to press on towards their objective, with the attack set to resume at 1430 hrs. But 20 minutes beforehand, the Germans launched a heavy counterattack with artillery, *minenwerfers* and numerous machine guns supporting their infantry, driving the advanced troops and the French on either flank back

---

46 TNA WO 95/2465: 103rd Infantry Brigade Headquarters.
47 TNA WO 95/2451: 34th Battalion, Machine Gun Corps, 29 July 1918.

to the GMP Line, the machine guns retiring to defensive positions on the front edge of the *Bois du Montceau* and the 5th Argylls conforming to this order.[48]

On the face of it, the delay of several hours appears to have been the main reason for the failure of the attack, allowing the Germans vital time to prepare their own counter-attack. Was it the British simply being too cautious at a time when prompt action was needed? Whilst it would take time for the support troops to reach the front line from their positions in the *Bois de la Baillette* and there were three battalions to co-ordinate, it had taken longer than anticipated for them to complete the movement. Had Nicholson received reports of heavy casualties or the failure of *68e Division* to come up on his right, or was he simply complying with *30e Corps'* orders, worried that after the performance on the 23rd, failure to accord with his superiors might result in censure? It was certainly true that there was still plenty of daylight to permit a resumption of the attack, so maybe he wanted to receive further reports first? Throwing all of his reserves into the resumption of the attack in the hope that it would be decisive was a high-risk strategy because if it failed or if the Germans counterattacked (as they surely would), General Penet might release the corps reserves, but he just as easily might not and there was nothing else available. Likewise, if he pushed them in too early with the picture still unclear, then he risked causing unnecessary casualties, which could not be easily replaced.

On the ground, time was rapidly ebbing away in which to press their advantage, and events were already overtaking Nicholson's ability to react, with the situation quickly deteriorating for the attackers and all momentum risked being squandered. The advance had been so rapid that the infantry had overran the barrage, and French and British artillery now began shelling their own positions, with runners unable to get messages back to the guns quickly enough to prevent a number of casualties. An alternative hypothesis was that some of the shells began dropping short of their target, but whatever the cause, 103rd Brigade began to take casualties, forcing the Scots to retreat to a safe distance. As early as 0800 hrs, D Company of the 5th KOSBs had been driven out of its positions by this 'friendly fire', and a further barrage at 1300 hrs, put down by the French to the rear of the front line, compounded the problems.[49] To the east, the men from the Queens stretched up the hill towards *Côte 189*, not along it as intended. Their unexpected advance, well ahead of other units, now meant the 4th Royal Sussex, 2nd Loyal North Lancs – with Captain Atkinson and his remaining men – and a small group from the 5th KOSBs would have to hold this precarious position for the remainder of the day, knowing that the Germans, determined to wrest back control, would inevitably counterattack. The rest of the 5th KOSBs, together with the 8th Scottish Rifles, had been held up in front of Beugneux and *Côte 158*, and they in turn were still not in touch with the *68e Division* of the French *11e Corps* on their right. The situation was becoming increasingly confused and rapidly spiralling out of control.

The fierce fighting had reduced the defenders from the German 19th Ersatz Division to just 1,000 effectives, which due to its combat losses and confusion had lost touch with the 40th Infantry Division holding Beugneux and the woods to the west. Nevertheless, a hastily organised German counterattack by two regiments of fresh troops from the Guards Ersatz Division between Beugneux woods and Grand Rozoy, together with continuing enfilade machine gun fire and German field artillery guns firing salvoes at point-blank range from *Côte*

---

48 TNA WO 95/2436: General Staff, 34th Division, narrative of operations with *Xe* French Army, events of 28–29 July. See also, TNA WO 95/2451: 34th Battalion, Machine Gun Corps, 29 July 1918.
49 Scott Elliot, p. 246. TNA WO 95/2466: 5th KOSBs, 29 July 1918.

189, proved a decisive moment. They forced the hand of Captain Middleton and the 4th Royal Sussex, who found it necessary to withdraw their line back down the hill to the relative safety of the south side of the Grand Rozoy–Beugneux road at around 1410 hrs, with the French *25e Division* also abandoning Grand Rozoy. In spite of being behind the protection of a small bank on the south side of the road, it was too small to offer much cover. Men of the Queens were frantically digging, being urged on by an injured officer who was wounded in both arm and leg by shrapnel. However, even here things were scarcely any safer for the men, with enemy machine guns continuing to enfilade these new positions from both flanks, forcing them to withdraw a second time to the GMP Line, just north of the *Bois du Montceau*, where they dug in and consolidated their positions. The German infantry, having crossed to the south side of the road in pursuit of the retiring British forces, withdrew at 1600 hrs into the cover of the wood.[50]

Shortly after 1330 hrs, the 2/4th Somerset Light Infantry, transferred from Divisional Reserve and attached to 102nd Brigade, together with the 7th Cheshires and a company of the 34th Machine Gun Battalion, received their orders to restart the attack at 1430 hrs, with the objective of capturing Beugneux. Unfortunately for the Somersets, they were nowhere near the starting line, and despite setting off as quickly as they could, they failed to arrive in time to take advantage of the artillery barrage laid down in front of them. In any event, their efforts were redundant, the Germans massing on the ridge east of Grand Rozoy and counterattacking down the hill 15 minutes before the attack was set to go in. This intervention was fortunate for the 7th Cheshires, who according to reports from the 2/4th Somersets, were not in a fit condition to take part in the attack anyway. In spite of engaging the enemy with Lewis and machine guns, the whole line was observed to be falling back and the attack was immediately postponed without it ever commencing, all units consolidating back on the GMP Line, the point from where the attack had been launched.[51] Captain Atkinson, now commanding the remnants of the 2nd Loyal North Lancs, was able to hold the advanced positions until 1400 hrs, when enfilading fire from German machine guns also forced him to retire. The after-action report for 102nd Brigade concluded that the attack had broken down because it had been given insufficient notice and had failed to keep pace with the barrage. But the war diary of 103rd Brigade is clear who it blamed for the failure, stating that firstly the French, then 102nd Brigade fell back, leaving the 8th Scottish Rifles and 5th Argylls completely in the air, Colonel Findlay left with no option but to order his men to conform to the movement and fall back on the Paris Line; Lieutenant Richardson of the 5th KOSBs also ordered his men to retire, returning to their positions in considerable confusion and suffering further casualties as they withdrew. Initially, only 220 men of the 5th KOSBs could be accounted for, but steadily more men began to dribble in, many having become mixed up with other units during the fighting, and eventually the KOSBs could muster 330 all ranks, with almost two-thirds of the battalion having become casualties.[52]

At 1300 hrs, the remaining 50 troops from A Company, 2nd Loyal North Lancs, advanced to reoccupy a spur on *Côte 189*, but the counterattacking Germans beat them to it, killing or

---

50   TNA WO 95/2458: 4th Royal Sussex, 0800 hrs, 29 July 1918. TNA WO 95/2442: Commander Royal Artillery, 29 July 1918. TNA WO 95/2462: 7th Cheshires, report on the operations extending from 22 July to 2 August 1918.
51   TNA WO 95/2451: 2/4th Somerset Light Infantry, 29 July 1918 and WO 95/2462: 4th Cheshires, Brief account of operations from 22 July to 2 August 1918.
52   TNA WO 95/2466: 5th KOSBs, 29 July 1918.

capturing the two Lewis gun teams holding the position, it having been vacated earlier due to friendly fire shelling. Having lost this position, Captain Atkinson ordered the remnants of 2nd Loyal North Lancs and the Argylls – around 200 rifles in total – to throw out a defensive line, but this too was enfiladed from both flanks, making the new line untenable and forcing a second withdrawal shortly after. At 1340 hrs, a message was received by Atkinson (sent at 1145 hrs) from OC, 101st Brigade, stating that 102nd Brigade would attack Beugneux at 1230 hrs. Being certain that no such attack had actually taken place, Atkinson ordered the remaining men to withdraw under cover of the wood between Grand Rozoy and Beugneux to Grand Rozoy station, where it re-assembled and reorganised, with just six officers and 230 other ranks available.[53]

With the French *68e Division* of the neighbouring *11e Corps* to their immediate right also failing to get forward, and a number of *poilus* from *25e Division* on their left driven out of the *Bois de la Terre à l'Or* and then out of Grand Rozoy by a fierce mid-afternoon German counterattack which included hand-to-hand fighting, the order was given for a general withdrawal. This initially forced the Royal Sussex and 2nd Loyal North Lancs back to the south side of the Grand Rozoy–Beugneux road, before another bout of German shelling led to them and several of the machine gunners withdrawing to the second GMP Line, 600 yards to the rear, between 1430 and 1500 hrs, halfway back to the jumping-off line. These moves allowed a brief respite in order to reorganise and form a defensive line but forced Nicholson to abandon his plans to resume the attack. Beugneux had changed hands three times during the day, but like the Scots to the north at Buzancy, the 34th Division had been unable to retain possession of the village for more than a few hours. At 1655 hrs, 152nd Brigade RFA reported from its observation post in the *Bois de Montceau* that whilst the GMP line was strongly held, there were no troops east of it.[54]

There is little doubt that many of the men would have been hugely disappointed by having to withdraw from what looked like a winning position.[55] Here, Findlay is critical of the 5th KOSBs, describing the remnants of the battalion as "melting away", rather than halting on a line to support his Scottish Rifles and "stop the rot". But he does concede that not all men did this. Many were wounded and some continued to maintain their positions as long as they were able. But perhaps the die was cast much earlier, with Edmonds commenting that the halt on the intermediate line for almost an hour during the first couple of hours of the attack was a mistake, since it allowed the Germans to bring up reinforcements, with all subsequent attacks being immediately counterattacked by the Germans.[56] Maybe the 34th Division was a victim of its own success, having captured the first objective so quickly (quicker than anticipated) that it felt it ought to stick to the timings and use the time to consolidate before pushing on? It certainly didn't want to risk walking into its own barrage, which would simply result in unnecessary casualties.

53 TNA WO 95/2457: 2nd Loyal North Lancs, record of operations of the 2nd Battalion Loyal North Lancashire Regiment from 23 July to 4 August 1918.
54 TNA WO 95/2442: Commander Royal Artillery 34th Division, 29 July 1918 and TNA WO 95/2451: 34th Battalion, Machine Gun Corps, 29 July 1918.
55 TNA WO 95/2461: 102nd Infantry Brigade Headquarters, 29 July 1918 and TNA WO 95/2465: 103rd Infantry Brigade Headquarters, 29 July 1918. See also, TNA WO 95/2466: 5th KOSBs, 29 July 1918.
56 Findlay, p. 169 and Edmonds, p. 284.

With Nicholson's troops now withdrawn a safe distance, British and French guns pounded the German positions in the village and the heights beyond (but with some shells falling short onto Allied lines), and by nightfall an outpost was established from the western foot of *Côte 158* to the Beugneux–Grand Rozoy road and west to the French line to the south of Grand Rozoy.[57] In order to minimise casualties, the 2nd Loyal North Lancs took up position 300 yards south of the line close to the station at Grand Rozoy in a new trench line they dug overnight, only moving back to the front line the following morning. With the patchy success of the participants leading to variable amounts of advance, *30e Corps*' line ran in a rather wavy fashion from *Bois de la Terre à l'Or* along the road to Grand Rozoy, through the north of the village. It then twisted southwards to a line 100 yards south of the road from Grand Rozoy to Beugneux as far as the eastern edge of the wood between the villages, through several stone buildings on the lower slope of *Côte 158* and along the south side of the Beugneux–Cramaille road.[58] At 1800 hrs, a German officer from the 6th Guard Infantry Regiment was captured just east of Beugneux and marched off to be interrogated. An hour later, verbal orders were given to the three brigade majors and the machine gun battalions to be reorganised, with all three being in the front line: 103rd Brigade on the right, 102nd Brigade in the centre and 101st Brigade on the left; each brigade was supported by a company of machine gunners but there was just one reserve battalion per brigade behind the line in the GMP Line, the 4th Cheshires being withdrawn to the safety of a ravine as Divisional Reserve.[59] The 5th Argylls, with a number of their officers still absent, either on leave or sick in hospital, had been pretty heavily mauled, losing three officers and 11 other ranks killed and 10 officers and 193 other ranks wounded. How much the late arrival of their CO and dearth of experienced officers had influenced their endeavours is difficult to say, but it cannot have helped their cause. It seems slightly odd that Lieutenant Colonel Barlow should allow Major Agnew (who had been commanding the battalion in Barlow's absence) to proceed on home leave on 31 July, especially given the fierce fighting and the heavy officer casualties suffered by the 5th Argylls, with just six officers and just 260 other ranks able to commence the attack the following morning.[60] There must have been an understanding between the senior battalion officers that when their turn for leave came, it would be honoured.

Shortly after dark, the remaining French troops were seen to walk out of Grand Rozoy and back across the road towards the Château-Thierry–Bethune (Soissons) road, despite there being no obvious German effort to evict them. The British who witnessed the French actions that evening (including Captain Atkinson of the 2nd Loyal North Lancs, who immediately informed 101st Brigade HQ)[61] were both perplexed and disheartened by what they saw, with some believing the French lacked the necessary fighting spirit. This, however, was not some defeatist move by the French. By this point in the war, they had learned an important and bitterly won lesson, whereby the Germans would either counterattack to recapture lost ground

57 Shakespear, pp. 260–61.
58 TNA WO 95/2436: General Staff, 34th Division, Operation Order No.241 and Shakespear, pp. 261-62.
59 TNA WO 95/2436: General Staff, 34th Division, Summary of operations and intelligence, 30 July 1918.
60 TNA WO 95/2466: 5th Argylls, 29 July-1 August 1918.
61 TNA WO 95/2457: 2nd Loyal North Lancs, Record of operations of the 2nd Battalion Loyal North Lancashire Regiment from 23 July to 4 August 1918.

or if it was towards the end of the day, would bombard French-held positions overnight, causing heavy casualties. By withdrawing to a safe distance and leaving a scattering of sentries in forward outposts, any shells would simply hit empty buildings but cause few casualties. But since the 34th Division's infantry (unlike the artillery) had no experience of fighting alongside the French on the Western Front and had not previously seen them make this orderly withdrawal overnight, many believed the French were wrong to leave their positions that they had fought so hard to capture, and none of this did anything to create an *esprit de corps* between the two belligerents.

So despite all their combined effort and endeavour, neither the British nor the French on either flank had made more than a few metres of progress yet had suffered heavy casualties throughout the fighting. Losses were estimated at 1,100 men for *25e Division* and more than 2,000 for the British.[62] Digging in on the GMP Line that night, which included a new trench for the support companies, the weary and dejected men began to take stock of the events of the day and briefly pondered what they could have done differently. Second Lieutenant Read of the 4th Royal Sussex described feeling deeply resentful of the way in which things had been bungled, with communications having completely broken down and support from 102nd Brigade failing to arrive.[63] But with the GMP Line being the obvious place for shelter and therefore a target for enemy shelling, German mustard gas shells began landing soon after nightfall and continued almost unbroken through the night, resulting in some casualties and little in the way of much-needed rest.[64] Yet in spite of their obvious disappointment at this latest setback, they had in fact inflicted severe casualties on the Germans, weakening them to a now critical level. A captured officer of the 6th Guard Infantry Regiment later revealed that his regiment had been reduced to just one officer and 136 other ranks.[65] The French *11e Corps* finally captured the remainder of Butte Chalmont, with this significant hill giving them a commanding and uninterrupted view both north and east. Forces from *VIe Armée* also made progress, gaining a footing in Fère-en-Tardenois as well as crossing the brook between it and Cierges, whilst to the east *Ve Armée* finally occupied the positions it had lost during the fighting on the 15th, a delighted Fayolle telegraphing his armies to urge them on: "The moment has come to gather the fruits of our counteroffensive that has lasted ten days. Forward, no matter how tired the troops are!"[66] It can't have been lost on the French high command that it had taken them 10 days to recapture what the Germans had taken two days to sieze in the first place, and it was going to take a lot more days of heavy fighting and effort to realise their goal of crushing the salient entirely.

62   TNA WO 95/2436: General Staff, 34th Division, Narrative of operations with Xe French Army, events of 28–29 July. AFGG, 30e Corps, 29 July 1918.
63   Read, p. 365.
64   A handwritten note on the back of the Operational Order of late on 29 July states: "At 12:45 the 5th Argylls managed to gain touch with the French at Point 118."
65   TNA WO 95/2436: General Staff, 34th Division, summary of operations and intelligence, 30 July 1918.
66   Code Telegram from Fayolle to his army commanders, No. 1.377/M, 2033 hrs on 27 July 1918 cited in *Woldike*, pp. 53, 162.

14

One more push to finally break the defenders?

Liaison overnight with the French on either flank was still proving extremely problematic, with *41e Division* to the right of 103rd Brigade believed to be dug in 400 yards south of *Côte 158*, but this was by no means guaranteed. A signal was issued at 2000 hrs that evening for the line to be advanced along the entire divisional sector overnight, with strong patrols pushed out in the darkness to probe the German lines. Lieutenant Colonel Kendrick commanding the 34th Machine Gun Corps, also ordered all of his available guns to move to positions along Ridge 836 as soon as the front battalions had moved forward, in order to support the advance if required. This order was signed by Lieutenant Colonel Dooner, GSO1 of the division, and is the last entry before he was killed by shellfire the next day.[1] With heavy casualties on both the 23rd and 29th, some reorganisation and switching of battalions in the front line was necessary: the 2nd Loyal North Lancs went to 101st Brigade's area and relieved the 4th Cheshires, who in turn moved into 102nd Brigade to relieve the 2/4th Somerset's, taking over a line of coffin trenches, the Somersets being withdrawn into Divisional Reserve in the *Bois de la Baillette*. That evening, 103rd Brigade was ordered to make another attempt to establish a line of advanced posts and to connect with *206RI* from the French *68e Division* on their right, with 101st Brigade ordered to do the same with the *98RI* (*25e Division*) on their left.[2] To the obvious frustration of General Penet, it is clear that there were still significant difficulties maintaining close liaison with the French on either flank and barely any evidence that the situation was improving, and he stressed that success could only come with constant liaison between the French and British attackers on their respective flanks; there was still much work to do to improve the situation.

Between 23 and 31 July, the 7th Cheshires had lost four officers killed and seven wounded, including their commander Lieutenant Colonel Moir, as well as 262 other ranks casualties. The sheer number of 7th Cheshire casualties left General Nicholson with little choice but to place the battalion into his divisional reserve on 1 August.[3] The casualties for the 2nd Loyal North Lancs had arguably been worse, having too lost its CO, Lieutenant Colonel Jourdain,

---

1 TNA WO 95/2436: General Staff, 34th Division, Operation Order No. 239, 29 July 1918 dictated at 1855 hrs, issued at 2140 hrs; GS286/70, 29 July 1918. TNA WO 95/2465: 103rd Infantry Brigade Headquarters, Signal BM180, 2000 hrs, 29 July 1918.
2 TNA WO 95/2436: General Staff, 34th Division, Operation Order No. 240, 1945 hrs, 30 July 1918. TNA WO 95/2462: 4th Cheshires, brief account of operations from 22 July to 2 August 1918.
3 TNA WO 95/2462: 7th Cheshires, Report on the operations extending from 22 July to 2 August 1918.

killed and Captain A.F.P. Knapp, his second-in-command, wounded, but fortunately not badly and able to continue at his post. Jourdain's replacement, Captain Atkinson, was amongst the walking wounded, together with Captain G.R. Brockbank and Second Lieutenants J.A. Mercer and C.G. Nightingale, but Lieutenant H.P. Soppitt, Adjutant J.B. Martindale (who died of his wounds on 1 August), Lieutenants H.B. Leonard and H. Wilkinson, Second Lieutenant E.W.W. Brown and Company Sergeant Major Owen Jones were all wounded and would take no further part in the fighting. A further 31 other ranks had been killed or died of wounds, with another 149 wounded and 21 reported missing. With such heavy casualties to both officers and men, Nicholson also put the 2nd Loyal North Lancs into divisional reserve on the 30th but hoped that it would prove to be a purely temporary measure. Captain R.V. Taylor and 80 other ranks arrived on the evening of the 31st from the Divisional Reinforcement Camp at Largny, a much-welcome addition to the depleted battalion, the injection swelling its ranks to seven officers and 380 other ranks.[4] The losses of the 2nd Loyal North Lancs is in stark contrast to the 22 casualties suffered by the 2/4th Somersets, which had spent much of the day in divisional reserve and had been unable to get up to support the attack; the slowness of action would have to be addressed by Nicholson.[5] Overnight, a heavy mustard gas bombardment of the 8th Scottish Rifles' positions on the GMP Line resulted in a number of casualties, with many men exposed to the gas whilst sleeping. By midday the following day, there were 19 casualties requiring hospital treatment for severe gas poisoning, including Lieutenant Colonel Findlay, Lieutenant Lyle, Sergeant Major W. Gray and Sergeant Wylie, with Gray succumbing to his injuries. All of the gas casualties were evacuated by ambulance to 63 Casualty Clearing Station at Senlis, before being transported by train to No.2 Red Cross Hospital, Rouen, with Captain W. Whigham Ferguson, MC, taking temporary command of the 8th Scottish Rifles on 30 July, before Acting Major G.R.V. Hume-Gore arrived from leave to take command at 2200 hrs on the 31st.[6]

By putting 102nd Brigade together with the 2/4th Somersets and his heavy machine gun reserves into action, Nicholson had gambled his hand, playing what he believed would be a decisive card. He had calculated that by adding his remaining reserves to the attack, he would be able to drive the enemy out of Beugneux and back off the ridge above and collect his winnings from this massive gamble. But on this occasion his hand was not strong enough, the mid-morning halt allowing valuable time for his opponent to reinforce his positions, combined with the crucial delay in getting his own reinforcements up to the line. In reality it was the Germans who held the winning hand, launching their strong counter-attack to drive the attackers back at exactly the right moment, recapturing Grand Rozoy from the French, retaining possession of Beugneux and the ridge above and forcing the French and British to withdraw, bloodied and having suffered heavy casualties. Any chance of success had also been fatally undermined when his own artillery began shelling his positions, allied to the failure of the French *68e Division* to get forward on his right. Thus for a third time Beugneux had resisted every effort to capture it, both attackers and defenders suffering heavy losses in the process. Although the village itself was nothing out of the ordinary, the stone buildings being a typically solid obstacle, its location

---

4   TNA WO 95/2457: 2nd Loyal North Lancs, record of operations of the 2nd Battalion Loyal North Lancashire Regiment from 23 July to 4 August 1918.
5   TNA WO 95/2451: 2/4th Somerset Light Infantry, 29 July 1918.
6   Findlay, pp. 171-74. Findlay was temporarily blinded by the mustard gas and his face and head badly blistered.

at the foot of the ridge made it the key strategic position that would unlock the ridge to the rear of the village. The Germans, perfectly understanding the strategic importance of this hill and having been ordered to retain the ridge at all costs, would not cede its control without one hell of a fight, and they weren't done yet.

Having received written permission from the Kaiser to withdraw his troops on the 23rd, Ludendorff was still refusing to face the reality in front of him and had to be persuaded by Crown Prince Wilhelm to proceed with the retirement to the *Blücher Stelling*. The German Crown Prince pointed out that he only had 13 exhausted and weak divisions in line compared to the 23 he had started with. Wilhelm also reiterated that he would need 17 divisions to hold this new position long enough to allow an orderly retirement of the German forces still in the Marne salient. Ludendorff retorted that he didn't have to be told by the Crown Prince how difficult the manpower situation was; he could see it for himself!

Elsewhere on Mangin's front, there had been more success, with the *69e Division* spearheading an attack to capture ground close to Soissons, advancing towards Le Pentes and Vauxbuin and putting the city under imminent threat of being recaptured by the French. He also withdrew into reserve the *48e Division*, which had been heavily mauled and reduced to being combat ineffective, with the *127e* and *17e divisions* due to arrive later that day.[7]

In spite of the progress made by *Xe Armée*, especially in the period between 18 and the 23 July, Pétain grew increasingly concerned by the limited success since the 23rd, worried that if Mangin was struggling to make headway, with fierce resistance by an enemy who appeared determined to hang on to the territory whatever the cost, then the grand counteroffensive needed a rethink. This view was reinforced by the fact that the Germans had established themselves on the high ground of the ridge and 15 days of heavy fighting had failed to dislodge them. There were growing signs too that extreme fatigue and continued heavy casualties were becoming major factors amongst the Allies. Pétain therefore decided to shift the main emphasis to the south and east, with *Xe Armée* advancing towards Arcy-Sainte-Restitue and Braine alongside *VIe Armée*, which would now be the focus of effort. To make matters worse for Mangin, Pétain confirmed that he could not be further reinforced, with troops needed more urgently elsewhere. The Commander-in-Chief ordered that he did not yet want *1er CA* to attack Soissons, even though they were virtually at the city gates, with only local mopping-up attacks to take place, believing that the Germans would simply decide that retaining Soissons was untenable and evacuate the city in due course, resulting in fewer casualties than a street-to-street urban battle. Although it was no consolation to 'The Butcher', Pétain also informed Berthelot that he could not be reinforced, and worse, that he would have to release the two divisions from XXII Corps – 51st (Highland) and 62nd (West Riding) Divisions – back to the British by the end of the month. The two in Mangin's *Xe Armée* – the 15th (Scottish) and 34th Divisions – were also mooted for imminent departure, and with the loss of American divisions back to Pershing's command, the *Xe* and *Ve Armées* were now likely to be too weak to make the main attacks, necessitating this different approach he now suggested. Degoutte in contrast, still had four American divisions under his command, with the double-strength 28th and 42nd divisions in line. Consistent with his previous messages, but contradicting Foch, Pétain concluded his correspondence saying that

---

7 Greenwood, p. 164. Zabecki, *The Generals' War* (Indiana University Press, 2018) states the Germans had 23 divisions between Soissons and Reims, with eight in reserve.

Fayolle and Maistre, his army group commanders, must employ their forces methodically and leave their reserves intact, sparing more casualties. This, he said, would ensure that the enemy would not be able to make sudden counterattacks whilst retaining sufficient infantry for future operations. A further letter to Foch crystallised his feelings on the current situation, stating that 58 French divisions had been engaged in the fighting in the Marne salient, with only a single fresh reserve division available to reinforce the line. French casualties had been heavy, losing 120,000 men in the infantry alone, with just 19,000 reinforcements available to Pétain and maybe another 29,000 after that, but these would only arrive in the next two or three months. He now intended the British, having had three months of very little fighting, and the Americans, now arriving in vast numbers, to take up the baton and take the fight to the Germans further north, with their renewed attacks to start in a few days.[8] To Foch it was just the same old Pétain: pessimistic, negative and too conservative. But when Fayolle weighed in, making a similar complaint and requesting that Foch allow him some breathing space, he paused for a moment, surprised at the comments from his long-standing friend who was certainly more in the mould of Foch than the Commander-in-Chief. However, he still rebuffed him, saying that although Fayolle's troops were dropping with fatigue, the Germans were doing so even more.[9]

Just as they had walked out of the village the previous night, the French walked back in and recaptured Grand Rozoy without opposition by 0600 hrs on the 30th, almost without a shot being fired, the Germans having themselves vacated the village in the early hours.[10] This was a huge bonus to the British to the immediate east of Grand Rozoy on two counts: firstly, by securing their left flank, the French had removed a potentially dangerous situation, preventing the enemy enfilade; and secondly, seeing them return to the fight helped to restore confidence in the fighting spirit of their French comrades. Although there was a noticeable lull on the 30th, hostile aeroplanes were particularly active, firing on the French and British lines, but at the cost of German flying ace Lieutenant Heinrich Drekmann in his Pfalz D. III biplane, shot down in the evening moments after he had shot down his 11th and final victim, a French SPAD belonging to *Escadrille 278*. The pilot, Corporal Adolphe Cabouillet (*Croix de Guerre*), and his 25-year-old observer, Lieutenant Albert Rapilly (*Croix de Guerre* and *Médaille Militaire*), had been returning from a reconnaissance mission behind German lines when they were intercepted by Drekmann over Grand Rozoy and crashed near the *Bois de la Terre à l'Or*, north-east of the village. A monument to Cabouillet and Rapilly was erected on the northern edge of Grand Rozoy to commemorate the fallen French aviators. Twenty-two-year-old Drekmann, from Harburg in northern Germany, was from a family of flyers, with two other brothers also being in the German Air Force, while he had been a member of von Richthofen's 'Flying Circus'.[11]

According to *30e Corps*' diary, the *25e Division* captured 14 officers and 484 men, the 34th Division capturing one officer and 81 other ranks, the Germans belonging to four different

---

8   Greenwood, pp. 165-67 and Zabecki states this letter was 31 July, not the 29th.
9   Greenwood, p. 172.
10   TNA WO 95/2436: General Staff, 34th Division, narrative of operations with *Xe* French Army, events of 30-31 July 1918 and Read, p. 367.
11   TNA WO 95/2451: 34th Battalion, Machine Gun Corps, 30 July 1918 and Franks, Norman, Bailey, Frank and Guest, Russell, *Above the Lines – The Ace and Fighter Units of German Air Service, Naval Air Service and Flanders Marine Corps 1914–1918* (London: Grub Street, 1993); Twitter <https://twitter.com/ron_eisele/status/1246563917222023169/photo/1>

divisions.¹² Many of the German prisoners who had been captured during the fighting on the 29th needed little persuasion to talk about conditions and recent events and revealed important information. They had been warned at 2200 hrs on the 28th that a French assault was planned for the following morning and that it was expected to come from further north. As a consequence, the 7th Guard Infantry Regiment had its three battalions in line, facing north towards the expected direction of attack, and was forced to quickly change positions when the attack commenced from a southerly direction. Crucially, the German prisoners revealed that manpower was at crisis levels, with one company only 80-strong and others as weak as 40 all ranks, having suffered heavy gas casualties earlier in the month which had not been replaced, most companies being amalgamated into composite units due to low strength. Another prisoner reported that morale too was extremely low. The 19th Ersatz Division had become so depleted by casualties that it was totally withdrawn on the 31st, with the Guards Ersatz Division replacing it in the line.¹³ The reduced strength also meant that there were no German *minenwerfer* in line in front of the British and only four machine guns per company. If anything, the position for the German artillery was even worse, the 47th Ersatz Field Artillery Regiment of the 19th Ersatz Division only in possession of 10 working 7.7in field guns on the ridge above Grand Rozoy and Beugneux, but these had been so heavily shelled during the attack that they were unable to open fire. Yet not everything was negative for the Germans, with the prisoners captured from the Bavarian and Guard Ersatz divisions still reporting strong morale amongst the troops. One thing, however, was unanimous amongst the prisoners: none of them spoke of any intended German offensives on this or any other part of the Western Front, and this important fact would need to be relayed back up the chain of command.¹⁴

12   AFGG, 30e Corps, 29 July 1918.
13   Takle, p. 238.
14   TNA WO 95/2436: General Staff, 34th Division, summary of operations and intelligence, 29 July 1918.

15

30-31 July: Time for a rethink?

General Pétain had been dissatisfied with events of 29 July, not just in *Xe Armée* but across the whole front, with only *VIe Armée* – together with the right of *Xe Armée* (having slightly extended their positions on the Butte Chalmont) – escaping significant criticism. The French Commander-in-Chief issued a new instruction to the five armies attacking the Marne salient, modifying the focus of attack. He did, however, recognise that much of *Xe Armée*, notably *30e* and *11e Corps*, was at the very limit of endurance, warning his army group commanders to ensure the methodical use of forces in order to spare the infantry as much as possible.[1] Pétain wrote:

> The enemy appears to be too strongly established on the plateaux south of Soissons and on the heights between the [River] Vesle and the [River] Ardre to admit of any hope that these two pillars of resistance can be broken and the German forces south of the [River] Aisne be destroyed. Henceforward our aim must be to hustle their retreat so as to upset their plans of evacuation and devastation of the country, and to hasten the moment when the Marne railway can be made ready again for traffic. The *VIe Armée* which now possesses the largest resources is charged with the principal role. It will push forward vigorously without interruption on its whole front in the general direction of Fismes and Bazoches, its left establishing itself in the Saponay area, so as to facilitate the advance of the right of the *Xe Armée* towards Cramaille. From midnight of the 29th/30th the *VIe Armée* will take over the *3e Corps*, the left of the *Ve Armée*, so that the boundary between the Groups of Armies of the Centre and Reserve will be Verneil–Saint-Gemme and then northwards to the east of Fismes. *Xe Armée* cannot count on any more reinforcements after receiving the *17e Division*, [and] will continue to act in the direction of Braine. It will make its principal effort with its right; but the centre will participate in the movement so as to occupy progressively the heights on the left bank of the [River] Crise. *Ve Armée* cannot count on any reinforcements either and must also release the British XXII Corps on the 31st, [and] will act preferably south of the Ardre northwards on the axis Lagery–Crugny, so as to support the right of *VIe*

---

1   Woldike, p. 56; Letter No.38.770 from Pétain to Fayolle and Maistre, 29 July 1918 cited in Woldike, p. 170, and Letter No. 1512/M, 1750 hrs on 31 July 1918 cited in Woldike, p. 173.

Armée. The commanders of Groups of Armies are requested to see that the forces are methodically employed, [and] to insist that each Army engaged is echeloned in depth so as to facilitate the employment of reserves and to guard against enemy action, which might entirely compromise our advance by a counter-offensive suddenly launched either between [the Rivers] Oise and Aisne, or against the Reims salient.[2]

Ever the pragmatist, Pétain recognised that the stubborn enemy resistance meant that he was no longer able to cut off the Germans in the *poche*, and consequently changed the focus away from Mangin's *Xe Armée* on the western flank and Berthelot's *Ve Armée* on the eastern flank towards the south of the now dwindling salient, with additional support for *VIe Armée*, which would take up the baton of leading the fight. His natural caution is also very evident, being anxious that the Germans might still counterattack, not helped by the grudging acceptance that the British XXII Corps would soon have to be withdrawn and return to British command. Two days later, Pétain wrote to General Pershing and General Fayolle commanding *Groupe d'armées de reserve* explaining his thinking:

The state of the forces at our disposal at the moment obliges us to give the battle a new "allure" which will economise infantry to the maximum. In consequence regulate your efforts by your resources. The object to attain is to throw back the enemy on the Vesle gradually by successive efforts in accordance with my directive of the 29th July, giving the American forces of the Sixth Army more and more of [the] principal role so that towards the 15th August they will hold all the front of that Army.[3]

This was absolutely classic Pétain: telling his senior commanders that the attack, whilst being successful, had not been decisive; that he was in charge, directing his armies, and they would do things the way he felt was most effective and with the necessary level of caution. It also indicates his strong sense of pragmatism and realism, which some have incorrectly interpreted as Pétain being negative and pessimistic. Some even go so far as calling Pétain "defeatist", but this too is wrong. Whilst perhaps not popular, since many relied on their Commander-in-Chief to be the cheerleader for French morale, he had no interest in sugar-coating the reality, presenting events in a matter-of-fact manner typical of his character. This was certainly not Foch's way of doing things, but Pétain was not Foch; he would do things in his own way and consistent with his personality, where he valued an honest opinion and presenting the facts. For example, he had no reinforcements to give any of his armies, so he explained the situation simply and with no room for confusion. Sending a memorandum to Foch on the 31st, he gave a frank evaluation of the remaining effectives available to him, stating that there were no more fresh reserves and he had a current deficit of more than 120,000 troops. He added that he could only identify 19,000 replacements, with just 29,000 more coming available in the next two to three months; numbers hardly adequate for the battle underway, let alone any future operations. Seventy-one divisions were in line and 20 of which had been in the line for a month and 18 for more than two months. Many of the reserve divisions were still weak, with four-fifths of them engaged in the recent

---

2 Edmonds, pp. 285-86.
3 Edmonds, p. 286.

fighting, and a total of 58 divisions were involved in the current battle. There was not, he said, a single fresh division in his "precautionary reserve", and whilst the men coming out of battle still had strong morale, they were extremely tired and "we are at the limit of our effort".[4]

No decision Pétain ever made would do anything which wasted the lives of his men unnecessarily, which was the reason behind him ordering attacks to be fought more methodically, with troops echeloned in depth. His natural caution may have resulted in him overestimating the enemy strength and ability to resist, as well as being concerned about a potential German counterattack to regain lost territory, but these are hardly damning criticisms. Having said that, he had perhaps lost sight of previous German tactics, such as during their retreat to the *Siegfried Stellung* (Hindenburg Line) in 1917, where upon withdrawing (as opposed to retreating during battle) they had laid waste to the ground as they left, burning buildings, looting stores and setting booby traps. Although they would still make local counterattacks and offer stiff resistance, this wanton destruction was not the action of an army intent on launching an immediate counteroffensive, because they would have to occupy ground deluged with gas and unfit for habitation. Ultimately, the buck stopped with him and he knew that the enemy, whilst battered and bruised, had not yet been defeated in the field; a wounded opponent remained a danger and could still strike at any moment. Foch, however, had already come to the conclusion that further German attacks were impossible, or at least extremely unlikely, with the enemy "occupying a defensive position behind a river, which we cannot attack immediately; this in all likelihood will permit him to reorganise his forces, so that in the course of time he may make some of them available for use elsewhere".[5] Colonel Desticker, Foch's Assistant Chief-of-Staff and artillery advisor, arrived with a Special Directive detailing the new offensive, involving the French *1er Armée* (General Debeney) and British Fourth Army (General Sir Henry Rawlinson), to commence in a few days' time.[6] The French GQG also ordered the withdrawal of the two French cavalry corps, with one to support the Anglo-French offensive at Amiens and the other to aid the Franco-American operation on the Meuse at Saint Mihiel. To this Pétain added a note to Fayolle, urging him to utilise the growing number of American forces to reinforce *VIe Armée*, with a view to allowing the AEF to progressively shoulder more of the effort and in due course take up the principal role. Reorganisation on the 29th also impacted Mangin's *Xe Armée*, frustrating him greatly, since he believed that the removal of *5e* and *1er divisions* would curtail his ambitions to finish the job. In typical Mangin fashion, he refused to be satisfied with playing a supporting role to Degoutte's *VIe Armée* to his right, claiming that he could still secure a decisive success by carrying the heights northeast of Grand Rozoy. Nevertheless, despite his complaints and protestations to the Commander-in-Chief, both divisions were needed elsewhere and were duly transferred to *IIIe Armée* to the north, with just the *128e Division* moving into *Xe Armée* in return.[7]

---

4 Letter No. 1512/M, 17:50 on 31st July 1918, cited in Woldike, p.173.
5 Edmonds, pp. 286–87.
6 Edmonds, p. 287. According to Elizabeth Greenhalgh's *Victory Through Coalition* (Cambridge: Cambridge University Press, 2005), pp. 9, 229-31, 337. Weygand could not speak enough English to "sustain a conversation", with German being the second language for most French officers. Clayton, p. 179.
7 Woldike, pp. 57–60.

With the apparent failure of the attack on 29 July, Ludendorff enquired whether it might be possible to hold the Ziethen or small bridgehead position for a considerable time. But upon hearing this, German Crown Prince was furious, protesting "energetically" against the very notion of retaining the position needlessly and suffering additional casualties, restating the reasons laid out in his telegram of the 24th, saying that he could not advise such a course unless the OHL demanded it. Despite the events of the 29th, when the Germans had counterattacked at exactly the right moment and had been able to hold the line under immense pressure, the mere prospect of converting a retirement into an advance would be virtually impossible with the beleaguered resources at his disposal. Both von Below (Ninth Army) and von Boehn (Seventh Army) concurred on this point, stating that it would be impossible to retain the position for more than a day or so. Even though Ludendorff was increasingly out of touch with reality, several key members of the OHL were not, and on 30 July the Supreme Army Command fixed the date for the beginning of the retreat to the night of 1/2 August.[8]

To the east, the two British divisions (the 51st and 62nd) of XXII Corps were being prepared for withdrawal, with the French *77e* and *14e Divisions* ordered by General Berthelot to extend inwards on the night of 30/31 July in order to cover the British. The British divisions had performed well, advancing roughly 4 miles and capturing 21 officers and 1,148 other ranks from seven different divisions, together with a haul of 185 machine guns and 32 recovered French and Italian guns. The 51st (Highland) Division was reported to have lost 115 officers and 2,950 other ranks, the 62nd (West Riding) Division 118 officers and 3,865 men.[9] Whilst fighting had been fierce and the cost in casualties high, General Godley was very pleased with the contribution of his two divisions, who alongside the Italians and French were likely to have made one of the largest, if not *the* largest, advances per man lost since the autumn of 1914. However, Godley did not say anything about the performance or contribution of the 15th (Scottish) and 34th Divisions. General Penet, commanding *30e Corps*, had also taken the opportunity to relieve several of the more tired and depleted French divisions in the line, with the *68e Division* now to the right of 103rd Brigade, but the *25e Division* remained on the left of 101st Brigade.[10]

Recapturing Grand Rozoy created a strong defensive flank and removed the risk of enfilade fire from the west. In reality, most of the machine gun fire during the 29th had come from Beugneux and the wood between the two villages, with the defenders in Grand Rozoy firing at the attacking French rather than the British to the east. The 1st Herefords suffered a number of casualties during a German artillery bombardment, with mustard and lachrymatory gas landing in their lines, killing five men and wounding 14, forcing the men to wear their respirators once more.[11] On the afternoon of 30 July, 103rd Brigade held a conference to outline the plans for a second attack on Beugneux at 0500 hrs on the 31st. However, at 2000 hrs that evening the attack was postponed by a day to allow for further recuperation of the tired assaulting forces. On the same evening, Lieutenant Colonel Dooner, chief of staff of the 34th Division, was killed by shellfire whilst visiting the headquarters of 103rd Brigade in the *Bois de la Baillette*, having travelled from the Advanced Divisional Headquarters at Ferme Giroménil to explain the plans

---

8   Edmonds, pp. 291-92.
9   Edmonds, p. 288.
10 TNA WO 95/2465: 103rd Infantry Brigade Headquarters, Operation Order No. 240 issued 1945 hrs, 30 July 1918.
11 TNA WO 95/2462: 1st Herefords, 30 July 1918.

for the following day's operation.¹² The key role of the division's GSO1 was taken by Lieutenant Colonel R.M. Tyler, DSO, Assistant Adjutant and Quartermaster General (QMG) of the 34th, but Dooner's contribution to decision making and his experience were sorely missed by General Nicholson at this critical moment.¹³

With the partially successful operations of the 29th, *30e Corps* now held a line which snaked from the *Bois de la Terre à l'Or* to Point 183, the south edge of Grand Rozoy, the Beugneux road, the crossroads at the eastern end of Grand Rozoy, approximately 100 yards south of the Grand Rozoy–Beugneux road and the western border of the wood south of the road. From there it stretched eastwards to buildings 500 yards southwest of Beugneux itself and along a line south of and parallel to the Cramoiselle–Cramaille road. The 34th Division would continue to be the right-hand division of *30e Corps*, with *206RI* of *68e Division* (*11e Corps*) on its right and *98RI* of *25e Division* on its left. The *68e Division* was targeting a line from Servenay to the north-west corner of the *Bois d'Arcy* and from there towards the hamlet of Arcy itself, whilst *25e Division* was aiming for the line from Orme du Grand Rozoy (a large elm on the skyline above the village) to *Côte 203*. Sandwiched between the two French divisions, the 34th Division would head north-eastwards, aiming to reach the same Brown Line objective which they had failed to obtain on the 29th.¹⁴ The French *127e Division* was in support, ready to pass through the *25e Division* and secure first the high ground from Servenay to the Orme du Grand Rozoy and then the next ridge, just south of Droizy. The *2e Corps* to the right (south-east) was to outflank Saponay from the east whilst *20e Corps*, including the 15th (Scottish), held itself ready to press forward towards Droizy as soon as the main attack had been successful.¹⁵

The detailed Operation Order issued by *30e Corps* on 31 July was an absolute godsend for the 34th Division, since crucially, most of the detail including the main objectives were the same as the attack on the 29th. The order stressed the need for the British to capture the Brown Line and ensure it was retained in the event of a German counterattack. Given they were attacking over ground they were now much more familiar with, there were only very minor adjustments to boundaries and they were able to adapt the existing maps issued several days before. Included was the instruction that 103rd Brigade could cross the southern divisional boundary into territory of the French *206RI* troops of *68e Division*, in the neighbouring *11e Corps*, if so required, in order to turn Beugneux from the south.¹⁶

Once again it would be 101st and 103rd brigades in the lead, with 102nd Brigade brought up to reinforce the attack as and when required. On the right would be 103rd Brigade, with 101st Brigade on the left, each with one company of the 34th Machine Gun Battalion. The three companies of Royal Engineers and the Machine Gun Battalion in Divisional reserve were to be assembled in the *Bois de la Baillette*, ready to move forward alongside the infantry when it

---

12 Dooner had only been appointed as GSO1 in May 1918, replacing Lieutenant Colonel Sir T. Cunninghame, who had been appointed Commandant of the School of Instruction for the American Army.
13 Shakespear.
14 TNA WO 95/2436: General Staff, 34th Division, Operation Order No. 241, issued at 1700 hrs on 31 July 1918 and TNA WO 95/2465: 103rd Infantry Brigade Headquarters, Operation Order No. 241, 31 July 1918.
15 Edmonds, p. 293.
16 TNA WO 95/2436: General Staff, 34th Division, Operation Order No. 241, issued at 1700 hrs on 31 July 1918.

attacked at 0400 hrs. B and C Companies of the 34th Battalion, Machine Gun Corps, would have moved up from the *Bois de la Bailette* during the night into dugouts in the GMP Line in order to be as far forward as possible, giving them the best positions to cover and support the action of the infantry. These positions offered some limited cover yet would expose the machine guns to fire from the Germans but were deemed necessary under the circumstances and a risk worth taking. Being so far forward would also allow the machine guns to change positions and give suppressing and supporting fire to the infantry as required. Units of 102nd Brigade would be withdrawn that night to divisional reserve, with 101st and 103rd brigades extending their flanks right and left respectively to cover the front vacated by 102nd Brigade, taking up their fighting formations with the leading waves dug in as close as possible to the starting line, all to be completed no later than midnight. Given that they were already in line, the moves having been successful during the night, it would allow the men to grab a few hours of much-needed sleep before the attack took place at dawn. The divisional artillery, anticipating success, took up fresh positions on the 30th and 31st, some 2,000 yards further forward of their previous emplacements.[17]

The Order of Battle for the attack was as follows:

Left
- 101st Brigade plus one company from 34th Battalion, Machine Gun Corps;
- 4th Royal Sussex on the right (three companies in the front line) advancing in two waves;
- 2/4th Queens (three companies in the front line);
- Brigade Reserve: 2nd Loyal North Lancs.

Right
- 103rd Brigade plus one company from 34th Battalion, Machine Gun Corps;
- 5th KOSBs (three companies in the front line) with its left on the right divisional boundary;
- 5th Argylls (three companies in the front line);
- 8th Scottish Rifles (two companies in the front line);
- Brigade Reserve: two companies of 8th Scottish Rifles.

Divisional Reserve
- 102nd Brigade less two battalions the 4th Cheshire's and the Herefords being selected to support 101st and 103rd Brigades respectively.;
- 2/4th Somerset Light Infantry (pioneers);
- 34th Battalion, Machine Gun Corps (less two companies).
- 207th, 208th and 209th Field Companies, Royal Engineers.[18]

---

17   TNA WO 95/2436: General Staff, 34th Division, Operation Order No. 241, issued at 1700 hrs on 31 July 1918 and TNA WO 95/2436: General Staff, 34th Division, narrative of operations with *Xe* French Army; events of 1 August 1918. TNA WO 95/2451: 34th Battalion, Machine Gun Corps, 31 July 1918.
18   TNA WO 95/2436: General Staff, 34th Division, narrative of operations with *Xe* French Army; events of 1 August 1918 and TNA WO 95/2442: Commander Royal Artillery, 31 July 1918.

Chastened by the experience of committing his reserves at the wrong point of the fighting on 29 July, General Nicholson would have to take the same gamble again. This time, however, he hoped to have better intelligence of how events were unfolding, which would allow him to push the reserves into action at the right time. The divisional artillery was supplemented for the attack by two regiments of French field artillery and two groups of six 155mm howitzers, giving Brigadier General Walthall, CRA, a total of 108 field guns and 32 howitzers, but this was 24 fewer heavy guns than had been available on the 29th, since guns were needed elsewhere.[19] There would be one gun for every 15 yards of front. The loss of so many heavy howitzers would no doubt be keenly felt amongst both artillery and infantry, and it must have played on Nicholson's mind in the small hours of the night. But at this late stage there was nothing he could do to increase his firepower and he would have to make the best of the situation. Matters were made worse since heavy casualties meant that there was going to be a shortage of machine guns for the attack, with A Company only able to man 10 guns, less than ideal support for the infantry. He also worried whether 101st and 103rd brigades would be strong enough to take a full part in the fighting, with the 5th Argylls having just six officers and 260 other ranks available for the attack. The shortage of troops forced his hand somewhat, and Nicholson decided to place three companies of each battalion into the front line instead of two. In many places, however, the three companies of 1 August were fewer in number than the strength of the two that had entered battle on the 29 July. The plan included additional support from 102nd Brigade, in divisional support, to push two battalions up, leap frogging and passing through the leading brigades as soon as they reached their objectives. They were then to capture and hold the high ground just short of the two farms, le Mont Jour and Bucy le Bras, at the northern extreme of the advance, roughly 1,500 yards ahead. These farms would form the forward boundary of the advance, and it was hoped that the infantry dug in there would be able to provide flanking fire for the French coming up on either side.[20]

The artillery would commence counter-battery fire 45 minutes prior to H-hour, as well as targeting Beugneux. At H-hour, the field artillery would open on the initial barrage line for four minutes, after which it would advance 100 yards every three minutes in a double barrage of first high explosive and then timed shrapnel until it passed the Brown Line, where it would remain for 30 minutes before ceasing.[21] Learning from the mistake on the 23rd, the key difference that Nicholson put in place was that there would be no intermediate halt, meaning that the Germans would have no respite and hopefully no opportunity to mount a counterattack. The artillery would then support consolidation and any advancing troops which required it, whilst A/152 and B/150 Brigades, Royal Field Artillery, would move forward, coming under command of the GOCs of 103rd and 101st brigades respectively, to support the infantry. A small detachment of French tanks operating on the right flank of the French *25e Division* (to the left of the British) was to work its way north-eastwards to deal with any German machine gun nests.[22] In

---

19 TNA WO 95/2436: General Staff, 34th Division, narrative of operations with *Xe* French Army; events of 1 August; TNA WO 95/2442: Commander Royal Artillery, 31 July 1918 and TNA WO 95/2436: General Staff, 34th Division, Operation Order No. 241, issued at 1700 hrs on 31 July 1918.
20 Takle, pp. 237-38.
21 Takle, p. 237.
22 TNA WO 95/2436: General Staff, 34th Division, Operation Order No. 241 issued at 1700 hrs on 31 July 1918.

order to ensure contact with the advancing infantry units, an Advance Divisional Headquarters was established at Ferme Giroménil, with Advanced Quartermaster stores remaining at Ferme d'Edrolle, 2,000 yards west of Billy-sur-Ourcq, and the main Divisional Headquarters at La Loge Ferme.[23]

The infantry emerging from their trenches 150 yards behind where the creeping barrage fell were to hug it closely and capture Beugneux. Once they reached the Brown Line objective, they would consolidate on that position. The order stated that the village and *Côte 158* were not to be attacked frontally. Instead, 103rd Brigade was to turn both of these obstacles from the south, with special parties detailed to mop up any resistance once the leading waves had passed through; it was essential that momentum be maintained. The right flank of 101st Brigade was to push well to the north of Beugneux and mop up the village from the north. Several copses south of Le Mont Jour, north-east of *Côte 199* and *Côte 172*, were also to be cleared of enemy, particularly any machine guns, with parties from 102nd Brigade detailed to support. The 34th Machine Gun Battalion, positioned under cover in the *Bois de Montceau*, was readied to cover and support the infantry if so required, including moving their positions forward.

Casualties for the division between 29 and 31 July had been heavy, as the following table reveals, with almost all of the 1,775 casualties occurring during the attack on the 29th:[24]

Casualties 29–31 July	Officers	Other Ranks	**Total**
Killed	16	206	**222**
Wounded	61	1,356	**1,417**
Missing		136	**136**
Total	77	1,698	**1,775**

23 TNA WO 95/2436: General Staff, 34th Division, GS286/201, 31 July 1918 and TNA WO 95/2439: Adjutant and Quartermaster General, 34th Division, 29 July 1918.
24 Shakespear, p. 266.

Casualties for 103rd Brigade during July were as follows:[25]

Unit	Officers				Other Ranks			
	Killed	Wounded	Missing	**Total**	Killed	Wounded	Missing	**Total**
5th KOSBs	2	5		**7**	18	227	27	**272**
8th Scottish Rifles	3	14		**17**	44	265	19	**328**
5th A&SH	3	12		**15**	15	232	5	**252**
103rd LTMB						5		**5**
103rd Brigade HQ					1	9		**10**
Total	8	31		**39**	78	738	51	**867**

For the 5th KOSBs, casualties had been particularly heavy. Two officers and 18 other ranks had been killed and five officers and 254 men either wounded or missing, with all of the missing either killed, wounded or taken prisoner.[26] The 8th Scottish Rifles' casualties were four officers killed and 10 wounded, plus 41 other ranks killed, 226 wounded and 19 missing.[27] The 4th Royal Sussex had lost three officers and 42 other ranks killed and four officers and 154 other ranks either wounded or missing, with Captain S.K. Reid, MC, succumbing to his wounds on the following day. Also wounded on the 29th was Reverend W.H. Aglionby, CFMC, the battalion's padre.[28] The casualty return for the 4th Royal Sussex listed just two officers and 210 other ranks answering the roll call that night.[29] Crucially, two battalions had also lost their CO during the attack on the 29th, with leadership passing to junior commanders. The two attacks had cost the 34th Division more than 3,000 casualties in total. Perhaps even more important was the loss of a further 77 officers, adding to the 45 from 22–28 July, meaning that many platoons and even some companies were now commanded by junior NCOs, having been shorn of many of their officers. For instance, the Argylls could call on just six officers and 260 other ranks, and they were by no means the worst affected.[30] For 102nd Brigade, which was involved in fighting on both the 23rd and 29th, two officers and 79 other ranks had been killed and 20 officers and 617 other ranks wounded, with a further 23 other ranks missing. Additionally, two officers and 240 other ranks were evacuated as gas casualties, with their absence of any experience of gas attacks undoubtedly contributing to their total of almost 1,000 casualties.[31] Not all battalions suffered such egregious losses. The 2/4th Somersets, being in divisional reserve for virtually the

---

25   TNA WO 95/2465: 103rd Infantry Brigade Headquarters, July 1918.
26   Scott Elliot, p. 246.
27   TNA WO 95/2467: 8th Scottish Rifles, 29-31 July 1918.
28   TNA WO 95/2458: 4th Royal Sussex, 29 July 1918.
29   Read, p. 367.
30   Shakespear, p. 263.
31   TNA WO 95/2461: 102nd Infantry Brigade Headquarters, 31 July 1918.

entire time, only had four casualties on 28/29 July, 22 on the 30th and 24 on the 30th/31st, of which just 12 were killed.[32]

The location of the 34th Division, miles from any other British unit – with the exception of the 15th (Scottish), embedded in *20e Corps* to the north, which was itself heavily engaged and taking similar casualties – only exacerbated the problem, since it was impossible to despatch replacement officers quickly. The 4th Royal Sussex, for example, only received four officers from England and 12 other ranks, all returned from hospital during this period. Whilst it swelled its ranks by an underwhelming 16, it had lost nine officers and 271 other ranks during the combat, with a further one officer and 46 other ranks lost through sickness, a net loss of 311 all ranks.[33] Even if the reinforcements departed now, they would have to follow the same circuitous day-long route that the 34th Division had taken previously, meaning they would only arrive on 2 August, which would be too late to take part in the attack. Consequently, the division was forced to make a difficult choice: either continue with its dwindling resources of just 350 effectives per battalion and risk being too weak to be effective, or request relief from the French. The 4th Royal Sussex was perhaps one of the better equipped, having been spared much of the fighting, but even they had been reduced to a trench strength of just 23 officers and 636 other ranks after only a single day's fighting. For Nicholson, whilst the first option was unpalatable and risky, the second was unthinkable. By putting his third brigade into action on the 29th, he had already acknowledged that his preferred option was to try to force the Germans back off the ridge and that he was willing to give it one last renewed effort.[34]

32 Wryall.
33 TNA WO 95/2458: 4th Royal Sussex, 31 July 1918.
34 The figure of 350 effectives per battalion for the attack on 1 August is mentioned in Shakespear, p. 265. Takle, p. 236.

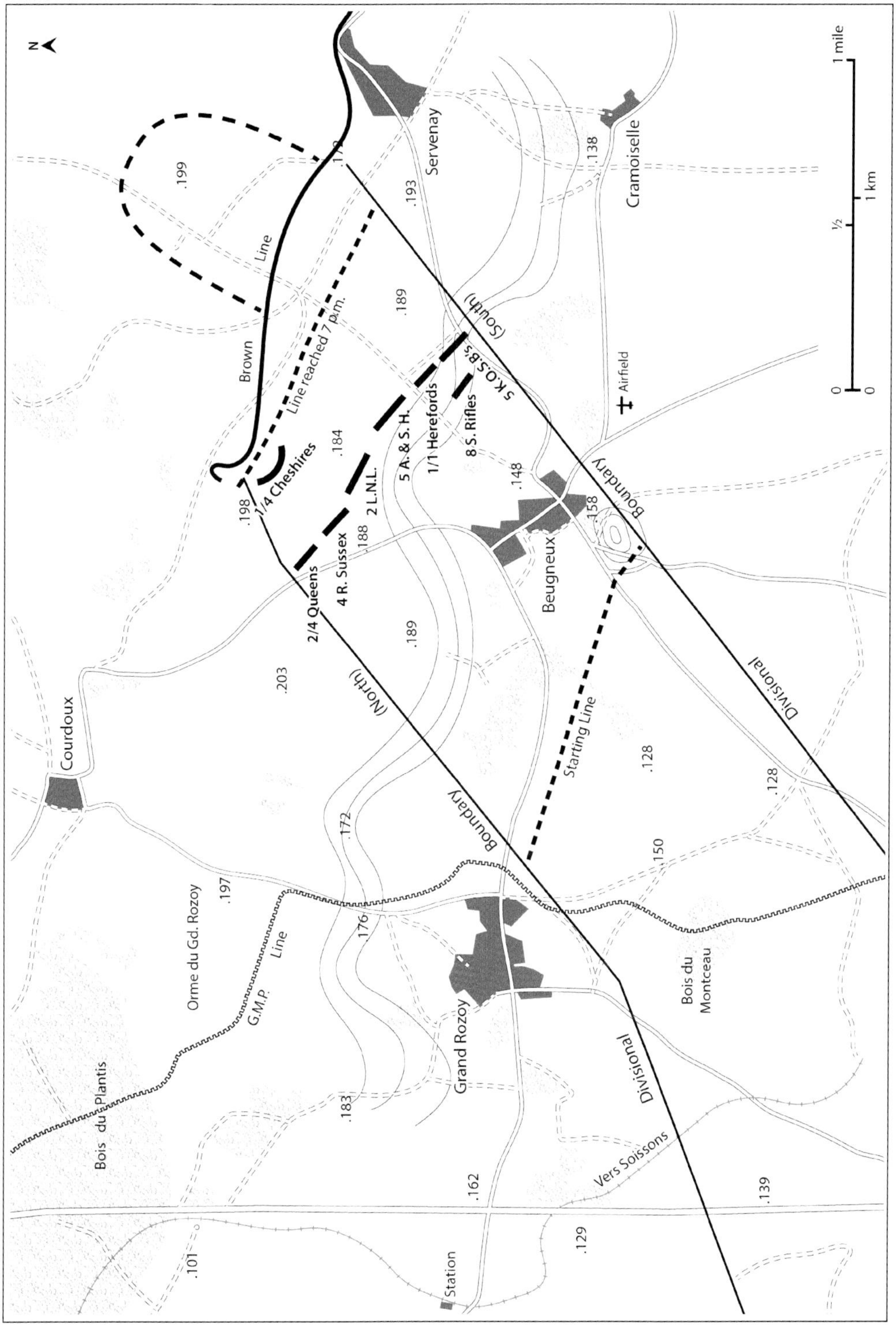

30–31 July: Time for a rethink? 183

Map 10. Advance of 34th Division, 1 August 1918.

16

1 August: Monumental events

For this assault, one last knockout blow to try to force the Germans back off the ridge, the 34th Division had several major advantages over the two previous engagements. Firstly, it had attacked the ground two days earlier, so was now more familiar with the terrain and any obstacles it needed to overcome. Secondly, Nicholson and his brigade commanders had sufficient time to go through the attack plan in detail, with diagrams and deployments explained to all senior officers. A third factor was that 103rd Brigade was authorised to cross the southern divisional boundary and into the sector held by *11e Corps* in order to make a wide enveloping movement and turn the village of Beugneux from the south if necessary. Another factor at play was the change to the artillery tactics, with a 45-minute preparation by all available guns prior to the attack. Crucially, the attack would also benefit from a detachment of approximately 30 French Renault FT-17 tanks earmarked to support the *25e Division*'s assault through Grand Rozoy to the left of the British, which would move in a north-easterly direction towards the objective, dealing with any stubborn resistance along the way, especially German machine guns.[1] Although more lightly armed, the Renaults, with a two-man crew, were smaller, lighter at only 6.5 tonnes and were able to travel at 7km per hour, making them much faster and more nimble than the lumbering Schneider or Saint-Chamond monsters, thus ideally suited to crossing the rolling terrain which had few if any trenches and shell holes. Their innovative design, with a 360-degree rotating turret, added to their flexibility and made them a fearsomely effective mobile artillery fighting machine. Yet even the lighter Renault tanks would probably be worn out quickly, so they had to be used at exactly the right moment to maximise their value.[2] Another change to the plan of attack was possibly the most important of all – there would be no intermediate halt, with all troops ordered to press on towards the Brown Line objective without pausing to consolidate. Since many of the tanks were likely to withdraw from the action after only a short period of involvement, the infantry would have to make rapid progress towards the objectives without their support.

---

1   TNA WO 95/2465: 103rd Infantry Brigade Headquarters, Operation Order No. 241, 31 July 1918, War Diary of 101st Brigade, BM.50/36 on 31 July has the tanks supporting as the French *95e Division* and TNA WO 95/2461: 102nd Infantry Brigade Headquarters, Brigade Order No.230, 31 July 1918.
2   Goya, p. 220.

The objective of the attack on 1 August was a repeat of that of the 29th, to force the Germans to abandon their defensive positions on the ridge and retire northwards towards the River Vesle, or further if possible, maybe even clearing the Marne salient entirely. Foch had arrived at *Xe Armée* headquarters to discuss the plans with Mangin, with the pair deciding to delay the attack by one day until 1 August, to give the commanders more time to co-ordinate their plans. It is interesting to speculate about the dynamic of that meeting. Would Foch have responded differently had it been Pétain making the request instead of 'The Butcher' himself, with Mangin much more in the Foch mould than of the Commander-in-Chief? Would the decision have been different if Pétain had arrived instead of Foch? Would Foch have listened to Pétain's explanation and reasoning with the same open mind that he granted Mangin, or would he have been deaf to his demands and insisted the attack go ahead as planned the following morning? There is no doubt that Foch had chosen the right man to head up *Xe Armée* – they were perfectly in step both strategically and tactically, and Mangin would not have forgotten that. Nevertheless, there is no doubt that Mangin would have faced some stiff questions and probing from Foch, who remained keen to put his stamp on the operation, with 'The Butcher' being extremely receptive and prepared to accept the meddling of the Generalissimo in tactical matters. After much discussion, the two men were able to agree on the plan and Foch confirmed a repeat of the attack on the 29th. The *30e CA* was to drive north-east between the Allont crest and Servenay in the direction of Launoy, between *25e* and *127e divisions*. To support *30e CA*'s thrust, *11e Corps* – sandwiched between *11e CA* and Degoutte's *VIe Armée* – would advance towards the *Bois d'Arcy* using *68e* and *41e divisions*, whilst to the left, *19e Division* and *20e Corps* would attack through Droizy as soon as the southern flank had been secured. As before, Mangin intended the attack to be decisive, rupturing the enemy's front and allowing the advanced units to progress as far as the high plateau between Launoy and Bucy-le-Bras, the success of *20e CA* being wholly dependent on that of *30e CA* to its right.[3]

With further Entente attacks on the German line now absolutely certain, and with ever-decreasing manpower resources spread dangerously thinly, the OHL was left with no option but to order a retirement back to the *Blücher Stellung* for the night of 1/2 August. According to the Staffs at Crown Prince Wilhelm's headquarters, the rearguard troops, unable to be reinforced, would be able to hold out for one more day but no more, and only then if their luck held and the men stood fast, with orders issued to hold the position of the Orme du Grand Rozoy to the last man.[4]

During the night of 31 July/1 August all troops edged forward into their jumping-off positions under the cover of darkness from 2200 hrs onwards. Learning from their recent experience, they were ordered to complete their assembly no later than midnight, with the men to dig in as best they could – and silently if possible – to protect from any enemy counter-preparation fire. As with the attack on the 29th, they were not to attack Beugneux and *Côte 158* frontally, but 103rd Brigade would turn them from the right (east). From left to right, Nicholson deployed the 2/4th Queens and 4th Royal Sussex of 101st Brigade and 5th Argylls and 5th KOSBs of 103rd Brigade, closely supported by two companies of the Scottish Rifles to 'mop up' Beugneux, all in contact with the French *68e Division* to their right. Whilst being in divisional reserve,

3　Greenwood, pp. 168-69.
4　Greenwood, pp. 169-71.

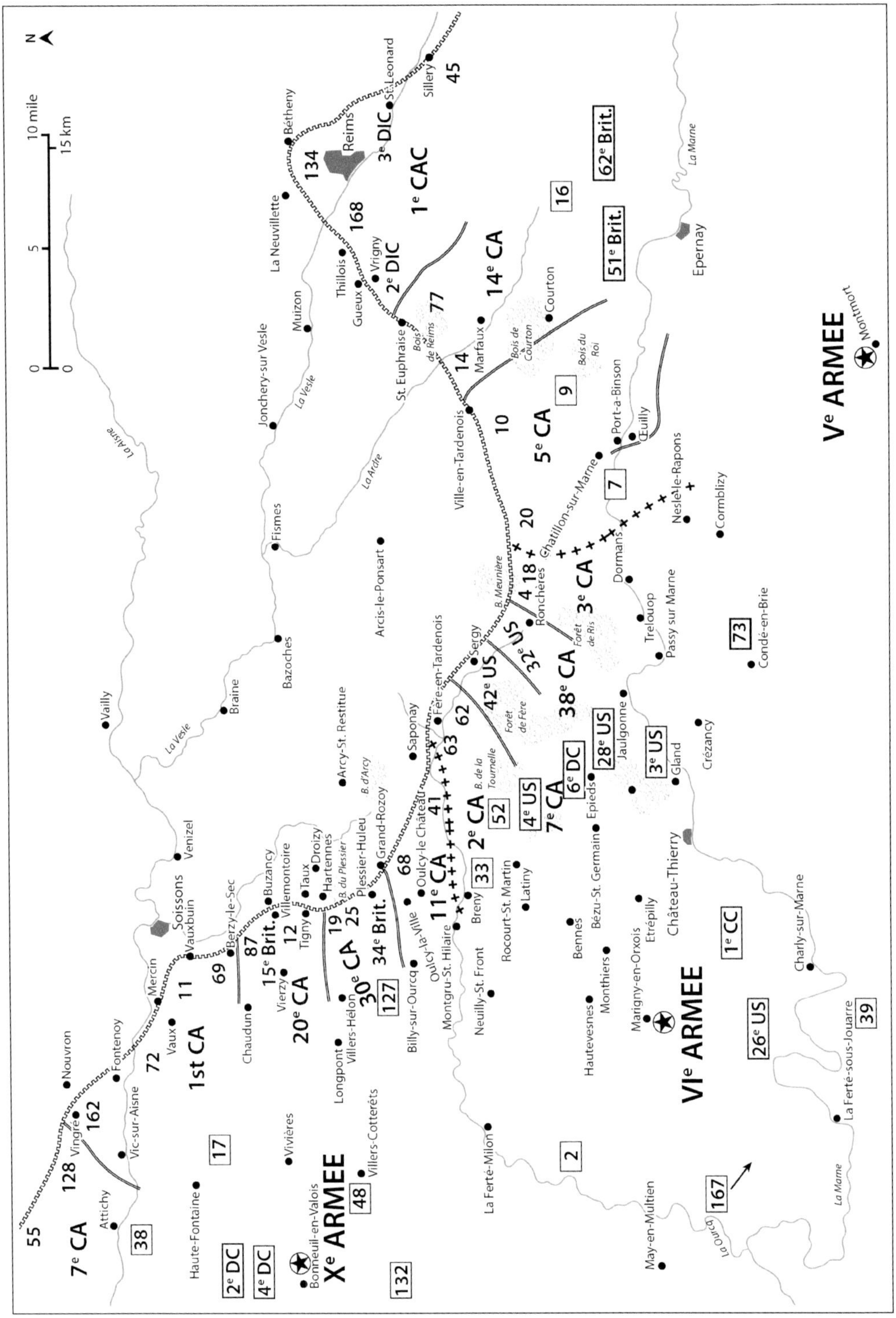

Map 11. Marne Salient, 1 August 1918.

102nd Brigade was ordered to stand ready to advance and support any exploitation, with the 4th Cheshires immediately behind 101st Brigade, having the objective of La Mont Jour, up on the plateau, almost 3km north of Beugneux, where it would occupy two small wooded copses that were certain to hide German defenders. The 1st Herefords would advance in the rear of 103rd Brigade to capture Bucy le Bras Ferme.

Mangin informed Nicholson of the importance of succeeding in this third attack, since it would influence his ability to commence attacks elsewhere. In turn, Nicholson wrote to his brigade commanders, stating: "The Divisional Commander has just been informed by the General Commanding the 10th French Army that the earliest possible information of the capture of the objective is one of the greatest importance in view of the fact that the commencement of other operations depends on it."[5] Reinforcing the point, General Penet issued another instruction later that night, placing *127e Division* in readiness to move through the *25e* and *34th divisions* north-east towards Launoy from its assembly positions in the *Bois de la Baillette* in order to exploit this success once the capture of the initial objectives had been achieved. The 34th Division would cover the right of the advance of *127e Division*, occupying the high ground at Le Mont Jour and the spur south-east of Bucy le Bras. The passing through of attacking units pressing the offensive by leapfrogging the front line, whilst by this period of 1918 fairly familiar to many troops on the Western Front, was not something that the infantry of 34th Division had encountered before. Two battalions were earmarked for the task, with one to cover the flank of *68e Division* advancing towards Arcy-Sainte-Restitue, 5km north-east of Beugneux. The infantry of *127e Division* would pass through British lines and constant liaison would be essential.[6] At 1600 hrs, all of the 5th KOSB company commanders met for a conference at the battalion headquarters, where the attack was explained in great detail and instructions for forming up were issued, then at 1930 hrs, Special Instruction No.3 was issued detailing the specific liaison between the British and three French divisions (*25e*, *68e* and *127e*) across two corps, underlining just how complicated the situation had become. Even though they had received their orders several days before, with so many moving parts still to be organised, it must have been a sleepless night for many of the division's senior officers, especially having lost Lieutenant Colonel Dooner, their GSO1.[7]

The *Bois de la Baillette* was jammed full of British and French troops and their equipment, making it an obvious target for enemy shelling, but conditions improved when the 34th Machine Gun Battalion moved during the night to a new position along the Soissons–Ouchy railway line and in the *Bois du Montceau*. However, with the northern edge of the wood only 200 yards south of Grand Rozoy, the machine gunners simply exchanged additional space for significantly greater danger, with the wood targeted repeatedly by German artillery. With the plan being for the guns to stretch west to east in the field between the railway line and the wood, there was no protection for the machine gun teams and no time to construct any meaningful defences. The ground around their new positions was virtually flat and ill-suited to the siting of machine guns,

---

5   TNA WO 95/2442: Commander Royal Artillery, Special Instructions No. 2, GS286/105, 31 July 1918.
6   TNA WO 95/2436: General Staff, 34th Division, GS 286/100, issued at 1830 hrs on 31 July 1918 and TNA WO 95/2461: 102nd Infantry Brigade Headquarters, Brigade Order, No. 230, 31 July 1918.
7   TNA WO 95/2466: 5th KOSBs, 31 July 1918 and TNA WO 95/2442: Commander Royal Artillery, Special Instructions No.3. GS286/109, issued at 1930 hrs on 31 July 1918.

with the gunners hoping that infantry had created some slit trenches which they might occupy or that the Germans wouldn't notice their arrival. If the enemy did spot the machine guns, then they were sure to be shelled.

The 2/4th Queens were ordered to watch their left flank very carefully and to guard against any enemy counterattacks debouching from Grand Rozoy, which had caused severe casualties three days earlier. This particular instruction appears inexplicable, since the French occupied Grand Rozoy, having captured the village on the 30th without opposition. Nicholson further stressed that the advance should not stop and instructed all attacking battalions to throw out defensive flanks should either their right or left be held up. The 4th Cheshires were under strict instructions to maintain touch with the French *25e Division* on their left and the 1st Herefords with the French *68e Division* on their right, with French-speaking officers allotted to the task of liaison.

The 4th Royal Sussex were assembled 100 yards south of the Grand Rozoy–Beugneux road in four lines of companies, one behind the other, getting as close to the road as they dared.[8] The 5th KOSBs moved into its attack positions in a cornfield behind a railway embankment, with two platoons per company available. The manpower situation was slightly improved when a draft of 120 men arrived at 2200 hrs that evening, most of whom had previously served with the 5th KOSBs, and these welcome additions were immediately distributed amongst the companies in the field. As the battalion moved forward, with its left on the Beugneux–Oulchy-le-Château road, the officer commanding the leading company gave the order for his company to quick march, two companies further to the right taking this as their signal to move too. However, instead of heading in the intended direction, they went off through the cornfield into the dark in entirely the wrong direction. Fortunately this was quickly rectified and the battalion was in position just after midnight.[9] To the west, the three Field Companies, Royal Engineers and the remaining half of the machine gun battalion were assembling in the *Bois de la Baillette*, ready to move off in support of the attack at 0400 hrs. With machine gun casualties being a constant concern, further heavy losses might hamper their contribution and it was therefore decided to utilise a single section to support the infantry, with other guns kept in reserve to assist with any consolidation, giving covering fire from the *Bois du Montceau*. This was later amended, with the machine gun battalion moving to the Soissons–Oulchy railway and the *Bois du Montceau* no later than 0330 hrs. In order to combat the expected German counterattacks, special parties were also detailed to occupy several of the small copses dotting the landscape to prevent the enemy from using them. With supply problems now seemingly resolved, two Stokes mortars were ordered to support each attacking battalion, but 101st Brigade could call on just three available mortars, with two of them allocated to 2/4th Queens.[10]

The attack on 1 August was noticeably better organised in other respects too. The horse and motor transport was now able to take two different circular one-way routes, meaning that evacuation of casualties and resupply of materiel was simpler and much less prone to congestion, which had dogged the earlier attacks. They also avoided travelling along the routes most likely

---

8   TNA WO 95/2458: 4th Royal Sussex; TNA WO 95/2456: 101st Infantry Brigade Headquarters, Order No.219, 28 July 1918 and TNA WO 95/2456: 101st Infantry Brigade Headquarters, Order No. 221, 31 July 1918.
9   TNA WO 95/2466: 5th KOSBs, 31 July 1918.
10 TNA WO 95/2456: 101st Infantry Brigade Headquarters, Operation Order No. 221, 31 July 1918.

to be targeted by German artillery.[11] With the division also benefitting from a couple of days in which to systematise their casualty evacuation procedures, the Advanced Dressing Stations at Billy-sur-Ourcq and Oulchy-la-Ville, the Main Dressing Station at Chouy and Walking Wounded Collecting Post at Billy-sur-Ourcq meant men could be either evacuated or returned to the line more quickly. This solution was particularly impressive, as the division had only been in the sector for a short period but had overcome the logistical nightmare of how to move around along the narrow country roads and tracks.[12] Franco-British liaison was also noticeably improved, with a Liaison Detachment of one (French-speaking) officer, half a section of infantry and two signallers from 103rd Brigade earmarked to meet a French detachment of similar strength from *68e Division* at midnight, whilst a similar arrangement was organised between 101st Brigade (and 102nd Brigade in reserve) and the French *25e Division*.[13] The 108 field guns and 32 howitzers at the disposal of the division would bombard the German positions for 45 minutes from 0400 hrs, graduating from harassing fire into a heavy and destructive bombardment. This was longer than the previous two engagements on the 23rd and 29th, and this final factor was perhaps the most crucial of all. Not only was the division's firepower significantly strengthened compared to previous action, but the concentrated nature of the firing and added firing discipline, rising to a destructive crescendo at 0445 hrs, would, it was hoped, allow the attackers the best opportunity to overcome the beleaguered and weakened defenders and capture their positions.[14]

The 4th Cheshires were tasked with following the extreme left of the divisional boundary, keeping pace with the French *127e Division* to its left. The 2/4th Queens on the left and 4th Royal Sussex on the right would form the attacking units of 101st Brigade, with the 2nd Loyal North Lancs in a railway cutting as Brigade Reserve. The 5th KOSBs were to envelop and turn the wooded knoll of *Côte 158* from the south and the 5th Argylls from the north, a particularly difficult task. The 5th Argylls were already in position, holding the line of a light single-track railway, but were precariously close to the enemy, being just 200 yards from the German front line; at 2100 hrs, as darkness enveloped the battlefield, the companies moved out from the GMP Line. Having suffered heavy casualties on the 29th, the 5th Argylls had been reduced to just three companies, all of which were in the line. To the extreme right of the divisional boundary, the 5th KOSBs occupied a line 100 yards wide, with A and D Companies in support 150 yards to the rear, the battalion headquarters making up a third line 200 yards behind. With each company reduced in size to just two platoons, they were augmented at the last minute with the arrival at 2200 hrs of a draft of 120 men re-joining their companies.[15] In the darkness, with German shells landing on the GMP Line which it had just vacated, the 5th KOSBs moved east by north-east, with its left flank on the track leading from Oulchy-le-Château to Beugneux, locating the 5th Argylls holding the railway line, where it was led into position at 0030 hrs on 1 August. The battalion headquarters was in a clearing in a cornfield; the men dug in and some

---

11 TNA WO 95/2439: Adjutant and Quartermaster General, Administrative Instructions No.56, 28 July 1918.
12 TNA WO 95/2465: 103rd Infantry Brigade Headquarters, Operation Order No. 241, 31 July 1918.
13 TNA WO 95/2465: 103rdrd Infantry Brigade Headquarters, Special Instructions No. 3, 31 July 1918.
14 Scott Elliot, p. 248.
15 Scott Elliot, p. 247. TNA WO 95/2465: 103rd Infantry Brigade Headquarters, 0330 hrs, 1 August 1918 and Shakespear, p. 264.

even tried to catch a bit of sleep, in spite of heavy shelling.[16] The 8th Scottish Rifles arrived at their jumping-off positions 90 minutes later, with Y and Z Companies leading off. Their positions were 500 yards south-west of the enemy's front line, with 102nd Brigade in position 150 yards south of the Beugneux–Grand Rozoy road by 0330 hrs.[17] Likewise, the 2nd Loyal North Lancs reached their assembly positions without incident at 0130 hrs, well in advance of the attack, with strict orders to ensure that they maintained 150 yards between each company, with platoons in single file 50 yards apart, the 4th Cheshires in support a further 150 yards behind.

The attack duly commenced at 0400 hrs with the planned 45-minute heavy artillery bombardment, aimed at neutralising German positions in Beugneux and in the wood between the village and Grand Rozoy, as well as hostile batteries on the reverse slope of the ridge beyond. The gunfire intensified towards H-hour at 0445 hrs. This was a carbon copy of the artillery bombardment three days before. The field artillery then struck up promptly at 0445 hrs for four minutes on their designated starting line, before the creeping barrage rolled forward at a rate of 100 metres every three minutes. D Company, 34th Battalion, Machine Gun Corps, added the extra firepower of a dozen Vickers machine guns to the barrage. Their task was to fire on the high ground behind *Côte 158* and Beugneux, and thereafter to move forward in support of the infantry attacking both sides of *Côte 158*, before taking up positions north-east of Beugneux. According to reports from 103rd Brigade, this time the barrage worked according to plan, being much more effective than the previous one. As the barrage rolled forward with the tanks in support, the men had already emerged from their positions wearing their respirators, advancing into a dense fog of thick shell-smoke tinged with mustard gas, hugging the barrage as closely as they dared. A combination of their respirators and the thick smoke meant that vision was limited to just 15 yards, with officers navigating by compass.

The initial advance was immediately successful, with the headquarters of the 5th KOSBs able to move forward at 0451 hrs. Some resistance was encountered by machine guns in the *Bois du Beugneux*, but these were quickly silenced by the Stokes mortars of the 101st LTMB. At 0500 hrs, just 15 minutes after the commencement of the advance, two 18-pdr batteries – A Battery from 152 Brigade and B Battery from 160 Brigade Royal Field Artillery – each with a section of howitzers attached, limbered up and, with cheers from the French artillery fighting alongside them, moved forward to their advanced positions to help consolidate the gains.[18] This is yet more evidence of the strong camaraderie and respect that existed between the French and British artillery units. The same could not be said of the two infantries, where suspicion still pervaded relations. Once the barrage had ceased, all of the remaining artillery in turn advanced to new positions 3,000–4,000 yards forward of their original positions, where they remained for the rest of the day.

---

16 TNA WO 95/2466: 5th KOSBs, 31 July 1918.
17 Findlay, p. 174 and TNA WO 95/2461: 102nd Infantry Brigade Headquarters, 0330 hrs, 1 August 1918.
18 TNA WO 95/2456: 101st Infantry Brigade Headquarters, 1 August 1918. The war diary of 103rd Brigade notes the field artillery of A/152 pushed forward at 103rd0 hrs to *Côte 158*, with the war diary of 34th Divisional Artillery reporting them to have completed their advance to new positions by 0625 hrs. See also TNA WO 95/2466: 5th KOSBs, 1 August 1918.

Beugneux church.

Grand Rozoy church.

According to Shakespear, "the advance was entirely successful", 1 August being characterised by him simply as "a good day", whilst Edmonds remarked that the offensive caught the Germans making ready for a further retirement and met with considerable success.[19] But as will be evident, these descriptions, particularly the one by Shakespear, were a typical British understatement of the events which unfolded during the day

Within 20 minutes, the 2nd Loyal North Lancs in the centre had advanced as far as the *Bois de Beugneux*, with part of the wood stretching to the south side of the road, right up behind the barrage, which was advancing in bounds of 100 metres every three minutes. Reaching the wood, B Company in the lead made a left wheel to mop up the wood from east to west, whilst the rest of the battalion continued in a north-easterly direction. Crossing the Beugneux–Grand Rozoy road, they encountered heavy enemy machine gun fire, but prompt action from the Lewis gunners neutralised them. This was followed up by a rapid advance with fixed bayonets, supported by a section of the 101st LTMB, which overcame all enemy opposition in the wood, with 50 Germans killed and another five taken prisoner, together with a dozen machine guns. The fleeing Germans were pursued out of the wood, with several more being killed and another 41 captured.[20]

The objective assigned to the 5th Argyll and Sutherland Highlanders and 8th Scottish Rifles was to clear the heavily defended *Côte 158*, supported by the 5th KOSBs, with their left on the south-eastern corner of the hill. *Côte 158* was little more than a small circular wooded 20ft-high mound at the southern edge of Beugneux. In spite of its modest size, the surrounding area was almost entirely flat, meaning that the hill commanded a wide field of fire in three directions, giving ample protection for the village. Looking at the map, it was easy to understand why the Germans believed that holding onto the hill was of significant strategic importance, and they would have to be driven off it by force. As soon as the Scotsmen emerged from their slit trenches and moved forward at 0449 hrs, the remaining German machine guns opened fire. With visibility reduced to a mere 15 yards in places, the 5th Argylls – already with just six officers – immediately lost Lieutenant Saunders killed and Lieutenant Grant wounded, before it had even reached the edge of *Côte 158*, whilst Lieutenant C.D. Robertson was wounded on the hill itself. Lieutenant R.R. French and a section of 12 men detailed to act as liaison with the *68e Division* to their right got themselves lost and failed to gain contact with the French at all, coming under heavy fire but fortuitously escaping without casualties. Now down to just three officers, Lieutenant Fleming led the 5th Argylls' attack over *Côte 158*, with CO Lieutenant Colonel Barlow and Lieutenant Thomson flanking it from the left, whilst two companies of the 5th KOSBs cleared a trench to the right of the hill at the point of the bayonet, which had been causing havoc enfilading the attackers, capturing 20 prisoners. *Côte 158* was finally wrestled from the enemy at the second attempt, with a battalion commander, his adjutant, two officers and 40 other ranks of the 18th Bavarian Regiment being captured, alongside 10 machine guns.[21] But the hill's capture had come at a heavy price, with the loss of Lieutenant Colonel Barlow, Officer Commanding the 5th Argylls, killed whilst urging on the leading troops, as were Regimental Sergeant Major C.S. Monteith, Company Sergeant Major McNabb and 30 other

---

19 Shakespear, pp. 262–63. Edmonds, p. 293.
20 TNA WO 95/2457: 2nd Loyal North Lancs, record of operations of the 2nd Battalion Loyal North Lancashire Regiment from 23 July to 4 August 1918.
21 Scott Elliot, p. 248. Takle, p. 237.

men. With Lieutenant Colonel Barlow killed, Lieutenant Fleming took over command of the remnants of the 5th Argylls. The Beugneux–Courdoux road was crossed around 0600 hrs and the Brown Line objective of Mont le Jour occupied 50 minutes later.[22] Three machine guns from A Company moved forward and took up positions near *Côte 199*, with four more near *Côte 198* and another three 800 yards to the rear, where they could cover the whole front.[23] The 2nd Loyal North Lancs now had Captain Atkinson commanding the battalion and the 5th Argylls a mere lieutenant (Fleming) as their senior officer, leading the troops up the hill towards the plateau, but despite their extraordinarily heavy losses, they had captured their objective in a little under seventy-five minutes. All they had to do now was to hold onto it and consolidate.

With *Côte 158* now captured, the 5th Argylls could turn their attention to taking Beugneux itself, with instructions to envelop or turn the village from both north and south. This they did with apparent ease, leaving a single company of each brigade to mop up any remaining resistance. The 5th KOSBs, meanwhile, had skirted *Côte 158* to clear the aerodrome wood to the east before pressing on north, but elements now found themselves too far to the east, having lost their bearings in the thick mist and smoke. Instead, they advanced through the now abandoned German airfield and up through a copse 500 yards east of Beugneux at 0605 hrs, before managing to reorientate themselves by swinging round northwards, with the French securing the aerodrome. At this point, the supporting company and battalion headquarters were also thrown into the fighting to reinforce the attack, striking the south-west corner of the wood, but were fired on at close quarters by a German machine gun which had been missed. A platoon from A Company, under Second Lieutenant Graham, then attacked the gun from the right, putting it out of action and enabling the headquarters and the remaining men to proceed to take their final objective, a point east of *Côte 189*, 1,200 yards north of Beugneux, gaining touch with the French upon their arrival. An airman's report at 0625 hrs confirmed there were friendly troops at position 49.12 but that they were being enfiladed by fire from Servenay to the north-east and from *Côte 199*. Unable to make further progress, they dug in as best they could, with a company of the 8th Scottish Rifles attempting unsuccessfully to press forward to protect the right flank, and enemy machine gun fire only ceased when the *68e Division* captured Servenay at 0910 hrs, the men having been under fire for almost three hours.[24] But it took until 1400 hrs for the remaining guns of No.3 and 4 Sections of B Company, Machine Gun Corps – released from divisional reserve – to get forward into position 500 yards north of Beugneux in support of the Scots.[25]

With just a sole officer still unwounded, the remaining 100 or so men of the 5th Argylls reached the north side of *Côte 158* and gained touch with the 5th KOSBs, who had come up the east side of the hill. They loaned Second Lieutenants Gillespie and French to the 5th Argylls to allow them to push on north, with the Argylls now led by only three junior officers.

---

22 TNA WO 95/2465: 103rd Infantry Brigade Headquarters, 1 August 1918. War diary 102nd Brigade, 0600 hrs, 1 August 1918 and TNA WO 95/2466: 5th Argylls, 1 August 1918. Lieutenant Fleming was awarded the *Croix de Guerre* by the French on 3 August 1918.
23 TNA WO 95/2451: 34th Battalion Machine Gun Corps, 1 August 1918.
24 Shakespear, p. 263; TNA WO 95/2442: Commander Royal Artillery, 1 August 1918 and TNA WO 95/2466: 5th KOSBs, 1 August 1918.
25 TNA WO 95/2451: 34th Battalion Machine Gun Corps, 1 August 1918. Of B Company MGC's 16 guns, two were completely put out of action and four more temporarily so during their operations.

Nevertheless, with a cheer from the remaining men of the Argylls, the two officers joined the advance and dashed up the hill towards the main objective, capturing a number of machine guns, two officers and about 50 other ranks along the way.[26] Meanwhile, the situation for Y Company of the 8th Scottish Rifles was particularly distressing, with their commander, Captain W.W. Ferguson, receiving two officers as reinforcements at 0200 hrs, but both Captain D.C. Johnston and Lieutenant Hardie were seriously wounded during the advance across *Côte 158*, with Hardie injured on his first day under fire.[27]

As the morning wore on, there was growing confusion between the infantry and artillery. Around 0700 hrs, the French *127e Division* requested that *30e Corps* advance its artillery batteries so that they could fire on Launoy and the *Bois de Six Sous*, from which the Germans were enfilading its troops. Fifteen minutes later, both 101st and 103rd brigades were reported to be on their objectives, with the artillery ordered to immediately lift its barrage north of the line through Le Mont Jour and Bucy le Bras Ferme, so as to avoid hitting its own troops. To their left, the *25e Division*'s artillery reported that fellow French troops had reached the *Bois du Belier* at 0750 hrs, with some *poilus* on the southern outskirts of Servenay shortly after and infantry from *25e Divi*sion reaching the Orme du Grand Rozoy, whilst *68e* and *41e divisions* outflanked Cramaille from either side, capturing the village but being unable to press north and take Saponay. With attacks appearing to have been successful up and down the line and fire superiority becoming ever more one-sided in favour of the French, Mangin ordered General Penet to send *127e Division* into action to exploit the success that he was seeing. But no sooner had *127e Division* entered the line and crossed the crest of the ridge, than a ferocious German bombardment halted its progress short of Courdoux with heavy casualties.[28]

To the west of the 5th KOSBs, the 1st Herefords were ordered to press north-eastwards towards a highpoint at *Côte 194* and a German strongpoint at Bucy le Bras Ferme, but were unable to make any progress owing to heavy enfilade fire from the crossroads just west of the farm, and dug in on their current positions at 1135 hrs. A small group of Germans suddenly appeared 120 yards ahead of the battalion HQ party, firing on the Herefords and causing several casualties, including Major A.G.R. Whitehouse, who was killed.[29] A brief skirmish ensued, resulting in the capture of several men and a large-bore anti-tank rifle, a prized possession for the Herefords.[30] Around 1235 hrs, troublesome enemy machine guns firing on the Scots from the crossroads west of Bucy le Bras were dealt with by a burst from a couple of British 18-pdrs.[31]

---

26 Shakespear, p. 263; TNA WO 95/2436: General Staff, 34th Division, narrative of operations with *Xe* French Army events of 1 August 1918 and TNA WO 95/2466: 5th KOSBs, 1 August 1918. Edmonds, p. 294, claims that every officer from the 5th Argylls had become a casualty.
27 Findlay, p. 175. Captain Johnston died of wounds at Rouen on 13 September 1918. Educated at Malvern College, he had played two first-class cricket matches for Oxford University. His name is absent from the roll of officers killed whilst serving with the 8th Scottish Rifles.
28 TNA WO 95/2442: Commander Royal Artillery, 1 August 1918 and Woldike, pp. 61–62.
29 Shakespear, p. 263 and TNA WO 95/2462: 1st Herefords, 1 August 1918.
30 Edmonds, p. 295.
31 Scott Elliot, pp. 249-50 and TNA WO 95/2442: Commander Royal Artillery, 1 August 1918.

Scott Elliot described the action involving the Argylls:

> Our scheme was to carry on to the right of a wood [*Bois de Beugneux*] full of machine guns. The Argyll's [*sic*] were attacking in front of the village and on the left of this wood. As we were advancing we met with very heavy shell-fire of all descriptions, and a rain of machine gun bullets was being poured into us. Our advance took us through fields of green corn, and the German bullets were whacking into this corn – a most disturbing sound. At one point we were held up by a nest of machine guns close at hand. Lieutenant Gillespie made reply with his Lewis guns, but Lieutenant Graham must have cleared it, as he appeared from the wood chasing the Germans at the point of the bayonet. When they saw us they at once [said], 'Kamerad.' We raced through the village and clearing it, ran into heavy machine gun fire from a wood on our right. Towards this we swung and going among the trees found that the machine guns were both to the right, in front, and to the left and only seventy or eighty yards away. I ordered the men to get down and take cover behind the trees. The Germans were firing wildly at us, and our men poured rapid fire into them. At this point, Corporal Kevan showed us all a brilliant example. Scorning to get down, he stood quite in the open, his Lewis gun on his shoulder, and played on the Germans. The gun on the right which Lieutenant Gillespie spotted was silenced first, and then the gunners in front were riddled with bullets. That gun silenced, we went forward at a bound, but the Germans ran to earth and only a bomb brought them from the depths. Two officers and sixty prisoners were sent to the rear under escort.[32]

Reaching the crest of the hill, the 5th KOSBs linked up with the 1st Herefords and 2nd Loyal North Lancs, the French consolidating their positions to the right. Having an extensive view to the north and east, there appeared to be no sign of an imminent German counterattack developing so the companies dug in on the plateau, taking the opportunity to reorganise. The Germans began shelling their positions at 0730 hrs, but with the bombardment being fairly feeble it caused few casualties and they were able to remain there for the time being.[33]

To the left of 103rd Brigade, 101st Brigade had a much stiffer test, but in most respects it was even more successful than the Scottish brigade, making rapid progress. At 0445 hrs, the men of the 4th Royal Sussex moved forward and their line initially advanced rapidly through the torn and splintered trees of the *Bois de Beugneux*. The Germans were seen retiring in disorder, forced out of the wood, and a dozen machine guns and 50 prisoners were captured or bayoneted during this textbook operation. The support given by the Stokes mortars of the 101st LTMB had proved crucial in dealing with the enemy machine guns. For a second time, Second Lieutenant Read led a party to rush and capture a German heavy machine gun nest, killing all six of the occupants.[34]

---

32 Scott Elliot, pp. 250–51.
33 TNA WO 95/2466: 5th KOSBs.
34 TNA WO 95/2458: 4th Royal Sussex, 0445 hrs, 1 August 1918; TNA WO 95/2436: General Staff, 34th Division, narrative of operations with *Xe* French Army; events of 1 August; Read, p. 370 and Takle, p. 238.

Having captured Grand Rozoy with little opposition, the French to the left were now able to push on up the hill beyond the village and reached the Brown Line around 0630 hrs, a shade under two hours after the attack had started. If anything, 101st Brigade's advance had been even more rapid than the French, with the efforts of the Queens, the Royal Sussex and Loyal North Lancs, together with a section from the 101st LTMB and supporting machine guns, all combining to capture the crest of the ridge near their Brown Line objective at around 0550 hrs, also capturing 12 machine guns and killing or taking prisoner 96 Germans. At the same time and in the absence of the French *25e Division*, which had yet to arrive, D Company of the 2nd Loyal North Lancs, under orders from Brigadier General Woodcock, advanced and carried *Côte 205* northeast of Grand Rozoy, throwing out a defensive flank to its left along the Brown Line in an attempt to protect the advancing Frenchmen. Shortly after 1000 hrs, orders were issued for the 4th Royal Sussex to be withdrawn to Brigade Reserve and for the 2nd Loyal North Lancs and 2/4th Queens to extend their inner flanks. However, with communication to the front lines nigh on impossible, the decision to extract the Royal Sussex was rescinded and instead they were ordered to maintain contact with the Queens on their left and 103rd Brigade on their right. Reports began to arrive suggesting that the 4th Royal Sussex had overshot the Brown Line and crossed the Beugnuex–Courdoux road, becoming the battalion to make the deepest advance north.[35] However, a reconnaissance at 1100 hrs revealed that the brigade was in fact 600 yards short and orders were immediately issued to advance to the Brown Line. Despite 101st Brigade being in contact with the French on their left and 103rd Brigade on their right, heavy casualties meant this order could not be attempted until support was received.[36]

Fierce enfilade fire from *Côte 203* was quickly silenced by Captain Atkinson. The CO of the 4th Cheshires, 44-yearold Lieutenant Colonel Swindells, was killed close to Le Mont Jour whilst leading the advance of his battalion in the successful capture of its objectives, Lieutenant J.A.L. Barnes thereafter assuming command of the battalion. Swindells had been seen to fall, wounded by machine gun fire, at approximately 0730 hrs, but his men had been unable to bring him in owing to the weight of fire where he fell; all efforts only resulted in more casualties, with the plan being reluctantly abandoned. Prior to the outbreak of hostilities, Swindells had been the manager of a cotton mill at Clough Bank in Cheshire, and just like Lieutenant Colonel Jourdain, he was vastly experienced, having commanded the 4th Cheshires since October 1914 and being wounded at Suvla Bay in 1915.[37] Also killed was the unfortunate Captain R.V. Taylor of the Royal Warwickshire Regiment, attached to 2nd Loyal North Lancs, who had only joined the battalion the previous day, and Captain J. Jaffe, MC, of the Royal Army Medical Corps, attached as Medical Officer of the 2/4th Somerset Light Infantry, whose body was discovered at the crossroads on the eastern end of Oulchy-la-Ville.[38] The new line ran from 849.809 to 846.814 (map coordinates) and was held by the 4th and 7th Cheshires, as well as two sections

---

35 TNA WO 95/2458: 4th Royal Sussex, 0600 hrs, 1 August 1918. The war diary of 101st Brigade has the Brown Line objective reached at 0630 hrs, the same time as the French. Rawson, p. 18.
36 TNA WO 95/2458: 4th Royal Sussex, 0645 hrs, 1 August 1918. It is unclear why this was not done until 1900 hrs.
37 TNA WO 95/2462: 4th Cheshires, 0730 hrs on 1 August 1918. Rawson, p. 18. St Oswald's Church, Bollington <https://stoswaldbollington.org.uk> TNA WO 95/2462: 4th Cheshire's, brief account of operations from 22 July to 2 August 1918.
38 TNA WO 95/2443: Assistant Director Medical Services, 1430 hrs on 1 August 1918.

of the Machine Gun Corps, with the 7th Cheshires, having been pressed into action by General Nicholson, moving cautiously through Beugneux to a ravine 400 yards north-east of the village in support of the other battalions from 102nd Brigade.[39] After holding the left flank for some time, the 2nd Loyal North Lancs were finally able to hand it over to the *25e Division* coming up in support on their left, amongst whom were a number of men from the 4th Cheshires who had become disoriented and mixed up in the ensuing melee, but had joined the advancing Frenchmen. At around 0900 hrs, a dozen French medium 'Whippet' tanks appeared 150 yards to the left of where the Royal Sussex were holed up at 847.812. The tanks' progress was halted when a cornfield was set on fire, the ripe corn burning fiercely, caused either by a German *flammenwerfer* (flamethrower), tracer fire or an exploding anti-tank shell, which caused nearby a German ammunition dump to explode, killing several men as they advanced, including Adjutant Captain J. Holding of 4th Royal Sussex. A number of wounded men also perished, unable to get away from the flames around them.[40]

The 4th Cheshires withdrew to some dead ground 100 yards to the rear, where they sheltered and reorganised in several newly created shell craters around 1100 hrs.[41] *30e Corps* received reports that the infantry had substantially gained their objectives as early as 0600 hrs, which included *2e CA* to the immediate right of *30e CA*, advancing their line towards Saponay from the east and towards the west of some woods near Fère-en-Tardenois.[42] General Penet immediately decided to launch *127e Division* to exploit the success by passing through the 34th Division towards Courdoux and Launoy, with Servenay and the *Bois de Belier* reportedly safe in French hands, captured by the *68e* and *25e divisions* respectively. More importantly, the success of *30e CA* allowed General Mangin to issue the order for *20e CA* to attack Droizy.[43]

Sergeant Pugh of the 1st Herefords described the events of 1 August:

> We next went over cornfields with a wood on our right where there were many Germans, and we got machine gunfire [*sic*] very hot on the right flank. We had a good many killed about this time one was Major Whitehouse; especially when we were going through the cornfield where the Germans were with machine guns. That cornfield was ripe for cutting and really was in no man's land. It was fine cover for snipers and machine guns. We attacked in open formation expecting to drive the Germans out of the Woods but the machine guns stopped us. In that attack there were lots of whippet-like tanks rendered useless from the German gas, not through gas affecting the crews but affecting the petrol engines so that they would not work. They were practically in no man's land. … There were a lot of his wounded in that action and a good many wounded fellows and others gassed passed through us on the way to the rear helping each other as best they could. Some had been blinded temporarily with the gas. It was here that I saw a platoon of the Cheshire's cut up, a big shell dropping amongst them.

---

39   TNA WO 95/2462: 7th Cheshires, 1345 hrs on 1 August 1918.
40   Read, pp. 371–72.
41   TNA WO 95/2462: 4th Cheshires, 0900 hrs on 1 August 1918.
42   Greenwood, p. 176.
43   Greenwood, p. 176; Shakespear, p. 264; TNA WO 95/2457: 2/4th Queens mention German *flammenwerfer* in their war diary of 1 August and TNA WO 95/2442: Commander Royal Artillery, 1 August 1918.

> A lot of the poor fellows were blown to pieces, so that one could not recognise them at all, some were cut through the middle and others had their arms and legs blown off. It was here that we suffered most of our casualties, we had to wait till night time to fetch the wounded in – that is to say those who could not come in themselves.[44]

In spite of the French putting 45 light tanks into action on the 1st around the area of Grand Rozoy, many were quickly put out of action, including an entire tank company destroyed by two German 77mm guns firing with pinpoint accuracy.[45] Even though there had been setbacks, reports to corps and *Xe Armée* headquarters indicated that the line was progressing along the entire front. To the north-west, the wooded Hartennes plateau, Tigny and the Crise stream were all taken, and the Scots and French were advancing through Buzancy. To the east, the Dormans–Reims road was crossed, Ville-en-Tardenois was encircled and the valley of the River Ardre was finally cracked open by an attack of the two British formations, 51st (Highland) Division and 62nd (West Riding) Division, and the French divisions in Godley's XXII Corps.[46]

Around 1100 hrs, French reconnaissance planes reported that German troops (from the 18th Württemberg Division) were massing behind the *Bois de Bousse* and in the Droizy ravine, ready to counterattack and recapture Bucy le Bras Ferme and Launoy, but the reports also confirmed that French artillery was firing on the German positions and preventing the attack from forming. Unfortunately for General Mangin, he had no more troops to send into the attack, having already deployed the fresh *128e Division,* inserted into the line between the *18e* and *1er CA* to reinforce his left flank. He might be able to find a couple of reserve brigades here and there but putting them into the fighting was a risky choice that went totally against Army doctrine; if he failed or if Pétain found out, then he would not survive a third time. So for once Mangin paused, weighing up the right course of action and impatiently awaiting further news of how the battle was developing. That news duly arrived, with the now clear skies witnessing numerous dogfights and allowing the aerial observers a good view of the fighting below.

The reconnaissance aircraft reported that numerous fires had broken out in the main centres, including Soissons, Fismes, Loupiegne, Arcy-Sainte-Restitue, Branges, Lhuys and Orton, as well as seeing several long columns of German troops retiring north towards the Vesle valley. The news of large numbers of the enemy withdrawing was just what Mangin had long dreamt of, meaning that he would not after all have to take the gamble of throwing more men into the fight. However, he wanted to chance his arm and see if his exhausted troops had one final attack left in them: a sharp assault on the strongpoint of the Orme du Grand Rozoy across to Servenay would disrupt the German retreat and, if strong enough, might even break open the enemy line entirely.[47]

By 1700 hrs, it had become evident to the attackers that the line had not been advanced quite far enough, with enemy guns in the valleys on either side of Bucy le Bras Ferme and in the Arcy valley able to fire on the French *68e Division* holding Servenay, causing a number of casualties. After consulting with General Menvielle commanding *68e Division*, Nicholson issued verbal orders to Brigadier General Walthall, CRA, and his three infantry brigadiers for

---

44 Sergeant Pugh, 1st Herefords cited in 'Herefordshire Regiment: Their First World War Story'.
45 Goya, p. 221.
46 Michelin, p. 33
47 Greenwood, p. 176.

an advance of 300–400 yards to commence at 1900 hrs, supported by a rolling barrage. The barrage, supported by heavy howitzer fire on *Côte 199*, would advance 100 yards every four minutes and finish 300 yards beyond the Brown Line, where it would remain for a quarter hour, before lifting, supported by howitzers firing on *Côte 199*. Around 1900 hrs, the 1st Herefords on top of *Côte 189* were relieved by 103rd Brigade and concentrated on a reverse slope 600 yards to the rear, halfway between the heights and Beugneux, whilst the Royal Sussex, with the Queens on the left and the 8th Scottish Rifles on the right, following verbal orders received at 1750 hrs, advanced to the Brown Line with little opposition, capturing six more machine guns and consolidating their new positions. The *68e Division* to the right of 34th Division advanced the left of their line to *Côte 172*. Advanced posts were thrown out and liaison with the French was maintained.

The Operation Order also stressed the need for vigilance and for positions to be consolidated in depth, with use made of machine guns and Lewis guns to cover the front.[48] With Nicholson worried about potential German counterattacks, the two companies of the 34th Machine Gun Battalion in reserve were ordered to fire on the valleys east and west of *Côte 199* to search out any Germans sheltering there, supported by artillery harassing fire on the same area. The barrage commenced at 1900 hrs, with the line advancing the necessary distance and *68e* and 34th divisions reaching *Côte 172*, but with some casualties in 101st Brigade on the left. A patrol by the *1er Zouves* brought in seven men from the 7th Guards Regiment suffering from being mustard gassed. These prisoners confirmed that *Bois du Plessier* had been evacauated. Having consolidated their positions, the men settled down in the shallow trenches or shell holes, hoping for a quiet night.[49]

General Fayolle reported the situation at 1900 hrs that evening, with *VIe Armée* having reached Plateau 230 (Reddy Ferme) beyond Cierges and holding *Bois du Meunière* and Goussancourt. Meanwhile, *Xe Amée* occupied the entire crest running from the Orme du Grand Rozoy to Servenay, together with the villages of Grand Rozoy, Beugneux, Cramoiselle, Courdoux, Cramaille and Servenay, having captured another 600 German prisoners during the fighting. Fayolle stressed the need to maintain reserves so as not to jeopardise the evident success and to spare the infantry as much as possible by reducing the pace of further attacks, confining them to the more important locations. He also ordered future attacks to be prepared with the utmost care and maximum use of artillery, ensuring *VIe* and *Xe Armées* maintained constant contact, with the boundary south of La Râperie. With the imminent departure of the two British divisions and no more reserves available (they having been moved north for the Amiens offensive), Fayolle ordered Mangin to continue the advance of his right flank in the direction of Arcy-Sainte-Restitue, but the remainder of *Xe Armée* was now to adopt a defensive attitude.[50]

---

48 There is a handwritten note in TNA WO 95/2436: General Staff, 34th Division, which reads: "Very doubtful if 1/4 Cheshires did reach Le Mont Jour." The war diary also suggests the 4th Cheshires were relieved by the French *127e Division*.
49 TNA WO 95/2436: General Staff, 34th Division, Operation Order No.242, issued verbally at 1750 hrs and later in written format at 1900 hrs, 1 August 1918. TNA WO 95/2458: 4th Royal Sussex, 1900 hrs, 1 August 1918; TNA WO 95/2465: 103rd Infantry Brigade Headquarters, Operation Order No.242, 1 August 1918 and TNA WO 95/2466: 5th KOSBs, 1 August 1918 and AFGG, *30e Corps*, 1 August 1918.
50 Instructions to the Sixth and Tenth Armies, No. 3.874, at 1900 hrs on 1 August 1918 cited in Woldike, pp. 174–75.

The following day, he wrote again to Mangin and Degoutte: "The Château-Thierry 'pocket' is being emptied. It is the crowning achievement of the counter-offensive started on the 18th by the *Xe* and *VIe Armées*."[51]

An 'SOS' signal went up at 2100 hrs, indicating a German counterattack was imminent, so the Herefords reoccupied their front-line positions once again. But in spite of heavy German shelling, no counterattack materialised, the 'SOS' being a false alarm. The Herefords were relieved by the 7th Cheshires under the cover of darkness at 2300 hrs. The 2/4th Somersets, attached to 103rd Brigade as its reserve from 1830 hrs onwards that evening, accompanied by a section of the machine gun battalion, advanced and by evening were also dugin in a small valley east of Beugneux, protecting the brigade's right flank. Tellingly, the 103rd Light Trench Mortar Battery had played no part in the success, having not fired a single round all day.[52] This last point is surprising, since the Stokes mortars were sufficiently close to have been able to shell *Côte 158* during the attack. With the division being in place on the GMP Line for two days, the LTMB had time to bring up sufficient shells for the task, so a lack of ammunition seems unlikely. Nor had it suffered any significant casualties in the preceding days. The most likely explanation for lack of action of the 103rd LTMB therefore is that the speed of advance prevented it from keeping pace with the fast-moving infantry, yet this contrasts sharply with the contribution of the 101st LTMB supporting 101st Brigade. The war diary describes the action of the artillery, both in the initial bombardment and providing covering fire, to have been very effective, and there is no doubt that it played a significant role in securing Beugneux and the ridge above. Two of the field batteries were able to move forward as early as 0500 hrs, with all remaining batteries doing so as soon as the barrage ceased. Many of these were able to push forward by 3,000–4,000 yards, making a significant contribution towards supporting the infantry during the remainder of the action.[53] Once again, the adage 'artillery conquers, but infantry occupies' was perfectly true here.

To Scott Elliot, it was a thrilling moment and a magnificent victory. The formidable and fortified entrenchments of Beugneux village and the dominating heights beyond, held with great determination by the Germans, had, after three resolute attacks, at last been captured. By the end of the day, the front line ran from the French *127e Division*'s positions at *Bois nr.4*, along a track to the crossroads 68.07, to a track running north-west to 59.09 and to the *68e Division* at *Côte 172*.[54]

The night of 1/2 August passed noticeably quietly, apart from a few long-range shells falling beyond the front line, and according to Read the quiet across the battlefield was strange and eerie as peace descended over the men of 34th Division dug in on the ridge trying to sleep despite heavy overnight rain.[55] The capture of a couple of prisoners revealed that the Germans had withdrawn just before midnight to new defensive positions further north, and by early the

---

51   Instructions to the Sixth and Tenth Armies, No. 387, at 1900 hrs on 2 August 1918 cited in Woldike, p. 179.
52   TNA WO 95/2462: 1st Herefords, 1 August 1918 and TNA WO 95/2465: 103rd Infantry Brigade Headquarters, 1 August 1918.
53   TNA WO 95/2436: General Staff, 34th Division, narrative of operations with *Xe* French Army events of 1 August 1918.
54   TNA WO 95/2436: General Staff, 34th Division, narrative of operations with *Xe* French Army events of 1 August 1918.
55   Read, p. 377.

next morning the eastern horizon was aglow with burning ammunition dumps, indicating the enemy setting fire to and destroying anything they could not carry away.[56] After an advance of several hundred yards and encountering no German opposition, the front line was pushed forward. At 1115 hrs, orders were received that the French *25e Division* would pass through the 34th Division later that day, to make contact with and harass the retiring Germans. At 1500 hrs, the Frenchmen duly arrived, to cheers from the British, in pursuit of the retreating Germans, allowing the 34th Division to withdraw to the rear and to send salvage parties as far as Le Mont Jour and *Côte 199*.[57] Captain Ferguson observed the remarkably stolid and cheerful appearance and fine physique of the Frenchmen marching past their weary allies,[58] a far cry from the image of the French as a 'spent force' that some might imagine when reading about the French Army of the summer of 1918, believed unable to make any meaningful contribution to victory. On the night of 2 August, the Germans began to occupy new positions on the River Crise about Ambrief, Mareuil-en-Dole, Dravegny and Lhery, 3 miles to the north, and withdrew from Soissons, allowing the French *11e* and *69e divisions* to reoccupy the shattered city at 1900 hrs that evening. The Germans bombarded the eastern portion of Soissons as they fell back, making the French occupation somewhat precarious.[59] With von Boehn's army falling back a fourth time, this time in a more general retirement, Mangin issued one final rallying cry to the commanders of his remaining divisions, saying that they must pursue the enemy and be on the Aisne and the Vesle by the evening.[60] This would keep up the pressure on the Boche and might also assist the impending Allied offensive due to commence on 8 August.

56   Scott Elliot, p. 251.
57   TNA WO 95/2462: 7th Cheshires, 2 August 1918.
58   Findlay, p. 175.
59   Takle, p. 239; Neiberg, p. 176 and Woldike, p. 63.
60   Greenwood, pp. 178-79.

17

Paying the 'Butcher's Bill'

17.1 Summary of casualties sustained, 22 July-3 August

With the Germans driven back to newly prepared positions on the River Vesle, this was finally the decisive victory Foch and Pétain had craved for and the successful termination of Foch's first "hook to the right".[1] Yet more heavy rain fell on 2 August, soaking the men to the skin. With the exhausted and drenched troops having no greatcoats, except those they could collect from their foe, they headed back down into Beugneux for a hot meal and some much-needed rest in one of the bombed-out buildings. On the 3rd, several members of the 8th Scottish Rifles were awarded the *Croix de Guerre* by a representative of *Xe Armée*, including Lieutenant Colonel Findlay, who also received the *Légion d'honneur (Chevalier)*, France's highest award for gallantry.[2] At 0715 hrs on the 4th, the fourth anniversary of the outbreak of war, the 5th KOSBs departed Beugneux, marching to the crossroads on the Oulchy-le-Château–Soissons road, where they were met by a fleet of French buses, Ferguson recalling the welcome sight of London buses to convey the 8th Scottish Rifles west.[3] With the battalion unable to take all of their rations with them, the grateful *poilus* quickly rushed up to take advantage of the left-behind booty of a large number of tins of bully beef and cheese. Motoring through the delightful French towns and villages of Villers-Cotterêts, Vez, Crepy and Dammartin, before arriving at Rouvres at 1800 hrs, spirits began to lift with the joyful sights they encountered along the route. But at the end of the long journey there was a sight even more welcoming: a decent bath and the chance to clean up and soak their weary bodies in the warm evening sunshine. The officers and men, many of whom were able to find a bed for the first time in weeks, bedded down for a night of blissful sleep, with their slumber finally undisturbed by the sound of artillery. To the north the fighting continued for a few more days but the involvement of the 34th and 15th (Scottish) divisions had come to an end.

Whilst the 34th Division must have felt somewhat frustrated that it was not given the opportunity to rout the enemy, most recognised that it was now too exhausted and too weak

---

1   Scott Elliot, p. 252.
2   Findlay, p. 176.
3   Findlay, p. 177.

to do so and welcomed their relief on the night of 2/3 August after three major engagements over 12 arduous summer days. On 4 August, the division moved – some by bus and others on foot – back to the entraining area and from there back to Bergues, their site of departure three weeks previously. The embussing schedule for 4 August, shown below, gives some indication of the level of casualties suffered by the division. For example, 103rd Brigade, which contained the three Scottish battalions, walked out with less than a thousand men.[4]

101st Brigade HQ (1,340 all ranks)	70
1 MG Coy	125
A Bn	264
B Bn	273
C Bn	323
TMB	35
207th Fd Coy & No. 2 Coy Train	120
104th Field Ambce	130
102nd Brigade HQ (1,305 all ranks)	120
1 MG Coy	125
A Bn	220
B Bn	440
C Bn	280
208 Fd Coy & No.3 Coy Train	120
103rd Brigade HQ (924 all ranks)	56
1 MG Coy	125
A Bn	236
B Bn	181
C Bn	153
209 Fd Coy & No.4 Coy Train	120
TMB	53
DHQ & Signals (40) (1,241 all ranks)	150
HQ RE & HQ Train	36
HQ MG Bn & 1 Co	155
102 Fd Ambce	130
103 Fd Ambce	130
2/4 Som LI	640

[4] TNA WO 95/2436: General Staff, 34th Division, Operation Order No. 243 issued at 1915 hrs on 3 August 1918.

Although perhaps not quite as high as during the previous two attacks, casualties had once again been severe, particularly among the already depleted officers, with most battalions reduced to less than 250 men by the time they withdrew on 2nd August:

Casualties 1–3 Aug[5]	Officers	Other Ranks	**Total**
Killed	12	138	**150**
Wounded	18	479	**497**
Missing	1	31	**32**
Total	**31**	**648**	**679**

The 5th KOSB's casualties amounted to 12 officers and 213 other ranks, the battalion being reduced to a mere 330 all ranks, with 1 August 1918 regarded as one of the three worst days experienced by the battalion after 12 July 1915 at Gallipoli and the First Battle of Gaza in March 1917.[6]

5th KOSB casualties	Killed		Wounded		Total casualties	
	Officers	Other ranks	Officers	Other ranks	Officers	Other ranks
22–28 July			1	14	1	14
28–31 July	2	17	5	21	7	38
31 July–5 Aug	2	25	2	136	4	161
Total	**4**	**42**	**8**	**171**	**12**	**213**

A battlefield casualty return states that the battalion had a strength of 39 officers and 826 other ranks on 30 June, and 31 officers and 491 other ranks on 9 August (two officers and 62 other ranks joining on 8 August). Casualties were listed as follows on 9 August:[7]

	Officers	Other ranks	Total
Killed	3	43	46
Wounded	8	339	347
Missing	1	51	52
Total	**12**	**433**	**445**

By the time darkness fell on 1 August, the 5th Argylls could muster just two officers and 130 other ranks, plus a Medical Officer. This contrasts with the losses from the 4th Royal Sussex and 4th Cheshires, who were both in the thick of the fighting throughout the day. Losses for

---

5   Shakespear, p. 266.
6   Scott Elliot, pp. 254–56.
7   TNA WO 95/2466: 5th KOSBs, 9 August 1918.

the Sussex totalled just 41 other ranks – 10 men killed, 28 wounded and three missing – with casualties of just seven officers and 59 other ranks for the Cheshires, although these figures did include the Battalion CO, Lieutenant Colonel Swindells, and his Adjutant, Captain Holding, both of whom had been killed. The officers were buried at location 827.787 and other ranks at 846.807.[8] One of the reasons for the relatively low casualty numbers of several battalions was that their attack was successful much earlier in the day, with the Royal Sussex reaching their objective by 0600 hrs after just over an hour of fighting. The 8th Scottish Rifles, largely in support of the 5th KOSBs and 5th Argylls, also had comparatively few casualties: five officers wounded, plus nine other ranks killed and 43 wounded.[9]

The 2nd Loyal North Lancs casualties comprised Captain Taylor and 20 other ranks killed, three other ranks who died from wounds, three missing and 55 other ranks wounded. When it embussed on 4 August in yet more rain, it departed with seven officers and 359 other ranks. Presumably the only reason there were not more casualties amongst the officers was that there were only seven to start with.[10] Despite being held back as Divisional Reserve and only arriving at 1830 hrs once most of the fighting had subsided, the 2/4th Somerset Light Infantry suffered a total of 68 casualties, including four officers, primarily from shelling and gas.[11]

According to the ADMS, casualties for 34th Division during this period were as follows:[12]

- 7 officers and 264 other ranks for the period until noon on 1 August;
- 12 officers and 368 other ranks for the period until noon on 2 August;

Summary of casualties sustained 22 July – 3 August[13]

	Killed		Wounded		Missing		**Total**	
	Officers	Other ranks	Officers	Other ranks	Officers	Other ranks	**Officers**	**Other ranks**
22–28 July	2	128	43	1,095		26	**45**	**1,249**
29–31 July	16	206	61	1,356		136	**77**	**1,698**
1–3 Aug	12	138	18	479	1	53	**31**	**670**
Total	30	472	122	2,930	1	215	153	3,617

In total, the 34th Division lost 153 officers and 3,617 men during the 12 days of fighting, almost all of whom were casualties on three days: 23 and 29 July and 1 August. For the Germans fighting in the battle, their casualties had been nothing short of horrific: their total casualties

---

8   TNA WO 95/2458: 4th Royal Sussex, 1 August 1918 and TNA WO 95/2462: 4th Cheshires, 1-2 August 1918.
9   War diary 8th Scottish Rifles, 1 August, 2030 hrs.
10 TNA WO 95/2457: 2nd Loyal North Lancs, record of operations of the 2nd Battalion Loyal North Lancashire Regiment from 23 July to 4 August 1918.
11 TNA WO 95/2451: 2/4th Somerset Light Infantry, July-August 1918.
12 TNA WO 95/2443: Assistant Director Medical Services, 2 August 1918.
13 TNA WO 95/2439: Adjutant and Quartermaster General, 12 August 1918.

for the period 15 July to 2 August were estimated at over 168,000, with more than 29,000 taken prisoner. Across the whole of the GAR, they had taken prisoner 689 officers and 27,424 other ranks, as well as capturing 4,400 machine guns and 600 *minenwerfer*. The attacks on 1 August around Grand Rozoy and Beugneux resulting in the capture of four officers and 250 men by *25e Division* and four officers and 246 men by 34th Division.[14]

17.2 The significance of the capture of the ridge north of Grand Rozoy and Beugneux and the action of the British 34th Division

"The battle of Soissons was a great tactical and strategic success for the Allies, striking a blow to the German army that it never recovered from."[15]
"The victory of August 1st completes the victory of July 18th and ends in pursuit."[16]

The fighting of the British 34th Division was but one small part of *the* turning point of the Great War and its impact on the outcome of the Second Battle of the Marne should not be overstated. After all, there were just four BEF divisions involved in the battle, representing only 10 percent of the total Allied troops engaged, and the battle is rightly classed as a Franco-American victory. It should not be forgotten that it was the French, not the British, who made the first great counter-punch on 18 July 1918, even though the British had enjoyed three months of relative calm on their front since Operation *Georgette* had wound down. That said, the British did play their part in this battle, repaying in small part the losses that the French had suffered when they came to the aid of the BEF during Operations *Michael* and *Georgette* in the spring, with a total of 47 French divisions having been sent north to prop up the British defences. Unfortunately, when it came the turn of the British to repay that debt they were found wanting, sending just four divisions, some armoured cars and a brigade of aircraft to the *poche*. This once again validates two important factors. Firstly, that the French were still the senior partner in the Entente, with arguably the most effective and certainly the most mechanised of all belligerents still involved. Pétain recognised the threat and was willing to rapidly send massive amounts of support to the BEF on both occasions when the British front was attacked. Foch, although newly appointed as Generalissimo, had less of an influence during these early days and wasn't appointed until several days of Operation *Michael* had elapsed. This alone shows the best leadership qualities of Pétain, and whilst he certainly had his character flaws – as well as his critics – a reluctance to see the bigger picture with an urgent need to support his key ally under attack was not one of them. Secondly, it shows that when the shoe was on the other foot and it was the French requiring support from their ally, then the British were largely deaf to their needs. Haig worried too much about his own sector and failed to support the French in the same way, either in May (*Blücher-Yorck*), June (*Gneisenau*) or July (*Marneschutz-Reims*), sending virtually nothing south. Even for the counteroffensive, Pétain only received four British divisions, and these were very nearly sent back before they had even arrived. This forced the French to instead rely on the largely untried and under-prepared AEF divisions for the task.

---

14 Greenhalgh (2011), p. 403; (2014), p. 323. Fayolle, p. 124. AFGG, *30e Corps*, 1 August 1918.
15 Gale, p. 146.
16 Mangin (1950), p. 287.

Despite the criticisms, especially the small size of Godley's XXII Corps sent by Haig, the four fresh and rested British divisions had helped to reinject some impetus to the counteroffensive and to finish the job of recapturing the ground lost in those frantic few days at the end of May, which had begun on the morning of 18 July. It is therefore somewhat ironic that XXII Corps had originally been intended for use by the GAC primarily in a defensive role, to relieve the tired and depleted Italian II Corps from Berthelot's *Ve Armée* which had been hard pressed in defence. But whilst on their way, two divisions had their destination changed and all four divisions ended up being involved in offensive rather than defensive action, as Haig had hoped they would. Whilst it is true that it had taken the Allies twice as long to retake the ground that they had lost at the end of May, they *had* done it and the victory was theirs, with the attack on 1 August being the decisive engagement. The Germans retired the same distance between 31 July and 3 August as they had done in the 13 days from 18 July, and this was especially true for *Xe Armée*.[17] At times, the advance – especially in the early days of the counteroffensive on the 18th and 19th – had verged on turning into a rout, breaking through German lines to the open countryside behind. But the stubborn German defence had progressively slowed the attacks down, allowing the Boche to retire to their new defensive positions.

17.3 34th Division casualties, including major engagements[18]

It is true to say that the number of casualties in this battle was relatively low when compared to other battles fought by the 34th Division during the Great War. Yet considering the success of the division during the battle and the unique circumstances facing it, and that the entire infantry was completely new, then the results achieved were remarkable. Whilst casualties were lower than in either March or April when attempting to stem the German Spring offensives, both of these were defensive battles; and on no other occasion during an offensive battle did the 34th Division achieve a bigger advance and a larger prize than it did in late July and early August 1918.

---

17 Rawson, p. 19.
18 Shakespear.

	Killed		Wounded		Missing		Total	
	Officers	Other Ranks	Officers	Other Ranks	Officers	Other Ranks	Officers	Other Ranks
Somme	84	1,103	145	2,880	23	2,356	252	6,339
1916	158	1,364	439	9,301	125	3,015	722	13,680
Arras	58	517	140	3,103	40	1,517	238	5,137
Poelcapelle	16	287	76	1,013	11	394	103	1,694
1917	129	1,446	392	8,262	56	2,218	577	11,926
Michael	20	192	56	1,005	62	1,844	138	3,041
Georgette	50	549	227	3,564	48	3,041	325	7,154
Marne	30	472	122	1,944	1	193	153	2,609
1918	115	1,317	420	8,254	121	4,746	656	14,317
Total	402	4,127	1,251	25,817	302	9,979	1,955	39,923

Elizabeth Greenhalgh makes an accurate assessment of the importance of seizing the initiative from the Germans during this battle. Had Pétain been overcome with a sense of pessimism, overridden Foch's urgings and halted the counteroffensive when it started to bog down around 21/22 July, or even postponed the attack of 18 July entirely, then she believed the war might well have continued into 1919, with unknown consequences for the Entente. Doughty, meanwhile, asserts that neither Pétain nor Haig recognised as fully as did Foch the strategic opportunity opening before the Allies as a result of the counteroffensive that commenced on the 18th, which proved to be one of the most important operations of the entire war, precipitating the disintegration of the German Army and unquestionably removing the threat to the French capital. Michael Neiberg goes even further, saying that the victory changed the entire tenor of the war and made victory in 1918 possible.[19] Its place in the history of the Great War is therefore as *the* pivotal moment, *the* turning point of the entire war.

One result that the success definitely achieved was that it was the master key which unlocked the wider Western Front, enabling future offensive battles to be contemplated and Foch's *grande offensive* – a co-ordinated series of Allied attacks – to become operational, commencing on 8 August with the Battle of Amiens. In July the Germans had to throw in 73 divisions to defend their gains, with the irony that it was Crown Prince Rupprecht rather than the Allies who was forced to send 13 of his divisions south to stem the Allied advance, and all to no avail.[20] This left Ludendorff's much-hoped-for *Hagen* offensive in complete tatters, with a reluctant Quartermaster General forced into a humiliating climbdown of first postponing the attack and then cancelling it entirely. Worse still, it had been the Germans and not the Allies who had to reinforce their lines with divisions pulled down from the north. All that did was weaken the Flanders defences further, making them increasingly vulnerable to attack and the fighting between 18 July and 2 August 1918 which unlocked the final Hundred Days of the war.

19 Greenhalgh (2011), pp. 405-06 and Doughty, p. 473. Neiberg, p. 186.
20 Greenwood, p. 174.

Takle describes the battle as an "epochal turning point in the course of the long struggle of attrition between the Allies and the Germans".[21] His assessment is absolutely correct. These commenced with the Battle of Amiens, where the British Fourth Army under General Sir Henry Rawlinson and French *Ier Armée* (General Debeney) attacked the German Second Army of General Georg von der Marwitz at daybreak on 8 August. To many British historians, 8 August is considered to be the turning point of the war. But they are wrong, because it had already been turned on its apex on the morning of 18 July, when the initiative was convincingly torn out of the Germans' grasp once and for all. The German plans to win the war in 1918, so vaunted by Hindenburg and Ludendorff, were now an impossibility. Worse than that, the defeat had damaged the credibility of the German Army with its allies, and few still believed that Germany could win the war. At home and at the front, the morale of the German people, already suffering significant shortages – especially of food – began to plummet. Desertions rocketed and discipline ebbed away yet further, as ordinary troops realised that their hoped-for victory was now just a phantom.

Although Haig remained reluctant to send XXII Corps, with its four divisions, south to support the French, he was eventually persuaded by both Foch and Pétain of the merits of their plans. He should take credit, since he also resisted the urgings of the British government to stop XXII Corps' movement shortly before their departure. It would have been very easy for Haig to cave in to his government and reverse the decision, but he chose to ignore it. Whatever the rationale, Haig eventually demonstrated strong and decisive leadership at a time when he could have claimed otherwise, with Franco-British relations especially weak during this period. After all, he'd been very keen to complain that the French had not played a full part when the British were attacked in March and April but been much less vocal when the boot was on the other foot, with the French front being attacked in May and June but sending no divisions south to their aid. Having suffered severe casualties in the first few days, French manpower was stretched to the very limit, with almost no reserves to call on to support the attack, and it is likely that they would have had to call a halt to the counteroffensive without the British reinforcements. They could of course have requested additional American divisions from General Pershing, but these were still in training, few had seen any sort of fighting and almost none were anywhere near being combat-ready. It is likely, therefore, that additional AEF divisions would have performed poorly if called upon. Had either the British declined to send XXII Corps or the novice AEF divisions been thrown into battle, then the counteroffensive would have probably ground to a halt or been stopped by Foch. If that had happened, then it is likely that Ludendorff would have decided to launch Operation *Hagen* in Flanders during August, with some of the heaviest guns being moved there on the morning of 18 July.[22] The other factor coming into play was the undoubted fighting quality of the four British divisions, all of which were able to add impetus to the attack at the crucial moment. The 15th (Scottish), 51st (Highland) and 62nd (West Riding) divisions were all veteran formations, with vast amounts of experience. Although the infantry of 34th Division had never experienced fighting on the Western Front, all of the infantry battalions had considerable battle experience in other theatres, notably Gallipoli and more recently Palestine, and all could be said to be battle-hardened. On top of that, the other

21 Takle, p. 246.
22 Takle, p. 245.

troops of the division – the artillery, machine gunners, trench mortar batteries, engineers etc. – were all Western Front veterans, as was its General Staff. Even if they were unused to working together, this knowledge, flexibility and experience inevitably came into play during this time and compensated for a lack of time spent together. Takle describes the wider battle in which the action of 34th Division was part of a "narrow but stunning victory, which had an instant impact in dislocating key elements of Ludendorff's meticulous plans", forcing him to first postpone on 20 July and then abandon entirely his plans for Operation *Hagen*, as well as further attacks on Reims and Épernay.[23] Although they were unable to completely sever the jugular vein and cut off the German Seventh and Ninth Armies in the Marne salient, nevertheless, the success of the counteroffensive was still a decisive blow from which the Germans would not recover and truly represents ***the*** turning point of the Great War.

Edmonds, the official British historian, described the battle as being over by the 24th, bar a few local affairs and a final "flare-up" on 1 August. He continues that it became no more than a "follow-up", the Germans retiring in their own time "behind the Vesle and the Aisne below Condé, covering their night marches by bombing of the Allied bivouacs and leaving behind gas 'booby traps' in the numerous large caves to be found in this part of the country".[24] Was it really little more than following up and harassing a retiring enemy? Edmonds is, however, correct when he asserts that although the Allied troops had been fighting alongside each other for four years, they knew very little of each other's methods, with the small amount of "mingling" of the two combatants in the intervening period often creating more difficulties than they solved. He mentions the differences in language, co-operation at the junctions of the two armies and a lack of effort made to familiarise staff officers with the organisation and methods of their ally. He also says that the Germans were absolutely determined to hold the neck of the pocket open for as long as possible, in order to allow their troops in the Marne salient to withdraw, with orders for them to fight to the last man.

But the differences between the British and the French go much deeper than what Edmonds describes. Something as simple, yet as vital, as a map was a perfect example of the challenges the British faced. The scales were different (British maps being in Imperial measurements and the French in metric), and they required practice in reading them and time to do so, which simply was not available. Moreover, there was a shortage of these maps, which would not have been such a problem if the British had been familiar with the territory they were attacking. But without the opportunity for more than a cursory reconnaissance (if one was possible at all), many of the officers went into an attack almost blind. Hardly any of the technology or equipment worked across both armies, from the simple rifle to the different calibre of the artillery, the telephone system and even the form of measurement requiring translation. This meant that neither ally could use the other's equipment, so when they did become involved in joint operations, such as during this battle, the obstacles to success were considerable and probably insurmountable.

There are just too many examples of delays to orders, especially during the early part of the battle, for this fact to be ignored. Despite General Nicholson seeing a significant improvement in the level of information arriving before the attack of 29 July, this was likely to have been due to nearly a week having passed between the attacks on the 23rd and the 29th, giving ample time

---

23 Takle, pp. 245–46.
24 Edmonds, p. 269.

to prepare very detailed plans for the subsequent attack. This contrasts starkly with the events leading up to the first attack by 34th Division on 23 July, with orders little more than verbal instructions; almost nothing in the way of written orders or maps were received early enough to be of practical use. Then there was the different approach to battle adopted by the two nations by the middle of 1918. The British, chastened by the terrible losses of the Battle of Passchendaele in the autumn of 1917 and the reversals of the Spring offensives, were by now firmly espousing the tactics of 'bite and hold', with limited and constrained objectives delivered with masses of preparatory artillery fire prior to the attack going in – a classic example of 'artillery conquers, infantry occupies'. This battle was both similar and different from the British method: whilst the bombardments were fierce (similar to the British), they were, in contrast to their ally, relatively short-lived in duration. Both nations were completely aligned behind the idea that artillery was key to the success of any attack, and it is notable that General Penet felt that the British organic artillery was too weak and thus decided to augment the British guns with additional French heavy artillery and howitzers for both the 29 July and 1 August attacks.

Other differences had their own impact, which although not significant on their own, in combination contributed to some of the difficulties that the British experienced. For example, railway loading ramps were found to be too narrow to accommodate British transport equipment, requiring a hastily improvised fudge, with French bus capacity also smaller than British vehicles.[25] Men were often dropped several miles from their destination, requiring lengthy and tiring marches, which caused a number of them to fall out *en route*. With the 34th Division being displaced away from other British units, with the exception of the 15th (Scottish) to the north, they also experienced shortages of some key supplies, including food, tobacco and beer; one particularly intoxicating example was when the British thought they were drinking beer, only to find out that they had been downing bottles of French champagne! The challenges of relief were noted as one of the lessons learned, with the after-action report suggesting that relief could be easily and simply effected by attacking through divisions in line instead of relieving units in situ. This was a sensible idea and one which was deployed to good effect on 1 August.

Perhaps the biggest difficulty of all was that of communication, which at times all but broke down due to the fact that too few officers spoke the other's language. One of XXII Corps' lessons learned which found its way into the *Official History* was that very few British or French officers understood each other over the telephone, requiring liaison officers and translators to do much of the speaking, with consequent delays in orders and instructions being relayed between each other. It was also often difficult, if not impossible, to get telegraphic messages through on French lines, with messages taking as long as 24 hours to get from XXII Corps to French flank corps. The need to have effective and intelligent liaison officers was stressed in the after-action report, with the lack of warning orders issued by the French (assumed to be for reasons of secrecy) hindering operations somewhat and making things more difficult than they ought to have been. Edmonds states that more British officers spoke French than vice versa, so French was generally used at headquarters and during conferences but having effective liaison officers was viewed by Godley as more important than the ability to speak French fluently, perhaps because he spoke no French! Difficulties relating to language, translation and suspect interpretation and comprehension of details given in French were major obstacles and one such

---

25 Edmonds, p. 308.

instance almost ended in disaster: the delay in halting French artillery which was falling short onto the British front line caused a number of unnecessary British casualties. That is not to say that the French were solely to blame, since British guns had also shelled their own troops in the past and would do so again, especially when the position of the front line became blurred and confused. Nevertheless, the length of time it took to correct the error undoubtedly caused additional casualties. Edmonds concludes, however, that despite these clear obstacles, the four British divisions of XXII Corps equipped themselves well and did a great deal to restore good relations with the French which had been so badly damaged during the reversal in the spring of 1918.[26]

It should not be forgotten that the battle was a decisive victory for the Allies, both strategically and morally. There is no doubt that it wrested back the initiative from the Germans and was conclusive proof that their five major offensives had not broken the Allies. Indeed, the Allies were now so strong that they could start their own massive counteroffensive just three days after the Germans had launched Operation *Straßenbau*,[27] or their Peace Offensive, on 15 July, which put Ludendorff into a mental tailspin from which he struggled to recover. In almost every area where you care to look, the performance of the Entente forces was superior to that of the Germans. Whether it be planning, intelligence, organisation or tactics; whether it be equipment, materiel, technology or training; or whether it be leadership, command, co-ordination, adaptability or initiative: these things were all better for the Allies. But that should not underplay the bravery and tenacity with which the Germans fought, nor their skilful defence of the ground they held, only being forced out of Grand Rozoy, Beugneux and the ridge above once the positions had become untenable. The Allies bombardment, particularly on 1 August, was noticeably stronger, and the German resistance to it was quite remarkable, despite their divisions being classed as second- and third-class formations. They were able to defend each position before falling back to new lines in the rear, thereby shortening their front. Furthermore, the German gunners quickly became adept at knocking out the French tanks at close range through open sights, especially the slow and lumbering Schneiders and Saint-Chamonds. But the lighter and more nimble Renault FT-17s proved particularly useful for attacking the many German machine gun positions, especially those in the numerous small woods and copses, which the larger tanks could not navigate and the infantry found costly to clear.[28]

Tim Gale makes a strong argument that whilst Mangin's *Xe Armée* would have benefitted from additional tanks throughout the battle, there were just not enough to go around. Mangin already had the lion's share of tanks on 18 July, and this situation persisted for the duration of the fighting. The French GQG and Pétain would never have agreed to allow Mangin the luxury of having all of the available tanks under his control, not least because the Commander-in-Chief didn't trust him to throw them into the attack with sufficient care. With the French attacking through five armies, Pétain and Foch had a difficult juggling act to share out the finite number of tanks to where they might be most effective, whilst ensuring the infantry was protected and its casualties minimised. It thus made sense to have tanks with all of the

---

26   TNA WO 95/2451: XXII Corps, report on the operations of XXII Corps while employed with the French Army between 13 July and 2 August 1918. Edmonds, pp. 300–04.
27   Operation *Straßenbau* was originally called Operation *Marneschutz-Rei*ms, but was renamed in June 1918. It is also commonly referred to as Operation *Friedensturm*.
28   Gale, p. 146.

attacking armies.[29] This did, however, mean that with the exception of the morning of 18 July, Mangin was never able to have a critical mass of tanks to make the decisive breakthrough; by the time of the British involvement, the losses in the preceding days meant that on 29 July and 1 August, only a tiny fraction of his tanks were still available. They could only be used in penny-packets, significantly reducing their impact and effectiveness, which proved to be a costly mistake. Whilst the French divisions at least had some experience of fighting alongside tanks, it was an entirely novel experience for the British 34th Division's infantry and not one they had even had the opportunity to train for. Consequently, it is unsurprising that there was mixed success for the tanks and the infantry fighting alongside them; nor that infantry casualties were much higher than they might otherwise have been had more tanks been available. Although it was no comfort to the casualties, the need to deploy tanks *en masse* was a key lesson that the Allies had indeed learned: in all future engagements where tanks could operate, they would do so in number, taking a leading rather than supporting role in the fighting.

The truth is that the actions of the 34th Division from 23 July to 1 August were just one element in turning the tide of the Great War; a shift in momentum which had begun on the morning of 18 July and which concluded with the retirement of the Germans to the *Blücher Stellung* shortly after nightfall on the night of 1/2 August. Whilst they were already planning their withdrawal from the villages of Grand Rozoy, Beugneux and Cramaille and the high plateaux beyond, the Germans still had to be forced to abandon their strongly held defensive positions. The German Ninth and Seventh armies were able to withdraw most of their divisions from the Marne salient, leaving just 18 divisions that were by then denuded of the majority of their strength by the heavy casualties suffered during the fighting, ten German divisions being entirely broken up. The spoils of the victory were considerable and should not be underestimated: a haul of 793 German artillery pieces and 3,723 machine guns were captured, plus 659 officers and 28,708 other ranks taken prisoner, in the period between 18 July and 1 August, with four officers and 246 other ranks captured by the 34th Division alone on 1 August. Although French casualties were indeed heavy – 2,539 officers and 92,626 men – German losses were estimated at 168,000, and they had lost almost a million men since March.[30]

It is possible to contrast the performance of the 34th Division during this period with that of the 51st (Highland) and 62nd (West Riding) divisions, who were both fighting in General Berthelot's *Ve Armée*. Over the period of their engagement, the latter advanced 7,000 yards on a front of 7,000 yards, capturing 21 officers and 1,148 other ranks (621 by the 51st Division and 548 by the 62nd) from seven different German divisions, as well as 135 machine guns, five *minenwerfer* and two artillery pieces, also recovering 32 French or Italian 75mm field guns. During the fighting, the 51st (Highland) Division received reinforcements of 60 officers and 1,065 other ranks, whilst the 62nd (West Riding) Division received 69 officers and 1,712 other ranks, enabling them to maintain a strong attacking force, having suffered casualties totalling 265 officers and 7,435 other ranks. Whilst the reinforcements were insufficient to replace all of the losses suffered, they were far in excess of those received by either the 15th (Scottish) or 34th Divisions during the same period, meaning their combat effectiveness was better sustained. Things were equally uneven in terms of supplies of ammunition and rations, with General

---

29   Gale, pp. 148–50.
30   Edmonds, pp. 305-06 and Takle, p. 249.

Godley writing to General Sir Herbert Lawrence, Haig's intelligence chief, to tell him that the arrangements were working very well for XXII Corps. A visit by Brigadier General Charles Grant on behalf of General Du Cane to XXII Corps' headquarters on 20 July reported back that Godley was indeed satisfied with these arrangements. But the situation facing the two divisions to the west was very different, with a major shortage of artillery shells significantly hampering the early stages of their deployment.

The following remarks are found within XXII Corps' war diary:

> [B] Divisions adapted themselves readily to the semi-open warfare and wood-fighting in which they were engaged and came into action on unknown ground without delay or confusion. The Divisional artilleries were freely used in close support of the infantry, Artillery Brigades working with Infantry Brigades, and in cases Batteries with Battalions. Both Divisions were admirably Commanded and their Staff work was excellent. Brigades were very well commanded. The co-operation of Divisions and Brigades was remarkable and quite spontaneous. Liaison with French Divisions was very well maintained … I think it may fairly be claimed that the work of both Divisions has done much to increase the prestige of British troops in the eyes of our French allies, both for courage and efficiency.[31]

Whilst the remarks were actually written about the 51st and 62nd Divisions, they applied equally to the performance of the 15th (Scottish) and 34th Divisions, which received almost no coverage by XXII Corps. It is telling that there is not a single mention of General Godley in the official history of the 34th Division during this period. In his profile of Godley, Roy Grover concludes that he never fully appreciated the realities of 20th-century warfare, whilst Christopher Pugsley describes his performance on the battlefields of the First World War as "the elephant in the room" in that it was the subject no one wanted to talk about.[32]

It had been exceptionally hard to free the French mentality of static, fixed-line trench warfare which had pervaded for the previous three years into a war of movement. That it was even possible after such a long time is due in large part to Pétain's personal efforts. It was he who had created and published a new doctrine in the series of Directives from autumn 1917 onwards, and it was he who had then toured the front to explain the radical new direction to his subordinate commanders. This new direction was then fully endorsed and continued by Foch when he became Generalissimo. It had been a genuine struggle for Pétain to get his message across and get the officers to understand the rationale for this change, with even some of his army commanders – such as Generals Duchêne and Humbert – ignoring him in favour of flooding their frontline trenches with defenders, with disastrous consequences. Fortunately, some of the other generals, such as *IVe Armée*'s Henri Gouraud, were much more receptive to Pétain's Directive No.4, seeing the value of what their Commander-in-Chief was talking about. They consequently put in place sophisticated defence-in-depth systems, with their first positions only

---

31 TNA WO 95/2451: XXII Corps, report on the operations of XXII Corps whilst deployed with the French Army between 13 July and 2 August 1918.
32 Grover (2004) and Pugsley, Chrtis, *The New Zealand Division at Passchendaele* (Liddle ed., 1997), pp. 272-91.

lightly held, which would enable them to absorb any German attacks and then counterattack quickly themselves, capturing any lost ground. Indeed, Mangin later described the battle as

> "classic battle of manoeuvre. The battle opened with the driving back of the enemy line ten kilometres in the first two days under the shock of a sudden attack. Then he brought up reserves and rallied. After that the objective was clear and definite. It was the eastern end of the long ledge that runs unbroken save the Savières valley from west of Villers-Cotterêts forest to the region of Grand Rozoy and Arcy. That was the key position of the struggle, which was the bastion of the enemy's resistance. Once we were masters of that on August 2nd, the enemy's retreat was inevitable. He knew it, too, and the battle was won."[33]

Captured German orders revealed that seizing the ridge had finally induced the enemy to retire to new positions on the River Vesle, with the position captured by the 34th Division considered the key obstacle holding everything together. Once it was gone, it made the German defences untenable and forced them back to the positions on the north side of the River Aisne from which they had attacked at the end of May. It had been a decisive victory, with the German Seventh, First and Ninth armies retiring behind the line of the Rivers Vesle and Aisne and abandoning Soissons altogether at 1400 hrs on 2 August, with its bridges blown by the retiring enemy.[34] The French would not see their enemy occupying this ground again for the remainder of the war.

17.4 Message from General Penet

General Penet, commanding the French *30e Corps*, issued an effusive celebratory 'Order of the Day':

> At the time when the 34th British Division leaves the 30e French Corps d'armée, the General Commandant of the Corps is happy to express all his satisfaction, all his admiration to the Staff Officers, Officers, NCOs and troops who, during the period of July 21st to August 2nd, showed a remarkable energy, bravery and ardour. All have fully repaid the calls of the Commander who demanded a considerable effort from them, both in the execution of rapid movements day and night, as well as in the attack and defence of conquered positions. Success crowned this effort of the allied Divisions and the General Commanding the 30e CA is delighted to be able to say that the British 34th Division has taken a very large part.[35]

The mixed success of the French tanks should not diminish their overall contribution, particularly that of the light Renault FT-17 tank. For the 585 light tanks involved, the results obtained from 18 July onwards heralded the start of the type's rapid growth and contrasts with that of the 185 Schneider and 190 Saint-Chamond tanks, which proved once again to be ill-suited to the style of fighting, their lack of speed making them unable to exploit and support the rapid territory

---

33   Ryan, pp. 148-49 and Takle, p. 254.
34   Edmonds, pp. 308-09.
35   Shakespear, p. 267; Read, p. 381.

gains being made by the infantry. The rapid pace of innovation, both in design and how they were deployed tactically, as well as their superior reliability, meant that it would be the light Renault FT-17 which emerged victorious. It is striking that whilst it was only lightly armed in contrast to the medium tanks, 37 percent of the 140 medium tanks were seriously damaged in *Xe Armée*s attacks, compared to just 22 percent of the 129 Renaults. It won out because it was better able to stay in the fight over the duration of the battle, the availability of tank support proving an important factor to the overall success on 1 August. Furthermore, being two-manned, with just a driver and a gunner, casualties could be more easily replaced. With the light Renault FT-17 tanks being deployed in number only from May 1918, the obvious lack of experience of using them in combat, using them *en masse* and their extended deployment (with each battalion employed on average for one-and-a-half days) all contributed to heavy losses, with almost 900 casualties amongst the tank crews. Indeed, tactical deficiencies were already clear, with some officers from the light tank battalions arguing that they had been used too early during an attack, without sufficient thought given to the eventual exploitation.[36] It is important to remember that this was only the third time in which French tanks has been used in large numbers, so there was precious little knowledge of how best to use them at this point in the war. But whilst that is undoubtedly true, the mass deployment of tanks on 18 and 19 July was used to devastating effect, carving huge gaps in the German front line which the Boche rushed to plug with whatever reinforcements they could muster, very nearly resulting in an Allied breakthrough. On top of that, Mangin's inclination and ethos was to attack with all of the force available to him; he was never likely to hold back some of the tanks for use in coming days in an effort to "shake off the mud of the trenches."[37] He wanted to make a decisive attack on the neck of the salient, so every operational tank available to him would be used. Unfortunately, this meant that due to the losses, the tanks went from acting as a lethal spearhead on 18 July, punching a hole in the German front line, to being used in penny-packets by time of the final attack on 1 August.

The fighting under examination shows the value of preparation over momentum in a static battle against a resolute enemy. The hurried first attack on 23 July, without the benefit of adequate reconnaissance or sufficient artillery firepower, was an expensive failure. The 34th Division formed up in extended line, tactics employed and suited to trench warfare, but here in terrain almost devoid of any trenches, leaving the troops exposed to German machine gun enfilade fire. General Nicholson has to shoulder most of the blame for this failure and for the 1,300 casualties resulting from the fighting, having hastily agreed to adopt the attack plan of the French *38e Division* in its entirety, even though he was not ready to attack and wholly underprepared. It is worth noting that the *38e Division* had been unable to make any significant advance since it was forced to halt its own attack on the 19th, having suffered very heavy casualties in two days of fighting. In effect, this had allowed the Germans opposing the newly arrived British four days to recover from the fierce fighting, reinforce their lines and restore order.[38] At the exact same time on the morning of 23 July, the two BEF divisions fighting on the River Ardre were experiencing a very similar fate, with little or no reconnaissance, inadequate

---

36   SHAT. 16 N 2120. Carton 3, Dossier 4. Tableau des pertes en chars et personnels, GQG, 9 septembre 1919 cited in Goya, pp. 220–26.
37   Goya, p. 247.
38   Takle, p. 250.

artillery preparation and too hasty deployment resulting in 3,000 casualties suffered within a few hours. Furthermore, the artillery continued to suffer casualties throughout its engagement, due to effective and accurate counter-battery fire from German guns firing off large numbers of shells, many of which contained poison gas. Of course, the enemy could afford to be far less accurate with any gas shells, since these only needed to land close to a target to inconvenience the gunners and reduce their effectiveness. With the 34th Division's artillery having served on the Western Front for many months, at least they were well aware of the tactics of the German gunners and experienced in operating their guns whilst wearing their respirators; it is interesting to note that the artillery suffered relatively few gas casualties compared to the infantry, none of whom had much experience against a gas attack, other than a brief period of training in late June and early July.[39]

The attack on Beugneux and the ridge and plateau beyond on 29 July was very nearly a spectacular success, but it too ended as a costly failure, with little to show for their efforts, apart from mounting casualties. On this occasion, a well-timed counterattack by a fresh German division, along with a delay in getting reinforcements into action, were decisive in forcing all of the attackers back to their starting point with heavy casualties. Yet although they didn't know it yet, the fighting had inflicted very heavy casualties on the Germans, fatally weakening them, and this time there were no enemy reinforcements to help bolster their defences. They would have to defend their positions with whatever resources they could muster, ordered to resist at all costs. So when the final attack came on the morning of 1 August, to the same plan as that of 29 July – but this time with beefed-up artillery firepower, including additional French heavy artillery – the weakened defenders (both in number and effectiveness) were unable to resist the fearsome assault; Beugneux, the wood to the west and the strategically vital ridge and plateaux above the village were all quickly lost. The remaining German defenders then had no option but to make an overnight withdrawal to new defensive positions on the *Blücher Stellung*.

The Allied success here showed the skilled intermeshing of support weapons: as well as the use of French tanks, the heavy Vickers machine guns and trench mortars enabled a weakened attacking force of 101st Brigade to capture the *Bois de Beugneux* in just two hours, killing or capturing 100 men and taking a dozen German machine guns.[40] Goya describes the action well: "Once the Germans found their front had become untenable, they fell back to a new line with the Allies beginning a pursuit that resembled a war of movement."[41] The 34th Division had come a very long way in a very short period, and its infantry had gained extremely valuable combat experience fighting on the Western Front alongside the French. It would be this experience which it would take into later battles during the 'Hundred Days', where mobility finally returned to the battlefields of France and Flanders.

Nicholson emerges from the events of July 1918 with a huge amount of credit, both personally and as a leader, but not so General Godley. It is an incontrovertible fact that Sir Alex Godley was all but absent without leave, playing almost no part in the fighting of either the 34th Division or 15th (Scottish) divisions during their time on the Marne; he was almost solely focused on commanding the two divisions fighting further east in General Berthelot's *Ve Armée*. There are no mentions of visits by General Godley to 34th Division headquarters and precious little

---

39   TNA WO 95/2447: 160th Brigade, Royal Field Artillery.
40   Takle, p. 258.
41   Goya, p. 248.

in the way of instruction, guidance or anything else from the corps commander. It was left to Nicholson to make and deploy his plans alongside those of General Penet's French *30e Corps*. Nicholson should never have been put in the difficult position he found himself in, where time and again during the battle he was left on his own, with no guidance from his corps commander, and this failure rests entirely with Godley. That Nicholson was able to lead his division (and especially his infantry, which had no previous experience of fighting on the Western Front) so effectively during this terrifically difficult engagement says everything about his character while making the lack of direction and leadership from Godley all too evident for anyone to see. Takle describes Godley as a "self- obsessed officer who enjoyed living in a champagne château and was much involved with visits, lunches, dinners and social engagements".[42] In the immediate days prior to their engagement in battle, Godley had dined at the Ritz in Paris on his way to the front. Ironically, he even complained that all this socialising left him little time for planning! In reality, he left much of the planning work to his staff officers, which although fairly common, put them in an unduly difficult position, having to liaise with two French armies. It also appears that he made only a single visit to the front, right at the end of the fighting around Bligny, and made none at all to either the 15th or 34th Divisions. Admittedly he faced a challenging situation, with two divisions on the western flank of the salient and the other two 30 miles further east, where a journey by staff car would require a large detour away from the front. Perhaps one can be charitable and suggest he had considered the lengthy drive and thus decided he'd be better served staying in one location and remaining in contact with his other formations via telephone.

Godley prided himself on creating good relations with his senior commanders, and once he eventually arrived at his new corps headquarters, he wasted no time establishing himself with the French *Ve Armée* and corps staff, again more interested in social than military matters. Takle criticises the commander for acting more like a diplomat than the senior British officer under foreign command and responsible for the lives of his men. Keen to curry favour, Godley all too readily accepted the French plan presented to him for the attack on the 23rd in the Reims area, and there is no evidence that he saw any of the *30e Corps* plans for their attack on the same day. Whilst this might have made him popular with the French commanders, the attack without proper preparation and no time for reconnaissance certainly cost many unnecessary lives and deserves criticism on purely military terms alone.[43] He should have insisted, even enforced, a short delay to the attack to allow proper preparations to be completed, rather than agreeing to its commencement as per plan. Whether or not Nicholson would have benefitted or suffered as a result of Godley's advice (or interference) is open to question, but whatever the truth and however difficult the situation, he should have made at least some effort to support Nicholson. It is consequently difficult to argue against the suggestion that Lieutenant General Sir Alex Godley came as close as anyone in the British Army of 1918 to the caricature of a 'donkey' or 'bungler'.

Nicholson read out an order to all ranks on parade on 3 August from General Mangin, which read as follows:

---

42 Takle, p. 129.
43 Takle, pp. 129–30.

> General Mangin had instructed me to convey to you his personal thanks for the magnificent results achieved by the Division yesterday. The General says that yesterday's battle worked out absolutely according to orders and times and says that the [German] general retreat taking place today is entirely due to the success of yesterday. The General has instructed me to tell you of his gratitude and appreciation for the splendid success achieved by the 34th Division yesterday.[44]

As the 34th Division departed the battlefield, Nicholson and Mangin bade the men farewell, thanking them as they passed by. Second Lieutenant Read remarked that the French general looked "like a real soldier, and a pretty tough one at that … with swarthy features but impeccably turned out". Read felt that things had gone wrong for the Royal Sussex from the outset, being shorn of several senior officers and NCOs away on leave, with a shell wounding most of the officers before they even began fighting. A complete and disastrous breakdown in communication and absence of accurate and timely information pervaded events, and he felt fortunate to have survived the mauling on 29 July, but he was happy to have survived and taken his part in the victory of 1 August.[45]

So pleased was General Fayolle, commanding the GAR, with the contribution of the 15th (Scottish) and 34th Divisions, that he wrote to Douglas Haig expressing his appreciation for their service during the battle, adding that "both of them by their dash, their courage, and their devotion, have excited the admiration of the French troops in whose midst they fought".[46] Clearly, these divisions had gone some way to restoring good relations between the two allies. Indeed, on 4 August he sent out a General Order which further praised the efforts of the British troops fighting side by side with the French:

> The Second Battle of the Marne ends, as the First, in Victory. There exists no more a Château-Thierry 'pocket'. The VIe and Xe Armées, as well as the Allied troops who fought at their side, have taken the most glorious part therin. … These results are due to the energy and skill of the leaders and to the extraordinary gallantry of the troops, the greater part of whom have gone ahead while fighting without let-up for more than 15 days. … Let all be proud of the work that has been accomplished! It is great, for it has contributed forcefully to assure final victory and to hasten the hour thereof.[47]

---

44 Signed Major B.V. Jackson, liaison officer, French *Xe Armée* and TNA WO 95/2439: Adjutant and Quartermaster General, 34th Division, 2 August 1918.
45 Read, p. 381.
46 Takle, p. 247.
47 General Order, No. 4. 190, 4 August 1918 cited in Woldike, p. 186.

17.5 Mangin's General Order No.343

General Mangin, commanding *Xe Armée*, also issued General Order No.343 to both the 15th and 34th Divisions, congratulating and thanking them for their contribution to the victory:

> Officers, Non Commissioned Officers and Men of the 15th and 34th British Divisions, you entered the battle at its fiercest moment. The enemy, already once vanquished, again brought up against us his best divisions, considerably outnumbering our own. You continued to advance step by step, in spite of his desperate resistance, and you held the ground won in spite of his violent counter-attacks. Then, during the whole day of the 1st of August, side by side with your French comrades, you stormed the ridge dominating the whole country between the Aisne and the Ourcq, which the defenders had received orders to hold at all costs. Having failed in his attempt to retake the ridge with his last reserves, the enemy had to beat a retreat pursued and harassed for 12 kilometres. All of you, English and Scottish, young soldiers and veterans of Flanders and Palestine, you have shown the magnificent qualities of your race, courage and imperturbable tenacity. You have won the admiration of your companions in arms. Your country will be proud of you for to your chiefs and to you is due a large share in the victory that we have gained over the barbarous enemies of the free. I am happy to have fought at your head and I thank you.[48]

By masterminding the efforts to sever the Marne artery during July 1918, Mangin had cemented his reputation as one of the Great War's finest offensive generals. There is little doubt that he savoured the moment of his great victory with a huge amount of pride and satisfaction. But even for a man known for his belief in the mantra of *l'attaque à l'outrance*, he must have been mightily relieved that his offensive push east had finally succeeded, albeit after 15 days of intense and at times extremely trying combat. He had taken a monumental risk of being fired for a third time when he ignored Pétain's instruction to halt the attack when the Commander-in-Chief had visited *Xe Armée*'s headquarters on the evening of 18 July, but the gamble had paid off and the victory was his. Yet in judging his character, it is probable that he also had mixed emotions, especially about the performance of some of his fellow army commanders, with his overall mood perhaps tinged with an element of disappointment that they had been unable to sever the German jugular at the neck of Marne *poche* and cut off the retreating enemy, thereby allowing them to make their escape.

On 7 August, General Pétain issued a congratulatory *Ordre Général No.116* to his armies and those fighting alongside them:

> Four years of effort aided by our faithful Allies, four years of trial stoically accepted, commence to bear their fruit. Broken in the fifth of his attempts in 1918, the invader has recoiled. His effectives are falling, his morale is weakening, whilst on our side, our American comrades, just disembarked, have already made our disconcerted enemy feel the vigour of their blows. Yesterday I said to you: obstinacy, patience, your American

---

48 Translation in TNA WO 95/1930: 9th Battalion Gordon Highlanders, 5 August 1918.

comrades are coming. Today I say to you: tenacity, boldness, and victory must be yours.[49]

Writing to his men a few days later, Nicholson was also delighted with the contribution of the 34th Division and their conduct, steadiness and gallantry throughout the operations with *Xe Armée*. He concluded, somewhat prophetically: "It is perhaps too much to say that final victory is in sight, but it is getting nearer and the Division must be ready to take a hand in it."[50]

---

49 Edmonds, p. 306.
50 TNA WO 95/2439: Adjutant and Quartermaster General, 34th Division, 12 August 1918.

Appendix I

34th Division Order of Battle, 4 July 1918

Commander	Major General C.L. Nicholson, DB, CMG
ADC	Second Lieutenant N.H. Docker
GSO I	Lieutenant Colonel J.G. Dooner, DSO
GSO II	Major J.F. Harter, DSO, MC
GSO III	Captain H.A. Chisenhale-Marsh
AA and QMG	Lieutenant Colonel R.M. Tyler, DSO
DAAG	Major W.A.C. Lloyd
DAQMG	Major H.D. Parkin, MC
ADMS	Colonel E.W. Bliss, CMG, DSO
DADMS	Major D. Dougal, MC
DADVS	Major H.A. Stewart
DADOS	Major D.V. Strickland
APM	Captain J.A. Ashton
Officer Interpreter	Lieutenant E.P. Coquelle

101st Infantry Brigade

Commander	Brigadier General W.J. Woodcock, DSO
Brigade Major	Captain R.J. Cash, MC
Staff Captain	Captain F.L. Tempest, MC
2/4th The Queens 2nd in command Adjutant	Lieutenant Colonel W.J.M. Hill Major R.J. Few, DSO Captain P.C. Duncan

4th Royal Sussex Regiment 2nd in command Adjutant	Major G.S. Constable, MC Captain J.R. Warren Captain R.C.G. Middleton, MC
2nd Loyal North Lancashire 2nd in command Adjutant	Lieutenant Colonel C.E.A. Jourdain, DSO Major R.E. Berkeley, DSO Captain G.P. Atkinson, MC
101st Light Trench Mortar Battery	Captain A.W. Rawson

102nd Infantry Brigade

Commander	Brigadier General E. Hilliam, CMG, DSO
Brigade Major	Captain M. Carr, MC
Staff Captain	Captain A.B. Leake
4th Cheshire Regiment 2nd in command Adjutant	Lieutenant Colonel G.H. Swindells Major E.W. Morris Captain J. Holding
7th Cheshire Regiment 2nd in command Adjutant	Lieutenant Colonel H.L. Moir Major F. de W. Harman, DSO Captain G.E. Nelson, DSO
1st Hereford Regiment 2nd in command Adjutant	Lieutenant Colonel H.M. Lawrence, DSO Major A.G.R. Whitehouse, MC Captain W.F. Chipp, MC
102nd Light Trench Mortar Battery	

103rd Infantry Brigade

Commander	Brigadier General J.G. Chaplin, DSO
Brigade Major	Captain R.W. Rotherford, MC
Staff Captain	Captain W.O.G. Black
5th King's Own Scottish Borderers 2nd in command Adjutant	Lieutenant Colonel R.N. Coulson Captain P.S.L. Beaver, MC Captain T.D. Craig
8th Scottish Rifles 2nd in command Adjutant	Lieutenant Colonel J.M. Findlay, DSO Major G.R.V. Hume Gore, MC Captain E.R. Boyd

5th Argyll and Sutherland Highlanders 2nd in command Adjutant	Lieutenant Colonel C.L. Barlow, DSO Captain A.J. Campbell
103rd Light Trench Mortar Battery	Captain O.B. Palmer, MC

Pioneer Battalion

2/4th Somerset Light Infantry 2nd in command Adjutant	Brigadier General E.B. Powell, DSO Major E.W. Farwell Captain W.H. Miles

34th Battalion Machine Gun Corps

34th Battalion MachineGun Corps	Lieutenant Colonel E.H. Kendrick, DSO Captain D.B. Parkinson-Cumine, MC Captain B.P. Whillis, MC

Divisional Artillery

Commander	Brigadier General E.C.W.D. Walthall, CMG, DSO
Brigade Major	Captain G.O.S. Smyth, DSO, MC
Staff Captain	Captain A. Beal, MC
Staff Lieutenant	Lieutenant C. Thompson, MC
Units	
152 Brigade Royal Field Artillery	Lieutenant Colonel H. Allcard, DSO
160 Brigade Royal Field Artillery	Lieutenant Colonel W.M. Warburton, DSO
34th Divisional Ammunition Column	Colonel C.N. Simpson, DSO

Divisional Engineers

Commander	Lieutenant Colonel A.C. Dobson, DSO
Adjutant	Captain W.J. Webb
Units	
207th Field Company, Royal Engineers	Captain A. Rough, MC
208th Field Company, Royal Engineers	Major J. Russell, MC
209th Field Company, Royal Engineers	Major F.C. Cook, MC

| 34th Divisional Signal Company | Major G.H.P. Boyle |

Army Service Corps

34th Divisional Train	Lieutenant Colonel A.W. Alexander
SSO	Major R.A. Shebbeare, DSO
34th Divisional Motor Transport Company	Major J.W. Stevens

Royal Army Medical Corps

102nd Field Ambulance	Lieutenant Colonel R. Stevenson, MC
103rd Field Ambulance	Lieutenant Colonel J. Rowe
104th Field Ambulance	Lieutenant Colonel E. Beverley Bird, DSO

Army Veterinary Corps

| 44th Mobile Veterinary Section | Captain W.J. Bambridge |

Labour Corps

| 231st (Divisional) Employment Company | Captain H.H. Wilde |

Appendix II: 34th Division casualties

OFFICERS	22-28 July					29-31 July					1-3 Aug					TOTAL				
Unit	Killed	Wounded	Wounded (At duty)	Missing	Total	Killed	Wounded	Wounded (At duty)	Missing	Total	Killed	Wounded	Wounded (At duty)	Missing	Total	Killed	Wounded	Wounded (At duty)	Missing	Total
Divisional Headquarters					0	1				1					0	1	0	0	0	1
2/4th Queens (Royal West Surrey) Regiment		1	1		2	1	3			4	1	2			3	2	6	1	0	9
4th Royal Sussex Regiment	1	1	2		4	2	5			7		1			1	3	7	2	0	12
2nd Loyal North Lancashire Regiment	1	4			5	1	8	2		11	1				1	3	12	2	0	17
101st Light Trench Mortar Battery (LTMB)					0					0					0	0	0	0	0	0
1/4th Cheshire Regiment		4			4		3			3	3	4			7	3	11	0	0	14
1/7th Cheshire Regiment		2	2		4	1	3	1		5		1			1	1	6	3	0	10
1/1st Herefordshire Regiment		10			10		1			1	2	1			3	2	12	0	0	14
103rd Divisional Headquarters					0			1		1					0	0	0	1	0	1
1/5th King's Own Scottish Borderers (KOSB)		1			1	2	5			7	1	2		1	4	3	8	0	1	12
1/8th Scottish Rifles (Cameronians)		1			1	3	11			14		5			5	3	17	0	0	20

Unit																				
1/5th Argyll & Sutherland Highlanders	3				3	2	12			14	3	2			5	5	17	0	0	22
103rd Light Trench Mortar Battery (LTMB)					0					0					0	0	0	0	0	0
2/4th Somerset Light Infantry (SLI)					0	1	2			3					0	1	2	0	0	3
34th Bn Machine Gun Corps (MGC)	1		2		3	2	2			4					0	2	3	2	0	7
152 Brigade Royal Field Artillery	3				3					0					0	0	3	0	0	3
160 Brigade Royal Field Artillery	3				3					0					0	0	3	0	0	3
Divisional Ammunition Column (DAC)					0					0					0	0	0	0	0	0
207th Field Company Royal Engineers					0					0					0	0	0	0	0	0
208th Field Company Royal Engineers					0					0					0	0	0	0	0	0
209th Field Company Royal Engineers					0					0					0	0	0	0	0	0
RAMC					0					0	1				1	1	0	0	0	1
102nd Field Ambulance					0					0					0	0	0	0	0	0
103rd Field Ambulance					0					0					0	0	0	0	0	0
104th Field Ambulance					0					0					0	0	0	0	0	0
Divisional Signal Company	2				2					0					0	0	2	0	0	2
Army Chaplain's Department					0	1	1	1		2					0	0	1	1	0	2
OFFICERS	**2**	**36**	**7**	**0**	**45**	**16**	**56**	**5**	**0**	**77**	**12**	**18**	**0**	**1**	**31**	**30**	**110**	**12**	**1**	**153**

OTHER RANKS

Unit	22-28 July					29-31 July					1-3 Aug					TOTAL				
	Killed	Wounded	Wounded (At duty)	Missing	Total	Killed	Wounded	Wounded (At duty)	Missing	Total	Killed	Wounded	Wounded (At duty)	Missing	Total	Killed	Wounded	Wounded (At duty)	Missing	Total
2/4th Queens (Royal West Surrey) Regiment	14	69		2	85	20	102		13	135	15	47		6	68	49	218	0	21	288
4th Royal Sussex Regiment	14	51			65	43	147		30	220	11	29		3	43	68	227	0	33	328
2nd Loyal North Lancashire Regiment	14	122		8	144	27	157		21	205	20	59		3	82	61	338	0	32	431
101st Light Trench Mortar Battery (LTMB)		2			2		6			6		2			2	0	10	0	0	10
1/4th Cheshire Regiment	7	308		1	316	11	42		4	57	10	45		3	58	28	395	0	8	431
1/7th Cheshire Regiment	20	151		4	175	5	79		1	85		4		1	5	25	234	0	6	265
1/1st Herefordshire Regiment	30	247		11	288	7	29		1	37	7	29			36	44	305	0	12	361
1/5th King's Own Scottish Borderers (KOSB)	1	13			14	17	214		27	258	25	112		24	161	43	339	0	51	433
1/8th Scottish Rifles (Cameronians)	3	21			24	41	244		19	304	9	43			52	53	308	0	19	380
1/5th Argyll & Sutherland Highlanders	4	23			27	11	209		5	225	37	65		9	111	52	297	0	14	363
103rd Light Trench Mortar Battery (LTMB)					0		2			2					0	0	2	0	0	2

Unit	C1	C2	C3	C4	C5	C6	C7	C8	C9	C10	C11	C12	C13	C14	C15	C16	C17	C18	C19	C20
2/4th Somerset Light Infantry (SLI)		1			1	11	31	4	46		15			15	11	47	0	4		62
34th Bn Machine Gun Corps (MGC)	7	39			46	11	68	11	90	3	9		2	14	21	116	0	13		150
152 Brigade Royal Field Artillery	4	15			19	1	1		2	1	7		2	10	6	23	0	2		31
160 Brigade Royal Field Artillery	1	10			11	1	18		19		3			3	2	31	0	0		33
Divisional Ammunition Column (DAC)					0		1		1		1			1	0	2	0	0		2
207th Field Company Royal Engineers	1	2			3		3		3					0	1	5	0	0		6
208th Field Company Royal Engineers		1			1				0		3			3	0	4	0	0		4
209th Field Company Royal Engineers		1			1				0		1			1	0	2	0	0		2
RAMC																				
102nd Field Ambulance		6			6				0					0	0	6	0	0		6
103rd Field Ambulance	5	10			15		2		2		3			3	5	15	0	0		20
104th Field Ambulance	3	2			5		1		1		2			2	3	5	0	0		8
Divisional Signal Company		1			1				0					0	0	1	0	0		1
OTHER RANKS	**128**	**1,095**	**0**	**26**	**1,249**	**206**	**1,356**	**0**	**136**	**1,698**	**138**	**479**	**0**	**53**	**670**	**472**	**2,930**	**0**	**215**	**3,617**

Unit	22-28 July					29-31 July					1-3 Aug					TOTAL				
	Killed	Wounded	Wounded (At duty)	Missing	Total	Killed	Wounded	Wounded (At duty)	Missing	Total	Killed	Wounded	Wounded (At duty)	Missing	Total	Killed	Wounded	Wounded (At duty)	Missing	Total
Divisional Headquarters					0					1	0	0	0	0	0	1	0	0	0	1
2/4th Queens (Royal West Surrey) Regiment	14	70	1	2	87	21	105	0	13	139	16	49	0	6	71	51	224	1	21	297
4th Royal Sussex Regiment	15	52	2		69	45	152	0	30	227	11	30	0	3	44	71	234	2	33	340
2nd Loyal North Lancashire Regiment	15	126		8	149	28	165	2	21	216	21	59	0	3	83	64	350	2	32	448
101st Light Trench Mortar Battery (LTMB)		2			2	0	6	0	0	6	0	2	0	0	2	0	10	0	0	10
1/4th Cheshire Regiment	7	312		1	320	11	45	0	4	60	13	49	0	3	65	31	406	0	8	445
1/7th Cheshire Regiment	20	153	2	4	179	6	82	1	1	90	0	5	0	1	6	26	240	3	6	275
1/1st Herefordshire Regiment	30	257		11	298	7	30	0	1	38	9	30	0	0	39	46	317	0	12	375
103rd Divisional Headquarters					0	0	0	1	0	1	0	0	0	0	0	0	0	1	0	1
1/5th King's Own Scottish Borderers (KOSB)	1	14			15	19	219	0	27	265	26	114	0	25	165	46	347	0	52	445
1/8th Scottish Rifles (Cameronians)	3	22			25	44	255	0	19	318	9	48	0	0	57	56	325	0	19	400
1/5th Argyll & Sutherland Highlanders	4	26			30	13	221	0	5	239	40	67	0	9	116	57	314	0	14	385
103rd Light Trench Mortar Battery (LTMB)					0	0	2	0	0	2	0	0	0	0	0	0	2	0	0	2

Unit																				Total
2/4th Somerset Light Infantry (SLI)		1		1	12	33	0	4	49	0	15	0	15	12	49	0	4	65		
34th Bn Machine Gun Corps (MGC)	7	40	2	49	13	70	0	11	94	3	9	2	14	23	119	2	13	157		
152 Brigade Royal Field Artillery	4	18		22	1	1	0	0	2	1	7	2	10	6	26	0	2	34		
160 Brigade Royal Field Artillery	1	13		14	1	18	0	0	19	0	3	0	3	2	34	0	0	36		
Divisional Ammunition Column (DAC)				0	0	1	0	0	1	0	1	0	1	0	2	0	0	2		
207th Field Company, Royal Engineers	1	2		3	0	3	0	0	3	0	0	0	0	1	5	0	0	6		
208th Field Company, Royal Engineers		1		1	0	0	0	0	0	0	3	0	3	0	4	0	0	4		
209th Field Company, Royal Engineers		1		1	0	0	0	0	0	0	1	0	1	0	2	0	0	2		
RAMC					0	0	0	0	0	1	0	0	0	1	0	0	0	1		
102nd Field Ambulance		6		6	0	0	0	0	0	0	0	0	0	0	6	0	0	6		
103rd Field Ambulance	5	10		15	0	2	0	0	2	0	3	0	3	5	15	0	0	20		
104th Field Ambulance	3	2		5	0	1	0	0	1	0	2	0	2	3	5	0	0	8		
Divisional Signal Company		3		3	0	0	0	0	0	0	0	0	0	0	3	0	0	3		
Army Chaplain's Department				0	0	1	1	0	2	0	0	0	0	0	1	1	0	2		
TOTAL	**130**	**1,131**	**7**	**26**	**1,294**	**222**	**1,412**	**5**	**136**	**1,775**	**150**	**497**	**0**	**54**	**701**	**502**	**3,040**	**12**	**216**	**3,770**

Source: War Diary, A&Q Branch, 34th Division, 11 August 1918.

Appendix III

German Order of Battle, July 1918

21st July

The fresh **19th (Royal Saxon) Ersatz Division** going into the line on the 21st, having rushed from Verdun, relieving the exhausted and decimated **51st Reserve Division**.

23rd July

7th Guard IR (**Guard Ersatz Division**), 18th Bavarian RIR (**Bavarian Ersatz Division**), 234th RIR and 236th RIR (**51st Reserve Division**), 24th and 23rd Ersatz IR (**19th Ersatz Division**) and 47th [Ersatz Field Artillery Regiment (**19th Ersatz Division**). The German Order of Battle was 236th RIR, 234th RIR, both of 51st Reserve Division and 18th Bavarian RIR from the Bavarian Ersatz Division from north to south, with the Guards Ersatz Division holding the line from Cordoux to Beugneux, having been in the line since the 24th

29th July

At 18:00 a German officer from the 6th Guard Infantry Regiment [**Guard Ersatz Division**] was captured.

31st July

As a consequence, the 7th Guard Infantry Regiment [**Guard Ersatz Division**] had its three battalions in line, facing north towards the expected direction of attack. It was forced to change its positions when the attack began from positions further south. Crucially, the German prisoners revealed that one company was 80 strong, but many were was weak as only 40 all ranks, having suffered heavy gas casualties earlier in the month which had not been replaced whilst a prisoner from the **24th Ersatz Division** reported that morale was extremely low, with companies amalgamated due to low strength. The **19th Ersatz Division** had become so depleted by casualties that it was totally withdrawn on the 31st, with the **Guards Ersatz Division** replacing it in line. The reduced strength also meant that there were no German Minenwerfer in line in front of the British and only four machine guns per company. If anything, the artillery was even worse, with **47th Ersatz Field Artillery Regiment [19th Ersatz Division]** only in possession of ten working 7.7 inch field guns on the ridge above Grand Rozoy and Beugneux, but these had been so heavily shelled during the attack that they were unable to open fire. But it was not all negative, with the prisoners captured from the **Bavarian and Guard Ersatz Divisions** reporting strong morale. Whilst morale was mixed, one thing was unanimous: none of the captured men spoke of any intended German attack on this or any other part of the Western Front.

	21	22	23	24	25	26	27	28	29	30	31	1
19th (Royal Saxon) Ersatz Division	Y		Y								Y	
51st Reserve Division	Y		Y									
Guard Ersatz Division			Y						Y		Y	
Bavarian Ersatz Division			Y								Y	

19th (Royal Saxon) Ersatz Division

(United States Army, p.303-305.)
VALUE—1917 ESTIMATE.
The 19th Ersatz Division remained in Lorraine for a long time; it did not take part in any serious battles. After October, 1916, it only occupied quiet sectors on the Cotes de Meuse. It cannot be considered as an attack division.

1918.
The division occupied the quiet Beaumont sector until June 30, when it was put at rest near Longuyon until July 11. During this time the division was given training to fit it for a war of movement. On July 16 it was moved to the Rheims front. On the 17th it moved to the vicinity of Grand Rozoy.

From July 20 to 31 the division was engaged in severe fighting at Plessier-Huleu and Grand Rozoy. It rested near Marle until the 21st of August undergoing reconstruction. It entrained on that date at Voyenne and reached La Fere the next day, from where it marched to Barisis and Folembray.

VALUE—1918 ESTIMATE.
The division was rated as third class. In 1918 it saw but two weeks' service on an active front.

Order of Battle
45. Ersatz-Brigade

- Ersatz-Infanterie-Regiment Nr. 23
- Ersatz-Infanterie-Regiment Nr. 24
- Ersatz-Infanterie-Regiment Nr. 32

5 Eskadron/Kgl. Sächsisches 2. Husaren-Regiment Nr. 19

- Artillerie-Kommandeur 137
- Ersatz-Feldartillerie-Regiment Nr. 47
- Pionier-Bataillon Nr. 519

1 Ersatz-Kompanie/Kgl. Sächsisches 1. Pionier-Bataillon Nr. 12
1 Ersatz-Kompanie/Kgl. Sächsisches 2. Pionier-Bataillon Nr. 22
Minenwerfer-Kompanie Nr. 164
Divisions-Nachrichten-Kommandeur 569

51st Reserve Division

(United States Army, p.497-499.)
VALUE—1917 ESTIMATE.
The 51st Reserve Division was good at the beginning of the war, but now appears mediocre. Health conditions seem to be poor (August, 1917).

1918.
Champagne.
1. The 51st Reserve Division remained in the Vouziers being trained until about the 20th of January, when it relieved the 52d Division near the Butte du Mesnil. It was relieved early in March and went to the Vouziers-Rethel area, where it received some more training in open warfare.

Picardy.
2. On the 20th it entrained, and arrived at Etreux (north of Guise) the following day. From there it marched via St. Quentin-Ham-Roye-Faverolles to Montdidier, where it arrived on the 30th. The following day it reenforced the front near Ayencourt (south of Montdidier), relieving the 9th Division. It was relieved by the 2d Division during the night of the 1st-2d of May and went to rest in the Chimay area.

Aisne.
3. On the 30th of May the division, thoroughly rested and brought up to strength, reinforced the battle front near Vauxbuin (southwest of Soissons). Here it became heavily engaged and suffered severe losses, especially the first two days. It was relieved near Cutry (southwest of Soissons) on June 16, and went to rest near Oulchy-le-Château.

4. During the night of July 19–20, the division reinforced the front near Blanzy (south of Soissons). Here it became heavily engaged. It was forced back by the Allied counteroffensive, and was withdrawn from line south of Braine early in August. It went to rest near Marle.

VALUE—1918 ESTIMATE.
The 51st Reserve is to be considered a **good second-class division**. It did not distinguish itself by any brilliant fighting, but it did acquit itself in the battles of the Somme and the Aisne and during the Allied counteroffensive. It suffered exceedingly heavy losses, but these were in large measure made good by drafts of 1919 class recruits.

Order of Battle

102.Reserve-Infanterie-Brigade
Reserve-Infanterie-Regiment Nr. 234
Reserve-Infanterie-Regiment Nr. 235
Reserve-Infanterie-Regiment Nr. 236
Maschinengewehr-Scharfschützen-Abteilung Nr. 73
Reserve-Kavallerie-Abteilung Nr. 51

Artillerie-Kommandeur 51
Reserve-Feldartillerie-Regiment Nr. 51
I.Bataillon/Reserve-Fußartillerie-Regiment Nr. 11 (from April 16, 1918)
Pionier-Bataillon Nr. 351
Divisions-Nachrichten-Kommandeur 451

Guard Ersatz Division

(United States Army, p.26-28.)
VALUE—1917 ESTIMATE.
The Guard Ersatz Division was recruited all over Prussia just as all the other Guard divisions. **Good division**. The 6th and 7th Guard Regiments are not to be considered as tried troops. The 399th Infantry Regiment seems to have but a slight combative value. **The men are said to have shown dissatisfaction when they left Russia for the western front**. Desertions are said to have taken place en route. (Inter. pris. Dec. 15–17.)

1918.
The division remained north of Verdun until February 20, when it was relieved and went to Damvillers, entrained, and went to the Arlon area and was trained until March 15. It entrained at Arlon on that date and traveled via Charleroi to Mons, where it arrived the following day. By night marches the division passed through Maubeuge-Bavai-Englefontaine-Fontaine au Bois-Bazuel-Le Cateau-Busigny-Bohain-Fresnoy-Péronne, without taking part in any fighting. It came into line March 25–26, and was heavily engaged at Proyart the 27th. The division was withdrawn about April 6, after having large casualties, and reinforced the front near Hangard the night of April 9–10, not being relieved until about May 4. Flanking divisions extended their fronts. It rested northwest of Mons until the end of June.

It then went to reserve in Champagne, and entered line west of Auberive July 15. It was withdrawn on the 21st. **The division was identified in line north of Oulchy-le-Château July 29, where it fought until withdrawn, about August 9.**

VALUE—1918 ESTIMATE.
Reliable information is to the effect that the Guard Ersatz, the Guard Cavalry, and the Jaeger Divisions bore the title "**Oberste Heeresleitungs Angriffsdivisionen**," and that they were **held under the direct control of the Supreme Command**. Nevertheless, the **Guard Ersatz has always been considered as being in the second of four classes**.

Order of Battle

Garde-Ersatz-Brigade:
6. Garde-Regiment
7. Garde-Regiment
Infanterie-Regiment Nr. 399
MG-Scharfschützen-Abteilung Nr. 29
5. Eskadron/2.Garde-Ulanen-Regiment
Garde-Artillerie-Kommandeur 6:
7. Garde-Feldartillerie-Regiment
Fußartillerie-Bataillon Nr. 89
Stab Pionier-Bataillon Nr. 501:
Garde-Pionier-Kompanie Nr. 301
Pionier-Kompanie Nr. 302
7. Garde-Minenwerfer-Kompanie
Garde-Divisions-Nachrichten-Kommandeur 551

Bavarian Ersatz Division

(United States Army, p.13-15.)
VALUE—1917 ESTIMATE.
The Bavarian Ersatz Division is a very mediocre division.

1918.
The division held the quiet Verdun sector until July 12, when it was relieved by the 231st Division.

It was moved to the Vesle front and on July 25 relieved the 40th Division near Oulchy-le-Château. It remained in this sector until August 12, when it was withdrawn and sent to rest in the vicinity of Maubeuge.

VALUE—1918 ESTIMATE.
The division was rated as third class. It was used **only in defensive sectors during 1918**.

Order of Battle

3.Kgl. Bayer. Reserve-Infanterie-Brigade:
Kgl. Bayer. 4. Reserve-Infanterie-Regiment
Kgl. Bayer. 15. Reserve-Infanterie-Regiment
Kgl. Bayer. 18. Reserve-Infanterie-Regiment
1. Eskadron/Kgl. Bayer. 6. Reserve-Kavallerie-Regiment
Kgl. Bayer. Artillerie-Kommandeur 19:
Kgl. Bayer. Ersatz-Feldartillerie-Regiment
Fußartillerie-Bataillon Nr. 89
Stab Kgl. Bayer. 13. Pionier-Bataillon:
Kgl. Bayer. 4. Landwehr-Pionier-Kompanie
Kgl. Bayer. 6. Landwehr-Pionier-Kompanie
Kgl. Bayer. 100. Minenwerfer-Kompanie
Kgl. Bayer. Divisions-Nachrichten-Kommandeur 551

26th Division

The 26th Division, after having done very well in Italy in 1917, was transported to the Western Front, detraining in the Freiburg region (southeast of Dieuze), and remaining here until March 10 1918. The division entrained at Strassburg on the 11th and 12th, and detrained near Peruwelz on the 13th and 14th, remaining in the neighborhood of Valenciennes until the 17th; from here it proceeded by night marches via Denain and Aniche to the Estrées-Ecourt-St. Quentin region (south of Douai), where it arrived on the 20th. On the 26th March it went into close reserve near Fontaine les Croisilles, and the next day it entered line near Hamelincourt (south of Arras). It attacked the next day, but made no headway. It was relieved by the 111th Division on the 31st, and rested near Croisilles until April 3. 3. Then it marched via Bapaume and Miraumont and entered line south of Hébuterne (south of Arras), taking part in the unsuccessful attack of the 5th. It was relieved about the 12th of May by the 16th Reserve Division, and went to the Denain region to rest and refit. On June 15 it was in army reserve in the Roye-Carrépuis area.

About July 3 it went to the vicinity of Neuflize (northeast of Rheims); the 15th it entered line north of Prosnes (southeast of Rheims), and was withdrawn on the 17th. Travelling in trucks, the division reached Bazoches on the 21st; it remained in reserve the 23d and 24th, and relieved the 45th Reserve Division **east of Saponay (northwest of Fère-en-Tardenois and east of Cramaille) during the night of July 25–26.** The Allied push forced the front back here, and the division was identified north of Saponay on August 2, northeast of Fismes on the 18th, east of Braine on the 20th. It was relieved about the 10th of September and went to rest north of Pont Arcy (northwest of Fismes).

VALUE—1918 ESTIMATE.
The 26th is rated as a first-class division. While it was in Alsace (January, February, and the first part of March) it was thoroughly trained in open warfare, and so it was used as a shock division, but it did not succeed in making much headway in its first two engagements. It did fight tenaciously, however, then and in subsequent fighting, and was mentioned in the German communiques of October 27 and November 2 as having particularly distinguished itself. It suffered heavy losses, so that despite the large numbers of reinforcements sent it from time to time, its battalions were reduced to three companies.

Appendix IV

Allied formations engaged 18 July–6 August 1918

	Xe Armée	VIe Armée	IXe Armée	Ve Armée	Total
Front of departure (18 Jul)	27km	26km	32km	35km	120km
Front of arrival (5 Aug)	37km	13km		20km	70km
Maximum depth of advance	25km	40km	9km	30km	40km
No. sq km regained	500km^2	605km^2	83km^2	429km^2	1,617km^2
No. infantry divisions	18	8	6	10	44
No. cavalry divisions	3			3	6
No. artillery batteries	471	233	187	375	1,208
Tanks	375	171		147	693
Aircraft groups	41	28	7	62	145
Prisoners captured	453 Off. + 17,290 OR	71 Off. + 4,491 OR	4 Off. + 341 OR	51 Off. + 2,328 OR	579 Off. + 24,547 OR
Cannons captured	457	170		111	738

Bibliography

1. Primary Sources
1.1. The National Archives of the United Kingdom (Kew) WO 95 Series
TNA WO 95/9743: XXII Corps General Staff
TNA WO 95/9744: XXII Corps Adjutant and Quartermaster ("A" & "Q") General's Branch
TNA WO 95/2436: Headquarters Branches and Service – General Staff, 34th Division
TNA WO 95/2439: Headquarters Branches and Service Adjutant and Quarter-Master General 'A' & 'Q' Branch, 34th Division
TNA WO 95/2456: 101st Infantry Brigade Headquarters
TNA WO 95/2457: 2/4th Battalion Queens Royal West Surrey Regiment
TNA WO 95/2458: 4th Battalion Royal Sussex Regiment
TNA WO 95/2457: 2nd Battalion Loyal North Lancashire Regiment
TNA WO 95/2461: 102nd Infantry Brigade Headquarters
TNA WO 95/2462: 1st Battalion Herefordshire Regiment
TNA WO 95/2462: 4th Battalion Cheshire Regiment
TNA WO 95/2462: 7th Battalion Cheshire Regiment
TNA WO 95/2465: 103rd Infantry Brigade Headquarters
TNA WO 95/2466: 5th Battalion Kings Own Scottish Borderers
TNA WO 95/2467: 8th Battalion Scottish Rifles
TNA WO 95/2466: 5th Battalion Argyll & Sutherland Highlanders
TNA WO 95/2451: 2/4th Battalion Somerset Light Infantry (Pioneers)
TNA WO 95/2451: 34th Battalion Machine Gun Corps
TNA WO 95/2450: 34th Divisional Signals Company, Royal Engineers
TNA WO 95/2449: 207th Field Company, Royal Engineers
TNA WO 95/2449: 208th Field Company, Royal Engineers
TNA WO 95/2450: 209th Field Company, Royal Engineers
TNA WO 95/2442: Commander Royal Artillery, 34th Division
TNA WO 95/2448: 34th Divisional Trench Mortar Operations
TNA WO 95/2448: 34th Divisional Ammunition Column, Royal Field Artillery
TNA WO 95/2444: 34th Divisional Deputy Assistant Director Ordnance Services (DADOS)
TNA WO 95/2445: 152nd Brigade, Royal Field Artillery
TNA WO 95/2447: 160th Brigade, Royal Field Artillery
TNA WO 95/2443: Assistant Director of Medical Services (ADMS) 34th Division
TNA WO 95/2452: 102nd Field Ambulance
TNA WO 95/2453: 103rd Field Ambulance
TNA WO 95/2453: 104th Field Ambulance

TNA WO 95/2454: 34th Divisional Train, Army Service Corps
TNA WO 95/2444: Assistant Director Veterinary Services, 34th Division
TNA WO 95/2454: 44th Mobile Veterinary Section, 34th Division

1.2 Imperial War Museum
Private Papers of Major-General Sir (Cecil) Lothian Nicholson KCMG, KCB.

1.3 Service historique de la Défense (SHD), Château de Vincennes
Rapport de la Commission d'Enquête instituée par Lettre Ministérielle, No. 18.194 du 14 Juillet 1917, SHD 5N255.

2. Published Sources

American Battle Monuments Commission (AMBC) (1943). *32d Division. Summary of operations in the World War*. Washington, DC: US Government Printing Office.

Armées Françaises dans la Grande Guerre (AFGG) (1923) *Les armées françaises dans la Grande guerre. Ordres de bataille des grandes unités: Divisions d'infanterie, Divisions de cavalerie. France : Etat-major des armées. Service historique. Tome X, Premier Volume.*

(1923) *Deuxième volume. Divisions d'infanterie, Divisions de cavalerie.*

(AFGG) *GHQ, Appui des armées britanniques par les forces françaises, 10 avril 1918*, 613-1598.

(AFGG2) *GQG Le général commandant en chef au général le groupe d'armées de réserve, 8 Juillet 1918*, 623-1847.

(AFGG) *30e corps d'armée, 1er juin 1918-28 juin 1919.*

Atkin, Stephen (1998) *Pétain*. London: Longman.

Bugnet, Charles (1934) *Mangin*. Paris: Plon.

Clayton, Anthony (2003) *Paths of Glory. The French Army 1914-18.* London: Cassell.

Creagh, O'Moore Sir and Humphris, E.M. (1923) *The VC and DSO. The V.C. and D.S.O.: a complete record of all those officers, non-commissioned officers and men of His Majesty's Naval, Military and Air Forces who have been awarded these decorations from the time of their institution, with descriptions of the deeds and services which won the distinctions and with many biographical and other details*. Volume II. London: Standard Art Book.

Crookenden, Colonel A. (1938) *The History Of The Cheshire Regiment In The Great War*. Uckfield: Naval and Military Press reprint.

Doughty, Robert A (2005) *Pyrrhic Victory: French strategy and Operations in the Great War.* Cambridge, Massachusetts: Harvard University Press.

Edmonds, Brigadier General Sir James E (1939) *Military Operations France and Belgium, 1918, Volume III, May-July: The German Diversion Offensives and the First Allied Counter-offensive*. London: MacMillan & Co.

Estienne-Mondet, A (2010) *Le général J.B. Estienne, père des chars.* Paris, L'Harmattan.

Fayolle, Maréchal Émile (1964) *Cahiers secrets de la Grande Guerre.* Paris: Plon.

Findlay, Colonel James M. (1926) *With the 8th Scottish Rifles 1914-1919.* London: Blockie.

Franks, Norman L.R., Bailey, Frank W. and Guest, Russell (1993) *Above the Lines: The Ace and Fighter Units of German Air Service, Naval Air Service and Flanders Marine Corps 1914-1918*. London: Grub Street.

Gale, Tim (2013) *The French Army's Tank Force and Armoured Warfare in the Great War: The Artillerie Spéciale*. Routledge Studies in First World War History. Routledge., 2013
    (2016) *French tanks of the Great War*. Barnsley: Pen and Sword.
General Service Schools (1923) *The German Offensive of July 15, 1918* (Marne Source Book). Fort Leavenworth, Kansas: General Service Schools Press.
Godley, Alexander J. (1939) *Life of an Irish Soldier*. London: John Murray.
Goya, Michel (2004) *Flesh and steel during the Great War: The Transformation of the French Army and the Invention of Modern Warfare*. Barnsley: Pen and Sword.
Greenhalgh, Elizabeth (2005) *Victory Through Coalition: Britain and France during the First World War*. Cambridge: Cambridge University Press.
    (2011) *Foch in Command: The Forging of a First World War General*. Cambridge: Cambridge University Press.
    (2014) *The French Army and the First World War*. Cambridge: Cambridge University Press.
Greenwood, Paul (1998) *The Second Battle of the Marne*. Shrewsbury: Airlife.
Grover, Ray (1996) Godley, Alexander John. *Dictionary of New Zealand Biography*.
    (2004) Godley, Sir Alexander John. *Oxford Dictionary of National Biography*.

Harbord, James G. (1936) *The American Army in France: 1917-1919*. Boston, Massachusetts: Little, Brown, and Company.
Harper, Glyn (2007). *Dark Journey: Three Key New Zealand Battles of the Western Front*. Auckland: HarperCollins.
Haswell, Jock (1967) *Famous Regiments Series: The Queen's Royal Regiment (West Surrey) (The 2nd Regiment of Foot)*. London: Hamish Hamilton.

Johnson, Douglas V. II and Hillman, Rolfe (1999) *Soissons 1918*. College Station: Texas A&M University Press.

Keegan, John (1998) *The First World War*. Bodley Head.
Kinloch, Terry (2018) *Godley: The Man Behind the Myth*. Dunedin: Exisle Publishing.

Liddle, Peter (ed.) (1997) *Passchendaele in Perspective*. London: Leo Cooper.
Liddell Hart, Basil H (1932) *Foch: The Man of Orléans*. Boston: Little Brown.
Lloyd, Nick (2013) *Hundred Days*. London: Penguin.
Ludendorff, Eric (1919) *My War Memories 1914-1918*, Vol.2. London: Hutchinson & Co.

Macdonald, Andrew (2013) *Passchendaele: The Anatomy of a Tragedy*. Auckland: HarperCollins Publishers.
Mangin, Charles (1950) *Lettres de Guerre 1914-1918*. Paris : Librairie Arthème Fayard.
    (1920) *Comment finit la Guerre*. Paris: Revue des deux mondes, T.56.
Mangin, Louis-Eugène (1986) *Le général Mangin. 1866-1925*. Paris : Fernand Lanore.

Marix Evans, Martin (2002) *1918: The Year of Victories.* Arcturus Military History Series, London: Arcturus.
Menat, Candice (2013). *Les Chars et les Américains.* HAL. hal-01163530
Michelin (1919) *The Americans in the Great War, Volume 1: The Second Battle of the Marne.* Clermont-Ferrand: Michelin & Cie.
Maurice, Major-General Sir Frederick BM (1919) *The Last Four Months: How the War Was Won.* Boston: Little Brown & Co.

Neiberg, Michael S (2008) *The Second Battle of the Marne.* Bloomington, Indiana University Press.
(2003) *Foch: Supreme Allied Commander in the Great War.* Dulles: Brassey's Military Profiles.
Nelson, James C. (2009) *The Remains of Company D: A Story of the Great War.* New York: St Martin's Press.

Palmer, Frederick (1937) *Our Gallant Madness.* New York: Garden City.
Pedronici, Guy (ed.) (1992) *Histoire militaire de la France,* Volume 3. Paris: PUF.
Pershing, John J (1931) *My Experiences in the World War,* Volume II. New York : Frederick A. Stokes Co.
Poincaré, Raymond (1930) *Au service de la France — Victoire et armistice, Tome 10.* Paris: Plon.

Rawson, Andrew (2018) *Advance to Victory: July to September 1918.* Barnsley: Pen and Sword.
Read, I.L. 'Dick' (2013) *Of Those We Loved: A Great War Narrative Remembered and Illustrated.* Barnsley: Pen and Sword.
Ryan, Stephen (1969) *Pétain the Soldier.* London: Thomas Yoseloff Ltd.

Scott Elliot GF (1928) *The War History of the 5th Battalion King's Own Scottish Borderers.* Dumfries: Robert Diwiddie.
Serrigny (1945) *Maréchal Pétain.* Le Procès du Maréchal Pétain
Shakespear, Lieutenant Colonel John (1921) *The Thirty-Fourth Division, 1915-1919: The Story of its Career from Ripon to the Rhine.* London: HF and G Witherby.

Takle, Patrick (2015) *Nine Divisions in Champagne: The Second Battle of the Marne.* Barnsley: Pen and Sword.
Tournoux, Jean R. (1966) *Pétain and de Gaulle.* London: Heinemann.

United States Army (1920) *Histories of two hundred and fifty-one Divisions of the German army which participated in the war (1914-1918).* Washington, DC.

Warner, Philip L. (1918-21) *Harrow Memorials of the Great War.* Volume 6. London: Phillip Lee Warner.
Watson, David (1974) *Georges Clemenceau: A Political Biography.* New York: David McKay.
Westlake, Ray (1996) *British Regiments at Gallipoli.* London: Leo Cooper.
Wryall Everard (1927) *The History of the Somerset Light Infantry (Prince Albert's) 1914-1919.* London: Methuen.

Zabecki, David T. (2006) *The German 1918 Offensives: A Case Study in The Operational Level of War*. London: Routledge.
(2018*) The Generals' War: Operational level command on the Western Front 1918*. Bloomington, Indiana: Indiana University Press.

3. Journals
Western Front Association. Lancashire North Branch Despatch, Issue 21, May 2018.

4. Unpublished Sources
Blanchard, David (2016) 'The Annihilation of the British IX Corps on the Aisne, 27th May 1918'. MPhil thesis.

Brady, Frances M. (1931) Study of the Physical Geography of the Soissons, Crepy, Château-Thierry, Rheims Area.

Hodgkinson, Peter E. (2013) British Infantry Battalion Commanders in the First World War. PhD thesis, University of Birmingham.

Service Historiqe de l'Armée de Terre (1919) Ordre générale numéro 1 du général commandant L'AS du 1er janvier 1917. Rapport au sujet de la participation de l'AS aux opérations due 23 et 25 octobre 1917. 16 N 2120. Carton 3, Dossier 4. Tableau des pertes en chars et personnels, GQG, 9 septembre.

Woldike, Aage (2003) 'Report by the Field Marshal Commander-in-Chief of the French Armies of the North and Northeast on the Operations of 1918. The Offensive Campaign (18 July-11 November). II Part. Château-Thierry – Soissons counter-offensive (18 July-6 August)'.

Zabecki, David T. (2004) 'Operational Art and the German 1918 Offensives'. Unpublished PhD thesis. Cranfield University.

5. Electronic Sources
Bollington Parish Church St Oswald's <https://stoswaldbollington.org.uk/pages/war_dead_search_3.php?id=123>

Herefordshire Light Infantry Museum <www.herefordshirelightinfantrymuseum.com>

The Long, Long Trail <www.longlongtrail.co.uk>

Major General Edward Charles Ingouville Williams CB, DSO <www.worcestershireregiment.com/wr.php?main=inc/o_ingouville_williams>
Mémoire des hommes <www.memoiredeshommes.sga.defense.gouv.fr>

Senior Army Appointments 1860 – <www.gulabin.com/armynavy/pdf/Army%20Commands%201860-.pdf >

Index

A
Abbeville, 44, 66
Aisne, 24, 50–51, 65, 73, 95, 103, 124, 133, 215
Amiens, 17–18, 22–23, 54, 66, 68, 86, 98, 121, 123, 132, 208–9
Arras, 10, 13, 36, 47, 117, 208, 239

B
Barlow, Lieutenant Colonel C.L., 45, 166, 192–93
Battle of Amiens, 86, 208–9
Beugneux, 137–40, 143, 148, 150–51, 155–57, 159–66, 169, 176–77, 179–80, 187–90, 192–93, 195, 199–200, 206, 212–13, 217, 232–33
Billy-sur-Ourcq, 103, 144, 153, 180, 189
Blücher-Yorck, 4, 22, 25–26, 29, 206
Boehn, General Max von, 187, 194, 198
Bois de Baillette 122, 137–40, 143, 145, 148–49, 153, 157, 163, 168, 176–77, 187–88
Butte Chalmont, 97, 120–24, 138–40, 143, 147, 160, 167, 173

C
Chaplin, Brigadier General J.G., 41, 103, 105
Château-Thierry, 26, 28-29, 49, 65–66, 69, 72–73, 78–79, 85, 87-88, 96–97, 102, 107, 112, 114, 117–18, 122–23, 133, 143, 148–49, 153
Chavigny Ferme, 100, 102, 105, 108
Chemin des Dames, 24, 29, 50, 133
Clemenceau, Georges, 13, 16–17, 27–28, 30–31, 38, 67, 77
Compiègne, 29–30, 33, 66, 71
Constable, Lieutenant Colonel G.S., 47–48, 153
Coutremain, 100, 103, 106, 108–9, 114–15

D
Droizy, 65, 127, 177, 185

E
Ely, Brigadier General H., 80, 83
Espèrey, General Louis Franchet de, 26–27
Estienne, General Jean, 31, 89, 123

F
Fayolle, General Marie Émile, 14–16, 18, 30–31, 33, 67, 77–78, 84–86, 95, 120, 122–24, 135, 147, 171, 173, 199
Foch, Generalissimo Ferdinand, 8, 16-24, 27–31, 67, 69, 86–89, 94–96, 98–99, 118–23, 135, 147, 170-71, 174-75, 185, 202, 206, 208-09, 212, 214
Fère-en-Tardenois, 8, 72, 95, 98, 119, 121, 124, 132, 138, 143, 147
Fismes, 95, 124, 173, 198, 239
Forêt de Retz, 62, 82, 84
Formations
  American
  American Expeditionary Force (AEF), 13, 85, 106, 175

  I Corps, 82, 138
  III Corps, 85

  British
  First Army, 14, 41
  Fifth Army, 11, 13, 15-16

  VII Corps, 36
  VIII Corps, 35
  IX Corps, 24, 245
  XXII Corps, 8, 36-38, 66, 68, 70, 74, 78, 102, 123, 173-74, 176, 198, 207, 209, 211-12, 214
  Canadian Corps, 66

  15th (Scottish) Division, 7, 68, 75, 78, 97, 100, 102, 106, 111, 123, 137, 202, 217
  34th (New Army) Division, 9, 11, 14, 20–21, 35-38, 40, 42–47, 68–71, 74–75, 78–87, 97, 99–109, 111-13, 115–17, 123-25, 127–28, 135, 137–40, 144–45, 147-51, 155, 157, 163, 165, 167,170–71, 176, 177, 181–82, 184, 187, 197, 199–202, 205-07, 209–11, 213-21
  51st (Highland) Division, 37, 68, 71, 74, 78, 103, 129, 170, 176, 198, 209, 213-214 62nd

(West Riding) Division, 37, 68, 71, 74, 78, 170, 198, 209, 213-14

French
GAC (Groupe d'armées du Centre), 4, 71–72, 84, 119–20, 133, 207
Xe armée, 8, 16, 22, 28-30, 32, 38, 45, 50, 52-53, 58-60, 62-63, 71-75, 77-78, 81-88, 94-96, 98-99, 107, 111, 116, 118-25, 127, 132, 135, 147, 163, 170, 173-75, 185, 198-200, 202, 207, 212, 216, 221

German
Army Group Crown Prince Wilhelm, 49, 53–56, 59

First Army, 51-53, 55-58, 60, 65, 68, 123, 130, 133
Seventh Army, 33, 43, 49-57, 59, 96, 130, 176, 210
Ninth Army, 50, 55, 63-64, 70, 124, 129-30, 133, 176

Corps Conta, 56, 58
Corps Kathen, 54–56
Corps Schmettow, 54
Corps Schoeler, 121
Corps Wichura, 58
Flanders Marine Corps, 171, 243

19th Ersatz Division, 104, 163, 172
51st Reserve Division, 103, 129
Guard Ersatz Division. 172
Bavarian Ersatz Division, 58, 128-29
Friedensturm, Operation, 4, 49, 51, 53

G
Georgette, Operation, 4, 20–33, 46, 49, 206, 208
Gneisenau, Operation, 29, 34
Godley, General Alexander, 36, 68, 71, 74, 78, 154, 176, 214, 217
Grand Rozoy, 107, 121, 123, 137–40, 142–44, 148–50, 159–60, 162–66, 171, 175–77, 184–85, 187–88, 190, 198–99, 234

H
Hagen, Operation, 4, 25, 34, 50, 54–55, 57, 59–61, 63, 98, 210
Haig, Field Marshal Sir Douglas, 13–18, 20, 22–24, 27, 30, 36–38, 58–59, 67–70, 73–74, 96, 120, 123, 206–9
Hammerschlag, Operation, 4, 33
Harbord, General James, 7, 80, 82, 243
Hilliam, Brigadier General E., 127

Hundred Days offensive, 17, 217, 243

L
Launoy, 107, 185, 187, 194, 197–98
Lawrence, General Sir Herbert, 38, 223
Lossberg, Colonel Fritz von, 104
Ludendorff, Quartermaster General Erich, 14–15, 25–26, 49–50, 52–55, 57, 59–60, 63–64, 97–98, 124, 129–30, 133, 135, 170, 176, 209
Lys, 20–21

M
Maast-et-Violaine, 109, 143
Maistre, 120–21, 171, 173
Malmaison, 86, 93–94, 103
Mangin, General Charles, 4–5, 7–8, 28–33, 58–59, 62–63, 72- 74, 77–78, 84–86, 88, 93–99, 107, 117, 120, 122–24, 132–33, 137, 170, 185, 197-98, 212–13, 218-20
Marne, 5, 25, 27, 29, 37–38, 51–52, 54–60, 62, 85, 87, 89, 132–33, 206, 208, 217,
Marne salient, 90, 92, 97–98, 118, 121, 124, 126, 129, 131–32, 170–71, 173, 185–86, 210, 213
Marneschutz-Reims, Operation, 4, 7, 49–51, 53, 55, 206, 212
Marseilles, 40–41, 44–46
Missy-aux-Bois, 78, 87
Montceau, 148, 150, 153–54, 157, 162–65, 180, 187–88
Montdidier, 18, 29, 72, 121, 235
Montrambœuf Ferme, 100–102, 105, 108, 127
Moulins, 55, 57, 101
Mudra, General Bruno von, 51, 57, 60

N
Nicholson, Major General Cecil Lothian, 10, 21, 35, 37, 41, 74, 100, 102-3, 106, 111, 137, 144, 148–49, 154–55, 162–63, 169, 177, 179, 182, 184–85, 187–88, 198–99, 210, 216–18, 221–22
Nivelle, General Robert, 18–19, 88–89, 94

O
Oise, 13, 22, 24, 29, 66, 73, 118, 133
Oulchy-la-Ville, 117, 122–23, 128, 148, 151, 153, 161, 189, 196
Oulchy-le-Château, 75, 96, 121–22, 124, 128, 130, 138, 149–50, 157, 235, 237–38
Ourcq, 5, 7, 50, 63, 124, 132–45, 151, 220

P
Parcy-Tigny, 76, 105, 108-9, 111–13, 116
Penet, General Hippolyte-Alphonse, 97, 99, 103, 108, 111–12, 150–51, 163, 168, 176, 211, 215
Pétain, General Henri Philippe, 13–18, 20–28,

30–31, 56, 58–59, 66–67, 70–72, 74, 77–78, 85–86, 88–89, 91, 93–95, 98–99, 118–20, 122–23, 170–71, 173–75, 206, 208–9, 212
Ploisy, 78, 87
Poincaré, Henri, 17, 122, 244
Puiseux, 74, 101

R
Reims, 24–26, 28, 49, 52, 55–56, 58, 60, 63, 69–71, 78, 97, 102, 133
Renault FT-17, 215–16
Robillot, 84
Romilly-sur-Seine, 71

S
Saponay, 194, 197, 239
Senlis, 3, 71–72, 74, 102, 169
Servenay, 142–43, 149–50, 177, 185, 193–94, 197–99
Soissonais, 5, 132–45
Soissons, 24–26, 28, 50–51, 53–54, 64–65, 78–79, 95–97, 107, 118, 122–23, 133, 148–49, 153, 170, 187–88, 201
Soucy, 74–75, 77, 105
St Anand, 84
Steenwerck, 20–21

T
Tahure, 49, 54
Tigny, 100, 102–3, 106, 108–9, 111–14, 123, 127, 198

V
Vesle, 24–25, 72, 95, 124, 129, 133, 173-74, 185, 201-2, 210, 215
Villers-Cotterêts, 62, 70, 72, 74–76, 82, 84, 99, 102, 144, 202
Villers-Hélon, 101, 105, 127

W
Walthall, Brigadier General E., 108, 125, 141, 179, 198
Wilhelm, Crown Prince, 25, 27, 33, 52, 97, 104, 129, 170, 185
Woodcock, Brigadier General W.J., 41, 127, 154, 196

Y
Ypres salient, 11, 35